Introduction *to* Educational Research

SAGE | **50** YEARS

SAGE was founded in 1965 by Sara Miller McCune to support the dissemination of usable knowledge by publishing innovative and high-quality research and teaching content. Today, we publish more than 850 journals, including those of more than 300 learned societies, more than 800 new books per year, and a growing range of library products including archives, data, case studies, reports, conference highlights, and video. SAGE remains majority-owned by our founder, and after Sara's lifetime will become owned by a charitable trust that secures our continued independence.

Los Angeles | London | New Delhi | Singapore | Washington DC

Introduction *to* Educational Research

Craig A. Mertler

Arizona State University

Mertler Educational Consulting

Los Angeles | London | New Delhi
Singapore | Washington DC

Los Angeles | London | New Delhi
Singapore | Washington DC

FOR INFORMATION:

SAGE Publications, Inc.
2455 Teller Road
Thousand Oaks, California 91320
E-mail: order@sagepub.com

SAGE Publications Ltd.
1 Oliver's Yard
55 City Road
London EC1Y 1SP
United Kingdom

SAGE Publications India Pvt. Ltd.
B 1/I 1 Mohan Cooperative Industrial Area
Mathura Road, New Delhi 110 044
India

SAGE Publications Asia-Pacific Pte. Ltd.
3 Church Street
#10-04 Samsung Hub
Singapore 049483

Acquisitions Editor: Theresa Accomazzo

Associate Editor: Jessica Miller

Editorial Assistant: Georgia McLaughlin

Production Editor: Olivia Weber-Stenis

Copy Editor: Megan Granger

Typesetter: C&M Digitals (P) Ltd.

Proofreader: Theresa Kay

Indexer: Jeanne Busemeyer

Cover Designer: Rose Storey

Marketing Manager: Ashlee Blunk

Printed in the United States of America

Cataloging-in-publication data is available from the Library of Congress.

ISBN 978-1-4833-7548-9

This book is printed on acid-free paper.

SUSTAINABLE FORESTRY INITIATIVE
Certified Chain of Custody
Promoting Sustainable Forestry
www.sfiprogram.org
SFI-01268
SFI label applies to text stock

15 16 17 18 19 10 9 8 7 6 5 4 3 2 1

• Brief Contents •

• Detailed Contents •

PART III • COLLECTING AND ANALYZING DATA

PART IV• THE RESEARCH REPORT

14. Writing a Final Research Report   308

• Preface •

Preface . . . to the Preface

Each new edition of a textbook represents change, of some sort. Although it may not appear so to those who are unfamiliar with its "previous editions"—since this is a first-edition text—this text also represents substantial change from its earlier versions. For seven previous editions, I—along with my coauthor, Dr. Carol M. Charles—produced a textbook by the same name but with a different publisher. In early 2014, an opportunity arose for SAGE Publications to publish *Introduction to Educational Research*, as a first edition. Having worked on two previous textbook projects with SAGE over the past 10 years or so, I could not have been more excited and jumped at the opportunity to have the SAGE imprint on this textbook—especially since SAGE is the leading authority when it comes to publishing books on the topic of research methodologies.

This new version of *Introduction to Educational Research* represents a significant revision of previous editions. Chapters have been rewritten, and the organization of the book has been restructured. For those adopters who are familiar with the previous editions, I firmly believe that you will find this version of the text substantially more beneficial to both you and your students. Content coverage and integrated samples and examples have been thoroughly augmented, while the conversational writing style apparent in previous editions has been maintained throughout.

Purpose of the Text

This book has two main purposes that receive attention simultaneously. The first is to provide knowledge about educational research, sufficient for a clear understanding of the following:

- Exactly what educational research is and is not
- The nature of research and the scientific process it employs
- Identifying research problems and stating research questions and hypotheses
- The ethical responsibilities that must be adhered to by researchers
- The purposes and processes of conducting a review of related literature
- The various types of research methodologies and designs, along with their purposes, characteristics, strengths, and limitations
- Characteristics, sources, and techniques used in the collection of data
- Procedures for analyzing qualitative and quantitative data
- Procedures for writing research proposals and final research reports

The second purpose of this book—a purpose that has been given preeminence in this edition (in keeping with previous editions)—is to help graduate students conduct their own research. Toward that end, specific guidance is provided in the following areas:

- Identifying appropriate topics for research
- Properly framing research questions and hypotheses
- Identifying possible types of research necessitated by various topics
- Preparing a research proposal for an identified research topic
- Conducting a thorough search for related research literature
- Evaluating various types of research appropriate for investigating selected topics
- Identifying necessary data, sources of those data, and the procedures by which data are collected
- Analyzing data appropriately
- Answering research questions and testing hypotheses
- Stating findings and drawing conclusions
- Preparing research reports

Focused on the Needs of Educators and Graduate Students

Introduction to Educational Research, first edition, is designed specifically for educators who are new to research and seeking advanced degrees in graduate studies. Most users will be in-service teachers, administrators, special-education personnel, instructional coaches, and counselors, but the book is also appropriate for graduate students not yet actively teaching. No prior familiarity with the principles, procedures, or terminology of educational research is required to fully benefit from this text.

Text Organized Sequentially, Like an Educational Research Study

The text is composed of 14 chapters, an appendix, and a glossary. In keeping with the purposes of helping students organize and undertake research while simultaneously acquiring fundamental knowledge about research, the text is organized into four parts, as follows:

Part I: Initial Research Considerations

Chapter 1: What Is Educational Research?

Chapter 2: Overview of the Educational Research Process

Chapter 3: Identifying a Research Problem

Chapter 4: Ethics in Educational Research

Chapter 5: Reviewing Related Research Literature

Part I clarifies the nature of educational research, explains its characteristics, provides an overview of the entire process of conducting educational research, discusses mechanisms for identifying appropriate research topics or problems, and provides strategies for reviewing related research literature.

Part II: Designing a Research Study

Chapter 6: Qualitative Research Methods

Chapter 7: Quantitative Research Methods

Chapter 8: Mixed-Methods Research

Chapter 9: Action Research

Chapter 10: Writing a Research Proposal

Part II provides detailed descriptions of qualitative research methodologies and quantitative research designs, mixed-methods research designs, the process of conducting action research, and strategies for developing a written research proposal.

Part III: Collecting and Analyzing Data

Chapter 11: Qualitative Data Collection and Analysis

Chapter 12: Quantitative Data Collection

Chapter 13: Quantitative Data Analysis

Part III provides detailed descriptions and examples of data collection and analysis procedures for both qualitative and quantitative research studies.

Part IV: The Research Report

Chapter 14: Writing a Final Research Report

Part IV discusses various aspects of writing a final research report, including the importance of identifying the audience, conventions of academic-style writing and format, and practical guidelines for writing.

Back Matter

The back matter of the text consists of an appendix and glossary. The appendix contains a written research report that has been published in an academic journal. This research report appears in its entirety. The glossary of important terms includes well over 350 terms related to various aspects of educational research.

Pedagogical Features and Benefits for Students

In keeping with the main purpose of helping users clearly understand and apply research concepts, several pedagogical features have been included in the book. Each chapter contains the following features:

- **Student Learning Objectives (or SLOs)**—The SLOs serve several pedagogical purposes. They provide a preview for each chapter, list the 4 to 8 major targeted learning objectives for that chapter, and may also be used as a review upon completing study of the chapter.
- **Developmental Activities**—Each chapter includes five developmental activities, located at the end of the chapter. These developmental activities are designed to provide opportunities, at a variety of levels of depth and breadth, for students to apply concepts and skills they have learned throughout the chapter. These may be used effectively as course assignments, in-class activities, or as a basis for class discussions on topics addressed in the chapter.
- **Chapter Summaries**—Thorough and detailed summaries of key concepts, listed in bullet-point format, are included at the end of each chapter and provide focused reviews of chapter contents.

Other pedagogical features include the following:

- **Reprinted Research Report**—The appendix contains a complete published research article. This can serve as an opportunity for students to engage in a critique of a published article as well as to see the format and writing style appropriate for academic journals.
- **Glossary**—A glossary of more than 350 terms important in educational research has been provided for easy student reference. The terms are highlighted in boldface on their first appearance in the text. This is one of the most comprehensive glossaries presented in any educational research textbook.

Supplements

For Instructors

SAGE edge for Instructors supports your teaching by making it easy to integrate quality content and create a rich learning environment for students.

- **PowerPoint presentations** have been created for each chapter appearing in the text. Each PowerPoint file is ready for classroom use and can also be used to provide handouts to students. The PowerPoint presentations are highly detailed and consistently follow the content as presented in each chapter.
- **Test banks** provide a diverse range of pre-written options as well as the opportunity to edit any question and/or insert your own personalized questions to effectively assess students' progress and understanding.

- **A Respondus electronic test bank** is available and can be used on PCs. The test bank contains multiple choice, true/false, short answer, and essay questions for each chapter and provides you with a diverse range of pre-written options as well as the opportunity for editing any question and/or inserting your own personalized questions to effectively assess students' progress and understanding. Respondus is also compatible with many popular learning management systems so you can easily get your test questions into your online course.
- **Sample course syllabi** for semester and quarter courses provide suggested models for structuring your courses.
- **EXCLUSIVE! Access to full-text SAGE journal articles** that have been carefully selected to support and expand on the concepts presented in each chapter.
- **Multimedia content** includes original SAGE videos that appeal to students with different learning styles.
- **Lecture notes** summarize key concepts by chapter to help you prepare for lectures and class discussions.

For Students

SAGE edge for Students provides a personalized approach to help students accomplish their coursework goals in an easy-to-use learning environment.

- **Mobile-friendly practice quizzes** allow for independent assessment by students of their mastery of course material.
- **Mobile-friendly eFlashcards** strengthen understanding of key terms and concepts.
- An **online action plan** includes tips and feedback on progress through the course and materials, which allows students to individualize their learning experience.
- **Chapter summaries with learning objectives** reinforce the most important material.
- **SAGE Journal Articles** combine cutting-edge academic journal scholarship with the topics in your course for a robust classroom experience.
- Carefully selected chapter-by-chapter **video and multimedia content** which enhance classroom-based explorations of key topics.

• Acknowledgments •

First and foremost, I would like to acknowledge and sincerely thank Diane McDaniel and Terri Accomazzo (acquisitions editor for education) for wholeheartedly and excitedly agreeing to take on this "new" project as it begins its "second life." For more than 10 years, I have been more than thrilled with my working relationships with everyone at SAGE Publications. I would also like to thank the following individuals who contributed to the production of this text: Jessica Miller (associate editor), Olivia Weber-Stenis (production editor), and Rose Storey (designer).

As mentioned earlier in the preface, this book existed previously in seven different editions. I want to respectfully acknowledge and thank my coauthor on those previous editions, Dr. Carol M. Charles, for his diligent work and professional collaboration over the years.

Finally, I would certainly be remiss if I did not acknowledge the valuable comments, feedback, and suggestions provided by the reviewers of this initial edition of SAGE's *Introduction to Educational Research*:

Kenneth R. Austin, Stephen F. Austin State University

Bruce Biskin, Rider University

Ellina Chernobilsky, Caldwell College

M. H. Clark, University of Central Florida

Jacqueline S. Craven, Delta State University

Sunny R. Duerr, State University of New York at New Paltz

Gerry Giordano, University of North Florida

Rachael Goodman, George Mason University

Kathleen Hickey, Governors State University

Anju Jolly, Pennsylvania State University

Greg Knotts, California State University, Northridge

Zaida McCall-Perez, Holy Names University

Ani Moughamian, Saint Mary's College

Brian Myers, University of Florida

Karen Nespoli, St. Joseph's College

Kathryn Newman, Grambling State University

Arturo Olivarez Jr., University of Texas at El Paso

Rosalind Raby, California State University, Northridge

Melisa Reed, Marshall University

Shlomo Sawilosky, Wayne State University

Bennett Schepens, Nyack College

Karen Selby, University of Detroit Mercy

John Tiller, Tennessee State University

My most important acknowledgment and thanks are extended to my wife, Kate, for her never-ending support, encouragement, and advice. Extensive writing projects are difficult without the support, feedback, and "sounding board" provided by those closest to us. My thanks also go to our son, Addison, as he embarks on preparation for his own professional career.

Dr. Craig A. Mertler

• About the Author •

**Dr. Craig A. Mertler** is currently an Associate Professor at Arizona State University. He began his career as a high school biology teacher. He has been an educator for 30 years—20 of those in higher education at Bowling Green State University, the University of West Georgia, Lynn University, and Arizona State University, and 6 as an administrator (department chair, doctoral program director, and education dean). Over his career, he has taught courses focused on the application of action research to promote educator empowerment, school improvement, and job-embedded professional development, as well as classroom assessment, research methods, and statistical analyses. He has served as the research methodology expert on more than 100 doctoral dissertations and master's theses.

He is the author of 20 books, four invited book chapters, and 18 refereed journal articles. He has also presented more than 35 research papers at professional meetings around the country, as well as internationally. He conducts workshops for in-service educational professionals (at all levels) on classroom-based action research and on the topics of classroom assessment and assessment literacy, as well as data-driven educational decision making. His primary research and consulting interests include classroom-based action research, data-driven educational decision making, professional learning communities, and classroom teachers' assessment literacy. In his leisure time, he coaches high school volleyball and enjoys playing golf and traveling with his family.

Dr. Mertler owns and operates Mertler Educational Consulting (www.craigmertler.com/mec), and he can be reached at craig.mertler@gmail.com for consulting, professional development, and speaking engagements. Additionally, you can read his blog at www.craigmertler.com/blog.

INITIAL RESEARCH
CONSIDERATIONS

1

What Is Educational Research?

Student Learning Objectives

After studying Chapter 1, students will be able to do the following:

1. Name and describe four methods that can be used to seek out answers to important questions

2. Describe the scientific method and how it can be applied to educational research topics

3. Summarize characteristics that define what educational research is and is not

4. Identify and define key terms associated with educational research

5. Identify various methods for conducting educational research

6. List and describe the major steps of the educational research process

7. Articulate the importance of exploring research in your specific discipline

8. Evaluate the perceived importance of educators' conducting their own research

Whether we realize it or not, research is—and should always be—central to how we function as a successful and productive society. Whether we consider history, medicine, social group dynamics, psychology, or any number of areas for study in which we might be interested, research is the key to answering our questions, solving our problems, and fostering creativity, innovations, and advancements. Research in the broad field of education is certainly no exception to this fact.

Finding Answers to Questions

The basic goal in nearly all research studies is to find answers to particular questions. These may be questions about students, teachers, curriculum, attendance, graduation rates, extracurricular activities—the list is seemingly endless. Human nature characteristically prompts us to try to find answers to our questions as quickly as possible. The sources we pursue for possible answers are typically those that are most convenient to us. These sources include tradition, authority, and common sense. *Tradition* refers to how we have historically sought answers to our questions. For example, suppose that Adams School District developed an innovative science curriculum 25 years ago. It was very well received at the time of its inception, both locally and statewide—so much so that several other districts developed similar curricula. However, the topic of revising that curriculum was recently raised in a science committee meeting. During the discussion, several committee members explained how innovative the curriculum was when it was originally developed and that they shouldn't now want to abandon something so innovative. The general consensus of the committee was that the science curriculum was great when it was developed and has been working fine since then— so why change it now? This argument may be correct; however, a good deal of time has passed and numerous scientific advances have been made since the curriculum was originally implemented. While it may have been effective for Adams' students in the past, it may not be appropriately meeting their academic needs now. Relying on the "it worked in the past, so why change now" attitude might lead us to inaccurate answers to our questions about the appropriateness of the curriculum.

If tradition fails to provide us with suitable answers to our questions, we next look to *authority*, or seeking answers and opinions from individuals who have substantial expertise in the field and who, we hope, know what is best for us. This source remains very popular in the broad field of education and can be highly effective. However, its effectiveness in terms of answering our questions is not always a certainty. Consider the numerous "bandwagon" movements that schools have jumped on over the years. When it turns out that these are not effective solutions to our school-based problems, schools jump off of them almost as quickly as they jumped on, usually in search of a different "quick fix." To work effectively, authoritative answers to our questions must be "customized" to fit the specific needs of the target school, district, or setting. This approach can certainly prove effective, but it does not routinely occur. In many instances, experts simply try to apply their answers to our questions, regardless of our specific situations, conditions, demographic makeup, and so forth. In these cases, authoritative answers will typically prove ineffective. For example, what might prove an effective solution in Adams School District might not be as effective in Brighton School District, and could even be a miserable failure in Crestview School District.

If traditional and authoritative approaches to answering our school-based questions do not prove to be effective, we might decide to take matters into our own hands. After all, who knows the specific needs of our district, and our students, better than we do? Using a *common sense* approach, human reasoning—sort of figuring things out on your own—can be highly effective. However, common sense can be effective only if the information on which solutions are developed and decisions are based is reliable and accurate. For example, consider all the advances in medicine and technology over the past decade—and the numerous failures that often preceded those successes. (Please note that I am using the term *failures* very loosely, because if we have learned something that will ultimately benefit us in the long run, then it was not a failure, in the literal sense of the word.)

In actuality, both tradition and authority can provide additional information and guidance, should we decide to use a common sense approach in answering our questions. Personal experiences and expertise provide great insight to help us answer our questions, but those sources of information may be biased or incomplete; they are simply not enough. We still need information—reliable and accurate information—to help guide our approach to seeking out answers to our educational questions. Where do we find this reliable and accurate information that can serve as a basis for answering our questions? This type of information must come from a process that is both systematic and objective, thus providing us with information that is accurate and meaningful, and not distorted or biased (to the extent possible). This approach is best accomplished through the application and use of the *scientific method*.

The Scientific Method

The **scientific method** is a specific strategy used to answer questions and resolve problems. It is very likely that you remember the scientific method from a junior or senior high school science course when you were required to complete some sort of research study in the form of a science fair project. The origins of the scientific method date back to 1938, when American philosopher John Dewey described the process as a procedure for thinking more objectively (meaning that the results or answers are not influenced by personal feelings or opinions when considering and representing facts). The scientific method consists of a systematic, step-by-step set of procedures that are employed to objectively investigate some sort of phenomenon and answer specific questions about it. Dewey presented the process in the following steps:

1. Clarify the main question inherent in the problem.
2. State a hypothesis (i.e., a prediction of a possible answer to the question).
3. Collect, analyze, and interpret information related to the question, such that it will allow you to provide an answer to that question.
4. Form conclusions derived from the interpretations of your analyses.
5. Use your conclusions to verify or reject your original hypothesis.

The scientific method is essentially the process used in conducting a vast majority of research studies. However, it is important to realize that this is a "generic" set of steps and that all research studies may not follow these steps to the letter, or necessarily in this order. In situations where research studies do not follow the steps exactly, they will still share a couple of important concepts in common. First, all research studies will clearly specify a research question that will serve to guide the conduct of the study. Second, all research studies will include the collection, analysis, and interpretation of information. Applying the scientific approach to this second set of activities is what enables us to answer our questions objectively.

How, then, is the scientific method related to research in the broad field of education? In actuality, there is a great deal of overlap between the two. Simply put, **educational research** involves the application of the scientific method to educational topics, phenomena, or questions. The generic steps in the process of conducting educational research are as follows:

1. Specify the topic about which a concern exists.
2. Clarify the specific problem on which the research will focus.
3. Formulate research questions and/or hypotheses concerning the specific problem or topic.
4. Conduct procedures by which data (a more appropriate term for "information") are collected, analyzed, and interpreted.
5. State the findings that are generated as a result of the analysis of data.
6. Draw conclusions related to the original research questions and/or hypotheses.

Note the similarities between Dewey's steps of the scientific method and the steps involved in conducting educational research. The major, integral components are common to both lists. However, to reiterate, these steps do not always occur in practice as they are presented here, nor do they always follow this particular sequence—especially with respect to specific types of educational research, namely those that use qualitative methods.

Educational Research— What It Is and What It Is Not

Although educational research can be a fairly straightforward process, some educators have preconceptions—or, perhaps more appropriately, misconceptions—about exactly what constitutes educational research. To fully appreciate the potential benefits of educational research—both as a doer and a consumer—it is critical to have a foundational understanding of it. The following list—partially adapted from Leedy and Ormrod (2013)—is an attempt to describe what educational research *is* and what it *is not*.

- *Educational research is scientific.* As a process, educational research is a scientific endeavor. As we have previously discussed, educational research closely parallels the scientific method; however, labeling it a "scientific process" goes even further. To say that educational research is scientific is to say that it is characterized by the principles and methods of science and that it is systematic and methodical. As you will see later in this list, educational research is objective and open-minded about that which is being studied. The overall process involves a step-by-step methodology that, when followed appropriately, ensures this high level of systemization and objectivity.

- *Educational research begins with a question or problem, which serves as the purpose or goal of a study.* Schools abound with problems that need solving and questions that need answering—just ask any teacher or administrator. The logical starting point for any research study in education is to clearly articulate the question you ultimately want to answer or the problem you ultimately want to address. In turn, this provides a clear direction for the study—everything that follows, in terms of the development of your study, will logically relate directly back to the question or problem. Furthermore, by brainstorming various questions and problems to address, we typically identify even more concerns that require our scientific attention. Clearly stating these questions and/or problems is the first formal step to conducting educational research.

- *Educational research requires the formulation of a specific plan for conducting the research.* Once the inherent question or problem has been specified and clarified, one must develop a plan for just how this research will be conducted. The data necessary for answering the question or addressing the problem do not miraculously emerge out of thin air for the educational researcher to take and run with. The entire study must be well planned and carefully thought out, prior to its inception. These are the types of decisions and plans that must be made in advance:

  ✓ Who will you study?
  ✓ How many individuals will you need—or do you want—to study?
  ✓ What information will you collect from them?
  ✓ How will you collect those data?
  ✓ When will you collect those data?
  ✓ What will you do with (i.e., how will you analyze) those data once you have them in hand?
  ✓ How do you plan to interpret the results of those analyses?

All these methodological issues must be addressed at the outset of any research study. For reasons we will discuss later in this book, these types of decisions simply cannot be made "on the fly," in the midst of the research process.

- *Educational research requires the collection, analysis, and interpretation of data as a means of answering the inherent question or problem under investigation.* For many novice researchers, this part of the process of doing educational research—collecting, analyzing, and interpreting data—often proves to be the most daunting. However, the more attention paid to these steps of the educational research process, the better the quality of the research study's ultimate outcome. In some cases, research studies will involve the collection of existing data (e.g., school attendance records or standardized test scores), but they will most often require the collection of original, new data (e.g., surveys, interviews, or pre- and posttests) specific to the research questions the study is addressing. Regardless of the source of the data, they will still need to be analyzed (with the perspective of the research question or problem in mind) and interpreted appropriately. This is a commonality across all educational research studies.

- *In most cases, educational research tends to be cyclical or helical, as opposed to linear.* When we look at the specific process of doing educational research in Chapter 2, it will appear as if it is linear. In other words, Step 1 is followed by Step 2, which is followed by Step 3, and so on until the research concludes. While this is accurate (to a degree), research seldom, if ever, stops at the end of this process. More often than not, conducting educational research in an effort to answer one or two pressing questions will result in the generation of new, additional research questions—and typically a greater number than you started with. Therefore, it is probably best to view educational research as *cyclical* (i.e., with cycles of research studies that explore the same basic topic in subsequent years or classrooms) or even *helical* (i.e., with a spiraling effect, where the original research study spawns additional, follow-up, or extended studies addressing different aspects of the same broad topic). This is, perhaps, one of the most unique aspects of educational research—that it is never truly done and that one can continually investigate educational phenomena.

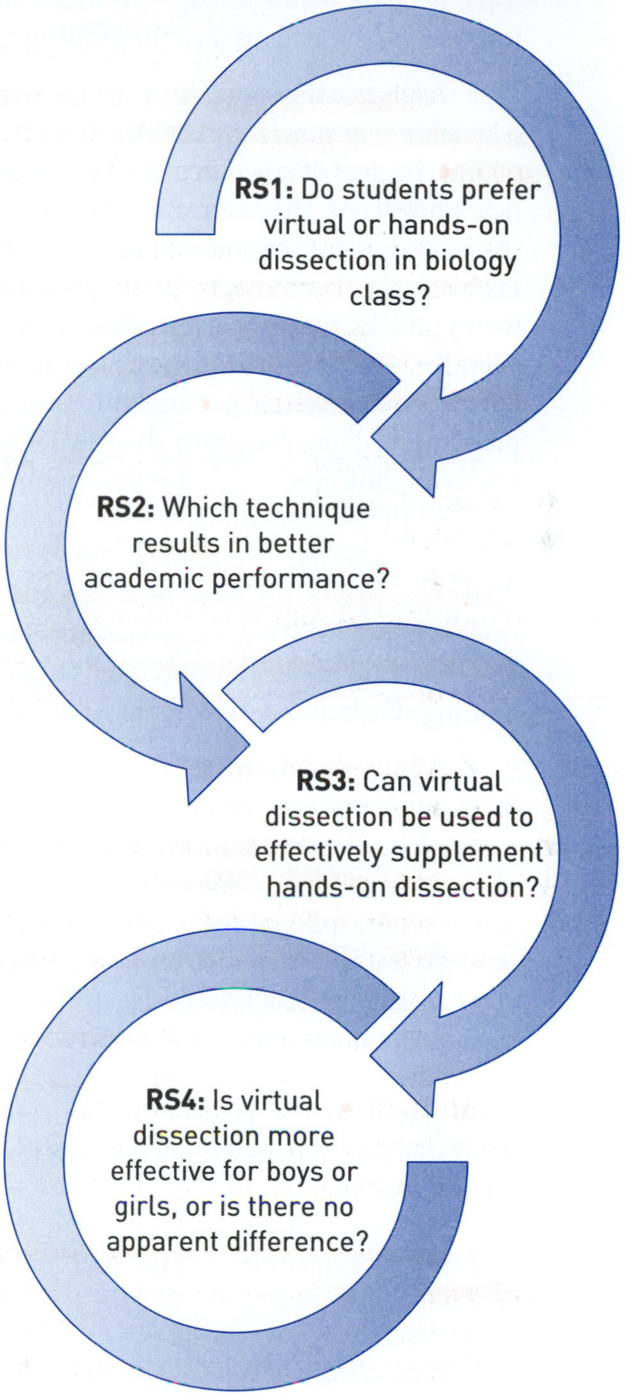

Figure 1.1 presents a scenario where a science department might want to investigate the benefits of a virtual dissection (e.g., using an iPad app) versus the more traditional, hands-on method. In Research Study 1 (RS1), the question focuses on the students' preferences for the two types of laboratory activities. The next study (RS2) focuses not on opinion or preference but, rather, on academic performance. RS3 investigates the use of the virtual dissection as a means only to supplement, not replace, the hands-on activity.

FIGURE 1.1 ● The Cyclical or Helical Nature of Educational Research

RS1: Do students prefer virtual or hands-on dissection in biology class?

RS2: Which technique results in better academic performance?

RS3: Can virtual dissection be used to effectively supplement hands-on dissection?

RS4: Is virtual dissection more effective for boys or girls, or is there no apparent difference?

In RS4, the department might now want to know if there is a difference—in terms of both preference and academic performance—between boys and girls in their use of virtual and hands-on dissections. In this scenario, notice (1) how the same broad topic is being investigated in all four studies but also (2) that different aspects of that topic serve as the focus (i.e., the guiding research question) for each subsequent study.

- *Educational research is, by its very nature, inquisitive, objective, and original.* Because educational research is scientific, it must be approached from the perspective of objectivity. The goal of any research study (regardless of the field of study) is the generation of new knowledge, the gaining of a better understanding of some issue or phenomenon, or the development of some sort of innovation. This simply cannot be accomplished if the researcher is biased or approaches a research study with some degree of subjectivity. That being said, it is critical to note that, as human beings, we all possess certain biases—for example, with respect to our view of the world, toward certain people, and even in our perspective on research. Human nature dictates that we will always have some sort of preconceived idea (i.e., *bias*) about what we may find as the result of any given research endeavor; however, the goal when conducting research in education is to *make every effort* to avoid the temptation to let those preconceptions guide how we conduct the study or interpret our results. Building on the previous example, I may honestly think that virtual dissection will be preferred by students and will result in better academic performance; however, I will still collect opinion and performance data from students on both virtual *and* hands-on dissection activities. This, in turn, will allow me to objectively answer my guiding research question about which learning activity is better.

- *Educational research should be beneficial, meaningful, and significant.* Topics or questions that are trivial in their nature should not be the focus of educational research studies. Educational research should be conducted so the results prove beneficial to someone, somewhere, somehow, someday. If you want to study something that will not potentially result in one or more of the above benefits, then I would strongly advise you to rethink your research topic. Educational research should be done to garner new knowledge and to shed light on the human condition and educational phenomenon. It should never be conducted as a means of doing harm to individuals or groups, or to denigrate, cast blame, find fault, deny opportunity, or stifle progress. The goal of the educational researcher is always to increase understanding and, whenever possible, to promote opportunity and advancement for the population at large.

Equally important, educators should understand what educational research *is not.*

- *Educational research does not have outcomes that are predetermined.* Following logically from an earlier bullet point, educational research does not pursue questions that either (1) have already been answered or (2) have a predetermined, desirable answer. This is an essential difference between *science* and *pseudoscience* (Johnson, 2008; Mertler, 2014). Science—and inquiry that results from the application of the scientific method—relies on perceived reality (typically in the form of collected data) to determine beliefs. In other words, and as we have seen, data are collected and analyzed to determine what is believed. In contrast, pseudoscience uses beliefs to determine perceived reality. That is, one begins with a strong belief and seeks out data that can be used to support that belief (Johnson, 2008). Pseudoscience is often used as a marketing tool by companies to sell products or by individuals or groups in attempts to demonstrate that their ideas, methods, or products are the most effective. Clearly, this approach is not systematic, nor is it objective, and it does not use the scientific method. Therefore, it is not science . . . and it is not research (Mertler, 2014).

● *Research is not simply gathering information.* When I was in the eighth grade, I did a research project on UFOs. I spent months reading books and articles with firsthand accounts of alien abductions, taking notes on 3-x-5 notecards, developing an outline, and then finally writing my research report. I learned a great deal in completing that project—not just about UFOs but also about organization, time management, and writing skills. It was a great learning experience; however, it was not "research." My overall experience and final report were not very *inquisitive*; I did not have any sort of clear and focused guiding question I was attempting to answer. They certainly were not *original*, since all I was really doing was collecting and organizing previously published stories and accounts. I might even argue that they were not objective, since I "captured" only one side of the story (i.e., information that supported the existence of UFOs). What I did was gather a lot of disparate information from a wide variety of sources and compile it into a cohesive written report—good work but clearly not research.

● *Educational research is not conclusive.* As we have discussed, educational research often generates more questions than were initially intended to be answered. In that sense, educational research is never conclusive. Perhaps more important, however, educational research typically involves the study of human beings and their behavior. The behavior of human beings is constantly in flux, changing in reaction to internal influences (e.g., age, natural growth and development, psychology, physical health, mental health) as well as external stimuli (e.g., technology, peers, family, teachers). What we research and conclude one day could easily change the next day if we study it in a different setting, with different students, teachers, curricula, classrooms, interpersonal relationships, and so forth. Along similar lines, the answers to the questions that guided our research should never be interpreted as right or wrong. Rather, they are answers appropriate for the given time and set of circumstances, including the particular data that were collected and analyzed.

● *Educational research is not trivial.* Over the past several years, there has been increased focus on the implementation of research-based strategies geared toward improved student performance. Research plays a very important role in today's educational climate, as well as in various school reform movements that we observe across our country and around the world. It is critical that educators at all levels see research as having substantial value for their practice, both individually (i.e., in their respective classrooms) and collectively (i.e., for the profession as a whole).

Educational Research as a Process

Earlier in this chapter, we discussed that educational research is a process, one that parallels the scientific method. Before we take a look at the specific process, we need to understand some of the guiding principles behind conducting research in education. The primary goal of most all educational research studies is "to describe, explain, predict, or control [educational] phenomena" (Gay, Mills, & Airasian, 2009). This is the case, regardless of the particular methods used to conduct the research (i.e., the techniques used to collect and analyze data). However, different research methods can produce different views of reality. The various research methods tend to be placed into two broad categories—quantitative approaches and qualitative approaches—based on different assumptions about how best to understand what is true or what constitutes reality (McMillan, 2012). Quantitative research methods require the collection and analysis of *numerical* data (e.g., test scores, attendance records, attitude scales, interest inventories); qualitative research methods require the collection and analysis of *narrative* data (e.g., observation notes, interview transcripts, journal entries).

Quantitative research methods use a deductive approach to reasoning when attempting to find answers to a research question. **Deductive reasoning** works from more general, broad-based ideas, concepts, observations, or experiences to the more specific, in a "top-down" manner (see Figure 1.2). You will notice that as one proceeds through the research process, there is a general funneling (i.e., narrowing) effect. As a purely hypothetical example, researchers conduct a survey of 1,500 educators regarding their opinions (i.e., *variety of data*) on the Common Core State Standards (CCSS). Those responses and opinions are aggregated, examined, and evaluated (i.e., *analyses of the data*), and it is determined that 65% of the respondents think that the CCSS will be beneficial for students and 35% believe that they won't (i.e., *specific conclusions*).

FIGURE 1.2   ●   The Process of Deductive Reasoning, as Applied to the Research Process

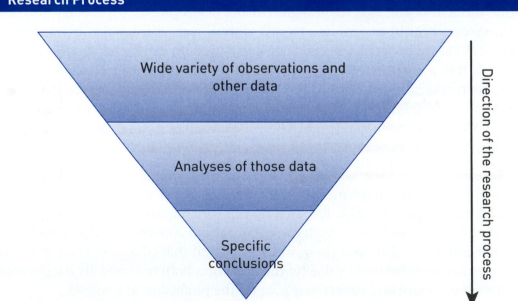

Wide variety of observations and other data

Analyses of those data

Specific conclusions

Direction of the research process

On the other hand, qualitative research methods use an inductive approach to resolving problems and answering research questions. **Inductive reasoning** works in a "bottom-up" manner, opposite to the direction used in deductive reasoning, and involves the development of broad, general conclusions from observations of a very limited number of events or experiences (see Figure 1.3). To build on our hypothetical example, imagine that a team of researchers observes a small group (i.e., 3–4 teachers) over the course of 2 months to see how implementing CCSS has (or has not) changed their instructional practices. Once the researchers have compiled their observation notes (i.e., *specific observations*) and examined them for any emergent themes or patterns in behavior (i.e., *analyses of the data*), they develop broad conclusions, hypotheses, or theories about teachers' instructional practices and the influence of CCSS (i.e., *broad conclusions*).

To accomplish the primary goal of a quantitative educational research study, researchers collect data on carefully identified **variables** (i.e., factors that may affect the outcome of a study or characteristics that are central to the topic or problems being addressed). Those data (by the way, the word *data* is always plural) are then analyzed and the results interpreted to test **hypotheses** (i.e., predicted outcomes of the study) or answer **research questions** (i.e., guiding questions that serve as the focus of the study). For example, a quantitative research study might require the collection of data on elementary school discipline referrals and absenteeism (numerical variables) to answer the following research question: Are there differences in the rates of disciplinary problems and absenteeism in schools with a K–8 grade span versus those with other grade span configurations (e.g., K–6, 6–8) (Mertler, 2014)?

The plan that will be used by the researcher to carry out the study is referred to as the **research design**. Quantitative research designs are either nonexperimental or experimental. In **nonexperimental research**, the researcher does not have direct control over any variable in the study, either because it has already occurred or because

FIGURE 1.3 ● The Process of Inductive Reasoning, as Applied to the Research Process

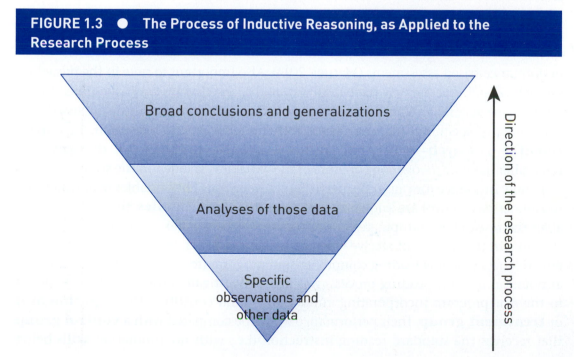

Broad conclusions and generalizations

Analyses of those data

Specific observations and other data

Direction of the research process

it is not possible (or, perhaps, ethical) for it to be influenced (Mertler, 2014). Another way of saying this is that, in nonexperimental research, variables cannot be controlled or manipulated by the researcher. The previous illustration of a study of school discipline and absenteeism problems is an example of a nonexperimental study, as the type of grade configuration, the number of discipline referrals, and the number of absences cannot be controlled or influenced by the researcher; those things occur naturally or have already occurred. That variables cannot be controlled in nonexperimental studies is an important distinction between nonexperimental research designs and experimental research designs, in particular when it comes to stating specific conclusions at the end of a study. This usually means that the conclusions to nonexperimental studies are able only to describe variables or the relationships between variables. Some examples of nonexperimental research designs include *descriptive, comparative, correlational,* and *causal-comparative* research (McMillan, 2012).

Descriptive studies are more basic, in that they simply report information—resulting from the collection of empirical data—about the frequency or amount of something (e.g., what percentage of the time do teachers use performance-based assessments in their classrooms?). **Comparative studies** build on descriptive studies by comparing two or more groups on one or more measured variables (e.g., is there a significant difference between elementary and secondary teachers' use of performance-based assessments?). **Correlational studies** measure the degree and nature of the relationship between two or more variables (e.g., what is the relationship between years of teaching experience and use of performance-based assessments?). Finally, **causal-comparative studies** (also sometimes referred to as ***ex post facto* studies**) compare groups—where group membership is determined by something that occurred in the past—on subsequent data on another variable in such a way that it makes possible drawing potential causal relationships between the two variables (e.g., do teachers who completed a stand-alone pre-service course in classroom assessment use performance-based assessment more than do teachers who did not complete such a course?). Notice that based on the sample research questions provided, it is quite possible to use any of the various types of nonexperimental research designs to study a given topic—in this case, classroom teachers' use of performance-based assessments (Mertler, 2014). Also important to note in the preceding sample research questions is the helical nature (i.e., varying research questions/studies on the same general topic) of educational research, as we have previously discussed.

Generally speaking and contrasted with nonexperimental research, in **experimental research**—which also includes **quasi-experimental designs**—the researcher has control over one or more of the variables included in the study that may somehow influence (or cause) the participants' behavior. The variables over which the researcher has control are known as the **independent variables**; these are the variables the researcher manipulates, meaning that the researcher determines which participants in the study will receive which condition (Mertler, 2014). For example, if the effectiveness of a new reading comprehension program (focused on the integration of annotation into the reading process) was being investigated, those students exposed to the *new* program incorporating annotation would constitute the **experimental or treatment group**; their performance would be compared with a **control group** that receives the standard reading instruction (i.e., with no annotation skills being taught, practiced, and reinforced). The ultimate variable of interest (i.e., the "behavior" variable mentioned above, perhaps "achievement in reading comprehension" in our example) is referred to as the **dependent variable** (since its value *depends* on the value, or group membership, of the independent variable).

Experimental research designs come in a wide variety, which will be discussed later in Chapter 7. However, a concrete illustration of an experimental research study might prove beneficial, at this point. Suppose a history teacher wants to determine whether students perform better when taught American history using the more traditional forward (i.e., past-to-present) approach versus a backward (i.e., present-to-past) approach (Mertler, 2014). She randomly assigns half of her class periods to be taught using the forward approach and the other half to be taught using the backward approach. The independent variable for her study is "the type of instruction." There are two *levels* to this variable (these two levels essentially "define" the two groups): The experimental group receives the innovative backward approach to instruction; the comparison group receives the more traditional forward approach. Finally, the academic performance (dependent variable) of all students is measured using the same instrument (e.g., a final exam) for both groups. The aspect that makes this study experimental in nature is that the teacher herself determines which group will receive which version of the treatment (i.e., instruction); in other words, she is *manipulating* or *controlling* the independent variable.

Data collected during quantitative research studies are numerical and are therefore analyzed statistically. Statistical analyses may include the use of descriptive statistics, inferential statistics, or both. **Descriptive statistics** enable researchers to summarize, organize, and simplify data. Some specific techniques include statistics such as the mean, median, mode, range, standard deviation, correlations, and standardized scores. **Inferential statistics** are more complex and permit researchers to test the statistical significance of the difference between two or more groups, or the degree of relationship between two variables. **Statistical significance** refers to a decision made from the results of statistical procedures that enable researchers to conclude that the findings of a given study (e.g., the size of the difference between two groups or the strength of the relationship between two variables) are large enough in the sample studied to represent a meaningful difference or relationship in the **population** from which the **sample** was drawn (Mertler, 2014). You will learn much more about statistical analyses in Chapter 13.

While quantitative research studies focus on a fairly small number of variables, qualitative research studies use a much more holistic approach to data collection. Qualitative research designs make use of systematic observation to gain knowledge, reach understanding, and answer research questions. In qualitative research studies, there is no attempt to control or manipulate any variable; researchers simply take the world as it exists and as they find it (Johnson, 2008). Qualitative research tends to emphasize the importance of multiple measures and observations. Therefore, the research questions—and/or associated problems that guide qualitative research—tend to be more broad and open-ended. This allows the researcher to collect a wide variety of data for the purpose of getting a more holistic picture of the phenomenon under investigation, and allows for triangulation.

Triangulation is a process of relating multiple sources of data to establish their trustworthiness or verify the consistency of the facts while trying to account for their inherent biases (Bogdan & Biklen, 2007; Glesne, 2006). It is important to note that conducting triangulation does not necessarily mean that the researcher is using three (as in *tri-*) sources of data; it simply means that there is more than one source of data. Perhaps a more appropriate term would be *polyangulation* (since the prefix *poly-* is defined as "more than one or many"; Mertler, 2014). This process of relating various sources of qualitative data enables the researcher to try to get a better handle on what is happening in reality and to have greater confidence in research findings (Glesne, 2006). For example, in a qualitative study, one might collect data through firsthand observations, videotaped observations, and interviews. Triangulating different sets of data from these sources would require them to be examined to determine, for example, if the behaviors exhibited and comments made by participants are consistent regardless of the type of data representing them. In other words, did a specific person act the *same way he said he acted*, or did he *verbally portray his behavior differently* from his actual behavior?

Similar to quantitative research, there are a variety of qualitative research designs, including phenomenology, ethnography, grounded theory, and case studies (McMillan, 2012; Mertler, 2014). **Phenomenological studies** engage the researcher in a—sometimes lengthy—process of individual interviews in an attempt to fully understand a particular phenomenon (e.g., what characteristics do teachers need to be viewed as compassionate by their students?). **Ethnographic research** describes social interactions between people in group settings (e.g., what meaning does the teachers' lounge have for the staff at Main Street Elementary School?). **Grounded theory research** attempts to discover a theory that relates to a particular environment (e.g., what types of personal and school characteristics serve to motivate teachers?). Finally, **case studies** are in-depth studies of specifically identified programs, activities, people, or groups (e.g., what is the nature of the school culture at Washington Middle School?).

The data collected during a qualitative research study may be quite diverse. Recall that qualitative data are typically narrative and consist primarily of observations, interviews, and existing documents and reports (McMillan, 2012). Resulting qualitative data are analyzed by means of a process known as **logico-inductive analysis**, a thought process that uses logic to make sense of patterns and trends in the data (you will learn more about this analytical process in Chapter 11).

While quantitative and qualitative approaches to conducting research are quite different on a variety of levels, they should not necessarily be considered mutually exclusive. It is not uncommon to see research studies, particularly in educational settings, that employ both types of research data. These types of studies are referred to as **mixed-methods research designs**. The combination of both qualitative and quantitative data tends to provide a better understanding of a given research problem than can one type of data in isolation. Perhaps the most appropriate way to think about mixed-methods designs is that these types of studies capitalize on the relative strengths of *both* quantitative and qualitative data. Creswell (2005) considers mixed-methods designs and **action research studies** to be very similar to each other, since they both often use quantitative and qualitative data. The only real difference between the two is the underlying purpose for the research. The main goal of mixed-methods studies is more traditional (i.e., to better understand and explain a research problem); the main goal of action research is to address local-level problems with the anticipation of finding immediate solutions. You will learn more about mixed-methods designs and action research in Chapters 8 and 9, respectively.

Now that we have a better grasp on some of the foundational aspects of educational research, let us consider a concrete example of the process of conducting an actual study. Remember that educational research is typically carried out as a process—that parallels the scientific method—using the following steps.

Step 1: Identification of an Existing Problem

An educational concern is identified for which there is no obvious answer. The concern may have arisen because of an identified need, an interest, a requirement, or a commissioned work, and may have been present for a long time or come up unexpectedly. For example, teachers in Adams School District recently identified a disturbing pattern of academic achievement in their schools—students from certain cultural and racial groups seem to progress more rapidly than others, despite the educators' efforts to provide equal educational opportunity for all. Initially, they can offer no substantive explanation for the occurrence, nor are they sure about which groups are performing differently.

Step 2: Clarification of the Specific Problem

Simply knowing that some student groups perform differently than others in some academic areas is not focused enough to guide a research study. The initial concern must be clarified and stated more succinctly, after which it becomes known as the **research problem**. In the case of Adams School District, and upon closer examination of existing data, teachers and administrators determine that there is a noticeable difference in academic performance in Algebra I courses, although they still are unsure as to why the difference exists. They decide to formally state their research problem as follows: *There is a differential level of academic achievement, as evidenced by scores on the state's end-of-course (EOC) exam in Algebra I, between various racial groups of students.*

Step 3: Formulation of the Research Question(s)

Now that the problem has been clearly identified, one or more research questions must be formally stated to provide specific direction for conducting the research study. In other words, the goal of this study will be to answer that research question. In the case of student performance in Algebra I, the educator-researchers in Adams School District state their research question as follows: *Is there a significant difference in Algebra I EOC scores based on students' racial classifications? If so, which racial groups outperform others?*

Step 4: Development of Procedures by Which Data Are Collected

When developing procedures for the collection of data, care must be taken to ensure that the data collected will "match" or "align with" the research question(s). If this does not occur, then it will be difficult, if not impossible, to accurately answer the research question at the end of the study. At the risk of oversimplifying our sample study, the research question would necessitate collecting data on (1) students' racial categorization and (2) EOC test scores.

Step 5: Specification of Procedures by Which Data Are Analyzed

Similarly, alignment between data analysis techniques and the original research questions must be ensured. Otherwise, you will have results of your data analysis, but they will not provide answers to your question, which defeats the purpose of research in the first place. Since our teachers and administrators are looking to compare students based on racial groupings, they will want to use a data analysis technique that focuses on group comparisons. They will likely use a *t*-test or ANOVA (you will learn more about these techniques in Chapter 13).

Step 6: Statement of the Findings Resulting From the Analyses

Once the results of data analysis have been obtained, the most straightforward way to state the findings is to use the results to provide a specific answer to the research question. Teachers and administrators in Adams School District would likely be able to use the results of their data analyses to determine that there is, in fact, a difference in Algebra I EOC performance based on racial classification. They would also be able to determine which racial groups scored higher than others. In other words, they would have successfully answered their research question as a result of conducting the study.

Step 7: Development of Conclusions/Recommendations Related to Question(s)

Once the research question has been answered, educator-researchers must then use that information to draw conclusions about the original problem that was identified and make recommendations about what to do in the future. This is the step that typically leads to the development or generation of additional research questions that build on the results of the current research study. Returning to our example, Adams School District may now want to seek answers to one or more of the following questions (among many other possibilities):

- What impacts on instructional methods result from some students outperforming others in the Algebra I EOC test?
- Are some students or sections of Algebra I taught differently?
- Are different teachers presenting the content and reinforcing mathematical skills differently?
- To what degree might this differential level of performance be based on whether the Algebra I class takes place in the morning versus afternoon?

In summary, the educational research process typically includes the following activities:

- Identifying an existing problem
- Clarifying and specifying the problem
- Formulating research questions concerning the central problem
- Determining and carrying out procedures by which data are collected and analyzed
- Stating the findings as determined through data analyses
- Developing conclusions and recommendations related to the original research question

Knowing Your Specific Discipline

One of the best things you can do to begin preparing yourself to be both a researcher and a critical consumer of research is familiarize yourself with your own specific discipline(s). Regardless of whether you plan to become a practitioner or a researcher in the future, knowledge and understanding of the research process, research methods, and appropriate ways to collect and analyze different types of data are essential *and critical* skills for keeping up with advances in your field (Leedy & Ormrod, 2013). These skills are crucial in guiding your ability to make accurate, well-informed decisions in your practice as a professional educator. Failure to gain *and* master these skills can only result in professional decisions based on faulty data, inappropriate interpretations and conclusions, or unsupported personal intuitions (Leedy & Ormrod, 2013).

One important way for you to be knowledgeable about your field is to read articles and other publications relevant to your academic discipline. As an educator, your "academic discipline" can be defined in many ways. You might read articles related to the subject matter you teach, or to the age or grade level you teach; perhaps you read articles about education in general; you might also read articles that address education policy or educational leadership—the list goes on and on and on. Along those lines, finding such articles and publications is not as difficult as you might think. A logical starting point is with your professors, who will have suggestions about journals that are particularly relevant to your field of study. Once you have a list of such journals, simply begin by browsing their tables of contents for articles that might grab your attention.

One additional piece of advice as you begin to explore research in your field is that you must be able to discern the general quality of the articles or publications you choose to read. One way to do this is by focusing your attention on research studies that have been refereed. A **refereed research report** is one that has been subjected to a review by colleagues and experts in a particular field. For the report to be published, it must have been deemed by experts in that particular field to be of reasonable quality. This is not to say that nonrefereed reports or articles cannot be beneficial or meaningful to you in your practice as a professional educator; the difference is that nonrefereed reports have not been subjected to this level of review. All research is and should be subject to critical review. Refereed articles have undergone this process, whereas nonrefereed articles leave that judgment purely to the reader's discretion.

As an educational researcher myself—and, perhaps more important, as a professional educator—I strongly believe that you owe it to yourself, and to your practice as a professional educator, to be educated in your profession.

Educators as Researchers

The act of studying and learning about the educational research process is valuable to your professional life as an educator, regardless of the setting in which you work. It is vitally important for educators, at all levels, to have a sound understanding of research methods for two basic reasons. First, at some point in your professional career, it may be highly beneficial for you to design and conduct, or otherwise become involved in, some sort of research study, as we will discuss momentarily. Second, having a foundational understanding of the research process enables you to be a more discriminating consumer of published research studies. This is important when it comes to identifying a particular study's strengths and weaknesses and determining the extent to which its findings may, or may not, apply to you and your setting.

Additionally, there are several common purposes—or *practical applications*, if you will—for studying educational research. These are just a few of the more common ways studying educational research can inform your professional practice:

- Writing grant proposals (including their evaluation components)
- Completing theses and dissertations
- Reading primary and secondary sources more critically
- Reviewing professional literature as a means of thinking more critically, and possibly more reflectively, about issues and problems related to your setting (e.g., your classroom, your students, your subject matter)
- Conducting more formal research projects

You may be wondering, in light of the required steps and processes considered so far, whether genuine research can be carried out by educators and, if so, whether such research can truly shed light on topics of educational concern. Rest assured that educators can, even while busy on the job, do research of quality and importance. For some time, practical inquiry undertaken by educators has been considered more likely to lead to classroom change than has formal research conducted by research specialists (Richardson, 1994). Radebaugh (1994) contends that educational research should not be left to experts but should involve educators much more extensively; educator-conducted research is especially powerful in shedding light on topics such as educators' personal and professional lives and the problems educators regularly encounter in their work (Fleischer, 1994; Goodson, 1994). I am a firm believer in the fact that educator-led research can be an extremely empowering professional activity.

Thus, be assured that not only can you involve yourself successfully in meaningful educational research, but any investigation you conduct likely will be more beneficial than formal research to your work in education, and probably more beneficial to other educators as well. You may even wish to involve your students as co-researchers in your investigations, which would logically invite them to take more responsibility for their own learning.

Developmental Activities

1. List and briefly describe at least five things within your classroom, school, or other educational setting that interest you and that you might want to pursue further. These might be problems you have become aware of, aspects of your practice you want to improve, or issues that concern you as a professional educator.

2. Based on what you learned in this chapter about educational research, for each of the problems or issues you generated above,

judge the extent to which you believe that each might be appropriate for an educational research study.

3. Based on your new knowledge, briefly discuss how you believe that educational research can prove to be personally and professionally beneficial to you. What concerns do you have about its potential shortcomings?

4. Sit with one or two educational colleagues (preferably ones who are not in this course with you) and discuss educational research. Are their opinions toward research similar to or different from yours? Do they believe that educational research can benefit them, either personally or professionally (or both)? What concerns about educational research do they express to you?

5. Do you believe that educational research can benefit your students or students in general? Why or why not?

Summary

- Research, in general, is important to how we function as a successful and productive society.
- The primary goal of virtually any research study is to find answers to our questions.

  o Typical sources for answering our questions (i.e., tradition, authority, and common sense) usually fall short in helping us find those answers.

- The scientific method is a systematic, step-by-step strategy used to answer questions and resolve problems.
- The main steps in the scientific method are as follows:

  o Clarify the main question inherent in the problem.
  o State a hypothesis.
  o Collect, analyze, and interpret information (i.e., data) related to the question.
  o Form conclusions derived from the interpretations of the analyses.
  o Use the conclusions to verify or reject your hypothesis.

- Educational research is a process that involves applying the scientific method to educational problems and phenomena.

- As a process, all educational research studies share the following characteristics:

  o Scientific
  o Begin with a question or problem that serves as the purpose or goal of the study
  o Require the formulation of a specific plan for conducting the actual research
  o Require the collection, analysis, and interpretation of data to answer the question under investigation
  o Tend to be cyclical, or helical, as opposed to linear
  o Inquisitive, objective, and original
  o Should be beneficial, meaningful, and significant
  o Do not have predetermined outcomes
  o Do not involve simply the gathering of information
  o Not conclusive
  o Not trivial

- Educational research relies on either deductive or inductive reasoning.

  o Deductive reasoning works from more general, broad ideas and observations to the more specific, in a top-down manner; it is commonly used in quantitative research studies.

- o Inductive reasoning works from specific observations toward the development of much broader conclusions or generalizations; it is commonly used with qualitative research studies.

- Data are collected on variables, and those data are analyzed to test hypotheses or answer research questions.
- Research designs describe the plan to be used by the researcher to carry out the actual study.

  - o Quantitative research designs can be either experimental or nonexperimental.

    - ✓ Nonexperimental designs include studies that are descriptive, comparative, correlational, or causal-comparative.
    - ✓ Experimental designs allow the researcher to have some degree of control over some variables; they involve the identification of independent and dependent variables, as well as experimental and control groups of participants.

  - o Qualitative research designs involve a broader, more holistic approach to collecting and analyzing data.

    - ✓ Triangulation, or polyangulation, is a process of relating multiple sources

of data to verify their trustworthiness, accuracy, and consistency.

- ✓ Qualitative designs include phenomenological, ethnographic, grounded theory, and case study research.

  - o Mixed-methods research designs, along with action research, typically involve the collection and analysis of both quantitative and qualitative data.

- The main steps in the process of conducting educational research are as follows:

  - o Identification of an existing problem
  - o Clarification of the specific problem
  - o Formulation of research question(s)
  - o Development of data collection procedures
  - o Specification of data analysis procedures
  - o Statement of the findings resulting from data analysis
  - o Development of conclusions and recommendations related to the question(s)

- Becoming familiar with your field of study by reading research articles is one of the best ways to begin your future as an educational researcher or consumer of research.
- Some of the most meaningful and beneficial research in education results from studies conducted by practicing educators.

⑤SAGE edge™

Sharpen your skills with SAGE edge!

edge.sagepub.com/mertler

SAGE edge for Students provides a personalized approach to help you accomplish your coursework goals in an easy-to-use learning environment. You'll find action plans, mobile-friendly eFlashcards, and quizzes as well as video, web, and resources and links to SAGE journal articles to support and expand on the concepts presented in this chapter.

2

Overview of the Educational Research Process

Student Learning Objectives

After studying Chapter 2, students will be able to do the following:

1. Summarize various activities that must be conducted during each step of the educational research process

2. Evaluate why specification of a research problem is so critical

3. Describe the importance of carefully stating the research question

4. List various reasons for conducting a review of related research

5. Identify various issues that must be addressed when developing a research plan

6. List and describe examples of techniques for collecting qualitative and quantitative data

7. Describe how and when data analysis occurs in qualitative and quantitative research

8. Describe the importance of results, conclusions, and recommendations in a research study

n Chapter 1, we looked briefly at the general process of conducting an educational research study. We outlined the main steps as follows:

- Identifying an existing problem
- Clarifying and specifying the problem
- Formulating research questions concerning the central problem
- Determining and carrying out procedures by which data are collected and analyzed

- Stating the findings as determined through data analyses
- Developing conclusions and recommendations related to the original research question

However, it is critical at this time that we begin to examine these steps more *specifically*, as each contains particular subcomponents. The focus of this chapter is to introduce the steps necessary in conducting educational research. The steps in the process (followed by the chapter of this book in which each is addressed) are as follows:

1. Identifying and limiting a research topic or problem (*Chapter 3*)
2. Formally stating and refining research question(s) (*Chapter 3*)
3. Reviewing existing literature related to the problem (*Chapter 5*)
4. Writing a literature review (*Chapter 5*)
5. Developing a research plan (*Chapters 6–10*)
6. Implementing the research plan and collecting data (*Chapters 11 and 12*)
7. Analyzing those data (*Chapters 11 and 13*)
8. Stating findings, conclusions, and recommendations in a written research report (*Chapter 14*)

This process is depicted in Figure 2.1. It is important to note, once again, the cyclical nature of educational research. Notice how the outcomes or results of one study can logically and informatively lead into the next phase of educational research. This figure is certainly not meant to imply that educational research is a linear process. As you read in Chapter 1—and, specifically, saw depicted in Figure 1.1—aspects of one study (e.g., conclusions, methods, literature reviews) may influence and guide subsequent studies.

Identifying and Limiting a Research Topic or Problem

The first—and arguably most critical—decision for any educational research study is exactly *what* to study. Often, personal and professional experiences lend themselves to the identification of educational research topics. For those of us who have conducted educational research studies, we typically choose topics we have had some previous experience with or exposure to. Topics for educational research studies should hold a good deal of personal interest for the researcher. If for no other reason, you are going to spend several months, if not years, researching the topic—so it most definitely should pique your interest. Personal interest, therefore, is a huge factor in deciding on an initial topic for educational research.

That being said, of course, there is likely nothing more important in terms of identifying an initial topic for research than an existing need. If a need has been determined, then there will be an audience interested in the results of a given research study. A need for research on a particular topic may stem from prior research conducted on that topic. It may also arise from various experiences of practitioners in the field related to the topic. Therefore, current and future research, as driven by this identified need, should likely make a contribution to the body of research in a particular field of study.

Another key factor in identifying a topic for a research study is verification that the potential topic is, in fact, a genuine problem. In other words, the researcher has a

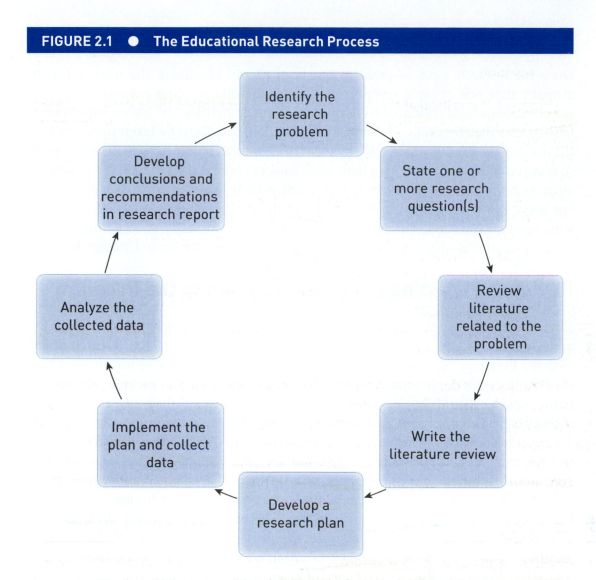

FIGURE 2.1   ●   The Educational Research Process

responsibility to provide a rationale for why this particular topic or problem is worthy of being studied. Arguably, the majority of the evidence for this justification and rationale will be found in the body of related research literature. The literature review should have a strong influence on the identification, specification, and articulation of the research problem. Similarly, specification of a particular research problem in subsequent cycles of research may be guided by various aspects of previously conducted research studies.

Other important factors include manageability and time. When conducting educational research studies, it is important to keep the ultimate goal in mind. Remember, the basic goal of nearly all research studies is to find answers to questions, or to help explain and understand some educational phenomenon. For example, if you are planning to conduct a research study and know that you must have it completed in roughly 4 to 6 months, knowledge of that fact will contribute a great deal to decisions about the specific topic you wish to research. Similarly, exposure to and familiarity with various research designs can be a great benefit when trying to gauge the manageability of researching a particular topic. Suggestions for identifying and narrowing the focus of educational research studies, along with other initial considerations, are discussed more extensively in Chapter 3.

Formally Stating and Refining Research Question(s)

Once the research topic or problem has been clearly identified, the next step is to formally state one or more research questions. Carefully wording a research question is a critical aspect of conducting educational research, because the research question is what guides the remainder of the study. In addition, care must be taken to ensure that the question is actually answerable by data the researcher is able to collect. Failure to do so may result in the collection of inaccurate data, or perhaps data that do not parallel or align with the research question. In cases such as these, unfortunately, you do not find out about the misalignment until the end of the study—when it is too late to restate your research question. Further discussions related to formally stating and refining research questions—including sample research questions—appear in Chapter 3.

Reviewing Existing Literature Related to the Problem

Examining existing research studies can provide a great deal of background information and guidance to the identified problem serving as the focus of the research study. "Related literature" can be loosely defined as any existing source of information that sheds light on the topic under investigation. These sources might include publications such as professional books, research journals, or unpublished research reports. Although there is really no limit to what can be used as background information on a given research topic, care must be taken to evaluate the existing literature against several criteria. These criteria include, but are not limited to, the following: the objectivity of the published research (and/or the extent to which an author has clearly identified and explained any potential bias); the specification of limitations inherent in the study; whether the research constitutes a *primary* (i.e., written by the individual who actually conducted the research) or *secondary* (i.e., someone's interpretation of another's research) source; whether the research is *empirical* or opinion-based; and whether it has been subject to a process of peer review.

Reviewing related literature is a critical part of any research study because it can inform so many aspects, including the specification of the problem, development of the research questions, and determination of research designs and methodologies. Suggestions and techniques for reviewing related literature are presented in Chapter 5.

Writing a Literature Review

For many researchers, one of the more challenging aspects of conducting a research study—and writing a research report—is writing a formal review of related literature. Compiling and synthesizing literature related to a given topic is not always as straightforward as it might seem. Adding to that challenge is the fact that every topic is different, especially in terms of the existing body of literature. Further, there is no "magical formula" that anyone can share with you regarding how to develop and formally write a review of literature. That being said, however, guidance regarding the development of a literature review can still be provided to the novice researcher. Suggestions and recommendations for writing a formal literature review are discussed in Chapter 5.

Developing a Research Plan

Specification of the research problem, development of research questions, and a thorough review of the existing body of literature provide the necessary groundwork to begin developing a plan to conduct an educational research study. The next step in the process is to specify exactly *how* a study will be conducted by answering several key questions related to the research plan, also known as the **research methods**:

- What data will be collected?
- Will those data be qualitative, quantitative, or both?
- Do the data already exist, or will original data be required?
- Will it be necessary to develop instrumentation (e.g., a survey or rating scale) or interview protocols?
- How and when will the data be collected?
- How will the quality of the data be ensured?
- If the data need to be collected from human participants, from whom will they be collected?
- How many participants will be necessary?
- What techniques will be used to analyze those data?
- Do all of the above align well with the research question(s)?

Additionally, care must be taken to ensure that all participants in your study are being treated ethically (see Chapter 4). Much more information regarding various research designs and the decisions related to a specific methodology are discussed in Chapters 6 (qualitative methods), 7 (quantitative methods), and 8 (mixed methods).

Implementing the Research Plan and Collecting Data

Once the plethora of decisions outlined in the previous section have been made—and aligned appropriately with the research question—it is time to implement the research plan and physically collect data. Fraenkel and Wallen (2003) suggest three broad categories of data collection techniques. First, data can be collected through the *observation* of participants in the study. These participants might include students, teachers, parents, administrators, or any combination of those groups of individuals. Observational data can be collected through the use of field notes, journals, or even videotaping.

A second category of data collection techniques involves collection of data by means of *interviews* with any of those groups of individuals involved in the educational process. Granted, when we think of interviews, we typically think of an oral question-and-answer exchange between participants in a study. However, interview data may also be collected through a pencil-and-paper—or even electronic—format. *Questionnaires* and *surveys* can be used to ask individuals about their personal opinions or perspectives on some aspect of the educational process under investigation.

The third category of data collection techniques involves examination of *existing documents* or *records*. Often, collection of existing data requires the least amount of time, since they have already been collected; it is the job of the researcher merely to *locate* those data. However, this process is not always so simple. Often, it may be difficult to physically locate these data, especially if a good deal of time has elapsed since their occurrence. Examples of existing documents might include attendance records, minutes of faculty meetings, policy manuals, and student portfolios—the list of existing data in schools is seemingly endless.

I typically add a fourth category of data collection techniques, composed primarily of quantitative measures such as checklists, rating scales, tests, and other formal assessments that are routinely administered in schools. Often, if we want to look at the effectiveness of instruction, for example, we may want to look at assessments that have been administered to students. Of course, within this category, we would also include scores resulting from the administration of standardized tests. It is important to recognize that the reader may see some overlap with the previous category of existing documents. This is certainly a reasonable perspective, as many quantitative measures that exist in schools naturally occur as part of the educational process. However, these are certainly realistic—as well as important and meaningful—sources of educational research data.

Much more specific information regarding various data collection techniques, instruments, and examples is provided in Chapters 11 (qualitative data collection techniques) and 12 (quantitative data collection techniques).

Analyzing the Data

Analysis of data occurs at different points in the process, depending on whether the study uses quantitative, qualitative, or mixed-methods designs and techniques. In quantitative research studies, data analysis typically occurs following the completion of *all* data collection. Once all data have been collected and organized appropriately (i.e., to correspond to the research questions and the intended analytical techniques), those data are then subjected to appropriate analyses through the use of some statistical analysis software program (e.g., SPSS, Excel, StatCrunch). Quantitative analysis of data is a very objective process; since the analysis is actually being done by computer software, the subjectivity and potential biases of the researcher do not impact the results. In other words, regardless of who analyzes the data, the results will be identical—although it is important to realize that there may still be a good deal of subjectivity when it comes to *interpretation* of the statistical results.

In contrast, during qualitative research studies, data analysis typically begins *during* data collection, continues throughout the *remainder* of the process of collecting data, and is completed *following* data collection. It is not uncommon for initial rounds of qualitative data analysis to necessitate the collection of additional or different qualitative data, to help fully answer the research question(s). The analysis of qualitative data is, by definition and design, a highly subjective process. In contrast to quantitative analyses, qualitative analyses are not conducted via a computerized (i.e., "nonhuman") process. Of course, computer software is available for *assisting* with coding in the transcription process; however, qualitative analyses are conducted exclusively by the human mind. Generally speaking, this technique consists of categorization based on logical analysis. The practice of *polyangulation* is critical during this analytical process. The researcher must read, reread, organize, condense, and synthesize all the qualitative data in an attempt to identify themes, categories, or patterns that emerge from those data. It is not uncommon—in fact, it is quite typical—for multiple researchers to arrive at very different results and conclusions after analyzing even a small set of qualitative data.

In essence, the analysis of data in mixed-methods research studies capitalizes on the best of both of the above "data analysis worlds." While the techniques for analyzing quantitative data and those for analyzing qualitative data within a mixed-methods study are the same as described above, the researcher must engage in a different sort of polyangulation to "merge" both kinds of data. By engaging in this process, the researcher gains a better understanding of how qualitative data and subsequent analyses can inform quantitative data analyses, and vice versa.

Discussion and examples of various data analysis techniques and procedures are provided in Chapters 11 (qualitative data analysis techniques) and 13 (quantitative data analysis techniques).

Stating Findings, Conclusions, and Recommendations in a Written Research Report

Once data analysis has been completed, the researcher has the responsibility of formally and succinctly stating the *results*, also known as *findings*, as well as *conclusions* and *recommendations* resulting from the study. This is the point in the study where the researcher actually provides answers to the originally stated research questions. However, this step in the process is not quite as simple as that. The researcher must then take the answers to research questions and contextualize them with respect to the broader field of education, the context of the study, the setting of the study, and so forth. In other words,

- What do the findings *mean* to the field of education?
- What are the *implications* for practicing educators?
- What *impact* might they have on students and parents?

Further,

- What *recommendations* for practice can be made?
- What *recommendations*, if any, regarding educational theory can be made?

With respect to a final written research report, this section potentially carries the most weight. Most readers of educational research reports will look to the substantive meaning of the researchers' final conclusions and recommendations that have resulted from the study. Although they will read the entire written report, this is a situation somewhat similar to when a person skips ahead to the last chapter of a novel to see how the story ends.

One additional—and vitally important—aspect of developing conclusions and recommendations is that they *must* follow logically from the research questions, the data that were collected, and the results of the analyses of those data. In other words, care must be taken so that conclusions and recommendations do not become so global that they extend beyond the parameters of the particular study. Recommendations and advice for developing a final written report upon completion of an educational research study are provided in Chapter 14.

The Educational Research Process—A Brief Example

Now that we have taken a concise look at each of the eight steps involved in conducting an educational research study, let us consider the following example (adapted from Mertler, 2014), where each step of a fictitious research study is briefly described. Our example begins with two researchers from the local university—one of whom specializes in social studies education and the other in research methodology. The social studies expert has been noticing for some time that high school students across the state have not been performing well in the state-mandated American history course. The course has always been taught in a traditional manner—with the content coverage beginning prior to the American Revolution and ending with more recent events. The social studies expert believes that there may be some merit in examining a "backward" approach to teaching history (i.e., beginning with current events and proceeding back through time to end at the American Revolution). He wants to investigate these two different instructional approaches and decides to enlist the help of a research methods colleague; she willingly agrees.

Step 1: Identifying and Limiting a Research Topic or Problem

The two researchers meet on a couple of occasions over the summer to identify the specific topic they hope to address through the examination and trial of this alternative instructional approach. Based on previous research and knowledge, they believe that students struggle most in making connections between seemingly unrelated historical events. The social studies expert argues that perhaps this backward approach (i.e., beginning with more recent historical events with which students will be more familiar) will have a positive impact on how well they are able to make these types of connections. The researchers decide to focus their attention on any differences in academic performance, as well as students' attitudes, related to the two instructional approaches.

Step 2: Formally Stating and Refining Research Question(s)

Now that they have narrowed the focus of their study, the researchers must formally state the research question that will guide it. They identify the key variables in their study as follows:

- Independent variable: instructional technique (i.e., forward vs. backward instruction)
- Dependent variables: performance on the state's end-of-course exam; students' attitudes and perceptions

Based on the identified problem, as well as the key variables in the study, the researchers state the following research questions that will guide their study:

1. Is there a difference in students' academic performance, dependent on the type of instruction received in an American history course? If so, what is the direction and size of that difference?
2. What are the students' attitudes toward and perceptions of these two types of instruction?

Step 3: Reviewing Existing Literature Related to the Problem

Although they are somewhat familiar with research in this area, the researchers decide to collect related, published research focused on the effectiveness of backward approaches to teaching historical, chronological events; how other history teachers may have implemented this type of instruction; and any problems they may have encountered. They decide to split the tasks, with the social studies expert identifying and reviewing published research studies on the topic and the methodologist identifying and reviewing studies that have examined differential instructional methods. After reviewing their respective bodies of literature, the two researchers revisit the research questions to determine if they are still appropriate or should be revised, as potentially influenced by the existing body of research.

Step 4: Writing a Literature Review

After a few months of identifying, collecting, reading, and synthesizing existing research on the topic, the researchers pool their resources and collaboratively draft a comprehensive literature review. Their formal review of related literature includes the following subtopics:

- Instructional methods
- Methods of teaching history
- Chronological methods of teaching history
- Differential effects of chronological teaching methods
- Student opinions of chronological teaching methods

Step 5: Developing a Research Plan

Following the review of published literature, the researchers have ample background evidence and support for the focus of their proposed study (i.e., the backward approach to instruction can be effective), although they also found some contradictory evidence (i.e., this approach is less or at least no more effective than the traditional approach). The researchers decide that the most appropriate design for their study is a comparative-type design, since the goal is to compare academic performance and attitudes of students taught using the forward approach with those of students taught using the backward approach. More specifically, they decide to use a mixed-methods design, where academic performance (i.e., Research Question #1) will be measured quantitatively and student attitudes (i.e., Research Question #2) will be measured qualitatively.

Step 6: Implementing the Research Plan and Collecting Data

Next, the researchers need to identify a couple of schools and several American history teachers in each. Several of those teachers will serve as the "comparison" group (i.e., they will teach their classes using the typical forward chronological method), whereas another set of teachers will serve as the "treatment" group (i.e., they will teach their classes using the backward approach). Further, they decide that the study will span an entire academic year, with the majority of data collection occurring near the end of the school year. The end-of-course exam in American history is administered in April; they will also survey the students at about the same time. They will use the school year to check in periodically with the teachers and to develop the qualitative attitude survey—containing open-ended questions—for students.

By the end of May, the student scores on the American history exam have been received from the state department of education. The researchers have also surveyed all the students involved in both groups of the study.

Step 7: Analyzing the Data

Immediately following the end of the school year, the researchers begin their data analysis. Test scores resulting from the administration of the end-of-course achievement test are statistically compared for the two groups (i.e., the backward group vs. the forward group). Upon interpreting the results of the analysis, it is determined that the test scores of the students who were taught using the backward instructional approach are significantly higher than those of the students taught in the more traditional manner.

The analysis of student perception data—and subsequent qualitative comparisons between the two groups—reveals some interesting results. Generally speaking, the students taught using the backward approach liked it but identified that this was largely because it was something different from what they were used to in a history course. They felt that they had a hard time adjusting to the different approach to studying history. Those taught using the forward approach liked the idea of being taught in the alternative manner but were apprehensive because they thought the material would be more difficult to grasp.

Step 8: Stating Findings, Conclusions, and Recommendations in a Written Research Report

With their findings in hand, the researchers develop conclusions and recommendations as part of a final written research report. They conclude that, while the backward instructional approach resulted in better academic performance, the students seemed very uncomfortable with the alternative method. They agree—and formally recommend—that it is imperative to continue studying the effectiveness of this approach in subsequent academic years, perhaps with a larger number of schools, teachers, and students. An additional recommendation includes the collection of data from teachers (i.e., what were their experiences and perceptions of the different teaching method?). Similar findings in the coming years would provide a much stronger case for permanently changing the approach to teaching American history—if, in fact, future data supported that recommendation.

Developmental Activities

1. In your opinion, which of the eight steps of the educational research process do you believe would be most difficult to carry out, in general and/or for you personally? Why?

2. In the Chapter 1 Developmental Activities, you brainstormed several possible topics for educational research studies. Select one of these topics and *briefly* outline how you would conduct this educational research study, corresponding to the eight steps presented in this chapter.

3. Revisit the sample study presented in the chapter. What questions or concerns came to mind as you read that example? Which of the eight steps concerned you or raised the most questions in your mind? Explain your answer.

4. The sample study presented in the chapter was done collaboratively between two researchers. Develop a list of pros and cons for conducting collaborative educational research.

5. Imagine that your school is experiencing problems related to its student dress code. Students are ignoring the code and in some cases are becoming extremely disruptive to the educational process as a result. How might you use the process of conducting educational research to investigate alternative solutions to the problem? What specific problems or research questions might you address? What sorts of data would you collect?

Summary

- The main steps in the process of conducting educational research are as follows:

  o Identifying and limiting a research topic or problem
  o Formally stating and refining research questions
  o Reviewing existing literature related to the problem
  o Writing a literature review
  o Developing a research plan
  o Implementing the plan and collecting data
  o Analyzing the collected data
  o Stating findings, conclusions, and recommendations

- Identification of the focus of the study is one of the most critical decisions in the process of conducting educational research.

  o The topic should be of personal interest to you and should be manageable.

- Care must be taken in formally stating research questions, as they will guide the remainder of the study.

- Reviewing existing literature and writing a literature review can provide a great deal of guidance to a research study.

  o Related literature can inform specification of the problem, development of research questions, and determination of research designs and analyses.

- *How* the research study will actually be conducted is known as the research method.

  - Many critical decisions about the research method must be made, including those related to data, participants, instrumentation, timeframe, research ethics, and data analysis.

- Methods used to collect data can be quite diverse.

  - Categories of techniques include observational techniques, interviews, existing data, and data collected through standard educational processes.

- Quantitative data analysis involves statistical techniques and is typically accomplished using statistical analysis software.

- Qualitative data analysis is an inductive process that must be facilitated in the mind of the researcher.

- Analysis of data collected in mixed-methods studies involves both kinds of data analysis and essentially merges the results.

- Findings, conclusions, and recommendations should be stated so they follow logically from all that has preceded in the study.

- The purpose behind stating conclusions and recommendations is to take the answers to the research questions and contextualize them with respect to the broader field of education.

- Extreme caution must be used so that conclusions and recommendations are not stated so globally that they extend beyond the parameters of the study.

- It is important to keep in mind that there is not a single way to research any given topic. Different approaches, methodologies, and data can be used to investigate the same or similar research topics.

⑤SAGE edge™

Sharpen your skills with SAGE edge!

edge.sagepub.com/mertler

SAGE edge for Students provides a personalized approach to help you accomplish your coursework goals in an easy-to-use learning environment. You'll find action plans, mobile-friendly eFlashcards, and quizzes as well as video, web, and resources and links to SAGE journal articles to support and expand on the concepts presented in this chapter.

3

Identifying a Research Problem

Student Learning Objectives

After studying Chapter 3, students will be able to do the following:

1. Identify and appropriately focus the scope of a research problem or topic

2. Recall and apply definitions of terminology necessary in conducting educational research studies

3. Apply these necessary terms when engaging in the preliminary development of an educational research topic

4. Translate a research problem statement into a guiding research question, following guidelines for both qualitative and quantitative research questions

The initial steps in any research study involve clarifying the topic to be researched as well as exploring the existing literature on that topic. These two broad steps and sets of skills will be our focus in this chapter and the next. As previously mentioned, decisions about these early steps of the process can be crucial to the success of a research study. Failure to clarify the focus of the project and inadequate examination of what has been done and is known about the topic may ultimately lead to an unsuccessful research study. Researchers must be mindful of these facts during the developmental stages of their research studies.

Identifying a Research Topic or Problem

I cannot reiterate strongly enough that careful identification of a research topic is one of the most important steps in the overall process. Nothing shapes the remainder of the study as much as the potential research topic or problem and the research questions that follow. If a research topic is too narrow, it may not be possible to collect adequate data to answer the research questions or solve the research problem. On the other hand, if the research topic is too broad, the researcher may become overwhelmed with too many possibilities (e.g., too many possible research designs, too much data, too many sources of data, too little time to complete such a broad study).

As educators—and I use this term to include all individuals who work in educational settings at any level—we all have concerns about educational matters, just as we all have questions for which we would like to find answers. For example, educators may want to know the ways multiculturalism can influence the teaching and learning process. They might want to learn more about the possible positive and negative effects of tablets and smartphones on student learning and engagement. Educators might be interested in learning more about how common standards will better prepare students for college and careers. University residence-life staff may want to learn about student satisfaction levels with various housing models. You might notice that, in this handful of examples, there is one commonality: The educators highlighted all seem to have some sort of a personal interest in the topic they propose to investigate. Having a personal interest in the topic that you will spend time exploring is critically important; however, interest is not the only factor in the decision.

Personal interest is a great starting point, but it is certainly not the only mechanism for identifying possible research topics. There are other excellent sources as well. For example, browsing almost any educational journal (in your university library or online) will likely generate ideas for potential research topics. National newspapers, which often report on issues and stories of an educational nature, can also be fruitful sources. Of course, simply talking with other educators will very likely result in a discussion of possible research topics. Regardless of the role you play or the position you hold in education—in K–12 schools, these roles include classroom teacher, administrator, teacher leader, counselor, psychologist, librarian, reading specialist, and intervention specialist; in institutions of higher education, they include faculty, student affairs staff, residence-life staff, counselors, and academic support staff—there are literally hundreds of topics that warrant investigation in our educational institutions. Regardless of your position, you will potentially find many of those topics appealing.

Preliminary Considerations in Selecting Topics

Because selecting a topic is so crucial to the success of a research study, researchers should evaluate a potential topic against several preliminary considerations. While it is not necessary to meet all these "requirements," care should be taken to balance these considerations and to make appropriate adjustments to a particular topic as necessary (Mertler & Charles, 2011).

1. *You should have a _personal interest_ in the topic you select to study.* Your level of interest in a topic often stems from its association with some sort of positive experience or unpleasant concern. In other words, you are not indifferent to the given topic—whether initially positive or negative, it has some sort of meaning to you. Additionally, I often stress to students who are new to research methods that they consider the amount of

time they will devote to thinking about, doing, and writing about this particular topic. Keep in mind that research studies in education may last anywhere from a couple of months to an entire school year, or beyond. Now consider how laborious the process may become if you do not really have a genuine interest in your topic—those several months could feel as though they are dragging on forever.

2. *Your potential topic should be <u>important</u> and likely to make a difference in some aspect of education.* As we have already mentioned, research studies in education should not focus on trivial ideas and concepts. If you really do not believe that investigation of your potential topic will result in a meaningful difference, I would argue that you should not conduct your research on that topic. Rather, the results of an educational research study *should* make some sort of difference—or should at least have *potential* to make a difference—in a given aspect of education. That means the difference could be felt or experienced by students, teachers, administrators, or another group. From a research perspective, our general hope is that by conducting research, we are making the educational process better for someone or some group involved in that process.

3. *The <u>newness</u> or <u>uniqueness</u> of a research topic can impact your enthusiasm.* While there is always value in repeating or replicating previous research, most research studies will result in the greatest amount of satisfaction if they are new, unique, and more original investigations. Original research has the potential to shed new light—and a greater amount of it—on the topic. I admittedly say this with some caution, as I do not want to give the impression that every study needs to be brand new. That simply is not feasible or realistic. However, if hundreds of research articles and volumes of books have been written on your topic, it probably does not warrant further study (unless you are incorporating or focusing on a newer aspect of that topic).

4. *You must always give consideration to the <u>amount of time</u> a research study will require.* Not all but most research studies are conducted for some overarching reason. For example, you might be doing a research study for a college course, as a master's thesis or doctoral dissertation, or with the goal of presenting at an upcoming conference. Even considering just these as situational alternatives, you can see that each of them has some sort of artificially imposed timeline or deadline. Therefore, the researcher must be able to plan ahead and determine roughly how much time it will take to complete the proposed study. You must consider and evaluate the potential time requirements of the study in relation to the time available. As we will discuss more in a bit, this activity often helps define (i.e., broaden or narrow) the focus of the study. All things being equal, if given the option, it is better to identify a topic (or scale back a broader topic) such that the study can be completed in the available time period. After all, this is far preferable to running out of time and not being able to complete your study.

5. *Similarly, you should consider the potential <u>difficulty</u> of a given research topic.* I have seen students become enamored with certain methodological approaches to conducting research studies that were unfortunately beyond their skill set. For example, I once supervised a graduate student who had originally planned to administer a quantitative survey to her students, then made the decision—on her own—to conduct a purely qualitative research study based on interviews with numerous students. The problem:

She had never received any training or coursework in collecting and analyzing qualitative data. She had effectively backed herself into a corner, where the requirements of the given methodology did not match her research skills. Her study, then, became much more difficult to complete than the one she had originally planned. Research topics must be practical, but so too must the methodologies used to conduct the investigation. In other words, a proposed research study must align with the research skills of the individual or individuals conducting the study.

6. *Consideration should also be given to any potential <u>monetary costs</u> of the study.* If you develop a topic that will ultimately require you to spend money on supplies, materials, travel, equipment, and so on, you may want to consider finding a different topic or, at a minimum, scaling back (i.e., narrowing) the proposed, original topic. There are many excellent prospective research topics in education that will involve little or no monetary expenditures on your part.

7. *All researchers need to be cognizant of <u>research ethics</u>.* As we will discuss in Chapter 4, it may be unethical—and potentially illegal—to conduct research that does physical, psychological, or emotional harm; that is punitive in any way; that slanders; or that promotes only one specific outcome. Any of these is considered mistreatment of human beings and is unacceptable in the field of educational research.

Limiting a Topic

Once a potential topic has been identified and evaluated against the considerations discussed above, it often must be "refined" before it can be effectively and efficiently researched. This is typically because most topics are too broad, too vague, or too complex (Mertler & Charles, 2011). First, the topic must be properly sized; that is, it usually needs to be reduced—or occasionally expanded—in scope. It is not uncommon for graduate students to select topics that are initially too broad to be dealt with expeditiously, especially within their constraints of time and monetary resources. The list of seven considerations presented above can be very effective in helping properly size a research topic. Although it happens less frequently, a research topic also may be too narrow. In this case, the topic must be fleshed out and expanded. This refinement is crucial largely because if a study does not have a specific and clear focus, it—along with the researcher—is likely to wander aimlessly, and the researcher may waste valuable time redoing aspects of the study. If time is valuable in the first place, then this situation will not help expedite the study in any way. Examples of research topics that are too broad or too narrow—along with their refined versions— are presented in Table 3.1.

Second, the topic may need to be clarified or reworded. A clear research topic will unambiguously identify the specifics of the investigation, along with the exact *variables* to be investigated and the participants if appropriate. Third, one or more *research questions* or *hypotheses* should be stated. As previously discussed, these provide specific direction for conducting the study. Specific discussions and examples of variables, research questions, and hypotheses are presented later in this chapter.

TABLE 3.1 ● Examples of Broad and Narrow Topics for Educational Research				
←Too Broad→		↑ Just Right ↓		→ Too Narrow ←
What teachers' lives are like outside of school	→	Leisure activities of elementary teachers and the amount of time spent on them	←	How second-grade teachers in Adams School District spend their time
Factors that affect learning among culturally diverse students	→	Hispanic students' perceptions of factors that make academic success more difficult	←	Things that keep Juan from being able to read at grade level
Importance of reading practice in developing reading skills	→	Effect of reading practice with fifth-grade "buddies" on the developing reading skills of first-grade students over a semester	←	Impact of having an older student read to a struggling first-grade reader
Virtual dissection versus real dissection of lab specimens	→	Tenth-grade students' perceptions of virtual and real animal dissections	←	Why students don't like to dissect starfish
Use of tablet computers and smartphones to improve learning	→	The effect of writing apps, providing immediate feedback, on students' abilities to develop thesis statements	←	How a particular spelling app helps underachieving students do better in school

Sample Educational Research Topics

Education—and all its related professional activities—offers us virtually limitless possibilities for educational research topics. Take a moment to think about all the aspects of the teaching–learning process that you encounter in a given day. My guess is that you could come up with numerous topics based only on the events that occurred that day. The following lists constitute a mere sampling of possibilities and are meant only to spark your own ideas. Possible research topics for teachers might include the following:

- *The classroom environment*
  - The effect that the physical arrangement of the classroom has on learning
  - The impact of the environment on the psychosocial development and interactions among students
  - The type and nature of interpersonal relationships and interactions among students

- o   The type and nature of interpersonal relationships and interactions between the teacher and students
- o   The potential impact on learning of alternative physical arrangements, time, movement between activities, and management of materials

- *Instructional materials*

  - o   The appropriateness of textbooks and other printed materials for a multicultural school
  - o   The effectiveness of supplemental, hands-on materials
  - o   The appropriateness for our students of the reading level of printed materials
  - o   The level of student engagement fostered by our instructional materials
  - o   The usefulness of all materials purely for academic achievement
  - o   The impact of instructional alternatives

- *Classroom management*

  - o   The operational efficiency of classrooms in our school
  - o   The efficiency of transitions within our school
  - o   The extent to which teachers believe that they can teach as they like
  - o   Pros and cons of our current methods of managing student behavior
  - o   The efficiency of classroom routines as efficient uses of time
  - o   The extent to which students learn without undue distraction

- *Instructional methods*

  - o   Factors that motivate and engage my students
  - o   Motivational and engagement factors that differ based on ethnic groupings
  - o   The best methods of teaching to reach our school's instructional goals
  - o   The nature, timing, and delivery of effective teaching methods and strategies
  - o   Students' responses to the nature, timing, and delivery of teaching methods and strategies
  - o   Effective methods for formative and summative assessment of student learning
  - o   Various questioning techniques and their relative effectiveness
  - o   The academic impact and student perceptions of "flipping" a classroom

Possible research topics for counselors and special educators might include the following:

- *Human intellectual, social, physical, and emotional growth and development*

  - o   Individual interests and learning preferences
  - o   Ideal rates of learning for individuals
  - o   The improvement of self-disciplined behavior
  - o   Effective ways to collaborate with classroom teachers

- *Exceptional populations*

  - o   Effective strategies for students with autism
  - o   Strategies for engaging students diagnosed with attention-deficit/hyperactivity disorder (ADHD)

    o Effective behavior management plans for students with varying exceptionalities

    o Effective ways to co-teach with classroom teachers

Possible research topics for school leaders might include the following:

- *Effective communication*

    o Appropriate communication styles in working with teachers

    o Appropriate communication styles in working with students and parents

    o Communication styles when working with the general community

- *Effective supervision*

    o Methods for mentoring new and experienced teachers

    o Strategies for motivating and assisting teaching staff

    o Effective means of formative teacher evaluation

- *Effective public relations*

    o Effective strategies for obtaining the support of parents and the community

    o The most appropriate strategies for general communications

- *Effective leadership*

    o Effective ways of organizing teachers, staff, and students

    o Methods for fostering collaboration among teachers, staff, and students

    o Techniques for supporting teachers, staff, and students

Possible research topics for university-level educators might include the following:

- *Student affairs*

    o Student preferences for various nonacademic student activities on campus

    o The integration of off-campus service activities with academic coursework

    o Effective models of student leadership

    o The perceived importance of spirituality on campus

- *Residence life*

    o Appropriate communication styles between students and resident advisors and other residence-life staff

    o Student opinions and preferences for various living arrangements within different housing models

    o Current trends in residence life

- *Academic affairs*

    o Student perceptions of various academic advising models

    o Student academic performance and perceptions resulting from "flipping" college classrooms

    o The appropriateness of various models for academic support centers and their integration with coursework

As mentioned above, these lists provide only a sampling of possible research topics in the broad field of education. The sky truly is the limit when it comes to identifying possible topics for educational research.

Necessary Terminology Related to Research

Once we have narrowed down a research topic, the next step is to develop research questions or hypotheses that will guide our study. However, before we look at the ins and outs of stating research questions, it is necessary to examine several research terms and phrases. The better we understand this terminology, the better we will be able to maneuver through the early—as well as latter—stages of research study development. Terminology we will examine in this section includes the following:

- *Problem statement*
- *Variables*
- *Research question*
- *Hypotheses*
- *Null hypothesis*
- *Research (alternative) hypothesis*
- *Directional research hypothesis*
- *Nondirectional research hypothesis*
- *Continuous variables*
- *Discrete variables*
- *Dichotomous variables*
- *Independent variable*
- *Dependent variable*
- *Confounding variables*

As we discussed earlier in this chapter, the research problem is essentially a research topic that has been appropriately refined (i.e., broadened or narrowed) to be researchable. As working examples, for the following research topics—that is, (1) the use of iPads in the classroom and (2) performance-based assessments and critical-thinking skills—the corresponding research problems might be stated as such:

1. The effect that incorporating iPads into instruction has on student engagement and attitude toward learning
2. Differences in measured problem-solving skills for students who receive performance-based assessments, integrated across the curriculum, and those who do not

Once we have identified the problem to be researched, the next step is to "convert" it into a problem statement. The **problem statement** is essentially a reiteration of the research problem as a complete sentence (or sometimes as several sentences, making up a complete paragraph). The purpose behind a restatement of the problem is simply to add clarity, in particular when the problem is being discussed in a research proposal (where it is written in future tense) or final report of the research (where it is written in past tense). For our two working examples, the respective problem statements might read as follows:

1. The purpose of this study will be to examine and describe the effects that incorporating iPads into instruction has on student engagement and attitude toward learning social studies among fifth-grade students.
2. The purpose of this study was to measure and compare the differences in problem-solving skills for high school students who received performance-based assessments, integrated across the math, science, and language arts curricula, and those who did not.

In each of the above cases, note the additional details about the study that have been provided in the problem statements. We learn more about the specific context of each study (e.g., grade levels and curricular areas), as well as the audience serving as the focus of the studies (e.g., fifth-grade and high school students). One of the things a researcher should try to accomplish in delineating the problem statement is specifying the main variables in the study. *Variables* are any sort of trait or characteristic that *differs* from one individual, object, procedure, or setting to another. Traits that do not differ from one person to another are known as *constants*. In educational research, we typically do not study constants, as we are concerned with studying things that differ from one person, place, or object to the next. You will learn more about variables in a moment.

The **research question** is the fundamental question inherent in the research topic and, in particular, in the research study at hand. It serves as the main guide to the remainder of the study, since the goal of the study will be to provide an answer to this question. In essence, the research question is typically the reaffirmation of the problem statement simply in the form of a question. It is often accompanied by a number of subquestions, designed to supplement the main research question with greater specificity. Returning to our working examples, we might state research questions as follows:

1. What effect does incorporating iPads into instruction have on student engagement and attitude toward learning social studies among fifth-grade students?
2. Are there differences in the problem-solving skills of high school students who receive performance-based assessments, integrated across the math, science, and language arts curricula, and those who do not? If so, what is the nature of the differences (i.e., which group showed higher problem-solving skills)? If separated out, are there differences in problem-solving skills among the three curricular areas? If so, in which area(s) do students demonstrate the highest level of problem-solving ability?

In the second research scenario, you should notice the greater degree of specificity guiding the research study, as provided by the subquestions. More detailed information regarding the development of research questions will be provided in the next section of this chapter.

The final set of terms we will consider here deal with hypotheses. Hypotheses are brief statements that parallel the research questions and predict the findings of the study. They essentially predict an answer to the stated research question. There are two types of hypotheses—null hypotheses and research or alternative hypotheses. A **null hypothesis** (typically symbolized as H_0) states that *no* effect will occur, *no* relationships exist between variables, or *no* differences will be found between groups. It essentially states that the variables being studied are not different among people, places, or things.

In contrast, a **research hypothesis** (typically symbolized as H_1)—also known as an **alternative hypothesis**—is most often a statement of what the researcher *actually* expects to discover in the study. These hypotheses state that there *is* an effect, a relationship *does* exist between variables, or there *are* differences between groups—in other words, the exact opposite of a null hypothesis. However, there may also be situations where the researcher actually expects *no* effect or *no* relationship to exist; that is, the research is being conducted in an attempt to support the fact that there is no effect or no relationship. In this case, the null hypothesis, in essence, states the expectation for the study, whereas the research hypothesis simply states the *opposite* potential outcome.

To add greater specificity, we can also more accurately state a directional or nondirectional research hypothesis. A **directional research hypothesis** indicates the direction of the results; in other words, it will include which group scores higher than the other, or if there has been an improvement or a decline in academic performance. A **nondirectional research hypothesis** will state that there is a difference but will not specify the direction of that difference.

Once again returning to our working examples, we can propose several appropriate hypotheses:

1. H_0: There will be no difference in measured student engagement or attitude toward learning social studies between fifth-graders who are exposed to iPads during instruction and those who are not.

    H_1: There will be a difference in measured student engagement and attitude toward learning social studies between fifth-graders who are exposed to iPads during instruction and those who are not.

2. H_0: There will be no difference in scores on a test of problem-solving skills between high school students who receive performance-based assessments integrated across the math, science, and language arts curricula and those who do not receive performance-based assessments.

    H_1: High school students who receive performance-based assessments, integrated across the curriculum, will score significantly higher on a test of problem-solving skills than high school students who do not receive performance-based assessments.

It is important to note several things about our sample hypothesis statements. First, notice that the research hypothesis in the first scenario is a nondirectional research hypothesis, whereas the one in the second scenario is a directional research hypothesis. Second, it is important to realize that the way hypotheses are stated will very closely parallel the way research questions are stated. Third, in reality, we would have listed several additional pairs of hypotheses in the second scenario based on the previously stated subquestions.

Mentioned earlier, variables are key components of research questions and hypothesis statements. The main reason for this is because variables should be identified clearly within research questions or hypotheses. Remember that questions and hypotheses serve to guide the study, and the researcher will address them upon completion of the study. Therefore, the researcher must clearly identify them at the outset. For example, in the scenarios above, it is clear that we would need to collect data on student engagement and attitudes (Scenario 1) and on problem-solving skills (Scenario 2); if we failed to do so, we would not be able to answer our research question.

Variables can be continuous, discrete, or dichotomous. **Continuous variables** measure gradational differences; individuals possess some amount of the same trait, which varies in small increments along a continuum. It is best to think of continuous variables as ones that could be measured along a number line or ruler:

| 0 | 1 | 2 | 3 | 4 | 5 | 6 | 7 | 8 | 9 | 10 | 11 | 12 | 13 | 14 | 15 | 16 | 17 | 18 | 19 | 20 |

Examples of continuous variables are height, weight, and age. Student scores on the test of problem-solving skills could also be a continuous variable, as could "achievement" (as measured by a standardized test).

Discrete variables are categorical in nature, meaning that they are divided into separate categories. Further, as a variable may be defined, it is not possible to have a score or value between adjacent categories. Depending on how they are defined, examples of discrete variables might include socioeconomic status, ethnicity, and school size (if measured as "small–medium–large"). **Dichotomous variables** are special cases of discrete variables with only two possible categories—for example, handedness (measured as left or right) and sex (measured as male or female). You might think of discrete, or categorical, variables as being grouped into file folders. One individual will have characteristics that place him or her in one file folder or another; the individual cannot be classified as being "in between" file folders.

It is absolutely crucial to note that a single variable can be continuous *or* discrete, depending on *how* the researcher chooses to measure or collect data on that variable. Consider the example of socioeconomic status (or SES) as a variable. A researcher could ask the following question of participants:

To the nearest thousand dollars, what is your total annual household income?

Participants would then respond with precise dollar amounts, such as $26,000, $55,000, or $94,000. In this case, SES is a continuous variable. On the other hand, the researcher might want only to *categorize* participants in terms of SES (e.g., low, medium, and high). In this case, the researcher would have to predetermine the cutoff points that separate the three categories. For purposes of her study, she might *arbitrarily* decide to establish the separation between low and medium SES at $25,000, and between medium and high at $75,000. Her question of participants might resemble the following:

> Based on your total household income, in which of the following categories would you place yourself?
>
> _____ Low (< $25,000)
>
> _____ Medium ($25,000–$75,000)
>
> _____ High (> $75,000)

In this research scenario, SES is a discrete variable. Notice that more precise data would be collected with the first form of the question, but this type of question would be much more difficult for people to answer. The second question, while not as precise, would pose an easier task for the participants. Both questions would result in the collection of SES data, simply measured differently.

Another mechanism for categorizing variables is by their level or scale of measurement. Although you will learn more about scales of measurement in Chapter 12, a brief introduction is provided here. Variables are measured according to four types of measurement scales: nominal, ordinal, interval, and ratio. **Nominal** scales involve the assignment of a label or name to a category; these variables are typically analogous to discrete or categorical variables. **Ordinal** scales build on the characteristics of nominal scales by also ranking individuals in order of the degree to which they possess a certain characteristic. **Interval** scales possess all characteristics of both nominal and ordinal scales, but the subsequent values represent equal intervals (i.e., the distance between scores of 90 and 80 is the same as the distance between scores of 60 and 50). Finally, the highest level of measurement is a **ratio** scale, which possesses the characteristics of the three preceding scales of measurement plus the additional characteristic of a true zero point—meaning that if someone scored a 0 on a particular measure, this would indicate a *complete lack* of whatever was being measured by that variable.

Independent and dependent variables are typically important in experimental and some comparative research. The terms *independent* and *dependent* are always used in association with each other; you cannot have a research study with an independent variable without also having a dependent variable, and vice versa. The *independent variable* precedes the dependent variable in time (i.e., it occurs or is measured first) and exerts influence on the *dependent variable*, which may change as a result. In our second working example, the independent variable is the "style of assessment" (i.e., performance based or not performance based), and it also happens to be a dichotomous variable (i.e., there are only two possible categories for students to "fit" in). The dependent variable is the "score on a test of problem-solving skills" (which is also a continuous variable). Exposure to the "style of assessment" occurs before measurement on the "test of problem-solving skills," hence the respective classifications as *independent* and *dependent* variables.

One final type of variable that is important for the researcher to be aware of is a confounding variable. **Confounding variables** are traits or conditions whose presence is likely not recognized or considered by the researcher and that may influence the outcome of the research study. Confounding variables take a variety of forms, including the following:

- Innate traits (e.g., motivation or intelligence)
- Permanent physical traits (e.g., poor eyesight, hearing, or coordination)
- Naturally occurring temporary conditions (e.g., fatigue, distraction, excitement, illness, or test anxiety)

The researcher must make a concerted effort to control for the effects of confounding variables if the research results are to be considered legitimate and valid. The conclusions drawn and recommendations offered from research studies where the effects of confounding variables were not controlled will very likely be misleading.

Research Questions and Hypotheses

Now that we have a basic understanding of what research questions and hypotheses are, we need to look at some additional specifics when it comes to framing research questions to guide a study. One of the initial decisions the researcher must make is whether to use qualitative or quantitative methods. Formally stating a research question can help the researcher determine the specific approach to use. On the other hand, it is often best to know which approach is intended *prior* to formally stating a research question (Mertler, 2014). Selecting the method in advance will typically lend focus to the research question. Leedy and Ormrod (2013) have developed a table of questions and answers—differentiated by qualitative versus quantitative approaches—to help guide the researcher in making this methodological choice. An adaptation of this table is presented as Table 3.2. The purpose of the table is to help researchers determine which approach will be most appropriate based on several factors, including the nature of the research topic and study, as well as various types of research skills necessitated by each approach.

Research questions are appropriate for any type of study, whether it uses a qualitative or quantitative approach. In general, qualitative research questions tend to be much more open-ended and holistic in nature than are those used in quantitative studies. The reason for this is to allow for possible outcomes the researcher did not anticipate. Further, these research questions are often worded so they can be answered with a great amount of detail and description. It is not uncommon to see words such as *how* and *what* in qualitative research questions, to allow the researcher to thoroughly describe the answers (Mertler, 2014). Sometimes researchers who use qualitative methods will not even state a research question at the beginning of the study; rather, they will wait until after some data are collected and analyzed so they have a better sense of the context of the study. Even after the qualitative research questions have been stated, they may be revised and updated to reflect the data (this, in essence, is known as an *emergent design*). In stark contrast, quantitative research questions are stated at the outset of the study and remain unchanged throughout its course.

TABLE 3.2 ● Distinguishing Characteristics of Qualitative and Quantitative Approaches to Research, Used to Guide Development of Research Questions

Characteristic/ Question	Qualitative Approaches	Quantitative Approaches
What is the main purpose for conducting the research?	• To describe and explain • To explore and interpret • To build theory	• To explain and predict • To confirm and validate • To test theory
What is the nature of the research process?	• Holistic • Unknown variables • Flexible guidelines • Emergent methods • Context bound • Personalized view	• Focused and narrow • Specific variables • Established and followed guidelines • Predetermined methods • Somewhat context-free • Detached perspective
What are the anticipated data, and how will they be collected?	• Textual and/or image-based data • Informative, small sample • Loosely structured or nonstandardized observations and interviews	• Numerical data • Representative, large sample • Standardized instrumentation
How will the data be analyzed?	• Search for themes and categories • Acknowledgment that analysis is subjective and potentially biased • Inductive reasoning	• Statistical analysis • Focus on objectivity • Deductive reasoning
In what format will the findings and conclusions be communicated?	• Words • Narratives, individual quotes • Personal voice, in literary style	• Numbers • Statistics, aggregated data • Formal voice, in scientific style

Source: Adapted from Leedy and Ormrod (2013).

When framing a research question from the problem statement, the researcher needs to be mindful of several important characteristics of research questions, listed and discussed below (Schwalbach, 2003).

- *Qualitative research questions should be stated in an open-ended fashion; quantitative research questions should be focused.* Since qualitative research focuses on a broad, holistic view of the research problem, the question should reflect this broad, open-ended approach to the study. For example, consider the following research question:

> How do students who are exposed to iPads during instruction feel about learning social studies?

Notice how this question is more open-ended than a potential quantitative research counterpart:

> What are the attitudes toward learning social studies of students who are exposed to iPads during instruction?

One might envision the qualitative question being answered through observations and interviews of many students over a long period of time, whereas the quantitative question might be answered simply by surveying students and asking them to indicate their attitudes on a scale of 1 to 10.

- *Regardless of methodology, research questions should not require a simple yes/no answer.* Consider the following research question:

> Is there a relationship between the use of iPads and attitude toward learning social studies?

In most every case, the simple answer to this question is going to be yes, since some sort of relationship is always likely to exist. Unfortunately, the researcher probably wants to know more than this. Now, consider a revised version of this research question:

> What is the strength and direction of the relationship between the use of iPads and attitude toward learning social studies?

Notice that, in this revised version, the focus remains on the same variables. However, this version allows the researcher to *discover* (i.e., provide an answer to) much more about the relationship, not simply whether or not one exists. In some situations, it may be acceptable to state a research question as a yes/no question but *only if* it is followed up with a more specific subquestion:

> Is there a relationship between the use of iPads and attitude toward learning social studies? If so, what is the nature and direction of the relationship?

- *Research questions should not be stated in a manner that assumes an answer even before data have been collected.* Here is another version of our working example research question:

> To what extent will use of iPads improve students' attitudes toward learning social studies?

In this example, the researcher has already assumed that iPads will, in fact, have a positive effect on students' attitudes (due to the use of the word *improve* in the question). If that were the case, there would likely be no reason to conduct the research study, since we would already know the answer. Research questions should be stated more objectively:

> To what extent will use of iPads affect students' attitudes toward learning social studies?

Through the use of the word *affect*, we are assuming that iPads will do *something* for student attitudes; the something could be positive or negative, which is why we are conducting the study. At this time, it is critical to raise an important point: The value of educational research does not lie *only* in finding positive results. When we learn that things do *not* work or that there is *no* relationship, we have still learned something valuable about our research problem.

- *Research questions should not be too broad or too specific in scope, especially in quantitative research studies.* Consider the following question:

> What will improve students' attitudes toward learning social studies?

This question is entirely too broad. One might design a whole host of studies that could investigate this research problem. Further, this question does not begin to suggest a methodology or approach for conducting the research study.

- *Research questions should be based in the body of literature related to the topic.* As we have briefly discussed, the reason behind reviewing related literature is to inform all aspects of your research study. A research problem and subsequent research questions should not develop out of the blue, without any substance to back them up.

- *Research questions must be answerable through the collection of available data.* Consider yet another version of our working example below:

> How will the integration of iPads into instruction affect students' attitudes toward world events in 30 years?

Honestly, I would not want to do this study. Based on the nature of the question, it would take me 30 years—if not more—to complete the study. The data necessary to answer this question are not available now, nor will they be anytime soon. A more acceptable version might be this:

> How will the integration of iPads into instruction affect fifth-grade students' attitudes toward social studies by the end of this school year?

Now, the data dictated by this question *are* certainly accessible. I could collect these data in many ways and could do so in the timeline outlined in the question.

- *Research questions must be ethical.* Recall from an earlier discussion that it is crucial for the researcher to ensure that all participants in the study are treated ethically. Researchers cannot expose participants to physical, psychological, or emotional harm of any sort, so they must make sure not to state research questions in a way that would require unethical methods.

- *Research questions should be important and feasible to answer.* Similar to the previous bullet, these are important characteristics that we have discussed in relation to research topics and problem statements. The idea that research topics must be both important and feasible to answer extends to the formal wording and statement of a research question.

Earlier in this chapter, in Table 3.1, we looked at several examples of research topics. The appropriately refined versions of these research topics and *potential* associated research questions are presented in Table 3.3. In most cases, you will notice that the wording of the research question very closely parallels that of the research topic, simply in the form of a question.

Hypothesis statements can also be used to guide research studies. They are tentative but well-informed guesses about the potential findings of the study, made before the study begins. However, compared with research questions, their use is much more limited. Hypotheses are used only in association with quantitative research studies, but they are not appropriate for all types of quantitative research studies. Hypotheses are only appropriate when the research design requires the use of inferential statistical analyses. Inferential statistics (which you will learn more about in Chapter 13) are also sometimes referred to as *hypothesis tests* for this reason. Hypothesis statements are usually included in experimental, correlational, and some comparative research designs, all of which are, of course, quantitative methodologies. The previously discussed guidelines for writing research questions also apply to the development of hypothesis statements.

TABLE 3.3 ● Examples of Research Questions Developed From Research Topics		
Research Topic		**Research Question**
Leisure activities of elementary teachers and the amount of time spent on them	→	What are the primary leisure activities of elementary teachers, and about how much time do they spend on them?
Hispanic students' perceptions of factors that make academic success more difficult	→	Which prohibitive factors to academic success do Hispanic students believe make their learning more difficult?
Effect of reading practice with fifth-grade "buddies" on the developing reading skills of first-grade students over a semester	→	What effect does reading practice with fifth-grade "buddies" have on the reading comprehension and phonemic awareness skills of first-grade students over the course of one semester?
Tenth-grade students' perceptions of virtual and real animal dissections	→	What perceptions do tenth-grade students hold regarding virtual and real animal dissections?
The effect of writing apps, providing immediate feedback, on students' abilities to develop thesis statements	→	What is the nature of the effect of writing apps, providing immediate feedback, on students' abilities to develop cohesive thesis statements?

Developmental Activities

1. In the Chapter 2 Developmental Activities, you brainstormed and outlined a possible educational research study. For that hypothetical study, develop the following:

   - A qualitative research question
   - A quantitative research question
   - A complete set of hypotheses (null, directional research, and nondirectional research)

2. Find a classmate and share the research questions and hypotheses you wrote in Question 1 above. Evaluate your classmate's statements against the guidelines and considerations presented in this chapter.

3. Other than their connection to the use of inferential statistics, discuss why you might prefer using hypothesis statements instead of research questions to guide a study.

4. Develop a list of 10 potential variables you might be interested in studying. Now classify each variable based on the following combinations of terms:

   - Continuous/discrete/dichotomous
   - Independent/dependent

5. For the hypothetical study you used in Question 1 above, identify five potential confounding variables and classify each as one of the following:

   - An innate condition
   - A permanent physical trait
   - A temporary condition

Summary

- Identification o f the topic to be researched is crucial, as it guides and shapes the remainder of the potential research study.
- Often, initial research topics must be broadened or narrowed to be appropriate in scope and size.
- Numerous preliminary factors must be considered when selecting research topics, including

  o personal interest,
  o importance of the topic,
  o newness of the topic,
  o amount of time that will be required,
  o potential difficulty of the topic,
  o potential monetary costs associated with the study, and
  o ethical design of the research.

- Most research topics must be refined before they can be effectively and efficiently researched.

  o This may require a narrowing or broadening of the topic, clarification or rewording of the topic, and a statement of the research question or hypothesis.

- Ideas for research topics in education can come from just about anywhere.
- Research problems are developed into problem statements, where key variables are delineated.
- Continuous variables measure a characteristic or trait along a continuum.
- Discrete, or categorical, variables measure characteristics that are divided into separate categories.

- Dichotomous variables are a special type of discrete variable, with only two possible categories.
- Variables may be continuous or discrete, depending on how the researcher measures or collects data on those variables.
- Variables may be measured on nominal, ordinal, interval, or ratio scales.
- Independent and dependent variables are designated in experimental and some comparative research.

  o An independent variable precedes the dependent variable in time and influences the dependent variable in some way.

- Confounding variables are measures of characteristics whose presence is not incorporated into the study but may influence the results of the study.

  o Examples of confounding variables include innate traits, permanent physical traits, and naturally occurring temporary conditions.
  o Confounding variables must be controlled if research results are to be considered legitimate.

- Research questions can differ depending on whether qualitative or quantitative methods will be used.
- Researchers must consider several important characteristics when stating research questions:

  o Qualitative research questions are open-ended; quantitative research questions are focused.
  o Research questions should require more than a simple yes/no answer.
  o Research questions should not be stated in a manner that assumes an answer before data have been collected.
  o Research questions should not be too broad or too specific in scope.
  o Research questions should be based in the body of literature related to the topic.
  o Research questions must be answerable through the collection of available data.
  o Research questions that guide research studies must be ethical.
  o Research questions should be important and feasible to answer.

- The two main types of hypotheses are null and research, or alternative, hypotheses.

  o The null hypothesis states that no effect will occur, no relationship exists, or no differences will be found.
  o The research or alternative hypothesis is a statement of the researcher's true expectations.
  o A directional research hypothesis indicates the direction of the results; a nondirectional research hypothesis states only that there is a difference and does not specify the direction of the difference.

⑤SAGE edge™

Sharpen your skills with SAGE edge!

edge.sagepub.com/mertler

SAGE edge for Students provides a personalized approach to help you accomplish your coursework goals in an easy-to-use learning environment. You'll find action plans, mobile-friendly eFlashcards, and quizzes as well as video, web, and resources and links to SAGE journal articles to support and expand on the concepts presented in this chapter.

Ethics in Educational Research

In this chapter, we consider one of the most important aspects of designing and implementing research studies in the broad field of education—that of ensuring the ethical behavior of the researcher. We examine critical issues and concerns that must be incorporated into the design of a research study. We discuss differences between ethical considerations in qualitative and quantitative studies, as well as the nature of institutional review boards. Finally, we review online courses that can assist in preparing researchers to address issues with human participants.

Ethical Considerations in the Conduct of Research

Similar to fields of study such as medicine, sociology, and psychology, educational research studies nearly always involve the collection of data from human beings as the main study participants. Regardless of the type of research being conducted or the type of research methods being employed—that is, qualitative, quantitative, or mixed methods—educational researchers must adhere to ethical considerations and ensure that the participants in their studies are protected, in a variety of ways. Leedy and Ormrod (2013) have identified four categories within which they believe most ethical issues in research fall. These issues typically apply across research studies, regardless of whether the research will use qualitative or quantitative methods. The four categories they have identified are

- protection from harm,
- voluntary and informed participation in the research,
- the right to privacy, and
- honesty with professional colleagues.

First and foremost, educational researchers must ensure that they are not exposing participants to *unnecessary and atypical physical or psychological harm*. When a study involves human participants, it is generally assumed that the risk associated with participating in the study should not be greater than the normal risks of day-to-day life (Leedy & Ormrod, 2013). Protection of research participants from harm includes protection from negative physical as well as psychological effects. Usually there is no risk of subjecting participants in an *educational* research study to physical harm, but there certainly is the potential of psychological harm, including undue stress, embarrassment, retribution, and the like.

In educational research settings, concern related to the protection of participants from potential harm is often a larger issue when dealing with participants from vulnerable populations. Examples of vulnerable populations might include individuals belonging to a particular gender, cultural background, or sexual orientation; pregnant teens; homeless students; students with exceptionalities; and very young children. Depending on the nature of a given study, these individuals might feel embarrassed, targeted, or otherwise uncomfortable. Additional care must be taken with such participants, especially if they cannot easily advocate for—or perhaps even voice—their own concerns about how they are feeling as a result of their involvement in a research study.

In some research studies, it may be necessary to create a small amount of psychological "discomfort" (Leedy & Ormrod, 2013). Simply put, even though great lengths may have been taken to minimize the negative effects, some may be unavoidable. In all studies, but especially ones where this discomfort is a factor, participants have the right to *informed* as well as *voluntary participation*. The combination of informed and voluntary participation is referred to as *informed consent*. **Informed consent** is defined as the act of participants—or their parents or legal guardians, in the case of children and other sensitive or vulnerable populations—agreeing to participate in a study once they know its nature and what their involvement will include (Leedy & Ormrod, 2013).

Informed consent is formally provided as a statement, or a longer form, that participants sign before they participate in the research (Creswell, 2005; Fraenkel, Wallen, & Hyun, 2012). The informed consent form actually describes what their participation will entail—including any potential risks they may face—and then requires them to sign the form if they agree to participate in the study. Participation in *any* research study should *always* be strictly voluntary. When participants over the age of 18 agree to participate in a research study, they are providing their **consent**. In situations involving minors (i.e., individuals under the age of 18), participants must provide **assent**. The rationale for the difference in terminology is that adults are able to *consent* to participate in research, meaning that they can decide for themselves whether they want to participate or not. Children cannot legally give consent to participate in research. Therefore, the parent or legal guardian must give permission for a child to participate; the child can only *assent* to participate (Mertler & Charles, 2011). An example of an informed consent form appears in Figure 4.1.

Leedy and Ormrod (2013) list several components that may be included on an informed consent form, such as the following:

- A brief description of the nature of the study
- A description of what participation will involve, in terms of activities and length of time
- A statement indicating that participation is voluntary and may be terminated without penalty at the participant's discretion
- A description of any potential risk and/or discomfort
- A description of the potential benefits of the study
- A guarantee that all data will remain confidential and anonymous
- The researcher's name and contact information
- Any office contact information, should participants have questions or concerns about the study
- An offer to provide a summary of the findings upon completion of the study
- A place for participants to sign and date the form, indicating whether or not they agree to participate

Researchers are sometimes faced with the dilemma of trying to determine exactly *how informed* potential participants should be (Leedy & Ormrod, 2013). Participants do not need to—nor do they want to—know *all* the details of a given research study in which they may participate. In fact, doing so may discourage them from participating altogether or cause them to behave or respond differently than they would under normal circumstances (Leedy & Ormrod, 2013). Essentially, potential participants need only know the details that will *directly* impact them as participants. This is known as *accurate disclosure*. **Accurate disclosure** to participants simply means that the researcher is obligated to *accurately* inform them about the general topic of the research, the nature of their participation, and any unusual tasks in which they may engage (Mertler & Charles, 2011).

Additionally, there is sometimes a question of how consent should be obtained. For example, the informed consent form shown in Figure 4.1 was administered face-to-face, requiring participants to complete and sign it in the presence of the researcher before any research could officially begin; however, this approach is not always feasible. Consider a possible research study where data are being collected entirely through the use of a mailed or web-based survey. It might not be practical to send out consent forms, require potential participants to sign and return the forms, and then mail out the surveys to the participants. In situations such as this, an informed consent cover letter can be used in place of a form requiring signatures. An example of this type of consent

FIGURE 4.1 ● A Sample Informed Consent Form, Highlighting Key Components

INFORMED CONSENT FORM

Principal Investigator (PI): Craig A. Mertler, Ph.D.   **PI Phone:** 419-372-9357

Project Title: *Development and Validation of the "Assessment Literacy Inventory"*

[Title of study and contact information]

You are invited to participate with no obligation in a research study which has as its main purpose the development and validation of an instrument designed to measure teachers' assessment literacy. Working with a colleague from Northern Illinois University, it is our intention to develop and validate a new instrument for future research endeavors with K–12 teachers on the topic of classroom assessment literacy.

[Description of the study (accurate disclosure)]

If you choose to participate in this research study, I would simply like to use the score you receive on a portion of your EDFI 402 final exam (consisting of the 35-item *Assessment Literacy Inventory*, or **ALI**). For purposes of the research study, all identifiers (i.e., names and identification numbers) will be removed from the scores. In addition, I would like to record the percentage of total points you have earned in EDFI 402. *The PI will not know who has or has not agreed to participate until after grades have been turned in at the end of the semester.* The information obtained from this study will be kept confidential and will only be reported in statistical analyses with no specific connections made to individuals. At no point will your identity be revealed. All data will be stored in a locked file cabinet, accessible only by the PI.

[Nature of participation; assurance of confidentiality and anonymity]

Your decision whether or not to participate will not interfere with your course grade, or current or future relationships with your instructor. You may choose to withdraw from the study at any time without penalty, and the PI may choose to cancel your participation at any time.

[Participation is voluntary; risk is minimal]

Do you have any questions? (*Circle one*)   **NO   YES**

If you circled YES, please contact the PI, Dr. Craig A. Mertler, at the above phone number or by email at mertler@bgsu.edu *before signing this form*. If you have questions or concerns regarding your rights as a research participant, you may also contact the Chair of the Human Subjects Review Board at BGSU at 419-372-7716, or at hsrb@bgsu.edu. Do not sign this form until these questions have been answered to your satisfaction.

YOU ARE MAKING A DECISION WHETHER OR NOT TO ALLOW THE PRINCIPAL INVESTIGATOR TO USE THE RESULTS OF A PORTION OF YOUR EDFI 402 FINAL EXAM (CONSISTING OF THE 35-ITEM *ASSESSMENT LITERACY INVENTORY*) FOR RESEARCH AND PRESENTATION PURPOSES ONLY. YOUR SIGNATURE BELOW ALSO INDICATES THAT YOU ARE OVER THE AGE OF 18.

[Specification of what participants are agreeing to do]

I **AGREE/DO NOT AGREE** (*circle one*) to participate in this research study.

[Indication of agreement and signature]

Participant's Name (please print): _____   Date: _____

Participant's Signature: _____

is provided in Figure 4.2. Notice that, in this study, consent to participate is provided by the participant's completing and submitting his or her survey responses. All other important aspects of an informed consent letter are included.

Third, research participants have a right to privacy. This is essentially achieved through providing assurances of *anonymity* and/or *confidentiality*. Study participants have **anonymity** when their identities are kept hidden from the researcher; researchers protect participant **confidentiality** when they know the identities of the participants but do not disclose that information to people outside of the research study (Gay, Mills, & Airasian, 2009). This includes protecting the anonymity of participants when writing final research reports. Unfortunately, these two terms are often confused and treated as if they are synonymous. If the researcher knows the participants' identities, the participants should be assured of confidentiality but not anonymity. Ethical researchers make sure that they know—and practice—the difference between these terms. Confidentiality is the *minimal* practice; at a minimum, data provided by participants should be kept strictly confidential and not shared with anyone. When practical and feasible, greater levels of objectivity can be provided in a study where participants' identities are kept anonymous.

Finally, researchers have the important obligation of reporting their findings in a complete manner, demonstrating the utmost honesty. Regardless of the nature of the research results—positive, negative, or somewhere in between—researchers must report the findings without intentionally misleading others (Leedy & Ormrod, 2013). Data should not be fabricated to support a preconceived conclusion. Similarly, conclusions should not be "manipulated" in an attempt to sway a research audience. My general rule of thumb is that, regardless of whether our research results turn out to be what we *expected* or even *wanted* to see, we have still learned something meaningful and beneficial about our topic of interest.

Ethics in Qualitative Versus Quantitative Studies

Up to this point, our discussion of ethical issues and researcher responsibilities has applied to both qualitative and quantitative research studies. However, qualitative research studies differ from quantitative research studies in at least two ways that impact decisions related to ethics (Gay et al., 2009). First, recall that many times qualitative research designs emerge, evolve, and change during the course of the study itself. The research design and plan for collection of data are preliminary, at best, when the study begins. Therefore, it may be difficult to know in advance what sorts of activities or tasks will be required or requested of potential participants. When these situations arise, unanticipated ethical issues will need to be resolved on the spur of the moment (Gay et al., 2009). Since the specifics of these issues cannot be anticipated, the qualitative researcher must be prepared to address them as they arise. Perhaps the most appropriate way to do this is to anticipate potential ethical issues at the outset of the study, including during development of the formal qualitative research proposal.

A second concern related to ethics in qualitative research is a direct result of one of the noted advantages of this type of research. Qualitative researchers are personally and intimately invested in the research setting. They must spend a great deal of time watching and conversing with their study participants. This prolonged amount of time spent together may result in a unique closeness. To reiterate, from a research

FIGURE 4.2 ● A Second Sample of an Informed Consent Form, Denoting an Alternative Method for Consent

Dear Ohio Teacher,

I am currently conducting an Web-based survey research study titled "**The Impact of NCLB on Teachers' Classroom Assessment Practices**," the purpose of which is examine how (or if) NCLB has affected the ways in which teachers assess the academic learning of their students.

Your superintendent has granted approval for teachers in your district to participate in the study as one of 150 randomly selected school districts in Ohio. The purpose of this email message is to ask for your participation in the study. I am asking you to participate in the study by simply completing the survey as honestly and openly as you can. The survey should only take about 10-15 minutes to complete. When you have completed the survey, simply click on the **SUBMIT** button located at the bottom of the page to send your responses to me. Please make sure you submit your responses only once! Additionally, please complete the survey by **September 30, 20XX**.

Please be assured that your responses will be anonymous. There will be no way for me to determine the origin of your responses. You will not be contacted for any further information. No one other than you will know if you have or have not participated in this study. Additionally, no individual information will be shared; only aggregate results will be reported. Finally, due to the Web-based nature of the survey, there exists a minimal chance that your responses could be intercepted, by individuals not involved with this study, while being transmitted.

Your participation in this study is voluntary. **By completing and submitting the survey, you are giving your consent to participate.** Please be assured that your decision to participate or not participate in this study will have no impact on your relationship with your respective school district. If you do not wish to participate, simply disregard this message. If you have any questions regarding this survey study, I may be contacted at *mertler@bgsu.edu*. You may also contact the Chair, Human Subjects Review Board, Bowling Green State University, (419) 372-7716 (*hsrb@bgsu.edu*) if any problems or concerns arise during the course of the study.

I would like very much for you to participate in the study by completing the brief survey which can be found by double-clicking on the following link: *http://edhd.bgsu.edu/mertler/nclbsurveya.php*

In advance, thank you very much for your participation in this research endeavor and best of luck in the remainder of your school year!

Best Regards,

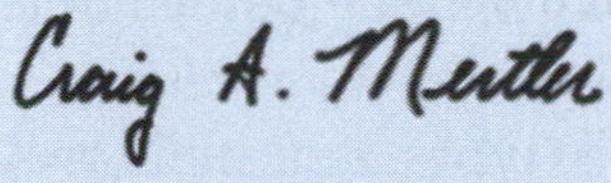

Craig A. Mertler

Craig A. Mertler, Ph.D.

Associate Professor of Assessment and Research Methodologies

APPROVED – BGSU HSRB

EFFECTIVE 8/22/20XX

EXPIRES 8/14/20XX

> Completing and submitting the survey serves as indication of agreement to participate

and data collection perspective, this is a wonderful thing. It results in richer, deeper data from the participants. However, it may also have an undue influence on the objectivity of the qualitative researcher, as well as on analysis of data and subsequent interpretation (Gay et al., 2009). Additionally, the qualitative researcher may observe behaviors that would otherwise be hidden, including those of an illegal or unprofessional nature. Gay and colleagues (2009) stress that in these types of situations, the researcher must make an ethical choice—to report the observations, realizing that the research study will likely end once participants discover the lack of confidentiality, or remain silent in the hope that the behaviors will be corrected naturally within the educational system. However, in the unlikely event that the researcher observes psychological or physical danger directed toward anyone in the setting, he or she is certainly obligated to inform the appropriate school authorities (Gay et al., 2009, p. 22).

Institutional Review Boards

In the 1970s, in response to prior abuses of human participants and because a vast majority of research in the United States is conducted in affiliation with a college, university, or research institution, the federal government created legislation intended to monitor these research activities (Creswell, 2005). Colleges and universities were mandated to create **institutional review boards (IRBs)** that review and approve both student and faculty research. An IRB is typically a committee made up of faculty members who review and approve research, ensuring that the rights of participants—as we discussed earlier—are protected. The role of the IRB is typically *not* to review and pass judgment on the research designs and methodologies; rather, its responsibilities lie solely in protection of the interests of human participants in those studies.

Leedy and Ormrod (2013) are quick to note that research is reviewed at the *proposal stage*; a proposal must be submitted to and approved by the IRB before the study can begin and before *any* data are collected. Additionally, this *must* be a *well-developed* proposal; in other words, it should delineate the nature of the qualitative study while leaving some degree of flexibility for a changing context. For example, the researcher may specify that the use of open-ended questions might be incorporated into an interview protocol. Further, the researcher may indicate that the original questions might diverge in some way during the course of the interviews, though still reflecting the nature of the originally submitted questions. It is important to remember that, once a research proposal has been approved by the IRB, the methodologies for data collection cannot be *substantially* revised without resubmitting a modified research proposal and going through the approval process all over again.

Leedy and Ormrod (2013) discuss the three types of possible proposal reviews conducted by IRBs, based on the extent to which the study imposes risks to participants. The IRBs for particular institutions may function somewhat differently, but generally speaking, they follow these protocols:

- *Exempt from review*—Research proposals may be declared exempt from review if they do not involve the collection of data from human participants at all. This might be the case for a historical research study where only 150-year-old documents and artifacts are serving as data sources.

- *Expedited review*—A research proposal receives an expedited review if participants will not be exposed to any noticeable risk. As an example, this is the appropriate type of review for a study where teachers are surveyed about their classroom assessment practices. An expedited review typically involves an assessment of the research proposal by a subset (e.g., two or three members) of the entire IRB.
- *Full board review*—A research proposal must receive a review by all members of the IRB in situations where participants are put at substantial risk or if the research proposes to collect data from minors. A study requiring the collection of data using videotapes of first-grade students reading aloud, for example, would require a full board review.

The process of obtaining approval from review boards differs from institution to institution; however, all researchers must complete some basic steps when seeking approval for a research study from their respective IRB (Creswell, 2005):

1. *Familiarize yourself with the process used by the IRB on your campus.* This includes obtaining all required application forms, knowing the submission deadlines, and finding out whose signatures are required on the forms.
2. *Determine what information about your project the IRB needs.* Most IRBs will require, at a minimum, the following:

   o A brief overview and purpose of the study
   o A listing of the guiding research questions
   o A (very) brief literature review
   o A description of how participants will be selected
   o Specifications of both risks and benefits of the study for the participants
   o A description of the proposed methodologies and data collection plans
   o Proposed plans for data analysis
   o Copies of all instrumentation and informed consent forms

3. *Develop all data collection instrumentation and related informed consent forms.* It is critical to keep in mind that, if your proposal is approved, you cannot change your instrumentation or consent forms without further delaying the start of your study.
4. *Complete the IRB application.* This is typically accomplished by providing all the required information (as outlined in Step 2 above).
5. *Submit your completed IRB application—including all required signatures—to the IRB for review.*

Once you have submitted your application, the chair of the IRB committee will determine what level of review it should receive. It will then be reviewed by the appropriate number of committee members; again, this time frame differs from campus to campus. If it is approved, you will receive notification from the chair of your institution's IRB. If your proposal is denied, you should be provided feedback as to why it was not approved so you can revise and resubmit your research proposal application.

Formal Preparation for Research With Human Participants

An additional aspect of ethical behavior not previously discussed in this chapter is the issue of *preparing* oneself to conduct research with human participants. One mechanism for facilitating this preparation to address issues related to the ethical treatment of participants in any type of educational research study is the requirement that *all* researchers—including graduate students, faculty, and full-time researchers—pass one of two self-paced, online research training courses. One is administered by the National Institutes of Health (NIH) Office of Extramural Research (phrp.nihtraining.com), and the other is administered by the Collaborative Institutional Training Initiative (CITI; www.citiprogram.org). The login screens for both sites are shown in Figure 4.3. For these training sites, registration and the courses themselves are available free of charge. It is important to note that many universities and schools require certification resulting from one of these two trainings before beginning any research study that involves human beings as participants.

Although some of the NIH course focuses on medical-type research, it provides an extremely thorough history and overview of aspects of the ethical treatment of human research participants. The entire NIH course takes roughly 90 minutes to complete and is divided into seven sections, four of which require successful completion of a brief multiple-choice assessment. The sections are as follows (asterisks indicate sections followed by an assessment):

- Introduction
- History
- Codes and Regulations*
- Respect for Persons*
- Beneficence*
- Justice*
- Conclusion

Once you have finished the course, you are provided with an electronic certificate of completion (see Figure 4.4).

The CITI course takes a bit longer to complete, as it contains additional modules. However, its use is recommended for social, behavioral, and educational researchers because it contains elective modules that can be tailored to a particular field of study (Fraenkel et al., 2012). These modules are as follows:

- Introduction
- Students in Research
- History and Ethical Principles
- Human Subjects Research Regulations
- Assessing Risk

FIGURE 4.3 ● Login Pages for NIH Training Course, "Protecting Human Research Participants," and CITI Training Course, "Human Subjects Research"

- Informed Consent
- Privacy and Confidentiality
- Research With Prisoners
- Research With Children

FIGURE 4.4   ●   Sample Certificate of Completion for NIH Training Course

Certificate of Completion

The National Institutes of Health (NIH) Office of Extramural Research certifies that **Craig Mertler** successfully completed the NIH Web-based training course "Protecting Human Research Participants".

Date of completion: 11/19/2012

Certification Number: 808521

- Research in Public Elementary and Secondary Schools
- International Research
- Internet Research
- Research and HIPAA Privacy Protections
- Vulnerable Subjects
- Conflicts of Interest in Research Involving Human Subjects

Similar to the NIH training course, users are awarded a certificate of successful completion at the end of the CITI course. Since both courses take some time to complete, the administrators of each have provided the option to save your work and return to it at a later time; the courses do not have to be completed in one sitting or session. Finally, it is important that all researchers and students check with their own institutions regarding specific policies and procedures related to these training courses. Typically, the certificate of completion must be included with any research proposal application materials submitted to an IRB.

Developmental Activities

1. Think of a possible research topic in any area of educational research that would require the inclusion of human participants. Identify aspects of researching that particular topic that would require you to take care to ensure the ethical treatment of your participants.

2. Develop a research question for a *qualitative* study in an area of interest to you. Next, draft

an informed consent form for your potential participants. Be sure to include references and assurances for all important ethical issues.

3. Develop a research question for a *quantitative* study in an area of interest to you. Next, draft an informed consent form for your potential participants. Be sure to include references and assurances for all important ethical issues.

4. What ethical issues would you be most concerned about when conducting classroom research with elementary students? As a responsible and ethical researcher, list possible ways you could address these issues.

5. For a research study involving students in Grade 2, draft both an assent form (for students) and a consent form (for parents/ guardians).

Summary

- Regardless of the approach used to conduct research, researchers must ensure that participants receive the following:

  o Protection from harm
  o The right to voluntary and informed participation
  o The right to privacy
  o Researcher's honesty with professional colleagues

- All research participants must be protected from unnecessary and atypical physical or psychological harm.
- Participants have the right to informed consent, which is a combination of informed and voluntary participation; they must provide informed consent to participate.
- Informed consent is typically provided by signing a form that describes what participation in the study will entail.
- When participants over the age of 18 agree to participate in the study, they are providing their consent.
- Minors involved in any research study can provide only assent, because they are not of legal consenting age.

- An informed consent form should always include the following:

  o A brief description of the study
  o A description of participant activities and duration of involvement
  o A statement indicating that participation is voluntary and may be terminated at the participant's discretion
  o Description of any potential risk as well as potential benefits
  o A guarantee that all data will remain confidential and anonymous
  o The researcher's name and contact information, as well as contact information for an official office
  o An offer to provide a summary of the findings of the study
  o A place for participants to sign and date the form

- Accurate disclosure is when the researcher informs participants only of the details that will directly impact them as participants in the study.
- Privacy can be attained through an assurance of anonymity, where identities are kept hidden from the researcher.

- Privacy can also be attained through assurance of confidentiality, where identities are known but not disclosed to people outside of the study.
- Regarding privacy, confidentiality is the minimal practice.
- Researchers have the important ethical obligation always to report their findings in a complete and honest manner.
- Ethical issues may be difficult to identify at the outset of a qualitative study, due to its emerging nature.
- Ethical dilemmas may arise during qualitative studies, due to the intimate nature of data collection and the close involvement of the researcher with participants in the setting.

- Researchers must ensure that their involvement and investment in the research setting do not jeopardize the quality of the research.
- Institutional review boards (IRBs) are committees at colleges, universities, or research institutions that review and approve research studies.
- Three categories of IRB review are *exempt from review*, *expedited review*, and *full board review*.
- Be sure to familiarize yourself with the process used by the IRB on your campus so you provide all the required information on your application.
- Two online courses for formal preparation to conduct research with human participants are offered by the National Institutes of Health and the Collaborative Institutional Training Initiative.

ⓈSAGE edge™

Sharpen your skills with SAGE edge!

edge.sagepub.com/mertler

SAGE edge for Students provides a personalized approach to help you accomplish your coursework goals in an easy-to-use learning environment. You'll find action plans, mobile-friendly eFlashcards, and quizzes as well as video, web, and resources and links to SAGE journal articles to support and expand on the concepts presented in this chapter.

5

Reviewing Related Research Literature

Student Learning Objectives

After studying Chapter 5, students will be able to do the following:

1. Describe the various purposes of conducting a review of related literature

2. Discuss what is meant by objectivity in a literature review

3. Distinguish between and provide examples of primary and secondary sources of information

4. Conduct searches for related literature using ERIC, Google Scholar, and ProQuest

5. List and describe various keys to organizing a literature review

6. Locate both primary and secondary sources of information appropriate for a topic of interest

7. Write a review of related literature for a topic of interest

Since the purpose of conducting any research study is to learn new things about a given topic, we must first understand what is known about that topic. Having a solid grasp of the research that has been conducted and the literature that exists on a given topic serves many functions for the researcher. In this chapter, we will examine the purposes and structure of a literature review, methods for finding sources for related literature, tips for searching online databases, and guidelines for formally writing a review of the literature as part of a research proposal or final research report.

What Is a Literature Review?

Generally speaking, a **literature review** is a comprehensive examination of the information and knowledge base related to a given research topic. Sources of this information include but are not limited to books, journal articles, conference presentations and papers, and evaluation reports. Conducting a systematic review of the related literature can provide numerous benefits as a researcher begins a study. Examining the literature can help the researcher identify a topic, narrow its focus, gather information about developing a research plan, and provide other general information regarding the overall project. The literature review enables the researcher to establish a connection between a proposed study and preceding research on the same topic. This can sometimes result in a revised approach to conducting a research study, because there is no need to replicate everything that has come before—reinventing the wheel, as the saying goes.

That being said, however, much can be learned from a comprehensive review of the literature. Decisions that researchers often struggle with during the preliminary stages of a research study can be facilitated more easily with knowledge of existing research on the topic. In turn, this typically results in a more efficient, more effective research study. Conducting a comprehensive review of the literature on any given topic enables you to become more of an expert in the area you are proposing to study, not to mention making you a more knowledgeable professional educator (Mertler, 2014).

Before you begin to search for literature related to your topic, it is important to be aware of several "characteristics" of this body of literature (Mertler, 2014). First, there is and always will be a wide range in terms of the *quality* of books, articles, and conference papers you will locate. There is a common misconception that the fact of being published signifies a work's quality. This is not *necessarily* the case. When you find an article or report, for example, you must consider whether it has been well researched or is simply someone's opinion. Often, opinion pieces can be valuable—especially if they are written by experts in the field—but we need to remember that such pieces are still based on individual *opinions*. In contrast, well-researched articles and reports are based on the collection of original data: These types of studies are referred to as **empirical research studies**. They are not inherently better and should not be taken at face value either; however, they are typically more rigorous since they are based on data and not just opinion. Furthermore, most articles that appear in academic journals, as well as research papers that are presented at conferences, have been through a peer-review process. These articles and papers are referred to as *refereed manuscripts*. This means that a group of experts in the field of study covered by the paper has reviewed the article, provided feedback on it, and deemed it worthy of publication, presentation, or another form of dissemination. Again, this adds another level of rigor and value to the research.

A second key feature of related literature is *objectivity*; that is, the literature should be *rigorously, ethically,* and *comprehensively* read and reviewed. In some cases, researchers have reviewed only literature that supported the conclusions they hoped to reach with their studies. Although some would argue that this is simply human nature and none of us can be truly objective, it is still a biased and unethical approach to reviewing related literature. A thorough, systematic, and comprehensive review of the literature will discover and present multiple perspectives on the phenomenon under investigation. You should include research that both supports *and* contradicts your views or anticipated results. This is a much more rigorous and ethical approach not only to the literature review but also to the study itself. It lets potential readers of a final research report know that the research was conducted as objectively as possible. For example, imagine that you are studying student perceptions of virtual versus real animal dissections and you personally think that virtual dissections will be better but know you still need to conduct the research to determine actual perceptions. You will want to be sure that your literature review includes research touting the benefits of virtual *as well as* live dissections. To be as objective as possible, the literature review will need to address the relative benefits and limitations of both methods.

Third, researchers must always be sensitive to the *timeliness* of the research they choose to include in the literature review. It is always important to examine the body of research in its entirety, but it is probably most applicable and meaningful to a proposed study to focus the review on the most current empirical research. If you consider only older, more historical research (say, research conducted 20 or 30 years ago)—and ignore that things change over time—you will likely miss newer, and possibly more innovative, research findings. Similarly, if you look only at research published in the past year or two, you might overlook some of the major advances or knowledge gained in the particular field of study. The span of years to be covered by a literature review will vary greatly from topic to topic; I wish I could provide a fast and firm guideline, but it simply is not possible. For example, some topics may have been heavily researched in the 1990s, and then interest waned but for some reason began to resurface in journals beginning in 2009. In this situation, you would likely *not* want to begin your literature review with articles published in 2009 but, rather, would go as far back as the height of this area of research in the '90s.

The final consideration related to the literature review is the number of sources needed. As a professor of research methods, I am probably most often asked by graduate students questions related to this area:

1. How many references do I need?
2. How much review of literature is enough?
3. How do I know when I'm done reviewing the literature?

These are excellent questions . . . to which I typically have no adequate response, at least from the students' perspectives. This is largely because every research topic is unique—as is the existing body of literature on that topic—in terms of both size and scope. It is important to realize that you must strike a balance between (a) getting bogged down in reviewing literature related to your topic, especially if you are examining a topic that has a large research/knowledge base, and (b) engaging in only a cursory examination of the literature, such that you miss out on important studies or contributors to the research body. My general recommendation is that you know you have done a reasonably good job of reviewing literature on your topic when you begin to see the same articles and the same authors cited across all the literature you are reviewing. Schwalbach (2003) has suggested that when you begin to recognize the major contributors in the field, you can be confident that you most likely have not missed important studies. Gay, Mills, and Airasian (2009, p. 81) have also offered some good advice for trying to strike this balance:

1. Avoid the temptation to include *everything* you find in your literature [emphasis added].
2. When investigating a heavily researched area, review only those works that are *directly* related to your specific problem [emphasis added].
3. When investigating a new or little-researched problem area, review *any* study related in *some* meaningful way to your problem [emphasis added].

Johnson (2008) has also provided a fairly good rule of thumb regarding the appropriate number of sources for a literature review, especially in graduate research projects. He has stated that master's theses should typically have a minimum of 25 sources, whereas doctoral dissertations will often require 50 or more. Finally, Gay and colleagues (2009) remind us of a key misconception: that the worth of a research topic is directly proportional to the amount of literature available on that topic. This is not an accurate assumption. Many new, yet important areas of study might have received a relatively small amount of attention in published literature simply because there has not been ample time for studies to be conducted and then published, presented, or otherwise disseminated. Some might argue that the *lack* of literature on a topic is reasonable justification for conducting new research on that topic. Similarly, just because a given problem area has received the attention of a thousand research studies does not mean that further research is unnecessary. In cases such as these, subtopics of the much broader research problem area are typically easy to identify and may serve as areas ripe for additional research.

Sources for Literature Related to Your Research Topic

Potential sources for literature related to your topic can be separated into primary sources and secondary sources. **Primary sources** are firsthand accounts of original research, such as journal articles, monographs, and papers presented at professional research conferences. In contrast, **secondary sources** are not firsthand accounts; they do not consist of original research but, rather, are summaries, compilations, analyses, or interpretations of primary research conducted by other individuals. Secondary sources include encyclopedias of research, handbooks of research, reviews of research, scholarly books (e.g., textbooks), and perhaps even magazine or newspaper articles (especially those written by experts in the field). Although your literature review should focus predominantly on primary sources of research information, secondary sources are a good place to begin your search for related literature, as they can provide some perspective on the body of literature you will be examining in greater depth.

Secondary sources are typically found in the reference section of the library and can be located by searching the library's main catalog. These catalogs used to consist of small index cards filed in drawers—which is how they became known as "card catalogs." However, most libraries now catalog all their reference materials electronically, enabling the user to search via computer. As an aside, this facilitates a much more efficient and expedient search through the wide variety of existing secondary sources. These are usually found in the library's main reference section and include such publications as

- *Encyclopedia of Educational Research,*
- *Review of Educational Research,* and
- *National Society for the Study of Education* yearbooks.

There are also several handbooks on a number of educational topics. These handbooks serve as collections of important articles related to the specific topic area, including the following:

- *Handbook of Research on Teaching*
- *Handbook of Research on Early Childhood Education*
- *Handbook of Research on Language Development*
- *Handbook of Research on Curriculum*
- *Handbook of Research on Math Teaching and Learning*
- *Handbook of Research on Multicultural Education*
- *Handbook of Research on Music Teaching and Learning*
- *Handbook of Research on Science Teaching*

On the other hand, primary sources are most often found by searching specialized indexes or databases. Most of what you will eventually locate by searching these databases is original research that has been either published in refereed journals or presented at professional research conferences. The purpose of the literally hundreds of academic journals published in the field of education is to inform the field, or more specific disciplines within the broader educational field, about current research (Johnson, 2008). Most of these articles are written by researchers or other academicians (i.e., college or university professors), or consultants. Drafts of manuscripts are submitted to the journal editor, who—because most journals are refereed—sends them out for peer review by anywhere from three to six experts in the field. Their responsibility is to check the manuscripts and studies for quality, accuracy, validity, and overall contribution to the field. Each reviewer provides evaluative comments to the editor and makes a recommendation for publication. Those decisions typically consist of "accept," "accept with revisions," or "reject." If an article is accepted for publication, it usually must undergo several rounds of revision before it appears in the journal. Depending on the journal, this process might take anywhere from a few months to a year. Getting an article published in a journal is no easy task; some journals have acceptance rates of 50%, whereas others may have acceptance rates as low as 5%.

Although there are numerous electronic databases for locating primary sources of educational research information, the ERIC database is arguably the most commonly used among education researchers (Mertler, 2014). **ERIC**, an acronym for **Education Resources Information Center**, was created in 1966 by the U.S. Department of Education and is the largest database for locating research in education. For many years, ERIC was a clearinghouse for research papers, including papers published in journals, research reports, and evaluation reports, and papers presented at conferences. Once a paper had been published or presented, one simply submitted it to ERIC to be included in the clearinghouse database. However, that process was substantially revamped in 2004 (Mertler, 2014). The new ERIC digital library uses two advisory panels to provide research, technical, and content expertise. One of these advisory panels is responsible for providing recommendations for selecting journal and nonjournal materials for inclusion in the ERIC database.

The searchable ERIC online database provides the worldwide educational community with the capability of searching more than 1.4 million citations dating back to 1966 (Institute of Education Sciences, n.d.). There are currently more than 650 journals indexed in the ERIC database, roughly 500 of which are indexed comprehensively—meaning *every* article in *each* issue is included. The remaining journals are indexed selectively—meaning only those articles pertaining to education have been selected for indexing. In addition, about 400,000 nonjournal items (such as conference papers and reports) are available as full text in PDF format for easy, free-of-charge downloading. The ERIC database can be searched from its main page (eric.ed.gov), affiliated with the U.S. Department of Education. The process of searching the ERIC database will be discussed in depth in the next section.

Of course, there are many other examples of searchable online databases; however, some of those require you to pay a subscription or user fee to search and download articles. Searching ERIC is a free service; all you need is access to the Internet. I will extend an important caution that you not limit yourself only to one database or only to full-text articles available online (Mertler, 2014). Granted, this is a quicker and easier way to gain access to and collect related literature; however, by doing so, you will limit your review of the *entire* body of literature to items available online and may give in to the allure of not having to leave your computer in search of hard-copy articles. Remember that some journals and other types of research reports are not indexed in ERIC. All it takes is a little bit of extra time—and some loose change—to visit your university library and make copies of articles that are available only in hard copy.

Another example of a free-of-charge Internet database is **Google Scholar**. According to its website (www.google.com/intl/en/scholar/about.html):

> Google Scholar provides a simple way to broadly search for scholarly literature. From one place, you can search across many disciplines and sources: articles, theses, books, abstracts and court opinions, from academic publishers, professional societies, online repositories, universities and other web sites. Google Scholar helps you find relevant work across the world of scholarly research. ("About," para. 1)

When you search for a topic in Google Scholar, Google provides a list of relevant articles but also ranks them in terms of the entire text of each document, including information on where it was published, who wrote it, and how often and how recently it has been cited in other research literature (Mertler, 2014). The process of searching Google Scholar will be presented later in this chapter.

ProQuest (www.proquest.com/connect) is another searchable online database that contains not only research articles and conference papers but also thesis and dissertation studies. Many of the articles accessible through the ProQuest database are available in full-text format—including theses and dissertations. In addition, you can purchase hard copies of theses and dissertations. You can also preview the abstract and a sampling of pages from theses and dissertations, prior to making a decision about downloading the entire manuscript or placing an order for a hard copy. The only potential limitation of ProQuest is that it is typically accessible only via a university library system, because ProQuest requires institutional memberships. Therefore, if you are a current student (as most of you are), you can access the searchable database through your university library's website, using your university log-in information. ProQuest is a great resource for accessing theses and dissertations in their full manuscript form.

Finally, the Internet itself and its multitude of search engines can be a valuable resource for information related to research topics, as well as for exploring initial ideas for topics. **Search engines**, of course, organize their findings by keywords (Mertler, 2014). When you use a search engine to find instances of a specific keyword—or keywords—the results will yield a list of related websites, typically in an attempt to rank them in terms of relevance to the topic. Additionally, there are numerous professional organizations in the broad field of education, and many of them maintain websites that include links to related webpages, typically chock-full of information. There are simply too many to list here, but it would be wise for you to explore resources available on the websites of many of these professional organizations. This can certainly be a great starting point in the process of gathering research literature related to your topic.

Searching the ERIC Online Database

The ERIC database of educational research consists of two indexes, both of which are searchable online and simultaneously. The *Current Index to Journals in Education* contains citation information and abstracts of journal articles that have been published in education and other closely related fields. On the other hand, *Resources in Education* cites and abstracts research documents that have not been published in education journals, including research papers presented at conferences, technical reports, reports of evaluations of federally funded programs, and any other original research that has not been published elsewhere (Mertler & Charles, 2011). The main entry page for the ERIC database is shown in Figure 5.1.

Notice, initially, that the main technique for searching the ERIC database is to use a single *keyword* or *descriptor*. However, due to the immense size of the database, this will often return an extremely large number of citations—often too many for a researcher to wade through. For example, if I was interested in locating research on the topic of "teachers' assessment practices," I would type that phrase into the search bar and click the **Search** button. Unfortunately—or fortunately, depending on how you look at it—ERIC returns nearly 10,000 citations matching that phrase (see Figure 5.2). Clearly, this is way too many articles for which to provide even a cursory review. This particular search needs to be

FIGURE 5.1 ● Main Entry Page for the ERIC Database (eric.ed.gov)

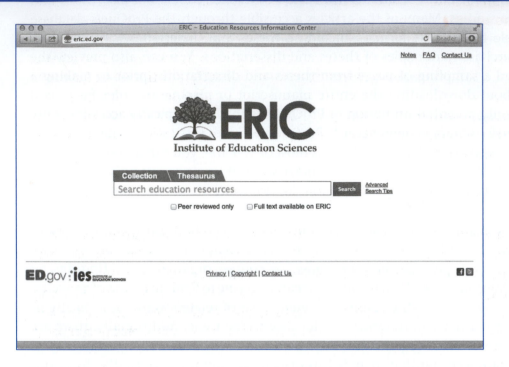

narrowed and specified. ERIC provides a mechanism for doing this—advanced search techniques. You can see how to use these techniques by clicking on *Advanced Search Tips* (eric.ed.gov/?advanced), located to the right of the *Search* button (see Figure 5.2).

FIGURE 5.2 ● Results From an Initial Search of ERIC, Showing a Large Number of Citations Returned

Collection	Thesaurus

Notes   FAQ   Contact Us

teachers' assessment practices   Search   Advanced Search Tips

☐ Peer reviewed only   ☐ Full text available on ERIC

Showing 1 to 15 of 9,977 results

Locating Interim Assessments within Teachers' Assessment Practice
Riggan, Matthew; Olah, Leslie Nabors – Educational Assessment, 2011

☑ Peer reviewed
☑ Direct link

Promising research on the teaching and learning impact of classroom-embedded formative assessment has spawned interest in a broader array of assessment tools and practices, including interim assessment. Although researchers have begun to explore the impact of interim assessments in the classroom, like other assessment tools and practices, they...

Descriptors: Homework, Student Evaluation, Observation, Formative Evaluation

Teacher Factors and Perceived Assessment Practices Needs of Social Studies Teachers in Cross River State, Nigeria
Ekuri, Emmanuel Etta; Eobai, Julius Michael; Ita, Caroline Iserome – Educational

Link to learn about advanced searching techniques

A large number of returned citations

The most effective method for either narrowing or broadening the search is the use of Boolean operators. **Boolean operators** are keywords that enable the retrieval of terms and specific combinations (Mertler, 2014). The most common Boolean operators are *and* and *or*. If *and* is used, only those documents that contain both keywords as descriptors will be retrieved (this will result in a narrower search, with fewer citations returned). If *or* is used, every document with either of these two keywords as descriptors will be retrieved (this will result in a broader search with more citations returned). Going back to our example, suppose I was interested only in the assessment practices of elementary school teachers. I would search for the following (exactly as it appears below):

"teachers' assessment practices" and "elementary teachers"

Notice in Figure 5.3 that I have now substantially narrowed my search for related literature, from nearly 10,000 citations to 31—a much easier review task for me. I will offer one substantial word of caution, however: It is ill-advised to assume that you now need rely only on those 31 citations. Once you have reviewed those, you may discover that you need to return to ERIC and slightly broaden your search. (As a side note, if I had searched for "teachers' assessment practices" *or* "elementary teachers," ERIC would have returned 18,340 citations!)

Before moving on, let us revisit Figure 5.3 to examine some of the other features ERIC provides along with the initial list of returned citations. On the left-hand side of the browser window, notice that ERIC has listed options for further narrowing your search. By clicking on any of the provided links, you can narrow your search according to

- publication date,
- additional or alternative descriptors,
- the source of the citation (e.g., specific journals, databases, or online submission—which means it was submitted directly to ERIC by the authors),

FIGURE 5.3 ● Results From an Initial Search of ERIC, Showing a Reduced Number of Citations Returned

Notes   FAQ   Contact Us

| Collection | Thesaurus |

"teachers' assessment practices" ℓ   Search   Advanced Search Tips

☐ Peer reviewed only   ☐ Full text available on ERIC

Showing 1 to 15 of 31 results

A much more manageable number of citations

The Impact of Extended Professional Development and a Comprehensive Approach to Assessment on Teacher Use of Assessment for Learning Practices
Robinson, Jack; Reed, William; Strauss, Richard – Online Submission, 2011

This study sought to examine the impact of teachers' participation in an extended period of embedded professional development (PD) emphasizing teachers' use of assessment for learning practices (AFL) in extended problem based units of instruction within a comprehensive AFL framework. The extended and comprehensive approach of using both course...

📄 Download full text

Descriptors: Student Evaluation, Learning Strategies, Faculty Development, Evaluation Methods

- author,
- publication type,
- education level, and
- audience.

Additionally, if you visit the *Advanced Search Tips* page (eric.ed.gov/?advanced), you will see several specific ways you can initially search the database. You're able to specify searches by the following ERIC field names:

- Abstract
- Audience
- Author
- Descriptor
- Education level ("educationlevel")
- Publication year ("pubyear")
- Source
- Title

For example, if I wanted to find all the citations in ERIC authored by myself, I would enter the following (exactly as it appears below) in the search bar:

author:"craig mertler"

In Figure 5.4, you can see that this search returns 29 citations. On the right side of each citation is a gray box that indicates the document's availability. Options here—along with their meanings—are as follows:

- **Direct link**—The document is not available in the ERIC database in full-text format, but a link to the document's location elsewhere online is provided.

FIGURE 5.4 ● A Sample Search by Author's Name

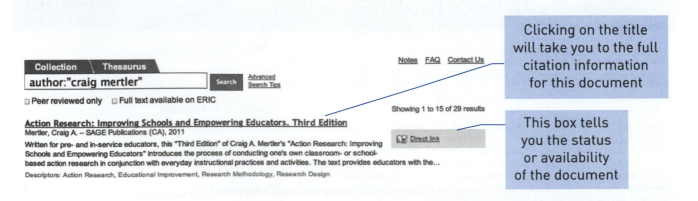

- **Peer reviewed**—This document, wherever it appeared, was peer reviewed or "refereed."
- **Download full text**—Clicking on this link will take you to the full document, ready for printing or downloading to your computer. Notice that under the search bar, there is an option for returning only articles available in full-text format, selected by clicking the box next to *Full text available on ERIC*.
- **PDF release pending**—ERIC is currently unable to release these documents electronically due to concerns about personally identifiable information that may exist in some older, non-peer-reviewed documents. These documents are being analyzed and, if found acceptable, will be returned to ERIC. In the meantime, these articles may be accessible through interlibrary loan and on microfiche in your university library.

Clicking on the title of an article—in this case, the fourth citation on the list—takes you to the document citation page (see Figure 5.5). Detailed information about the particular document or article is provided on this page, including

- the title;
- name(s) of author(s);
- reference citation information;
- the entire abstract;
- keywords/descriptors that were used to index the article;
- contact information; and

FIGURE 5.5　●　Sample Document Citation From ERIC

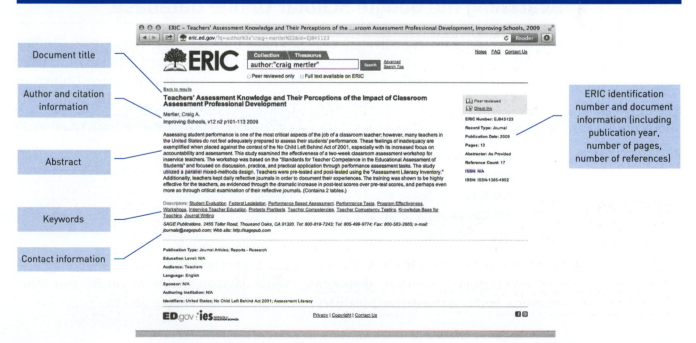

- other information related to the article, including the ERIC identification number, year of publication, number of pages, and number of references cited in the article.

Looking on the right-hand side of the screen, you will notice that all documents have a unique six-digit ERIC identification number *(ERIC Number)*. However, some citations have identification numbers that are preceded by the letters *EJ* and others by the letters *ED*. The letters *EJ* signify that the document was published in an academic journal, whereas the letters *ED* signify virtually any other kind of research document, including papers presented at academic conferences, technical reports, evaluation reports, position papers, and so on. If the document is available for download in full-text format, this identification number is not necessary; however, if the document is not available in full-text format, then the researcher will have to go to the library to try to locate it. Knowing whether the identification number is preceded by *EJ* or *ED* becomes important at this point. Generally speaking, documents identified by *EJ* will be located on the shelves of bound (i.e., hard-copy) journals. In contrast, documents identified by *ED* will likely be found only in your library's microfiche stacks.

Due to the flexibility and ease of searching the ERIC database, it does take some practice and experience to work with it effectively and efficiently (Mertler, 2014). The idea of combining keywords in a single search, using *and* or *or* as operators, or even combining keywords with authors' names can be somewhat intimidating to the novice researcher. However, beginning researchers should not hesitate to experiment with the searchable database. With its millions of indexed documents and convenient online access, ERIC is a valuable resource for researchers at any level of experience.

Searching the Google Scholar Online Database

Similar to the ERIC database, Google Scholar (scholar.google.com) will conduct searches for your topic across a broad cross-section of research and scholarly literature (Mertler, 2014). The default settings available in the main search screen (shown in Figure 5.6) will return citations from a wide variety of document types, including

- theses and dissertations,
- journal articles,
- books,
- abstracts,
- legal documents, and
- court opinions.

Furthermore, these documents come from a diverse list of sources, including academic publishers, professional societies, online databases, and university and other websites. Some of the distinct features of Google Scholar enable you to

- explore related works, citations, authors, and publications;
- locate the complete document online or through a local university library;

FIGURE 5.6 ●   Main Search Page for Google Scholar (scholar.google.com)

- track recent publications and trends in a specific area of research; and
- check who is citing your publications (if you are an author yourself) and how many times those publications have been cited.

Suppose I wanted to do a search similar to the one I previously conducted in the ERIC database. I would enter the phrase "teachers' assessment practices" in the search bar and click the search button, indicated by the magnifying glass symbol:

Examining the search results provided by Google Scholar, you will first notice that the search returned about 1,970,000 results (see Figure 5.7). I would probably want to narrow that a bit. Further, you should see that results are sorted by relevance; however, you can search by particular dates using the options in the left sidebar. If I was interested only in publications since 2013, I would simply select "Since 2013" in the sidebar. As shown in Figure 5.8, this would substantially reduce the number of hits to 28,600 (see Figure 5.8)—still too large to review efficiently and expediently. Additional information appears in the right sidebar, which contains links to online accessibility (i.e., full text or if accessible through a library, database, website, or journal).

You can search by author name using Google Scholar's advanced search feature, similar to the advanced search options in the ERIC database. From the search results page,

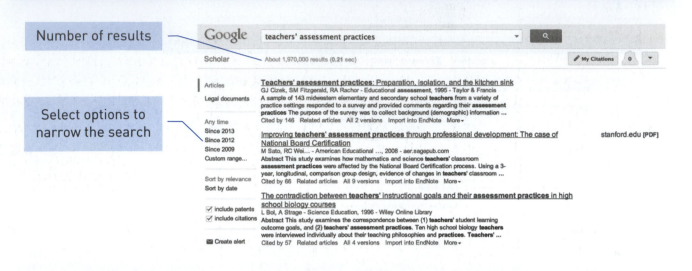

FIGURE 5.7 ● A Google Scholar Results Page

Number of results

Select options to narrow the search

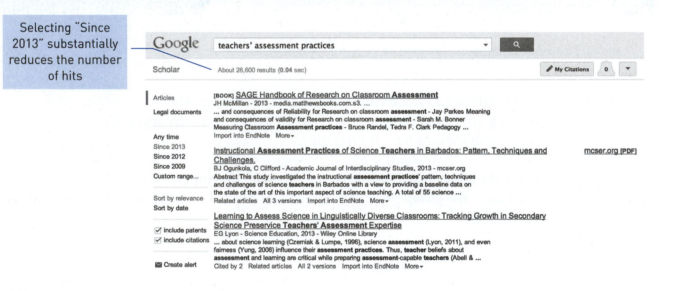

FIGURE 5.8 ● Same Google Scholar Search After Narrowing Search by Specific Dates

Selecting "Since 2013" substantially reduces the number of hits

select the downward pointing arrow, then select *Advanced search* (see Figure 5.9). This will open the window you see in Figure 5.10. For example, if you wanted to search for my name, you would simply enter

<u>*Craig A. Mertler*</u>

in the search bar, located to the right of *Return articles authored by*, then click the search button in the lower left-hand corner:

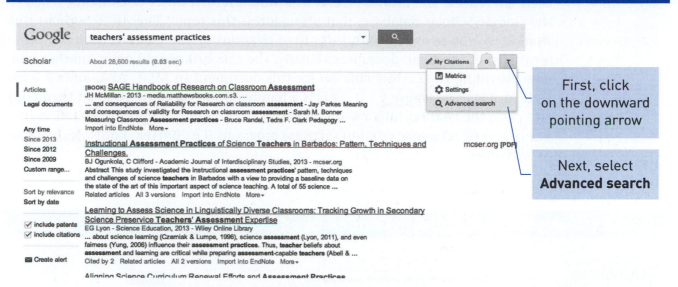

FIGURE 5.9 ● Accessing the Advanced Search Feature in Google Scholar

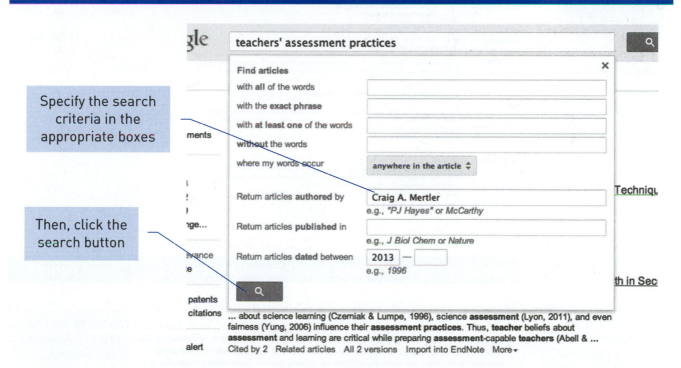

FIGURE 5.10 ● Advanced Search Window in Google Scholar

The results of this search are shown in Figure 5.11.

Figure 5.12 presents the elements contained in a single search result returned by Google Scholar. Clicking the title link—*Designing scoring rubrics for your classroom*—would download the article to your computer. If you clicked on *Cited by*

184, Google Scholar would return all 184 documents that have listed this article in their references. The *Related articles* link would return other documents, listed in the Google Scholar database, that also address this topic. The *All 27 versions* link would take you to a page with links to or citations of any other versions, or other locations, of the same document. Finally, the *Cite* link would open another window providing the correct citation for this document in MLA, APA, and Chicago style formats (see Figure 5.13). This is a handy option, because you can then copy and paste the citation into a word-processor document or import the citation into one of several reference citation software programs (i.e., BibTex, EndNote, RefMan, or RefWorks).

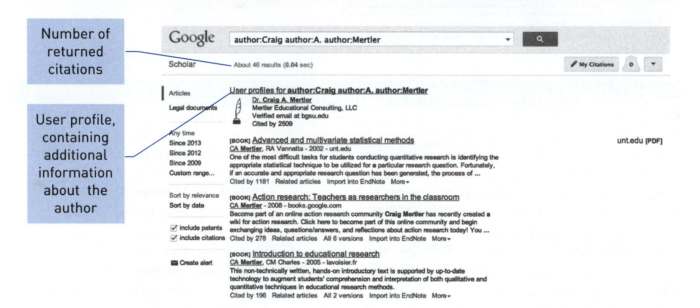

FIGURE 5.11 ● Results of an Author Search in Google Scholar

Number of returned citations

User profile, containing additional information about the author

FIGURE 5.12 ● A Single Google Scholar Search Result, Highlighting Additional Search Options

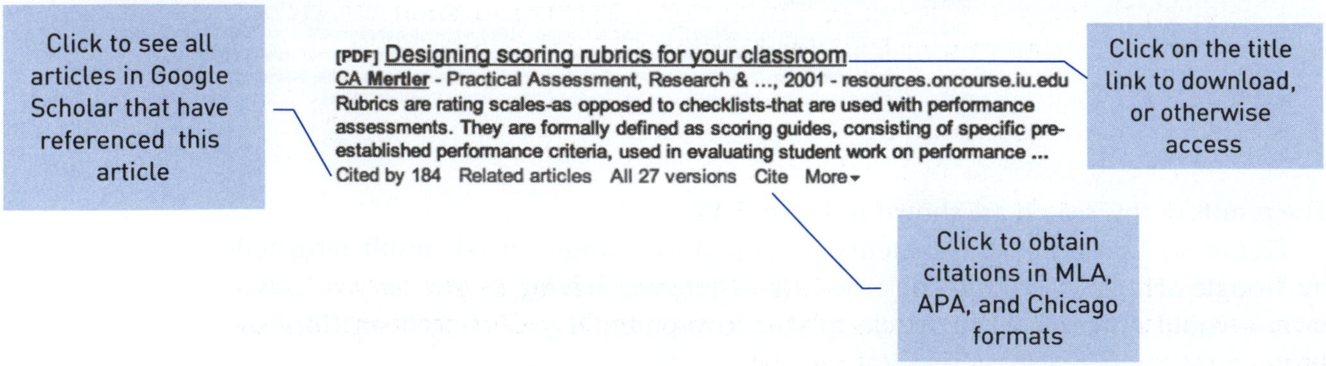

Click to see all articles in Google Scholar that have referenced this article

Click on the title link to download, or otherwise access

Click to obtain citations in MLA, APA, and Chicago formats

FIGURE 5.13 ● The Bibliographic Citation Option in Google Scholar

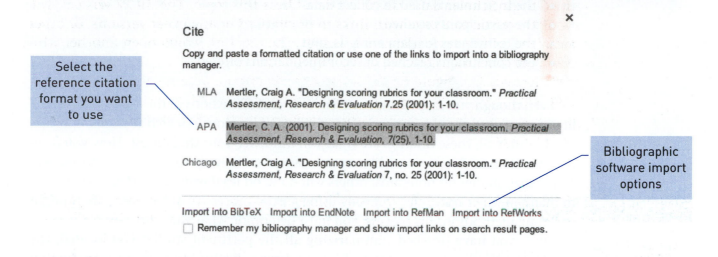

Writing Your Literature Review

Writing a review of related literature is, in my opinion, one of the more difficult aspects of writing any type of research proposal or report. There is no easy, step-by-step process for creating such a review (Mertler, 2014). What makes it so difficult is that every study and every body of literature is different; if I gave the same area of study and set of 50 to 60 research articles to 10 different people, I would likely receive 10 unique reviews of that literature. They would be organized differently, they would stress varying aspects of the body of research, they would use different subheadings, and so on. I believe that one of the best ways to learn how to write a literature review is to examine how others have accomplished the task, reading others' reviews carefully and critically, and paying close attention to *how* they are structured, organized, and written. Even though there is no step-by-step formula, I can offer several suggestions that I hope will help you organize your review and begin to get it down on paper.

It is critical to be mindful of the goals you're trying to accomplish by developing a written review of related literature (Mertler, 2014). The primary goal is to convey to all individuals interested in this particular topic—keeping in mind the various audiences who may read your review—the following information:

- The historical context of the topic
- The research trends related to the topic
- How theory has informed practice and vice versa

The first thing you should try to do is condense each study you review into a brief summary, stressing the aspects related to your topic and/or pertinent to your proposed study. These aspects might include

- the variables studied,
- the methodology employed,
- the instruments used to collect data,
- the participants studied,
- the techniques for data analysis, and
- the conclusions reached or recommendations offered.

Even though you may include references to and discussions of the aspects above, the literature review should emphasize the *findings* of previous research (Pyrczak & Bruce, 2003)—after all, these findings are what will influence your study most. How you facilitate this step in developing a literature review is entirely up to you. Some people will summarize studies on notecards; others will do so on legal pads; still others may decide to maintain their notes electronically using a word processor. Again, there are no right or wrong methods in this process; you must determine what will work best for you.

Once you have finished summarizing all the pertinent studies you located, the next step is to develop an outline for your review, beginning with an introduction that communicates its organization, often using subheadings (Pyrczak & Bruce, 2003). Your review's organization and subheadings should focus on the aspects of the body of literature that are relevant to your topic and study; these are the *key elements* for helping any reader of your literature review understand the main focus. As you begin to use this organizational outline to write the review, it is important that you *not* write it in the form of an annotated list or bibliography (i.e., one study summarized in a paragraph, followed by another summarized in the next paragraph) but, rather, as a cohesive essay that flows smoothly for the reader—from one paragraph to the next and from one section to the next (Pyrczak & Bruce, 2003). By doing so, you will create for the reader a better view of the trends your topic has seen over time. All literature related to a given subtopic should be cited during the discussion of that topic. This last characteristic may seem a bit odd, because you might talk about one particular study in four or five different places throughout your literature review. However, this is perfectly acceptable, since you will be focusing on different aspects of that study under different subtopics or subheadings within the review.

Another key organizational aspect of writing a literature review—and one with which a lot of novice researchers seem to struggle—is the order of the topics, from the beginning to the end of the review (Mertler, 2014). Generally speaking, a well-written literature review should begin with the subtopics—not *necessarily* studies or articles—that are *least* related to your specific proposed study. As you proceed through the development of your literature review, the subtopics should begin to focus more and more. In other words, they should become *more* closely related to your topic. This "design" has a funneling effect (see Figure 5.14). As you write—and someone reads through—your literature review, the scope of the research being summarized is continually narrowed; in other words, you are funneling the reader's attention in the direction of your specific topic. The logic behind this practice is that the final subtopics presented in your literature review

FIGURE 5.14   ●   Depiction of the Narrowing Focus in a Literature Review

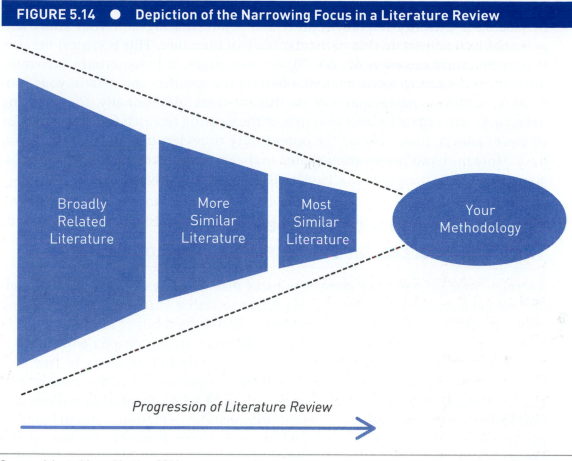

Source: Adapted from Mertler, 2014.

will be those most closely related to your study (which you will present next as your study's methodology; Mertler, 2014).

For example, a recent study of mine focused on teachers' perceptions of the influence of No Child Left Behind (NCLB) in their classroom assessment practices. The three *main* subheadings (beginning with the broader literature and progressing to the more focused) of my literature review were as follows:

- *The Impact of "No Child Left Behind"*
- *Teachers' Perceptions of "No Child Left Behind"*
- *"No Child Left Behind" and Classroom Assessment*

I think you can see how the literature review moves from research that is broadly related (i.e., the impact of NCLB in general) to research that most closely aligns with what I specifically studied (i.e., the connection between NCLB and actual classroom practice).

Finally, I am a firm believer in the inclusion and usefulness of concluding, summary paragraphs, as they provide a starting point for *your* study, based on what previous research has found (Mills, 2011). They also provide support for your study by placing it within a relevant context and demonstrating how your study will potentially contribute to that particular body of literature. This is critical because if your literature review is 50, 60, 70, or more pages, it is sometimes extremely difficult for readers to focus their attention on the specifics and details; your concluding, summary paragraphs will do this for them. Additionally, these closing paragraphs will provide a brief overview of the existing research for those who, for whatever reason, have not had the opportunity to review it as thoroughly as you have. More in-depth information related to the process of writing research proposals and reports is presented in Chapters 10 and 14, respectively.

Not Just for Conducting Research— Valuable Sources for Professional Development

Although your primary and immediate focus may be on learning about and conducting graduate-level research, it is important to realize that you may have a long career in education or an education-related field. The methods of locating research, both primary and secondary, presented and discussed in this chapter will continue to be excellent and invaluable techniques for finding up-to-date research. True education professionals continue to develop in their respective fields throughout their careers. These individuals maintain memberships in professional organizations and read journals and other sources of current information and research specific to their disciplines. As current or future members of your respective professions, you should also avail yourselves of such opportunities.

Developmental Activities

1. Reflect for a moment on your skills of reading, summarizing, and writing. What do you anticipate will be the most difficult aspect of writing a review of related literature?

2. Develop a list of advantages and limitations of locating research literature through ERIC and Google Scholar.

3. Do you believe that secondary sources are a good place to begin looking for literature on a given topic? Why or why not?

4. Searching research databases for related literature can seem daunting. Begin small by identifying a potential topic of interest and then locating one source from each of the following categories:

   - A refereed journal article
   - A paper presented at a professional conference
   - A website

5. Assume that you will write a literature review for the three items you located in Question 4. Develop a potential outline of your review based only on the contents of those three sources.

Summary

- A literature review is a comprehensive examination of the information and knowledge base related to a given research topic.
- A systematic review of the literature can provide numerous benefits to a researcher beginning a study—for example, in refining the topic and making decisions regarding methodology.
- Researchers must always be cognizant of the quality of the literature they choose to include in a review.
- Empirical research studies are based on the collection of original data. They are not inherently better but typically more rigorous than opinion-type articles and documents.
- Articles that have gone through a peer-review process prior to publication in a journal are called refereed manuscripts.
- Literature reviews should be as objective as possible, presenting all sides of a body of research.
- The research studies reviewed should be timely within the context of the topic.
- The adequate amount of research to be reviewed often varies by topic.

  o When you begin to read the same major contributors in the field, you can be confident that you have not missed any important studies.

- Sources for literature are classified as primary sources and secondary sources.

  o Primary sources are firsthand accounts of original research.
  o Secondary sources do not consist of original research but are summaries, compilations, or interpretations of primary research conducted by other individuals.
  o Literature reviews should focus on primary sources.

- Primary sources are typically found by searching specialized databases, such as ERIC, ProQuest, and Google Scholar.
- The searchable ERIC online database contains more than 1.4 million citations, 400,000 of which are available in full-text format.
- The ERIC database of educational research consists of two indexes—one that contains citation information and abstracts of published journal articles and another that cites and abstracts documents not published in journals, such as papers presented at conferences, technical reports, evaluation reports of grants, and reports of other original research.
- The primary method for searching the ERIC database is by keywords or descriptors, although searches can be done by author name as well.
- Searches can be narrowed or broadened with Boolean operators.

  o Using *and* between keywords will result in a narrower search; using *or* will result in a broader search.

- Searching Google Scholar offers some advantages over searching the ERIC database, such as access to articles that have cited a particular source as a reference and provision of citation formats.
- Writing a literature review is not an easy process, as every topic's body of literature differs.

- When writing a literature review, the goal should be to provide the historical context of the topic, its research trends, and how theory has informed practice (and vice versa).
- When summarizing articles, the emphasis should be on the findings of previous research studies.
- Once you begin writing the literature review, the organization and subheadings are key elements.
- A literature review should not be written as an annotated bibliography but, rather, as a cohesive essay that flows from paragraph to paragraph.
- Topics in a literature review should be ordered from those least related to your study to those most closely related to your study.
- Summarizing your literature review in a few concluding paragraphs is highly beneficial for readers.
- Even if you are not conducting a formal literature review, immersing yourself in research literature is a good practice for professional development.

$SAGE edge™

Sharpen your skills with SAGE edge!

edge.sagepub.com/mertler

SAGE edge for Students provides a personalized approach to help you accomplish your coursework goals in an easy-to-use learning environment. You'll find action plans, mobile-friendly eFlashcards, and quizzes as well as video, web, and resources and links to SAGE journal articles to support and expand on the concepts presented in this chapter.

DESIGNING A RESEARCH STUDY

PART II

6

Qualitative
Research Methods

Student Learning Objectives

After studying Chapter 6, students will be able to do the following:

1. Describe the nature and essential characteristics of qualitative research studies

2. Summarize and describe the steps in the process of conducting a qualitative research study

3. Identify various approaches to conducting qualitative research

4. Summarize the basic steps and procedures in conducting ethnographic research

5. Identify various limitations of ethnographic research

6. Summarize the basic steps and procedures in conducting narrative research

7. Identify various limitations of narrative research

8. Design qualitative research studies for a topic of interest

This chapter deals with qualitative research, a set of approaches that use narrative, nonnumerical data. The general purpose of qualitative research is to investigate the quality of a particular topic or activity. These approaches to conducting educational research have some unique characteristics that differentiate them from more quantitative methods. You will learn about these characteristics, the qualitative research process, and several different approaches to conducting qualitative research, with more specificity provided for ethnographic research and narrative research.

Characteristics of Qualitative Research

Qualitative research involves the collection, analysis, and interpretation of data, largely narrative and visual in nature, to gain insights into a particular phenomenon of interest (Gay, Mills, & Airasian, 2009). The focus of qualitative research tends to be on the *quality* of a particular activity, rather than on how often it occurs or how it might be evaluated, which is typically the focus of quantitative research (Fraenkel, Wallen, & Hyun, 2012). Since the focus of qualitative research is on the quality of a specific phenomenon, there is a greater emphasis on *holistic description*—that is, on providing descriptions in thick, rich detail—of the phenomenon, setting, or topic of interest. This type of description exists in stark contrast to that resulting from quantitative research, which can be thought of as a "snapshot" of the topic.

It is important to note that the term *qualitative* is used not necessarily because it describes a specific strategy of inquiry but, rather, because it easily differentiates this type of research from other specific strategies of research that we collectively consider to be quantitative forms (Gay et al., 2009). These include survey, correlational, causal-comparative, experimental, quasi-experimental, and single-subject research (which will be discussed in Chapter 7). These methods are classified as quantitative forms of research because they seek to represent data in numerical ways; in other words, if data do not exist as numerical, they may be quantified. Qualitative research does not incorporate the use of numerical data; in contrast, it involves the collection and analysis of nonnumerical (typically referred to as *narrative*) data, such as observational notes, interview transcripts, transcripts of video and audio recordings, as well as existing documents and records.

It is important to remember that both qualitative and quantitative research methods are valuable in their own right. One is not inherently superior or inferior to the other. Both approaches to research are "scientific" in particular ways, and each has its own strengths and weaknesses. Since they each contribute important research findings that help us better understand educational phenomena, most educational researchers would agree that educational problems are best investigated using whatever method or methods are most appropriate for the research situation (McMillan, 2012). It is best to begin with a topic of interest or specific research questions and *then* select the method that provides you with the most credible answers to those questions.

Bogdan and Biklen (2007) have described five essential features or characteristics of qualitative research. They point out that not all approaches to qualitative research display these characteristics to an equal extent; they do, however, all exhibit them to some degree. These five characteristics are as follows:

1. *Qualitative research is naturalistic.* One of the most distinguishing features of qualitative research is that it occurs in a natural setting. Researchers go directly to the particular setting of interest to collect their data. The reason behind this is that they are interested in observing human behavior in a specific context *as it naturally occurs*, as opposed to observing or interviewing people in a more "artificial" setting. For example, if we want to know how teachers behave in their classrooms, we should

observe them in that setting. If we take them out of that setting, we will likely observe different sorts of behaviors from them. In other words, in qualitative research, the setting itself serves as a direct source of data.

2. *Qualitative research is descriptive.* The data, as well as the results of analyses of those data, take the form of words or pictures rather than numbers. The intent is to provide rich descriptions of the phenomenon of interest, which could not be accomplished by reducing pages of narration into numerical summaries (McMillan, 2012). The written results often contain quotations taken directly from the data to illustrate, corroborate, and support the explanation of the findings. Qualitative researchers tend not to ignore any detail that might shed light on a particular topic; nothing in the natural setting is taken for granted.

3. *Qualitative researchers are concerned with process as well as product.* Qualitative researchers are concerned not only with the outcomes or products of a situation or program but also—perhaps more important—with *how* and *why* things occur as they do. For example, rather than focusing their attention on academic outcomes, qualitative researchers tend to be more interested in why certain students react positively to an instructional intervention program while others react negatively. They may seek answers to questions such as these:

- What did the program mean to students?
- Why were some students motivated while others were not?
- In what ways did the features of the program go beyond the intervention and extend into the rest of a student's school day?

4. *Qualitative researchers analyze their data inductively.* Typically, qualitative researchers do not formulate a hypothesis, then collect data in an effort either to prove or disprove it—recall from Chapter 1 that this process is known as *deductive reasoning.* In qualitative research, the ultimate findings of a study—and the "directions" traveled to arrive at them—can occur after some time has been spent collecting and analyzing data. Data are collected and then synthesized to produce generalizations—a process we have referred to as *inductive reasoning.* One may not even know what one is looking for until after a period of data collection. This process is important in qualitative research because the researcher wants to be open to new information and new ways of understanding the phenomenon of interest, regardless of the point in the study when they are discovered.

5. *Qualitative researchers are primarily concerned with how people make sense and meaning out of their daily lives.* This concept deals largely with people's individual perspectives on their lives. Qualitative researchers are typically interested in learning what participants in a study are thinking and why. Assumptions, goals, motives, reasons, and values are all of interest and are likely to form the focus of the research questions that guide a qualitative researcher's study (Fraenkel et al., 2012).

The Qualitative Research Process

In Chapters 1 and 2, you learned about a general process for conducting educational research studies. That basic series of steps is fairly consistent across different types of quantitative research, but the steps in conducting qualitative research are not quite as distinct. They may occur out of the sequential order in which they are presented, may overlap with each other, and are sometimes conducted concurrently. Although they are typically not followed in linear, sequential fashion, the main steps in the qualitative research process are as follows:

1. *Identification of the phenomenon to be studied.* As with any type of research study, the topic for investigation must first be identified. In qualitative studies, this initial topic is typically quite broad in scope and likely will be narrowed during the study. It is important to note that the purpose of a given study will often guide choices and decisions about the methodology to be employed.

2. *Review of related literature.* As you have learned, related literature is reviewed to identify useful strategies for conducting the study, as well as to determine what has already been discovered about the topic of interest.

3. *Identification and selection of participants.* In qualitative research, participants who will constitute the sample are selected purposefully, not randomly as they are in quantitative studies (you will learn more about this in Chapter 7). Characteristically, there are substantially fewer participants in qualitative research studies than there are in quantitative research studies.

4. *Collection of data.* Data collection in qualitative studies is a lengthy, ongoing process. Data are typically collected directly from participants through observations, interviews, and other types of records and artifacts.

5. *Analysis of data.* As previously mentioned, qualitative data are analyzed inductively by synthesizing all the information collected from various sources into common themes or patterns. The analytical process relies heavily on narrative summary and rich description.

6. *Generation of research questions.* Following an initial stage of data collection and analysis, a preliminary set of research questions is developed. At this point in the process, the questions may appear somewhat broad.

7. *Additional data collection, analysis, and revision of research questions.* This is the key step that differentiates qualitative research from quantitative research. Following an initial stage of data collection, data analysis, and research question generation, the researcher returns to the setting to engage in further data collection and analysis. This process may be seen as iterative or cyclical in nature. That is, data are collected and analyzed, and preliminary research questions are developed. More data are collected, combined with the initial data, and then analyzed. The researcher may reexamine the research questions, some of which may be discarded and others revised, based on the "new" data and resulting analyses. This process can continue for extended periods of time and ends only when the researcher is confident that he or she is uncovering nothing new through observations and interviews.

8. *Final interpretation of analyses and development of conclusions.* Although interpretation occurs continuously throughout the data collection and analysis process, there

is a final stage of interpretation of results. Once the qualitative researcher is sure that nothing new can be learned from further data collection, he or she develops a final, comprehensive interpretation of the data analyses and extends those interpretations into the study's conclusions.

Approaches to Conducting Qualitative Research

Similar to quantitative research, qualitative research encompasses numerous approaches to conducting research. The number of approaches differs, depending on the source you consult. Some sources and authors list as few as seven approaches to qualitative research, whereas others list nearly 30 different types (Mertler & Charles, 2011). A single chapter cannot do justice to the wide variety of options available when trying to select a qualitative research design; however, in an attempt to provide an *overview* of qualitative research approaches, we will focus our attention on six of the more commonly used qualitative approaches: ethnographic research, narrative research, historical research, grounded theory research, phenomenological research, and case study research. Brief descriptions of each approach are offered next, with greater detail for ethnographic research and narrative research provided later in the chapter. It is important to note that the in-depth discussions of ethnographic and narrative research are not intended to diminish the importance, relevance, or value of the other approaches to qualitative research; they are simply the most commonly used approaches to conducting qualitative research in education. It is equally important to note that the descriptions that follow, both the brief and more detailed ones, represent *generalizations—or generic descriptions—* of qualitative practice; in practice, qualitative approaches to research are often adapted in numerous ways, depending on the research situation. Qualitative research methods intentionally emphasize variation and customization.

Ethnographic Research

Ethnographic research, also known as ethnography, involves in-depth description and interpretation of the shared or common practices and beliefs of a culture, social group, or other community. A key assumption of the ethnographic researcher is that by entering directly into—and interacting with—the lives of the people being studied, one reaches a better, more comprehensive understanding of the beliefs and behaviors of those individuals (Mertens, 2005). To accomplish this, it is necessary for the researcher to immerse himself or herself in the setting over an extended period of time. Only through prolonged exposure and experience in the natural setting—and by establishing rapport with the individuals in that setting—can the researcher gain a complete understanding of the educational phenomenon (McMillan, 2012).

Ethnography is guided either by an explicit educational theory or an implicit personal theory about the way things work within that specific culture or group setting. Since this approach begins with a theory, the researcher must be willing to abandon or modify a theory that does not "fit" the data, keeping in mind that the data represent the reality of that culture (Mertens, 2005). You will read more about ethnographic research later in this chapter.

Narrative Research

The purpose of **narrative research** as a methodological approach to conducting qualitative research is to convey experiences as they are expressed in the lived and told stories of individuals (Creswell, 2007). Narrative research typically develops as a spoken or written account of an event or action, or a series of events that are chronologically connected. Focusing attention on one or two individuals, the researcher gathers data from their stories, which report their individual experiences, and chronologically orders the meanings of those experiences (Creswell, 2007). One of the primary goals of narrative research conducted in the field of education is to increase understanding of issues related to teaching and learning through the telling and retelling of teachers' stories from their professional lives (Gay et al., 2009). You will learn more about narrative research later in this chapter.

Historical Research

The purpose of **historical research** is to describe events, occurrences, or settings of the past in an attempt to better understand them, learn from past failures and successes, and see if they might apply to present-day problems and issues (Fraenkel et al., 2012). Historical research is different from many other types of qualitative research because it is often impossible to collect data directly from the participants being studied (i.e., primary data). If the event occurred many years ago, no one who was a direct participant in that setting and during that time is likely to be available as a primary data source. Therefore, the historical researcher typically relies on existing records (both numerical and nonnumerical), documents, journals, photographs, relics, and similar sources (i.e., secondary data). Once the data have been collected, however, the process of analysis and interpretation is quite similar to that described earlier in the chapter.

Of key importance in analyzing and interpreting historical data is something that differentiates it from other types of qualitative research: The historical researcher must be concerned with external evidence and internal evidence of the data's validity (Leedy & Ormrod, 2013). *External evidence* is primarily concerned with answering the following question: *Is the source or article genuine?* It is critical to determine whether or not the document was falsified. In other words, *who* wrote the document, *when* was it written, and under *what conditions* and *for what purposes* (Fraenkel et al., 2012)?

Once the historical researcher is satisfied that a source document is in fact genuine, internal evidence of validity must be collected. *Internal evidence* is concerned with the accuracy of the document's contents (Fraenkel et al., 2012). Just because we can verify that a certain historical figure authored a particular document (e.g., Abraham Lincoln and the Gettysburg Address), that does not *necessarily* mean the comments contained within the document accurately reflect the events of that time period. Both the accuracy of the information and the truthfulness of the author must be evaluated as part of the process of collecting and analyzing data when conducting historical research (Fraenkel et al., 2012). In our example, it would be the researcher's responsibility to determine whether the comments, statements, and implications in Lincoln's address actually reflect the events leading up to November 19, 1865. This would be done by verifying the author's credentials—was the author present at the event or during that time? Was the author a participant in or an observer of the event? Did the author have a vested interest in the outcome of the event?—and the contents of the document—do the contents make sense in relation to the events during that time period? Would people of that time have behaved in the ways suggested by the document? Is the language contained in the document appropriate for the time period, and/or does it suggest a bias of any sort? (Fraenkel et al., 2012).

Grounded Theory Research

The purpose of *grounded theory research* is to discover an existing theory or generate a new theory—resulting *directly* from the data—that broadly and conceptually explains a process, action, or interaction related to a substantive topic. The theory that develops is known as a "process" theory, since it explains an educational process that occurs over time (Creswell, 2005). These theories are not generated or stated prior to the study but, rather, are developed inductively from the data that are collected and analyzed during the study (Fraenkel et al., 2012). In this sense, the goal of grounded theory research is not to begin with a theory and then set out to collect data that will prove it; the goal is to begin with a particular educational phenomenon in mind and permit those aspects that are relevant to the phenomenon to *emerge during the study*. This is another way of saying that the theory is "grounded" in (or derived from) the data. It is appropriate to use grounded theory research when you need a broad theory or explanation of some process and existing theories do not address your problem or the particular setting you want to study (Creswell, 2005).

The data for this type of qualitative study are collected primarily through one-on-one interviews, focus-group interviews, and participant observation conducted by the researcher (Fraenkel et al., 2012). This is largely because grounded theory studies tend to focus on what happened to individuals, why they believe it happened as it did, and what it means to them (McMillan, 2012). As described earlier in the section outlining the qualitative research process, data collection and analysis are ongoing processes. The analytical process used in grounded theory research involves continually comparing the emerging themes and the developing theory to newly collected data; this is known as the *constant comparative method* of data analysis (McMillan, 2012; Mertens, 2005). Data are collected and analyzed, and a theory is proposed; more data are collected and analyzed, and the theory is revised; data continue to be collected and analyzed, and the theory continues to be developed until a point of saturation is reached.

Phenomenological Research

The intent of *phenomenological studies* is to describe and interpret the experiences or reactions of participants to a particular phenomenon *from their individual perspectives* (Fraenkel et al., 2012; Mertens, 2005). Key in such research is the person's *perception* of the meaning of an event, as opposed to the event itself (Leedy & Ormrod, 2013). For example, a phenomenological researcher might study the variety of perceptions and experiences of people who have homeschooled a child, or perhaps the individual perceptions held by teachers who recently attended the same 3-day professional development training session.

The underlying assumption in this approach is that there are multiple ways of interpreting the same experience, as well as multiple meanings to be derived from it (McMillan, 2012). The subjective meanings created within participants constitute *their* reality—in other words, the *essence* of the experience for each person (Fraenkel et al., 2012; McMillan, 2012). These individual experiences and subsequent meanings can, and do, differ from person to person. For this reason, the concept of participant perspective is central for researchers using a phenomenological approach.

A typical sample size for a phenomenological study is about 5 to 25 individuals, all of whom have had direct experience with the phenomenon being studied (Leedy & Ormrod, 2013). Data for phenomenological research are typically collected through the use of often lengthy (perhaps 1- to 2-hour), in-depth, semistructured or unstructured one-on-one interviews, where the participant clearly does most of the talking and the researcher does most of the listening (Leedy & Ormrod, 2013). The ultimate goal of the analysis, then, is for the researcher to attempt to identify and describe aspects of each participant's perceptions—and the associated meanings—in great detail. Phenomenological research is one of the more difficult types of qualitative research to conduct since the researcher must get the participants to *accurately* relive the experience in their minds, recalling their associated reactions and perceptions (Fraenkel et al., 2012).

Case Study Research

Case studies are in-depth analyses of single, restricted entities (Fraenkel et al., 2012; McMillan, 2012), known as cases. A case is often described as a *bounded system*—a unit around which there are boundaries, such that one can "fence in" what is going to be studied (Gay et al., 2009). A case might consist of one student, one classroom, one school, one program, or one community. For example, a researcher might study the instructional methods and techniques used by an exceptional teacher of high school science (Leedy & Ormrod, 2013), or perhaps the nature and implementation of an instructional intervention designed for a single student, including how that student reacts to the intervention over an extended period of time. As you can see from these examples, researchers typically focus on a single case because of its unique or exceptional qualities that could promote increased understanding or improve practice (Leedy & Ormrod, 2013).

There exists some debate as to whether case study research is a true research methodology (Gay et al., 2009). While many experts treat it as such, others believe that case study research is not as much a methodological choice as a choice of *what* or *who* to study. Case study research can be described as

- a qualitative approach to studying a phenomenon;
- focused on a unit of study, or a bounded system;
- not a methodological choice but a choice of what to study; and
- an all-encompassing research method (p. 426).

Case studies may involve both qualitative and quantitative data, which is why you will see this approach discussed again in Chapter 7. The basic purpose of a case study is to develop a highly detailed description and gain a better, more thorough understanding of the individual entity. The methods of data collection, analysis, and interpretation are essentially the same as those that have been discussed up to this point, the lone distinguishing factor being the single case situation. With case studies, more than any other type of approach to conducting qualitative research, generalizability of the findings is a concern. However, this concern can sometimes be addressed through the use of an approach known as *multiple* or *collective case study*, where two or more cases are studied independently to make comparisons or propose generalizations (Leedy & Ormrod, 2013).

For those who are interested in learning more about case study research, I direct you to *The Art of Case Study Research* by Robert Stake (1995) and *Case Study Research: Design and Methods* by Robert Yin (2009).

The distinguishing characteristics of the various approaches to qualitative research discussed above are presented in Table 6.1.

TABLE 6.1 ● Distinguishing Characteristics of Commonly Used Qualitative Research Designs				
Design	**Purpose**	**Focus**	**Data Collection**	**Data Analysis**
Ethnography	To understand the behaviors and culture of a group	A specific field site where a group of people share a common culture	• Participant observation • Structured or unstructured interviews with key informants • Artifact/document collection	• Identification of underlying structures and belief systems • Organization of data into some sort of "whole" (e.g., chronology, event)
Narrative research	To tell the lived and told stories of individuals	One to two individuals with interesting life stories or experiences to share	• Lengthy, in-depth interviews • Field notes • Journals • Other relevant data sources (as appropriate)	• Categorizing and restorying in chronological fashion
Historical research	To describe settings or events of the past	Gaining a better understanding of a specific setting or event	• Interviews • Documents • Artifacts • Records • Other sources	• Identification of categories or themes • Organization of themes into detailed description of the event or setting
Grounded theory research	To derive a theory directly from data collected in a natural setting	A process, including human actions/ interactions and how they affect one another	• Interviews • Other relevant data sources (as appropriate)	• Systematic method of coding data into categories to identify interrelationships • Continual intertwining of data collection and analysis • Construction of a theory from the categories and relationships

Design	Purpose	Focus	Data Collection	Data Analysis
Phenomenological research	To understand experiences from participants' perspectives	A particular phenomenon as it is experienced and perceived by different individuals	• In-depth interviews with 5 to 25 individuals	• Search for meaningful experiences (categories) that reflect different aspects of the phenomenon • Integration of the categories into a seemingly typical experience
Case study research	To understand one person or situation in great depth	One case or a few cases in its/their natural setting	• Observations • Interviews • Documents and other sources (when appropriate)	• Categorization and interpretation of data into common themes • Synthesis into an overall portrait of the case(s)

Source: Adapted from Leedy and Ormrod (2013).

More About Ethnographic Research

The word *ethnography* is derived from the prefix *ethno-* (meaning "human race or cultures") and the suffix *-graphy* (meaning "writing" or "a field of study"). Ethnography is a research process used in the scientific study of human interactions in social settings, focusing on their everyday behaviors with the intent of trying to identify and describe cultural norms, beliefs, social structures, and other patterns (Leedy & Ormrod, 2013). A key facet of ethnographic research is that the group being studied must share a common culture (Leedy & Ormrod, 2013)—however *culture* is defined for the purposes of a particular study. For decades ethnography has been the predominant research procedure used in anthropological studies, but in recent years it has become increasingly popular in educational research. It is used to develop detailed explanations and descriptions of the conditions and interactions of individuals and groups as they function within the schools and larger society (Wiersma & Jurs, 2005).

Ethnography is essentially a descriptive approach but is placed in a category of its own because (1) it is unique in focusing on *social behavior within natural settings*; (2) it relies on qualitative data, usually in the form of narrative descriptions made by an observer of, or participant in, the group being studied; (3) its perspective is holistic—observations and interpretations are made within the context of the *totality* of human interactions; (4) hypotheses and research questions may emerge *after* data collection is well under way, rather than being stated at the beginning of the investigation; and (5) its procedures of data analysis involve **contextualization**, where research findings are interpreted with reference to the particular group, setting, or event being observed.

Ethnographic research can thus be described concisely as follows:

1. Its *purpose* is to describe and explain a facet or segment of group social life as it relates to education.
2. The *hypotheses and research/questions* begin as broad statements about the purpose of the research. In some studies, they may be permitted to emerge more specifically as data are collected and analyzed.
3. The *data* consist of verbal descriptions of people, interactions, settings, objects, and phenomena within the context being studied.
4. The *sources of those data* include the people, settings, and relevant objects being observed.
5. *Data collection* is done by the researcher through observation, sometimes combined with interviews.
6. *Data are analyzed* through the presentation of verbal descriptions and/or logical analyses of information to discover salient patterns and themes.

Topics and Procedures in Ethnographic Research

Because the purpose of ethnographic research is to study people in small or large groups in an attempt to understand those groups and how they function, the range of possible topics in ethnographic research is quite broad. The following topics provide just a small sample:

- Faculty interactions in the lounge and workroom
- Kindergartners' behavior on the playground
- The daily routines and procedures of administrative personnel
- Students' lives at school and work
- The lifestyles of top student athletes
- The coping behaviors of students who consider themselves to be "outsiders"

This list could go on and on. Virtually any topic that involves social behavior and its impact on the teaching–learning process—or some other educational practice, routine, or activity—can be studied through the application of ethnographic research methods.

These general procedures are typically followed when conducting ethnographic research:

1. A question or concern serving as the focus of the research is formalized.
2. A group is identified for use in studying the concern. The group may be very small (consisting of two or three people) or quite large (consisting of hundreds of individuals).
3. The researcher introduces the proposed research to the group and obtains the group's agreement for participation in the study. After gaining entry to the group setting, the researcher must spend a good amount of time establishing rapport with and gaining the trust of the group's members (Leedy & Ormrod, 2013). However, the researcher cannot deceive members of the

group and must be honest with them about why he or she is there; it may sometimes be difficult or challenging to strike an appropriate balance.

4. The researcher may function as either a **privileged observer** (also known as a *nonparticipant observer*) or as a **participant observer** of the group. A privileged observer does not participate in the activities of the group, whereas a participant observer engages actively in all group activities as a regular member of the group being studied. Again, a balance must be achieved here, because if the researcher's role begins to change from "outsider" to "insider," he or she may become emotionally involved to the extent that ability to assess the situation accurately is lost (Leedy & Ormrod, 2013).

5. The researcher's role is to watch and listen attentively—using a procedure called **naturalistic observation**—and to record as accurately as possible all *pertinent* information. (Even though the ethnographic approach is holistic, no one individual can record every detail of events, interactions, objects, settings, etc. The investigator must exercise quick judgment regarding what is and is not worth recording.) Initially, the researcher should intermingle with everyone to get a general sense of the social and cultural context (Leedy & Ormrod, 2013). After spending more time in the natural setting, the researcher will typically identify group members who can provide better quality information and insights. These members are referred to as **key informants** (Leedy & Ormrod, 2013).

6. The observations and their recordings produce vast quantities of written notes, which represent the data obtained in the study.

7. The duration of ethnographic research may be as short as a week or two or as long as several years. However, in ethnographic research conducted by graduate students in educational settings, the duration should be adequate to obtain detailed information but usually not more than 2 months. That being said, typical ethnographic studies require substantial time in the field; prolonged engagement onsite, and with those individuals being studied, is critical to a successful ethnographic research study.

8. Data analysis, which often requires as much time as the actual collection of data, involves primarily narrative analysis and interpretation. As we have seen, qualitative data do not lend themselves to statistical analyses. Researchers must examine the data for patterns of language and behavior that provide insight into the group's concerns and functions. Once identified, these patterns are described carefully and in great detail. Patton (2001) considers this descriptive aspect crucial, believing that if descriptions are good enough, readers can make their own interpretations. However, ethnographic researchers are also obligated to interpret and explain the findings of their investigation. Reflecting on the following questions may help in formulating interpretations:

• What commonalities tie group members together? Did these commonalities or other factors make this group deserving of study?

- What seem to be the key life perspectives of this group? Do members feel isolated, put upon, prejudiced against, overworked, misunderstood? Do they feel superior in identifiable ways? Do they seem unusually able to exercise control over their fate?
- How do these perspectives, if identified, seem to cause the group to react to opportunity and threat? Do they tend to be aggressive, antagonistic, submissive, escapist? Do they complain, blame, and scapegoat? Do they reach out for greater challenges? Do they attempt to control or dominate?
- How does the group attempt to solve or otherwise deal with problems, expectations held for them, or demands made on them? What are the results of their efforts?
- What language patterns are associated with identified perspectives and behaviors? What special terms are used and with what meanings?
- What are the group's preferred activities? Is there evident linkage between activities and life perspectives?
- Which objects within the setting receive major attention (e.g., automobiles, electronic equipment, clothing, printed materials, weapons, sports paraphernalia)?
- What patterns of leadership, friendship, dominance, and submission are noted within the group? What are the effects of those patterns? What special words or terms are associated with them? What activities, events, or routines seem to strengthen the bonds that hold the group together?

Leedy and Ormrod (2013) stress that it is virtually impossible—and perhaps even *undesirable*—to analyze ethnographic data with total objectivity. Once immersion in the group has occurred, it becomes increasingly difficult for the researcher to step outside of the activities and culture of the group, as he or she—to some degree—is now a group member. Wolcott (1994) has suggested that the analytical goal be *rigorous subjectivity*, where the researcher aims for balance, fairness, completeness, and sensitivity, even though his or her personal attitudes and opinions are bound to become intertwined with the observations and, ultimately, analyses and interpretations (Leedy & Ormrod, 2013).

For those who are interested in learning more about the process of conducting ethnographic research, I direct you to the work of Harry F. Wolcott (1994, 2001), a longtime and leading expert on the topic of ethnographic methods. His books address such topics as how to collect data in the field, how to analyze and interpret ethnographic data, and how to write reports of ethnographic research studies.

Strengths and Concerns in Ethnographic Research

Much of the popularity of ethnographic research in education stems from its holistic nature. Some educational practitioners have expressed dissatisfaction with investigations that focus on highly concentrated aspects (i.e., one or two variables) of education or personal behavior, and their subsequent findings that appear isolated and unrealistic outside the normal context of an educational setting. Ethnography helps satisfy this concern by presenting what educators consider to be realistic pictures of group behavior. Educators often feel that they can derive better insights from these realistic portrayals than from traditional research, with the result that they are able to work more effectively with their students.

However, concerns about ethnography also exist, predominantly in relation to the reliability of data and, therefore, the validity of research conclusions. A major problem is that typically only a single researcher records the descriptions that constitute the data, leaving the research open to all sorts of questions concerning expertise, consistency, and potential bias. Recall our earlier discussion noting that bias is not inherently bad; however, researchers have a responsibility to recognize and make explicit any limitations of their individual and/or collective biases. Following from this, then, is the other major concern about the validity of ethnographic findings. It is difficult to resolve these issues, even when two or more researchers collect data as a check against each other. An additional problem with ethnographic research has to do with the generalizability of its findings. In far too many cases, it is clear that conclusions drawn from ethnographic research, even though they illuminate the *particular* group being studied, do not seem to be applicable to other groups and settings. As you can see, this potentially limits the practical value of ethnographic research.

More About Narrative Research

As mentioned earlier, the general purpose of narrative research is to tell stories, specifically the lived stories of individuals. Narrative research focuses on the process of studying one or two individuals through the collection of their *own* stories as the data and reporting them in chronological fashion—often by tying them to the main stages in the course of one's life (Creswell, 2007). The narrative researcher and participant(s) then *collaboratively* construct a narrative of the lived experiences and meanings the participant(s) attribute to those experiences (Gay et al., 2009). In other words, the story *itself* is the final outcome (the research report) of the research study.

Gay and colleagues (2009) stress that narrative research can prove incredibly beneficial in today's educational world. While schools and education professionals have always had to deal with certain issues—for example, the achievement gap, drug use, teen suicide, homelessness—these issues have deepened and spread over the past couple of decades. Mysteriously absent in many—if not all—of the political and educational policy debates is the voice of the educational practitioner. Narrative research can serve as the vehicle through which to increase understanding of central issues related to the teaching and learning process by telling and retelling teachers' stories. It is not always possible to reduce our collective understanding of educational issues to numbers and statistics; narrative research provides the educational researcher with a mechanism for validating the practitioner's voice in these sometimes heated debates (Gay et al., 2009). As is often the case, narrative research is about empowering the participant to tell his or her story.

Narrative research can be characterized by the following elements, as compiled by Gay and colleagues (2009, p. 387):

- A focus on the experiences of individuals
- A concern with the chronology of individual's experiences
- A focus on the construction of life stories based on data collected through interviews
- Restorying as a technique for constructing a narrative account
- Inclusion of, and close attention to, the context and place in the story
- A collaborative approach between researcher and participants in the negotiation of the final story
- A narrative constructed around the question, "And then what happened?"

Several forms of narrative research exist; in fact, Creswell (2005) has identified nearly 20 different types. They all tell the stories of lived experiences, but three general characteristics differentiate one type from another. The first characteristic is *who* is telling or writing the story, the key factor being the particular *perspective* of the storytelling (Creswell, 2005, 2007). For example, a **biographical study** is a form of narrative research where the researcher writes and records the experiences of another person's life. An **autobiographical study** is similar but is written and recorded by the individual who is the subject of the study.

The second characteristic concerns *how much* of a life story is being told and presented (Creswell, 2005). A **life history** portrays an individual's entire life, whereas a **personal experience story** is a narrative study of an individual's personal experience as related to a single or multiple incidents or private situations. Finally, an **oral history** is conducted by gathering the personal reflections of events, as well as implications of those events, from one or several individuals.

The third characteristic is the narrative research study's particular *theoretical lens* or *perspective* (e.g., from a feminist perspective, the perspective of Hispanic Americans, or the perspective of marginalized individuals). A **theoretical lens** is a guiding perspective or ideology that provides structure that ultimately advocates for specific groups or individuals, during both the research and the writing of the final research report.

Procedures in Narrative Research

The following are standard procedures in conducting narrative research (Creswell, 2007). As with many types of qualitative research, these steps should not be viewed as a definitive and linear process but, rather, as a general guide.

1. The researcher determines if narrative research is the most appropriate method for investigating the research problem or topic.
2. The researcher identifies one or two individuals who have interesting life stories or experiences to share. The researcher must plan to spend a considerable amount of time with each participant. Also critical in this process is establishment of the *relationship* between the researcher and the participant,

which should be characterized by caring, respect, and quality of voice (Gay et al., 2009). Stories can be collected in multiple ways (e.g., participants can record their own stories in journals, researchers can observe participants and record field notes, stories can be collected through interviews or written accounts with family members or other people who know the participants well, or more "official" data in the form of work-related memos and documents can be included).

3. Closely related to Step 2, information is collected on the *context* represented by the various sources of data. Stories must be situated in the appropriate context for accurate interpretation later. The experiences of the participants, and their related stories, might be situated in the workplace, in a personal family environment, or in a context related to their culture. This is important because the context often affects the nature or details of the stories being told.

4. The participants' stories are analyzed and "restoried" into a format that makes sense. The process of **restorying** is largely about organizing a good deal of personal story data into a presentation that will make sense to the intended audience. Creswell (2005, 2007) suggests that this may consist of

   - gathering the stories through in-depth interviews and transcribing the audiotapes as a record of raw data (including not just what is spoken but also laughter, frustration, facial expressions, etc.);
   - retranscribing the data to condense the original transcripts, focusing on the key elements identified in the stories; and then
   - organizing and writing the story in a chronological sequence, paying close attention to the setting, people, actions, problems, and solutions.

5. Throughout the process of conducting narrative research, the researcher collaborates with participants by actively involving them in the process of collecting, analyzing, and rewriting the stories. This allows for clarification and verification of the details of stories. Oftentimes, the meanings of particular events as told in the stories will lead to a negotiated—that is, between researcher and participant—meaning behind the stories. This activity will sometimes lead to **cpiphanies**, or key turning points, in the lives of the participants and perhaps in the life of the researcher as well.

For those interested in learning more about the process of conducting narrative research, you may want to examine Clandinin and Connelly (2000) and Czarniawska (2004).

Strengths and Concerns in Narrative Research

The clear advantage of narrative research is its ability to focus in great detail on the events of an individual's life, in an attempt to tie events together, examine relationships, and offer explanation and insight into that life within its specific context. It is a powerful form of qualitative research. That being said, it is not without its challenges.

Narrative research constitutes a lengthy process, wherein the researcher must spend a great deal of time collecting extensive information on the participant. As Gay and colleagues (2009) have stated, if you are a person who does not interact well with others, narrative research is probably not for you. Additionally, there needs to be a clear understanding of the context of the individual's life (Creswell, 2007). The goal is to explain the multiple, intertwined layers of context and experience that define us as human beings.

Developmental Activities

1. Making a decision regarding research methodology is critical in the process of conducting research. That decision is often guided by the characteristics of a particular methodology and the degree to which it fits a research topic. To pick the most appropriate methodology, the researcher must understand the pros and cons of a particular methodology. Describe what you see as the strengths and weaknesses of qualitative research designs.

2. The term *holistic* is used often in this chapter. Describe what you think is meant by *holistic*, especially in terms of data collection, analysis, and conclusions in a research study.

3. Brainstorm two or three possible topics for qualitative research studies. Recalling that qualitative research questions are typically stated in broader terms than are quantitative questions, draft possible research questions to guide these qualitative studies.

4. Research is often associated with *objectivity*. How does objectivity "fit" with qualitative research methods? Is this a strength or limitation of qualitative research? Why?

5. Do you think it would be possible for a qualitative research study to be both ethnographic and narrative? Why or why not?

Summary

- Qualitative research involves the collection, analysis, and interpretation of narrative data.
- The focus of qualitative research is typically on the quality of a particular activity.
- Holistic description of the phenomenon, setting, or topic of interest is a key characteristic of qualitative research.
- Both qualitative and quantitative research methods are valuable in their own rights.

- When deciding on a research methodology, it is best to begin with a topic of interest or specific question and then select the method that will provide you with the best answer to that question.
- Five essential features of qualitative research are as follows:

  o Qualitative research is naturalistic.
  o Qualitative research is descriptive.

- o Qualitative researchers are concerned with process as well as product.
- o Qualitative researchers analyze their data inductively.
- o Qualitative researchers are primarily concerned with how people make sense and meaning of their lives.
- Although the basic steps are fairly consistent, those used in conducting qualitative research may occur out of sequential order, may overlap, and are sometimes conducted concurrently.
- The general steps in conducting qualitative research are as follows:

  - o Identification of the phenomenon to be studied
  - o Review of the related literature
  - o Identification and selection of participants
  - o Collection of data
  - o Analysis of data
  - o Generation of research questions
  - o Additional data collection, analysis, and revision of research questions
  - o Final interpretation of analyses and development of conclusions

- Many different approaches exist for conducting qualitative research.
- Commonly used qualitative approaches include ethnographic research, narrative research, historical research, grounded theory research, phenomenological research, and case study research.
- Ethnographic research involves the in-depth description and interpretation of shared practices and beliefs of a social group or other community.
- Narrative research is an approach used to convey experiences as they are lived and told by individuals.

- Historical research describes events, occurrences, or settings of the past to better understand them.
- Grounded theory research is used to discover an existing theory or generate a new theory resulting directly from data.
- Phenomenological research is used to describe and interpret experiences or reactions of participants to a specific phenomenon from their individual perspectives.
- Case study research is an in-depth analysis of a single entity, known as a case.
- Ethnography is a research approach used to study human interactions in social settings.
- Important features of ethnographic research include the following:

  - o Ethnographic research focuses on social behavior in natural settings.
  - o It relies on narrative descriptions made by observers or participants in the group being studied.
  - o Its perspective is holistic.
  - o In some studies, research questions may emerge after data collection is well under way.
  - o Procedures of data analysis involve contextualization within the group, setting, or event being observed.

- A privileged observer, also known as a nonparticipant observer, does not engage in the activities of the group.
- A participant observer actively engages in all activities as a regular member of the group being studied.
- Naturalistic observation is a holistic technique where the researcher must record all pertinent information.
- A strength of ethnographic research is its holistic view of education or personal behavior.

- Concerns about ethnographic research involve the reliability of data and the validity of research conclusions, as well as the generalizability of findings.
- Several forms of narrative research exist; all forms tell stories of lived experiences, but they differ according to perspective, amount of life story told, and theoretical lens.
- A biographical study is a type of narrative research where the researcher records the experiences of another person's life.
- An autobiographical study also involves the experiences of a person's life but is told by the individual who is the subject of the study.
- A life history tells the story of an individual's entire life.

- A personal experience story is a study of an individual's personal experience related to a single or multiple incidents.
- An oral history is conducted by gathering personal reflections of events and their implications from one or more individuals.
- A key technique used in narrative research is restorying, a process of reorganizing personal information and stories into a format that makes sense for the intended audience.
- During the process of restorying, participants as well as the researcher may experience epiphanies.
- A clear strength of narrative research is its ability to tell detailed stories of people's lives.
- Narrative research, however, is a lengthy process wherein the researcher must uncover a multitude of details in people's lives.

$SAGE edge™

Sharpen your skills with SAGE edge!

edge.sagepub.com/mertler

SAGE edge for Students provides a personalized approach to help you accomplish your coursework goals in an easy-to-use learning environment. You'll find action plans, mobile-friendly eFlashcards, and quizzes as well as video, web, and resources and links to SAGE journal articles to support and expand on the concepts presented in this chapter.

Quantitative Research Methods

Student Learning Objectives

After studying Chapter 7, students will be able to do the following:

1. Describe the defining characteristics of quantitative research studies

2. List and describe the basic steps in conducting quantitative research studies

3. Identify and differentiate among various approaches to conducting quantitative research studies

4. List and describe the steps and procedures in conducting survey, correlational, causal-comparative, quasi-experimental, experimental, and single-subject research

5. Identify and discuss the strengths and limitations of various approaches to conducting quantitative research

6. Identify and explain possible threats to both internal and external validity

7. Design quantitative research studies for a topic of interest

This chapter focuses on research designs commonly used when conducting quantitative research studies. The general purpose of quantitative research is to investigate a particular topic or activity through the measurement of variables in quantifiable terms. Quantitative approaches to conducting educational research differ in numerous ways from the qualitative methods we discussed in Chapter 6. You will learn about these characteristics, the quantitative research process, and the specifics of several different approaches to conducting quantitative research.

Characteristics of Quantitative Research

Quantitative research relies on the collection and analysis of numerical data to describe, explain, predict, or control variables and phenomena of interest (Gay, Mills, & Airasian, 2009). One of the underlying tenets of quantitative research is a philosophical belief that our world is relatively stable and uniform, such that we can measure and understand it as well as make broad generalizations about it. You should note right away the stark contrast between this belief and those of qualitative research—namely, that the world is ever changing and the role of the researcher is to adapt to and observe those constant changes. Gay and colleagues state that, from a quantitative perspective, conclusions drawn about our world and its phenomena cannot be considered meaningful unless they can be verified through direct observation and measurement. Further, quantitative researchers typically base their investigations on the belief that facts and feelings can be separated, and that the world exists as a *single reality*—composed of facts—that can be discovered through observation or other measurements (Fraenkel, Wallen, & Hyun, 2012). Yet again, this belief operates in stark contrast to the assumption held by qualitative researchers that individuals, in essence, are responsible for developing their own separate and unique realities of the same situation.

The goal of quantitative research studies is vastly different from the qualitative goal of gaining a better understanding of a situation or event. When conducting quantitative research studies, researchers seek to describe current situations, establish relationships between variables, and sometimes attempt to explain causal relationships between variables. This type of research is truly focused on describing and explaining—sometimes in a somewhat definitive manner—the phenomenon under investigation (Creswell, 2005). Because of this singular perspective, quantitative research operates under widely agreed-on steps that guide the research process (Fraenkel et al., 2012). The quantitative research process—along with its various designs—is fairly well established; there is little flexibility in terms of the strategies and techniques used. Quantitative researchers believe that nothing should be left to chance; therefore, no aspect of the research design is permitted to emerge during the process, as it is in qualitative research.

The role undertaken by the quantitative researcher is very different from that of his or her qualitative counterpart. One of the goals of qualitative research is for the researcher to become deeply immersed in the setting and among the participants. However, a major goal of quantitative research is for the researcher to remain as *objective* as possible (although, as we have previously discussed, all researchers have biases and it is more important that they recognize those biases and discuss their limitations). The much more linear steps in the quantitative research process—as you will see shortly—constitute the preestablished routines and strategies that help enhance researcher objectivity. This focus on objectivity is what enables the quantitative researcher to *generalize* findings of a research study beyond the particular situation (e.g., setting, school, participants) involved in that study.

Some additional characteristics of quantitative research, summarized below, continue to differentiate its goals and strategies from those of qualitative research (Creswell, 2005).

1. While the *literature review* serves as a justification for the research problem regardless of the research type, its role is much more central to the design of a quantitative study than to that of a qualitative study. Not only does it provide background information for the study, but it serves to inform the methodologies, instrumentation, populations, and analytical techniques to be used in the study.

2. The *purpose* of quantitative studies is typically specific and narrow, focusing on only a handful of measurable variables. This is very different from the holistic perspective of qualitative research.

3. *Data collection* is one of the most thoroughly established aspects of quantitative research. While these strategies may emerge during a qualitative study, they must be well developed prior to beginning a quantitative research study. Furthermore, in a quantitative research study, data collection instruments, procedures, and sampling strategies typically do not change once the study has begun. Quantitative researchers operate in this manner because they believe that it enhances the objectivity of their studies.

4. Quantitative *sampling strategies* differ drastically from those used in qualitative studies. Their focus in quantitative studies is twofold: First, because generalizability of the results is a key aspect of quantitative research, sampling strategies tend to focus on the *random selection* of participants. Second, and again focusing on the idea of generalizing the results, quantitative researchers typically collect data from a large number of individuals in their studies. As you will read in Chapter 12, the reason for using large samples is to collect data from enough individuals that those data mirror the substantially larger population from which the sample was drawn.

5. Techniques for *data analysis and interpretation* are entirely statistical in nature. The focus is on the application of existing indices (e.g., calculating an average score), formulas (e.g., the formula for calculating a standard deviation), and statistical tests (e.g., an independent-samples *t*-test) that are consistent regardless of a particular topic or the variables being studied. In other words, if two researchers are analyzing the same quantitative data set and both are calculating an average score, their calculated score will be identical. The same can be said for interpreting the results of statistical analyses. For example, when interpreting the average test score for two groups of students exposed to different instructional methods, we would naturally interpret the higher average score to mean that *that* group outperformed the group with the lower average score. Of course, this is not the case when analyzing qualitative data, where interpretations can involve a great deal of subjectivity depending on the individual doing the analysis and interpretation. This is yet another aspect of quantitative research methods that introduces objectivity into the overall research process.

6. Finally, *reporting the results* of quantitative research almost always occurs in a standard, fixed format (as you will learn more about in Chapter 14). The results are reported in an extremely objective and unbiased manner, having not been subjected to the inherent biases of the researcher.

The Quantitative Research Process

The general steps involved in the process of conducting any research study—as discussed in Chapters 1 and 2—are typical for quantitative research studies. In nearly every quantitative study, the steps are followed in sequential order. Furthermore, one step is usually completed before the subsequent step begins, especially when it comes to data collection, analysis, and interpretation. Only once data collection has ceased does the analysis begin, followed—upon its completion—by the interpretation of those results. I will briefly reiterate the process, as it was presented in Chapter 2.

1. *Identification of the research problem to be studied.* As you have seen numerous times, clearly identifying a research topic is the first step in any study. Quantitative research studies tend to be narrow in scope, focusing on a handful of key variables. As has been previously noted, the purpose of any given study will often guide choices and decisions about the methodology to be employed in that study.

2. *Statement of one, or several, pertinent research questions and/or hypotheses.* The researcher must ensure that research questions and hypotheses are stated clearly and precisely, as they will guide the remainder of the study. Failure to do so at the outset of the study can lead to problems—that is, misalignment between research questions and necessary data or between collected data and proposed analytical techniques—as the study progresses.

3. *Review of related literature.* Reviewing related literature provides a great deal of guidance in quantitative research studies. Learning what others have done previously can inform decisions regarding research design, sampling, instrumentation, data collection procedures, and data analysis.

4. *Development of a written literature review.* Once the related literature has been collected and thoroughly reviewed, the researcher must synthesize the pertinent body of literature for a prospective reader of the final research report.

5. *Development of a research plan.* Taking what has been gleaned from the literature review, alongside the goals of the researcher, a complete research plan is developed. Included in the plan are strategies for selecting a sample of participants, an appropriate research design based on the nature of the research questions or hypotheses, and strategies for data collection (including procedures, instrumentation, informed consent forms, and a realistic time frame) and data analysis.

6. *Collection of data.* Data collection in a quantitative study tends not to take a great deal of time, depending on the particular design. Data are typically collected directly from participants through the use of instruments, such as surveys, inventories, checklists, tests, and other tools that will generate numerical data.

7. *Analysis of data.* Quantitative data are analyzed statistically, focusing on numerical descriptions, comparisons of groups, or measures of relationships among variables. Because samples tend to be large, data analysis is typically conducted through the use of statistical analysis software programs.

8. *Development of conclusions and recommendations.* Conclusions are drawn directly from the interpretation of results from the statistical analysis. The conclusions, as well as the recommendations for practice and future research, are typically connected back to the body of literature that served as the basis for the earlier literature review.

9. *Preparation of a final research report.* The final step in conducting a quantitative research study is to prepare the final research report. This report summarizes all aspects of the study; in other words, each of the previous eight steps are clearly and thoroughly described in the report.

Approaches to Conducting Quantitative Research

There are several commonly used approaches to conducting quantitative research studies in the field of education. These approaches typically fall into two categories: nonexperimental research designs and experimental research designs. Next, I will provide an overview of these two categories, in addition to descriptions of the specific approaches or designs within each.

Nonexperimental Research Designs

Nonexperimental research designs embody a group of techniques used to conduct quantitative research where there is no manipulation done to any variable in the study. In other words, variables are measured as they occur naturally, without interference of any kind by the researcher. This lack of manipulation may exist because the variable was naturally "manipulated" before the study began or because it is not possible, or feasible, for the researcher to manipulate a particular variable (Mertler, 2014). Three types of nonexperimental research designs are *descriptive research* (which includes *observational research* and *survey research*), *correlational research*, and *causal-comparative research*.

Descriptive Research The purpose of *descriptive studies* is to describe, and interpret, the current status of individuals, settings, conditions, or events (Mertler, 2014). In descriptive research, the researcher is simply studying the phenomenon of interest *as it exists naturally*; no attempt is made to manipulate the individuals, conditions, or events. Two commonly used quantitative, non-experimental, descriptive research designs are *observational research* and *survey research*.

Observational Research. Some of you may be thinking that this sounds more like a qualitative research design than a quantitative one. While observation is certainly important in the realm of qualitative research, we can also design observational research studies that rely on the collection of quantitative data. Quantitative observational studies typically focus on a particular aspect of behavior that can be quantified through some measure (Leedy & Ormrod, 2013). There may still be some confusion between the two observational research approaches, but the *quantification* of observations is the key distinction. For example, we might design a study that focuses on quantifying disruptive classroom behaviors demonstrated by a particular student or group of students. The teacher may notice that the behaviors occur sporadically throughout the day and may want to discover if there are particular times or activities during which the disruptive behavior arises. We might develop an instrument—essentially, a simple tally sheet—to record the number of times the disruptive behavior occurs during specific intervals throughout the day. We might include on the tally sheet a section to indicate the specific activity in which the student is engaged and any other students involved when disruptive behavior occurs. At the end of predetermined periods of time, we would count (i.e., quantify) the number of tally marks on the sheet (Mertler, 2014).

We might base our quantification in observational study on a number of different criteria (Leedy & Ormrod, 2013). In the previous example, we saw how the occurrence of behavior is *counted* to determine its overall *frequency*. However, in other situations, we might be concerned with the *accuracy, intensity, proficiency*, or *mastery* of a particular behavior. In these cases, our instrument would not be restricted to a simple set of tally marks. The researcher would need to design an instrument that allowed for the *rating*—on a continuum—of the particular characteristic serving as the focus of the study. Examples of these different types of instruments and scales will be discussed and presented in Chapter 12.

A strength of observational research is that it can yield data that depict the complexity of human behavior. With respect to some situations and research questions, it may provide a quantitative option to qualitative approaches such as ethnography and grounded theory research (Leedy & Ormrod, 2013). However, observational research is not without its limitations. An observational study tends to require considerable advanced planning, attention to detail, and often more time than other descriptive approaches to conducting quantitative research (Leedy & Ormrod, 2013).

Survey Research. A second approach to conducting descriptive research is survey research. The central purpose of **survey research** is to describe characteristics of a group or population (Fraenkel et al., 2012). It is primarily a quantitative research technique in which the researcher administers some sort of survey or questionnaire to a sample—or, in some cases, an entire population—of individuals to describe their attitudes, opinions, behaviors, experiences, or other characteristics of the population (Creswell, 2005).

In most cases, it is not possible or feasible to survey an entire population; therefore, a sample of **respondents** must be selected from the population. Since the purpose of survey research is to describe characteristics of a population, it is imperative that the sample be selected using a probability sampling technique to ensure more accurate representation of the population. No sampling technique will *guarantee* perfect representation, but probability techniques improve the odds. Accurate representation is necessary because the survey researcher is attempting to describe an entire population by collecting and analyzing data from a smaller subset of the larger group. If the sample does not approximate the larger population, then the inferences drawn about that population will be erroneous to some degree. (Probability sampling techniques will be discussed in Chapter 12.)

Survey research can be used in a descriptive manner, as has been explained; however, it may also be used to investigate relationships between variables (Fraenkel et al., 2012; McMillan, 2012). This process involves a combination of survey research and correlational research design (which you will learn more about shortly). Educational researchers use this approach when the purpose of their study is to describe the relationships between variables within a given population. Similarly, survey research may also be used in a comparative research design (McMillan, 2012). For example, if a researcher wished to examine the differences in attitudes between two or more subgroups of a population (e.g., based on gender, ethnicity, years of teaching experience, or school level), survey research would be an appropriate methodology to use. For these reasons, there is sometimes disagreement among educational research experts as to whether survey research should be categorized as a *separate approach* to conducting quantitative research or as a particular *data collection technique* to be employed when using other approaches to quantitative research.

When conducting survey research, the researcher can choose among several modes of data collection, including direct administration of surveys, mail surveys, telephone surveys, interviews, e-mail surveys, and web-based surveys (Creswell, 2005; Fraenkel et al., 2012; Mertens, 2005). **Direct administration** is used whenever the researcher has access to all, or most, members of a given group who are located in one place. The researcher administers the survey instrument in person to all members of the group, usually at the same time. This typically results in a high rate of response (also known as **return rate**), often near 100 percent. The cost of this mode is lower than most others; however, its main disadvantage is that gathering an entire group together in the same location at the same time is not always possible.

Mail surveys involve administering or distributing the survey instrument to the sample by sending a hard copy to each individual and requesting that it be returned by mail before a certain date. While the cost can be a bit prohibitive, the researcher does gain access to a wider sampling of individuals than through the use of direct administration. The trade-off, however, is that the response rate is typically much lower. Additionally, it is not possible to encourage participation when the researcher is not face-to-face with the respondents.

Telephone surveys can be quite expensive because they must be administered individually, as opposed to the simultaneous administration of direct and mail surveys. These surveys essentially require the researcher (and any assistants, who must receive training) to read each survey question to individual respondents. Therefore, data collection can take a good deal of time, depending on the size of the sample. Also, access to some individuals may be substantially limited (e.g., those without telephones, those with unlisted telephone numbers, or those who use only cell phones). However, telephone surveys are especially effective in gathering responses to open-ended questions.

Interviews are the most costly type of data collection in survey research, largely because they must be conducted individually and face-to-face. This usually means that either the researcher or the respondent (or possibly both) must travel to the interview location. It is easier in interviews to enlist the participation of respondents and probe for clarification of their answers, due to the more conversational style of data collection. Somewhat similar to telephone surveys, interviews require that any assistants or staff be trained in the administration of the interview protocol. This requires additional time and expense on the part of the researcher.

Finally, the rise of the Internet has resulted in a substantial increase in the use of *electronic surveys*. An electronic survey is distributed to potential respondents, usually as attachments to e-mail messages or as standalone webpages, each with its own unique URL or web address. **E-mail surveys** are delivered to potential respondents via e-mail and require an e-mailed set of responses in return. Individuals who complete **web-based surveys** are typically directed to a website through initial contact via e-mail. They complete the survey online and submit their responses via the Internet. The cost and time requirements for these electronic modes of data collection are low; however, both modes require access to technology—e-mail surveys require an active e-mail account, which must also be accessible to the researcher through some sort of existing database, and web-based surveys require access to the Internet via a web browser. Additionally, other limitations of electronic surveys include the fact that databases of current e-mail addresses often do not exist for larger populations (e.g., all teachers in a given state) and many people are not comfortable using websites or sending personal information via the Internet. Mertler (2002) has outlined some of the technological limitations of web-based and other electronic surveys, in addition to providing some guidelines for their use. These limitations include

- compatibility issues (e.g., older computers or web browsers that will not allow the respondent to view or complete the online survey),
- e-mails not delivered to potential respondents because they are sent to multiple recipients (and thus categorized as "spam"), and
- representativeness of the resulting sample (and, ultimately, generalizability of the study's findings).

The above concerns aside, the use of web-based technology for the collection of research data has exploded over the past decade. Below is a listing of several websites where researchers can develop surveys, have them published online, and use them to collect data efficiently. Most of these sites charge fees for hosting the survey and for storing data on their web servers, although the fees vary widely. These sites have many interesting features, and I encourage you to investigate them.

- KwikSurveys (www.kwiksurveys.com)
- Murvey (www.murvey.com)
- Qualtrics (www.qualtrics.com)
- QuestionPro (www.questionpro.com)
- SurveyGizmo (www.surveygizmo.com)
- SurveyGuru (www.surveyguru.com)
- SurveyMonkey (www.surveymonkey.com)
- Zoho Survey (www.zoho.com/survey)
- Zoomerang (www.zoomerang.com)

Table 7.1 presents a summary of the relative advantages and limitations of these various survey data collection modes.

Types of Surveys. There are three basic types of surveys: descriptive, cross-sectional, and longitudinal. It is important to note that a given research topic may be studied using any of the three types of surveys, as you will see in a moment, depending on the purpose of the research. Mertens (2005) explains the **descriptive survey** approach as a one-shot survey for the purpose of simply describing the characteristics of a sample at one point in time. In research of students' reading attitudes and behaviors, a descriptive survey study might be structured as follows: The researcher would randomly select students—possibly elementary or middle school students—and survey them in an attempt to describe their attitudes toward reading as well as their reading behaviors.

A **cross-sectional survey** involves the examination of the characteristics of—and possibly differences among—several samples or populations measured at one point in time. Using the same topic discussed above, an example of a cross-sectional survey study might involve the examination of—and comparisons among—the reading

TABLE 7.1 ● Relative Advantages and Limitations of Different Modes of Survey Delivery						
	Mode of Survey Delivery					
Characteristic	**Direct Administration**	**Mail Surveys**	**Telephone Surveys**	**Interviews**	**E-Mail Surveys**	**Web-Based Surveys**
Comparative cost	Lowest	High	High	Highest	Low	Low
Data collection time	Shortest	Short	Long	Longest	Very short	Very short
Response rate	Highest	Low	High	High	Low	Low
Group administration	Yes	Yes	No	Possibly	Yes	Yes
Permit follow-up questions	No	No	Yes	Yes	No	No
Permit random sampling	Possibly	Yes	Yes	Yes	Yes	Yes
Facilities required	Yes	No	No	Yes	No	No
Technology required	No	No	No	No	Yes	Yes
Training required	No	No	Yes	Yes	No	No

Source: Adapted from Fraenkel et al. (2012).

attitudes and behaviors of third-, fifth-, and seventh-grade students. All the students making up the sample would be surveyed at the same point in time. If a cross-sectional survey is conducted for an entire population, the resulting survey is known as a **census**.

Finally, in a **longitudinal survey**, individuals in one group or cohort are studied at different points in time. In other words, the same group of participants is studied over an extended period of time, which typically involves the administration of several surveys at particular time intervals. The longitudinal version of our hypothetical study would look somewhat similar in purpose but would address somewhat different research questions. The purpose would again be to examine the reading attitudes and behaviors of students, but this time the researcher would follow the same students over an established period of time. For example, the attitudes and behaviors of third-grade students would be measured. Two years later, the same group of students would again be measured as fifth-graders. Two years later, they would again be surveyed as seventh-graders.

Generally speaking, there are three main types of longitudinal surveys: trend, cohort, and panel studies (Creswell, 2005). A **trend study** is a longitudinal survey study that examines changes within a specifically identified population over time. An example might be a survey study of ninth-graders' attitudes toward and use of illegal substances for the 5-year period between 2010 and 2014, in an attempt to identify trends in those attitudes and behaviors. Different ninth-grade students would be surveyed each year; however, they would all represent the same population (i.e., ninth-grade students).

In a **cohort study**, the researcher studies within a specified population a subgroup (called the "cohort") whose members share some common characteristic. This subgroup, as defined by the characteristic, is then surveyed over time. Let us now extend our example of studying attitudes toward and use of illegal substances and apply a cohort design to it. If the researcher wanted to begin by studying ninth-graders (i.e., "ninth grade" would be the defining characteristic) in 2010, this same cohort (but not *necessarily* the same people) would be studied as tenth-graders in 2011, eleventh-graders in 2012, and so on. It is important to note that the group studied each year may or may not be the same individuals that began the study in 2010; remember, they are *selected* from and are *representing* a particular subgroup of a much larger population. To be a part of the group studied in each subsequent year, participants must have been in the ninth grade in 2010.

Finally, a **panel study** is most closely aligned with the fundamental description of a longitudinal survey. In a panel study, the researcher examines the exact same people over a specified length of time. In applying this design to our current example, the researcher would select and survey a group of ninth-graders in 2010, survey the same students in 2011, again in 2012, and so on. Therefore, a panel study is somewhat analogous to a cohort design that studies the same people throughout the length of the longitudinal study. The advantage of this type of design is that you are studying the same individuals; the limitation is that some of them may relocate and be difficult, if not impossible, to find. This tendency will likely result in an ever-decreasing sample size throughout the course of the study.

Cross-sectional survey designs are the most commonly used survey design method, especially when compared with longitudinal designs (Creswell, 2005). This is largely because they can be conducted in a shorter amount of time. Some researchers argue that a longitudinal study provides more meaningful information (i.e., *changes* in reading attitudes and behaviors can be examined for the *same* students). The trade-off, however, is the amount of time required for data collection in this type of survey study.

The Survey Research Process. As previously mentioned, the basic steps in conducting a quantitative research study are fairly consistent across different types of quantitative research. The steps in conducting a survey research study are no exception, although there are unique aspects to the process:

1. *Identification of the topic to be studied.* As with any type of research study, the topic for investigation should first be identified. The topic is often refined and narrowed during the next step.

2. *Review of related literature.* As you have learned, related literature is reviewed to identify useful strategies for conducting the study, as well as to see what has already been discovered about the topic of interest. Also, in survey research, related literature can be used to guide the development of survey or interview questions, as well as data collection protocols.

3. *Identification and selection of participants.* In survey research, the initial activity in the selection of participants is to identify the **target population**. This is the larger group of people to whom the researcher would like to generalize the results of the study. From that list of people, individuals are randomly selected for inclusion in the sample, using a probability sampling technique.

4. *Determination of the mode of data collection.* The researcher must determine the most appropriate method for collecting data—whether it be direct administration of a survey, a mail survey, a telephone survey, interviews, e-mail surveys, or web-based surveys—focusing on the advantages and limitations of each.

5. *Drafting the cover letter and instrument.* A **cover letter**, which will accompany a written survey or precede the interview process, explains the purpose of the study and describes what will be asked of participants. In addition, this letter also describes the potential benefits of the study. The survey instrument or interview questions must be developed based on the guidelines previously discussed. A sample cover letter used in a web-based survey study, along with the survey it accompanied, is presented in Chapter 12.

6. *Pilot test of the instrument.* For a researcher conducting a survey study, there is probably nothing more frustrating than sending out a survey only to discover later that participants did not understand the directions or the questions to which they were supposed to respond (Gay et al., 2009). A **pilot test** is a trial run of the data collection process to determine if any revisions should be made before *actual* data collection occurs. Using a small group—perhaps 15 to 20 individuals—selected from the population of interest, the cover letter and survey are distributed and completed. Upon completion, the researcher seeks feedback from the participants. This process gives the researcher an idea of how long it might take individuals to complete the instrument. It also provides feedback about specific questions that may need revision prior to actual data collection.

7. *Collection of data.* Data are collected through the administration of the survey instrument or by interviewing participants.

8. *Analysis of data.* Most analyses of survey data will involve the use of statistical procedures. These analyses may involve simple frequency distributions, descriptive statistics, correlations, or group comparisons.

9. *Answering research questions and drawing conclusions.* The results of the analyses should permit the researcher to answer the guiding research questions for the study. Once this has been done, inferences about the population may be drawn and conclusions about the study stated.

Strengths and Limitations in Survey Research. As with any research methodology, survey research has its advantages and its limitations. Among its advantages, survey research enables data collection from a large number of people (and can typically do so efficiently), allows for generalizability of results to large populations, and is versatile both in terms of what can be investigated and how (i.e., the various modes of data collection). As you read in this chapter, the wide variety of design options allows the researcher to "customize" survey research to meet the needs and goals of a given study (and its associated questions).

Limitations include issues related to low response rates as well as the time and financial requirements of some modes of data collection. Low response rates are always a potential concern in conducting survey research. Unfortunately, there is no single, widely accepted standard for the rate of survey response; it often depends on the nature of the survey study, the length of the survey instrument, and the population being studied. In some studies (such as those using a direct administration mode of delivery), the survey can be expected to receive nearly a 100% return rate. However, when using mail, e-mail, or web surveys as the mode of delivery, response rates of 50% to 75% may be acceptable. Even in these situations, characteristics of the population may result in response rates below this range. For example, some people (and, therefore, some populations) are constantly inundated with requests to complete surveys; educators are not immune to this experience. It is always advisable to "oversample" from the population (i.e., select substantially more individuals for potential participation than what you are hoping to get), anticipating some degree of nonresponse. Additionally, follow-up mailings or e-mails for requests to complete the survey are nearly always necessary and will result in improved rates of response. Of course, doing this may add to the monetary cost of implementing the survey study. That being said, Dillman (2000) has stated that repeated contact with respondents is the single most effective technique for increasing survey response rates.

The final limitation—or at least consideration—is that we are relying on *self-reported data* (Leedy & Ormrod, 2013); that is, people are telling us what *they* believe is true or what *they* have experienced. On the surface, this sounds like exactly what we want. However, researchers need to remember two important things when it comes to self-reported data:

- Even though people believe they are being accurate, they may in fact not be. Essentially, we are collecting information on their *perceptions* of what they believe to be accurate.

- Sometimes respondents to a survey will indicate answers they *think* we want to hear—especially if they are being asked questions of a sensitive nature; these are known as *socially acceptable responses*. Although this issue is unavoidable when conducting survey research, at a minimum, researchers have an obligation to recognize and acknowledge that respondents *may* be providing socially acceptable responses.

Correlational Research The purpose of *correlational studies* is to discover, and then possibly measure, relationships between two or more variables. From a research perspective, the word *relationship* means that an individual's status on one variable tends to reflect (i.e., is associated with) his or her status on another variable. Correlational research in education seeks out traits, abilities, or conditions that *covary*, or *co-relate*, with each other. Understanding the nature and strength of the relationship between two or more variables can help us

- comprehend and describe certain related events, conditions, and behaviors (correlational studies with this goal are typically referred to as **explanatory correlational studies**);
- predict future conditions or behaviors in one variable from what we presently know of another variable (these studies are generally referred to as **predictive correlational studies**); and
- sometimes obtain strong suspicions that one variable may be "causing" the other.

For example, we know that high school grade point average is correlated with subsequent student success in college. The correlation is far from perfect; in fact, perfect correlations are virtually nonexistent in education. Nevertheless, we can predict, with some degree of accuracy, a person's future college success by the grades he or she earns in high school.

In a correlational study, the researcher examines whether and to what degree a statistical relationship exists between two or more variables. Such a study is typically used to measure or describe existing conditions or something that occurred in the past (Johnson, 2008). The basic design for correlational research involves a *single* group of people who are quantitatively measured on *two* (or more) characteristics (i.e., variables) that have already happened to them. For example, we might be interested in measuring *if* there is a relationship—and if so, *how strong*—between the number of hours students spend studying independently and their scores on a unit test (Mertler, 2014). It is important to realize that, at the time we would collect data on these variables (i.e., "amount of time spent studying" and "test score"), they would have already occurred. Additionally, it is usually the case in a correlational study that the variables measured occur naturally. In our example, students would "naturally" study and they would "naturally" take a unit test. Therefore, when a correlational research design is used, there is no manipulation of any of the conditions being measured in the study.

The relationships investigated during a correlational study are measured statistically by calculating a *correlation coefficient* (symbolized by an italicized, lowercase *r*), which measures two aspects of the relationship between variables: the *direction* of the relationship and the *strength* of the relationship. You will learn more about correlation coefficients—along with their interpretations—in Chapter 12. However, a word of caution is warranted here. It is critical that the correlation coefficients—and, therefore, the results of a correlational study—not be misinterpreted. Proper interpretation of correlation coefficients allows the researcher to conclude that the relationship has a certain magnitude and direction. There is a common misconception—especially among laypersons and the public—that correlational research also implies causation between the two variables. This could not be further from the truth, and it is crucial to remember the following:

Correlation ≠ Causation

This misconception seems to play out quite frequently in the mass media, particularly on television news programs. It is not uncommon for a newscaster, in reporting the results of a study that undoubtedly was focused on measuring the degree of association between two variables, to imply causation between those variables.

A research is not permitted to conclude, simply because two variables are related, that one variable causes the other (Mertler, 2014). The reason for this is that there are likely to be *additional* variables—perhaps *numerous* additional variables—that have causal influences but were not included in the study at hand. Let us imagine for the sake of illustration that, in our example study above, the result was a *strong positive relationship* (i.e., as one variable increases, so does the other) between the "amount of time spent studying" and "scores on the unit test." It would then be accurate to say that increased time studying is *associated with* higher scores on the test. However, it would be completely inaccurate to conclude that studying for a longer period of time *will cause* improved test performance—although students have been trying to prove this one for years! There could certainly be numerous other variables that might influence higher test scores, such as the quality of time spent studying, the level of conceptual understanding of the material being tested, or perhaps even whether the student had a good night's rest before the test.

Although we cannot and should not use the results of correlational research to try to explain causal relationships between variables, we can certainly use them for prediction purposes. The basis for our ability to predict the value on one variable if we know the value on another variable is that we are capitalizing on the quantitative measure of the relationship that exists between the two (Mertler, 2014). If we know what the measure of the relationship is—as indicated by the direction and value of the correlation coefficient—and we know the number of hours a student has spent studying, then we can predict the test score the student will receive. There will typically be some degree of error inherent in our prediction; only in situations where the relationship is perfect (i.e., the correlation coefficient is equal to –1.00 or +1.00) will we be able to predict the value of the second variable with 100% accuracy. However, when studying human beings in educational settings, there is an infinitesimal chance of obtaining a perfect correlation between two variables. The degree of predictive accuracy is determined by the magnitude of the correlation coefficient; the greater the absolute value of the coefficient (i.e., the closer the $|r|$ is to 1.00), the more accurately the value of one variable can be predicted from the other. Still, it is important to keep in mind that this is *not* a prediction of causation but, rather, a prediction of association.

The Correlational Research Process. Similar to survey research and most any other quantitative research study, the basic steps in conducting a correlational research study are fairly straightforward:

1. *Identification of the topic/problem to be studied.* Since correlational studies are designed either to measure relationships between variables or to test hypotheses about predictions, the variables should be selected based on some *logical* rationale. Correlational research where the researcher attempts to correlate a large number of variables just to "see what turns up" is strongly discouraged (Fraenkel et al., 2012; Gay et al., 2009). This is more like a "fishing expedition" than a research study. Also important to note, when stating research questions or hypotheses, it is appropriate to use the terms *relationship* or *prediction* (e.g., *What is the relationship between chronological age and mathematical ability?* or *Can mathematical ability be predicted from chronological age?*). Researchers sometimes use these terms in research questions for other types of research; however, their use will clearly imply that a correlational design is being implemented.

2. *Review of related literature.* Reviewing the related literature is again useful to identify strategies for conducting a correlational study, as well as to provide guidance about what has previously been learned about the relationships between the variables of interest. As you will discover in Chapter 13, related literature can also help appropriately contextualize interpretations of correlation coefficients.

3. *Identification and selection of participants.* In correlational research, participants are selected through the use of an appropriate sampling method. The *minimally* acceptable sample size for correlational studies is 30 participants. If there is concern about the validity and reliability of the variables being measured, however, it is advisable to use a larger sample (Gay et al., 2009).

4. *Specification of the design and procedures for data collection.* The basic design of a correlational study is straightforward. Scores on two or more variables of interest are collected for *each* member of the sample. The pairs of scores making up the data set are then correlated, meaning a correlation coefficient is computed for the two sets of scores.

5. *Collection of data.* Data are collected in a manner appropriate for the variables of interest. For example, in the hypothetical study we have been using to examine correlational research, the researcher would ask students to report how many hours they studied and would then collect the actual test scores from the teacher. Care would need to be taken to ensure that, when the data were compiled into a database or spreadsheet, the scores were paired accurately for each participant. In other words, the number of hours Kate spent studying would need to be paired with *her* test score. If the scores were randomly mixed in the data file, the resulting correlation coefficient would be entirely inaccurate.

6. *Analysis of data.* The analysis of correlational data involves calculation of a correlation coefficient. You will learn in Chapter 13 that there are many different types of correlation coefficients, depending on the level of measurement for each variable.

However, the processes of data collection and analysis are essentially the same for any correlational research study.

7. *Answering research questions and drawing conclusions.* The results of the correlational analyses should permit the researcher to answer the guiding research questions, or address the hypotheses, for the study. Once this has been done, inferences about the nature of the relationship between the variables of interest within the population can be drawn and appropriate associational—but not causal—conclusions about the study asserted.

Strengths and Limitations in Correlational Research. Among the strengths of correlational research is the simplicity of its design. In its simplest form, data for only two variables are required. Again, depending on the variables being studied, this may be a relatively simple and straightforward task. Because of its somewhat simpler design, correlational research is often appropriate for novice researchers, provided they heed the warnings put forth earlier regarding correlational research and the dangers of inappropriately implying causation.

While the design is simple, researchers must ensure that the limited data they are collecting exhibit the qualities (i.e., sound validity and reliability) necessary to draw generalizable conclusions about the relationships between variables. Of course, a correlation coefficient can be calculated regardless; unfortunately, failure to ensure that the data are of high quality will likely result in the inaccurate interpretation of the calculated correlation coefficient. This can lead to erroneous and misleading conclusions for the research study.

Causal-Comparative Research Sometimes researchers are interested in exploring the reasons behind existing differences between two or more groups. Such studies are known as *causal-comparative studies*. In a sense, this type of research is similar to correlational research in that it intends to study conditions that have *already* occurred. Data are collected to try to determine why one group is different from another (Johnson, 2008; Mertler, 2014). Causal-comparative research designs are also referred to as *ex post facto*—or "after-the-fact"—designs. The reason for this is that the study first observes a difference that exists within a group of people, for example, and then looks back in time to determine possible conditions that might have resulted in this observed difference. The researcher is looking for a possible cause "after the fact," since both the precursory conditions *and* the resulting differences have already occurred; that is, the study is taking place retrospectively (Gay et al., 2009). Two or more groups are compared to find a "cause" for—or consequences of—existing differences in some sort of measurement or score (Fraenkel et al., 2012; Johnson, 2008). However, it is once again important to note that causal-comparative research cannot establish true cause and effect—as experimental research can—because no variables are being manipulated.

The most common situation appropriate for causal-comparative designs is one in which the presumed cause, or *independent variable*, has already occurred. The variable of ultimate interest is the *dependent variable*. The independent variable—also referred to as the *grouping variable* (Gay et al., 2009)—defines group membership, because these are typically naturally occurring conditions or ones that have already occurred as part of some process external to and preceding the research study at hand (Mertler, 2014). For example, researchers may informally observe that the range of scores on an annual standardized test of reading is quite large. In trying to identify possible causes for the differences in these scores—perhaps gender, single-parent versus two-parent homes, or school attended—they could use a causal-comparative design to explore differences in test scores between students belonging to the different groups. The main reason a causal-comparative design is appropriate in this situation is that none of those independent variables can be manipulated. In other words, as a researcher, I cannot assign students to different gender categories (other than the ones to which they naturally belong), nor can I assign them to live in a single-parent or two-parent home. Similarly, I cannot assign students to attend different schools just for the purposes of my research study. Those actions would not be ethical, nor would they be practical or feasible.

As another example, consider a situation where researchers want to know how effectively a new self-esteem program, being piloted in numerous schools throughout a large urban district, is working (Mertler, 2014). This study uses scores from a self-esteem inventory (i.e., the dependent variable) administered to students in schools throughout the district—some of which are piloting the program and some not (i.e., the independent variable). In this example, it is important to realize that the independent variable is a *preexisting condition*; that is, the program was already being implemented in some schools and not in others. The researchers are studying the effect of the program on students' self-esteem after the fact (i.e., after the program has already been implemented). Once the researchers administer the self-esteem inventory, scores are collected. The scores from students who have been exposed to the pilot program are then compared with scores from students in schools that do not have the pilot self-esteem program. If the scores on the inventory are significantly higher for the students who have been exposed to the program than for those students who have not participated in the program, the researchers will conclude that the new program is effective. In contrast, if the inventory scores are lower for the students exposed to the new program or if there is no difference in the scores between the two groups, the researchers will conclude that the new program has a negative effect or no noticeable effect, respectively.

Researchers must exhibit caution because interpretations of the results of causal-comparative research are limited; researchers cannot say conclusively whether a particular factor is a cause, or a result, of the behaviors observed (Fraenkel et al., 2012). The distinct value of causal-comparative studies is that they are capable of identifying *possible* causes of variations in behaviors, academic performance, and the like.

The Causal-Comparative Research Process. Similar to correlational research, the steps in conducting a causal-comparative research study are fairly simple. One of the substantive differences is that analysis of causal-comparative data can involve a wider variety of statistical techniques (Gay et al., 2009). The steps in conducting a causal-comparative research study are as follows:

1. *Identification of the topic/problem to be studied.* Problem identification in a causal-comparative study begins by identifying a phenomenon of interest and then considering possible causes for, or consequences of, that phenomenon (Fraenkel et al., 2012). Once possible causes have been identified, they are typically incorporated into a formal problem statement and research questions or hypotheses. Similar to the process in correlational studies, possible causes or consequences should be identified based on some *logical* rationale. Again, research attempting to investigate a large number of variables just to "see what turns up" should be avoided entirely. Potential research questions are stated in terms of group differences (e.g., *How does teacher training—traditional versus alternative—affect empathy in the classroom?* or *Does gender have an effect on mathematical problem-solving skills?*).

2. *Review of related literature.* Conducting a literature review in a causal-comparative study can provide guidance in the identification of possible causes or consequences of a particular phenomenon. Related literature may also aid the researcher in making methodological decisions, including those related to methods and instrumentation for data collection and data analysis.

3. *Identification and selection of participants.* One of the most important factors in selecting a sample in this type of study is to carefully define the characteristic(s) that will serve as the grouping variable(s), and then be sure to select groups that differ specifically and measurably on the characteristic(s). Further, and beyond consideration of the grouping variable, it is important to select groups that are as homogeneous on *other* factors as possible. Of course, this is impossible to accomplish with respect to all the other factors that can influence human behavior, but measures should be taken to try to control these other influences. Often, the success of a causal-comparative study depends largely on how carefully the comparison groups have been defined (Fraenkel et al., 2012). Typically, the groups will differ in one of two ways: (1) One group will possess a characteristic that the other group does not, or (2) both groups will possess the same characteristic(s) but to differing degrees or amounts (Gay et al., 2009). Since there is only limited control within a causal-comparative design, it is best to select participants randomly from the two (or more) well-defined populations, or groups. It is advisable to have a minimum of 30 participants in each group.

4. *Specification of the design and procedures for data collection.* At this point, I will introduce some common notation used to depict research designs. The symbols are as follows:

T = Treatment condition

O = Observation or measurement

EXP-GRP = Experimental group

CO-GRP = Control or comparison group

GRP = Nondescript group

GRP_1, GRP_2, . . . = Subscripts denote different groups

Using this notation, the basic causal-comparative design appears in Figure 7.1. In this design, two groups are determined based on the presence or absence—or differing

FIGURE 7.1 ●   The Basic Research Design for a Causal-Comparative Research Study

Group	Dependent Variable
GRP$_1$	O
GRP$_2$	O

degree—of the characteristic of interest. Each group is then measured on the dependent variable, and the subsequent scores are statistically compared by group.

5. *Collection of data.* There are essentially no limits to what can be used as instrumentation or sources for data collection in causal-comparative studies, provided that the resulting data are quantitative.

6. *Analysis of data.* The analysis of causal-comparative data involves calculation of both *descriptive* and *inferential* statistics, as well as the statistical comparison of two or more groups on some quantitative variable. In Chapter 13, you will learn that there are numerous methods for conducting statistical group comparisons. They vary depending on the number of groups being compared, the number of dependent variables being measured, and the underlying purpose of the causal-comparative research study.

7. *Answering research questions and drawing conclusions.* The results of the causal-comparative analyses should permit the researcher to answer the guiding research questions, or address the hypotheses, of the study. However, it is critical to remember that interpreting the findings of a causal-comparative study requires a good deal of caution on the part of the researcher. Even when taking measures to ensure that the groups being compared are relatively equivalent—with the exception of the grouping variable—it is difficult to establish any sort of cause-and-effect conclusions with any degree of confidence.

Strengths and Limitations of Causal-Comparative Research. Gay and colleagues (2009) discuss one of the major strengths of causal-comparative research. Even though true cause-and-effect relationships can be determined only through the application of experimental research (as you will read about shortly), an experimental study is often inappropriate, unethical, or impossible to conduct in many educational settings. Causal-comparative research is an effective alternative to experimental designs, particularly in situations where the independent/grouping variable cannot or should not be manipulated. The main limitation or weakness of causal-comparative research is that, because the cause under investigation has already occurred, the researcher has no control over it. This is incredibly limiting in situations where researchers are trying to conclude cause-and-effect relationships.

Consider a situation where researchers want to study the effect of drinking large amounts of soda on frequency of childhood obesity. They design the study comparing the frequency of childhood obesity in two groups of children—ones who drink soda daily and ones who do not drink soda at all. Realize that the researchers have no control over the participants in terms of soda consumption; these are preexisting conditions that defined the two groups. If it turns out that the group of children who consume soda on a daily basis experience a much higher rate of childhood obesity, the researchers cannot conclude that obesity is directly attributable to soda consumption. Since there was no control over the grouping variable, it is likely that numerous other conditions contributed to the occurrence of obesity, such as eating habits, environmental factors, and genetics. In situations such as these, it is impossible to identify a definitive cause-and-effect association.

Experimental Research Designs

The second category of quantitative research designs is collectively known as *experimental research*, a group of techniques where the researcher establishes different treatments or conditions and then studies their effects on the participants. It is because of this ability to manipulate the treatment conditions and control for many extraneous factors that experimental studies are the most conclusive of all research designs. There are four general categories of experimental research, with each category containing multiple designs: *preexperimental research designs*, *quasi-experimental research designs*, *true experimental research designs*, and *single-subject research designs*.

As has been mentioned, experimental research studies can demonstrate cause and effect the most convincingly of any research design. However, there are trade-offs for this desirable outcome. Students often ask, if experimental research can be so conclusive, why would we conduct any other type of research? The answer lies in the strict requirements of experimental research designs and the fact that many educational problems, settings, and situations do not lend themselves to these requirements. *Generally speaking*, the broad category of experimental research design requires the following components:

- A sample of participants who are *randomly* selected and/or *randomly* assigned to an experimental group(s) and control group(s), more appropriately referred to as a **comparison group**
- An independent variable—which, in experimental studies, can be referred to as the *treatment variable*, the *causal variable*, or the *experimental variable*—that can be selectively applied to the experimental group
- A dependent variable—which, in experimental studies, can be referred to as the *criterion variable*, the *effect variable*, or the *posttest variable*—that can be measured in an identical manner for all groups in the study

As you will see in a moment, there is some variation to these requirements, depending on the specific design we are examining. For example, if we wanted to conduct an experiment on sixth-grade classroom discipline, we would need to randomly select and randomly assign sixth-grade students to two or more classes, at least one of which would receive the experimental treatment while another, serving as a comparison group, would not receive the treatment. The experimental treatment (i.e., the manipulated independent variable) might be a new system of discipline. The dependent variable (which would be measured in both groups) might be the incidence and severity of student misbehavior. If, after the new discipline system had been in effect for a while, the experimental group exhibited behavior significantly different from that of the comparison group, we could conclude that a cause-and-effect relationship existed (provided we accounted for some other control measures, which we will discuss more extensively in Chapter 12). We could then conclude—with some degree of confidence—that the discipline system had caused better, or perhaps worse, student behavior.

It is important at this point to discuss the distinction between *random selection* and *random assignment*. Random selection of samples and random assignment of sample members to experimental and comparison groups are essential and distinguishing features of experimental design. The only exception occurs in single-subject designs, usually conducted on an individual diagnosed as having significant personal problems—for example, obsessive eating or uncontrolled outbursts. **Random selection** is the process of choosing, in random fashion, individuals for participation in a research study, such that every member of the population has an equal chance of being selected to be a member of the sample. Some of the random sampling techniques we will look at closer in Chapter 12 include *simple random sampling, stratified random sampling*, and *cluster sampling*. Once participants have been randomly selected to participate in a study, they undergo **random assignment** to groups (usually treatment and comparison groups). Random assignment means that every individual who has been randomly selected to participate in the experiment has an equal chance of being assigned to any of the groups (i.e., experimental or comparison groups) being compared in the study. Both random selection and assignment help ensure equivalence of groups, and control for many extraneous variables that might otherwise contaminate the results of the research study. When it is not possible to randomly select a sample of participants—this is typically difficult, if not impossible, in school settings—one must, if possible, randomly assign students to experimental and comparison groups. It is not always feasible to randomly assign students to treatment conditions in school settings; when random assignment is not possible, the result is a quasi-experimental study, rather than experimental research. To summarize,

Random selection + Random assignment = Experimental research

Random selection (only) = Quasi-experimental research

It is important to note here that, in experimental or quasi-experimental designs, there may be a need or desire to have multiple (i.e., more than two) groups. Clearly, in these cases, the researcher must be able to structure some sort of "alternative" treatment group. This means that there will typically be an experimental or treatment group (receives the treatment condition), a control group (receives nothing), and a third comparison group (receives *something* but not the treatment of interest).

For example, suppose a researcher wanted to investigate the impact of an Internet-based study site on student performance on a standardized achievement test. The treatment group would receive structured time to work with the online study site. The control group would not receive any form of direct study support in preparation for the achievement test. In addition, the researcher might hypothesize that *any* sort of supplemental study time or effort would be beneficial to student performance and may want to compare the effectiveness of this other type of study support against the online site (i.e., the treatment condition), as well as against the complete lack of support (i.e., the control condition). Therefore, the researcher may establish a third, "alternative treatment" group that receives a limited amount of study support supplied by the teacher. This group is sometimes referred to as the *comparison group*, although it is usually the case that any nonexperimental group may be referred to as the comparison group. The benefit of including an additional comparison group is that it can provide the researcher an additional level or type of comparison to better explain the effectiveness of the treatment condition.

There are two major classes of experimental research design: single-variable designs and factorial designs (Gay et al., 2009). **Single-variable designs** are those that involve only one manipulated independent variable. In contrast, **factorial designs** involve two or more independent variables, at least one of which is manipulated. Most of our discussion here will focus on single-variable experimental research designs. Single-variable designs fall into three of the four categories previously listed: preexperimental, quasi-experimental, and true experimental designs. The designs differ in their degree of control over extraneous variables that can jeopardize validity. Each of these three types of experimental designs is discussed below.

Preexperimental Research Preexperimental designs do not do a very good job of controlling for extraneous variables and should be avoided. Gay and colleagues (2009) have asserted that the results of a preexperimental study are so questionable that they may be useful only to provide a *preliminary* investigation of a problem. The first example of a preexperimental design is a **one-shot case study** (see Figure 7.2), involving a single group that is exposed to a treatment condition and then posttested. For example, researchers want to know if a new lab kit will improve student performance in science. The researchers select science teachers, all of whom use the kits with their science classes, and then administer an examination. The resulting exam scores are higher than normal, so the researchers conclude that the new lab kits are effective in helping students learn more.

The essential problem with this design is that even if the participants score high on the posttest, we have no idea what we should attribute their performance to, because we do not know what happened to them or with them before the treatment was administered. The students may have performed better with *any* set of lab materials or even *without* any lab materials, perhaps because they are naturally bright, among a variety of other possible reasons. Gay and colleagues (2009) offer the following advice: "If you have a choice between using this design and not doing a study, don't do the study. Do a different study with a better control design" (p. 253).

A second preexperimental design is known as a **one-group pretest–posttest design** (see Figure 7.3). While still not a strong design, it offers an improvement over the previous one. In this design, we still have only one group—so we have no "other" group for comparison purposes—but a pretest is added prior to the introduction of the treatment. Returning to our previous example, this would involve the administration of a pretest to the students prior to exposing them to the new lab kits. Lessons would then be taught by the teachers using the lab kits, followed by the administration of the posttest to the students. The success of the treatment would essentially be determined by comparing pretest and posttest scores (Gay et al., 2009). This design represents an improvement over the one-shot case study because the researcher will, at a *minimum*, know if some sort of change (i.e., an increase or decrease in scores) has occurred (Leedy & Ormrod, 2013). However, there could most certainly be other explanations for the change in scores, and these possible explanations are not accounted for in the design.

A third and final example of preexperimental design is the **static-group comparison design** (see Figure 7.4). This design offers a slight improvement, in that it introduces a second comparison group; however, the pretesting is not included. Additionally, the members of both groups have been selected in a nonrandom manner; they are in essence existing, intact groups—hence the use of the term *static group*. In this design, the experimental group is exposed to some sort of treatment or condition, and the comparison group is not. The purpose of the comparison group is essentially to demonstrate what the performance by the members of the experimental group *would have been* had they not received the treatment; however, this can happen only to the degree that the design ensures the comparison group is equivalent to the experimental group (Gay et al., 2009). This design is still weak, because no attempt is made to ensure that the groups are equivalent at the outset of the study or

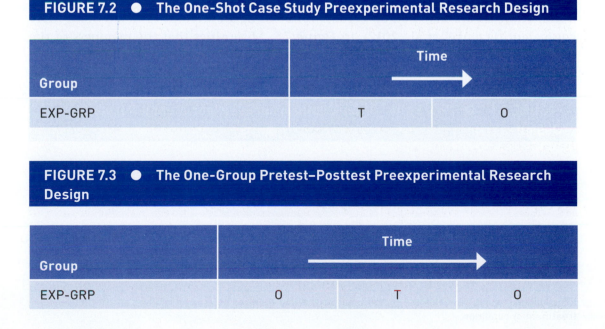

FIGURE 7.2 ● The One-Shot Case Study Preexperimental Research Design

Group		Time	
EXP-GRP		T	O

FIGURE 7.3 ● The One-Group Pretest–Posttest Preexperimental Research Design

Group		Time	
EXP-GRP	O	T	O

to determine what the groups may have been exposed to prior to the study; therefore, we have no way of knowing if the treatment resulted in any observed differences between the groups (Leedy & Ormrod, 2013).

Strengths and Limitations of Preexperimental Research. As you can see from our discussion, these preexperimental designs leave a lot to be desired. They are not strong in terms of their control over extraneous variables; either the "independent variable" doesn't vary (due to the fact that there is only one group), or the equivalency of the experimental and comparison groups cannot be established, or individual participants were not randomly selected. Therefore, these designs are very weak in terms of enabling the researcher to draw definitive conclusions about cause-and-effect relationships among variables in the study. These preexperimental designs should be used only as preliminary studies and followed up by more stringent designs (Leedy & Ormrod, 2013), which we will talk about next.

Quasi-Experimental Research Quasi-experimental research designs come the closest to true experiments; however, there is still no random assignment of the participants to groups, which weakens the ability to control for extraneous influences. Random assignment to groups is the aspect of experimental research design that ensures that the groups being compared are relatively similar. Since random assignment of students to groups is typically impractical—due largely to the fact that students are already "assigned" to numerous preexisting and intact groups, such as classes, grade levels, and so on—quasi-experimental designs are often appropriate for research in school settings.

The first quasi-experimental design we will discuss is the **matching posttest-only control group design** (see Figure 7.5). This design uses two groups of participants from the same population, such as two intact classrooms in the same school system. Since random assignment to treatment conditions is not possible in this scenario, students are matched on certain variables in an attempt to make them more equivalent (Fraenkel et al., 2012). In Figure 7.5, *M* signifies that the members of the groups have been matched on one or more variables. This design represents a slight

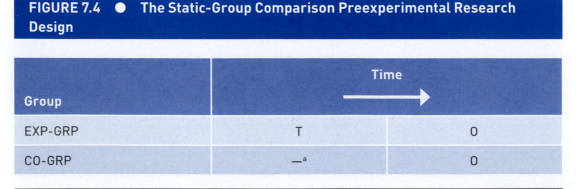

FIGURE 7.4 ● The Static-Group Comparison Preexperimental Research Design

Group	Time	
EXP-GRP	T	O
CO-GRP	—[a]	O

[a]The dashed line indicates that the comparison group either receives nothing or receives an alternative treatment or condition.

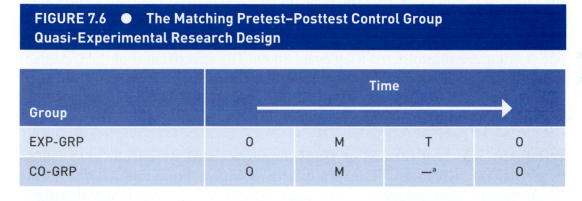

FIGURE 7.5 ● The Matching Posttest-Only Control Group Quasi-Experimental Research Design

Group	Time		
EXP-GRP	M	T	O
CO-GRP	M	—[a]	O

[a]The dashed line indicates that the comparison group either receives nothing or receives an alternative treatment or condition.

FIGURE 7.6 ● The Matching Pretest–Posttest Control Group Quasi-Experimental Research Design

Group	Time			
EXP-GRP	O	M	T	O
CO-GRP	O	M	—[a]	O

[a]The dashed line indicates that the comparison group either receives nothing or receives an alternative treatment or condition.

improvement over the static-group comparison preexperimental design, in that attempts—albeit weak attempts—have been made to establish the equivalency of the groups. Members of the groups are matched, one group is exposed to the experimental treatment or condition, both groups are given a posttest, and then those scores are compared to see if the groups differ on the dependent variable.

A variation of this design is the **matching pretest–posttest control group design** (see Figure 7.6). This is a slightly improved design because not only is a pretest administered, but the pretest scores serve as the basis for matching participants across the groups. In other words, a pretest is administered to all participants and, based on the results of the pretest, each participant is matched with another participant who has a relatively similar pretest score. Groups are then created by putting each person from the pair into a separate group (i.e., one into the experimental group and one into the comparison group; Johnson, 2008). The result is two groups that are relatively similar on the variable of interest, as measured by the pretest.

A **counterbalanced design** is the third type of quasi-experimental research design we will examine. In this research design (see Figure 7.7), each group is exposed to each treatment—however many there may be—but in a different order than are the other groups (Fraenkel et al., 2012). This design is another technique used for equating experimental and comparison groups. The only restriction on the design is that the number of groups must be equal to the number of treatments, although the order in which the groups receive treatment is randomly determined (Gay et al., 2009). Although the diagram in Figure 7.7 shows three groups and three treatments in the study, any number of group treatments may be studied.

A final type of quasi-experimental design is the **time-series design**. This design (see Figure 7.8) is essentially an elaboration of the one-group pretest–posttest design (Gay et al., 2009). In that design, observations in the form of pretests and posttests are taken immediately before and after exposure to the treatment. In a time-series design, however, an extensive amount of data is collected on one group by first pretesting the participants repeatedly until the pretest scores become stable. The group is then exposed to a treatment condition and then posttested repeatedly. If the group performs essentially the same on repeated pretests but then significantly improves on the posttests, the researcher can be more confident about the effectiveness of the treatment, compared with a situation where only one pretest and one posttest are administered (Gay et al., 2009). The effectiveness of the treatment is determined by analyzing the test scores to see if patterns exist; however, the typical statistical analyses appropriate for this type of design tend to be quite advanced (Gay et al., 2009).

Strengths and Limitations of Quasi-Experimental Research. In situations where random assignment is not feasible, quasi-experimental research designs are advantageous. They represent a vast improvement over preexperimental designs, which we identified as being extremely weak. While they allow for conclusions that may provide some degree of confidence, they still do not control for all extraneous and influential variables; therefore, researchers cannot completely rule out some

FIGURE 7.7 ● The Counterbalanced Quasi-Experimental Research Design

Group	Time					
GRP$_1$	T$_1$	O	T$_2$	O	T$_3$	O
GRP$_2$	T$_2$	O	T$_3$	O	T$_1$	O
GRP$_3$	T$_3$	O	T$_1$	O	T$_2$	O

FIGURE 7.8 ● The Time-Series Quasi-Experimental Research Design

Group	Time									
EXP-GRP	O$_1$	O$_2$	O$_3$	O$_4$	O$_5$	T	O$_6$	O$_7$	O$_8$	O$_9$ O$_{10}$

alternative explanations for the results they may obtain in quasi-experimental studies. The only solution to these concerns is to use true experimental research designs.

Experimental Research True experimental research designs share one important characteristic in common: They all involve the *random assignment* of participants to treatment conditions (Gay et al., 2009). Random assignment is one of the most powerful techniques for controlling for extraneous threats to validity (Fraenkel et al., 2012). An additional characteristic these designs share is that they all have at least one comparison group. The simplest experimental design is the **posttest-only control group design** (see Figure 7.9). This design closely resembles the static-group comparison design, with one exception: The participants have been randomly assigned—signified by *R* in the figure—to the experimental and comparison groups. The combination of random assignment and a comparison group controls for nearly all threats to validity. The one thing missing in this particular experimental design is use of a pretest as a means for providing additional control.

This missing element is addressed in the second experimental design, the **pretest–posttest control group design** (see Figure 7.10). This design requires at

FIGURE 7.9 ● The Posttest-Only Control Group Experimental Research Design

Group	Time		
EXP-GRP	R	T	O
CO-GRP	R	—[a]	O

[a]The dashed line indicates that the comparison group either receives nothing or receives an alternative treatment or condition.

FIGURE 7.10 ● The Pretest–Posttest Control Group Experimental Research Design

Group	Time			
EXP-GRP	R	O	T	O
CO-GRP	R	O	—[a]	O

[a]The dashed line indicates that the comparison group either receives nothing or receives an alternative treatment or condition.

least two groups, each of which comprises randomly assigned participants. All groups are administered a pretest, receive some sort of treatment condition (or, perhaps, the absence of a treatment condition), and are posttested at the end of the study. The combination of (1) random assignment, (2) the use of a pretest, and (3) the presence of comparison group(s)—in a minimal two-group design—makes this the most powerful experimental research design.

The final experimental design is actually a combination of several designs we have looked at thus far. The **Solomon four-group design** is a combination of the posttest-only control group design and the pretest–posttest control group design; therefore, this design provides the benefits of both wrapped into one. The Solomon four-group design (see Figure 7.11) first involves the random assignment of participants to one of four groups. Two groups are pretested, and two are not; one of the pretested groups and one of the non-pretested groups receive the experimental treatment. The other two groups receive nothing or an alternative treatment. Finally, all four groups are posttested using the same measure. As you can see in Figure 7.11, the benefit of this design is that numerous group comparisons are possible, allowing for determination of the effect of the pretest as well as that of the treatment. This design is actually stronger than the pretest–posttest control group design; however, it requires a substantially larger sample due to the inclusion of a third and fourth group.

The Experimental Research Process. The steps in conducting any type of experimental research study (i.e., preexperimental, quasi-experimental, or true experimental) essentially mirror the process for conducting causal-comparative research, as presented earlier in the chapter. The primary exception is the inclusion of random assignment in experimental studies. Those steps are as follows:

1. *Identification of the topic/problem to be studied.* Problem identification in an experimental research study begins by selecting a treatment condition and then considering ways to measure its effect. As in both correlational and causal-comparative

FIGURE 7.11   ●   The Solomon Four-Group Experimental Research Design

Group	Time			
EXP-GRP$_1$	R	O	T	O
CO-GRP$_1$	R	O	—[a]	O
EXP-GRP$_2$	R		T	O
CO-GRP$_2$	R		—[a]	O

[a]The dashed line indicates that the comparison group either receives nothing or receives an alternative treatment or condition.

studies, any possible cause-and-effect relationship should be determined based on some *logical* or *empirical* rationale.

2. *Review of related literature.* Reviewing related literature can provide guidance in the identification of key variables that should be measured and ways to control for extraneous influences within an experimental study. This review may also aid the researcher in making methodological decisions, including those related to experimental design, as well as methods and instrumentation for data collection and data analysis.

3. *Identification and selection of participants.* As you undoubtedly know by now, random selection and/or random assignment of participants is key in any sort of experimental research study. Decisions must be made about the feasibility of both random selection and random assignment. If random assignment is not possible, other mechanisms (e.g., matching) for establishing the equivalency of the groups involved in the study must be considered, and the appropriateness of their use must be evaluated. As with causal-comparative research, it is advisable to have a minimum of 30 participants in each group.

4. *Specification of the design and procedures for data collection.* Of course, specifying the design in any sort of experimental research study is of the utmost importance so that the various requirements, respective of a particular design, can be appropriately and ethically incorporated into the study.

5. *Collection of data.* There are no limits to what can be used as sources for data collection in experimental studies, provided the resulting data are, of course, quantitative in nature.

6. *Analysis of data.* Similar to causal-comparative data, the analysis of experimental data involves the calculation of both *descriptive* and *inferential* statistics, as well as the statistical comparison of two or more groups on the quantitative variable (i.e., the posttest). Again, these statistical techniques for conducting group comparisons will be presented in Chapter 13.

7. *Answering research questions and drawing conclusions.* The results of the statistical analysis should permit the researcher to answer the guiding research questions, or address the hypotheses, for the study. However, it is critical to remember that researchers must be extremely cautious when interpreting the findings of an experimental study. Even when taking measures to ensure that the groups being compared are relatively equivalent, researchers must factor into their conclusions the various threats to validity.

Strengths and Limitations of Experimental Research. The clear strength of experimental research designs is their capacity to draw strong cause-and-effect conclusions in a research study. As has been mentioned numerous times throughout this chapter, experimental research designs are the only type of study that can establish cause-and-effect relationships. However, these designs are not without their limitations.

The requirements for designing and conducting true experimental studies are extremely stringent and, in some cases, prohibitive. In addition, researchers must go to great lengths to ensure that their designs, data, and conclusions do not fall victim to the variety of threats to validity, which we will discuss momentarily.

Single-Subject Research As we have seen thus far, most experimental research is accomplished through the study of participants in groups. However, experimental-type studies can be conducted on individual participants. These types of designs are known as **single-subject experimental research designs**. Single-subject designs are typically used to study and promote a change in behavior as exhibited by an individual. Generally speaking, a participant is exposed to a nontreatment phase and a treatment phase, and performance is measured during each phase (Gay et al., 2009). Typically, the nontreatment phase is symbolized by A, and the treatment phase is symbolized by B. Suppose that researchers were asked to study a student who chronically misbehaved and did not respond to the disciplinary techniques used with other students. The researchers might decide to conduct a single-participant experiment to see if the student's behavior could be improved.

In such a study, the researchers would need to make accurate measurements of the student's behavior before applying an experimental treatment. Over a period of a week or two, the number of times the student exhibited various misbehaviors—such as shouting out, getting up and wandering around the room, provoking confrontations with other students, and refusing to comply with the teacher's directions—would be recorded. These data would serve as a baseline measurement against which to compare the student's behavior during and after receiving the experimental treatment. The researchers would then implement the experimental treatment, perhaps a special system of behavior modification. After implementation and at a designated time, the student's misbehaviors would again be recorded over a period of days. This process could be repeated several times.

There are various types of single-subject research designs. The simplest form is known as the **A-B design** (see Figure 7.12). In this design, baseline measures (A) are obtained over time and then a treatment (B) is implemented, during which time additional measures are recorded. If there is a change in behavior, then the treatment is said to have had an effect. Although this is a straightforward design, its results may be subject to numerous competing explanations, making it a weak design in the long run. As we have already seen with both experimental and quasi-experimental designs, other variations of this simple design introduce ways to control for the possibility of alternative explanations.

The **A-B-A design** (see Figure 7.13), also known as the **reversal design** or measurement-treatment-measurement design, is a much-improved single-subject design when compared with the A-B design. The A-B-A design begins in similar fashion by establishing the baseline (A) and then introducing a treatment (B). However, in the third phase (the second A), the treatment is reversed or, in actuality, removed or withdrawn. If the negative behavior returns after removing the treatment, this tends to show that the treatment had an effect. The substantial limitation of this design is

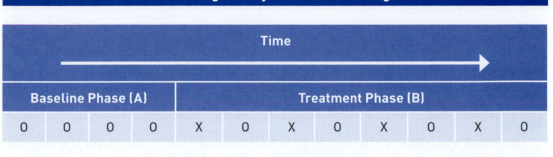

FIGURE 7.12 ● The A-B Single-Subject Research Design

Time →											
Baseline Phase (A)				**Treatment Phase (B)**							
O	O	O	O	X O	X O	X O	X O				

FIGURE 7.13 ● The A-B-A Single-Subject Research Design

Time →													
Baseline Phase (A)				**Treatment Phase (B)**							**Baseline Phase (A)**		
O	O	O	O	X	O	X	O	X	O	X	O O	O O	O

that many interventions cannot, or perhaps should not, be withdrawn. This may be due largely to ethical reasons (e.g., involving self-injurious behavior) or perhaps even some practical reasons (e.g., the intervention cannot be unlearned, like a skill).

A third single-subject design is the **alternating-treatment design**. This design is used to investigate and explain the comparative effect of two treatments. In the application of this design, two treatments are alternated in quick succession and changes in the participant's behavior are plotted on a graph to facilitate informal comparisons. Finally, in the **multiple-baseline design**, two or more (often three) behaviors, people, or settings are plotted in a staggered graph, where a change is made to one but not the other two, and then to the second but not the third behavior, person, or setting. Differential changes that occur to each behavior or person, or in each setting, help strengthen what is essentially an A-B design, with its problematic competing explanations for behaviors, by providing opportunities to examine those alternative explanations.

Strengths and Limitations of Single-Subject Research. The strength of single-subject research is its ability to focus on a single participant and study the effectiveness of treatment on *only* that participant. By focusing on one individual, one behavior, and one treatment, it is possible to scientifically impact and correct negative or undesirable behaviors. The limitations of this focused research effort lie in the fact that there will always be alternative explanations for *why* a behavior was corrected, or why it *failed* to be corrected. Effectively factoring out alternative explanations for the results of any sort of experimental study will always be a challenge for the educational researcher.

Threats to Validity in Quantitative Designs

"Validity of research" refers to the degree to which research conclusions can be considered accurate and generalizable. All types of quantitative research designs are subject to *threats to validity*, both internal and external. These threats must be controlled, or otherwise accounted for, so the potential error they might introduce into the research study does not jeopardize the legitimacy and accuracy of the research findings and conclusions.

Internal validity is the degree to which measured differences on the dependent variable are a direct result of the manipulation of the independent variable, and not some other variable or extraneous condition or influence (Gay et al., 2009). Researchers have an obligation to examine threats to internal validity that might negatively influence the outcome of an experimental study. The degree to which the conclusions drawn from experimental research studies are directly attributable to the independent variable and not some other explanation determines the degree to which the study is internally valid (Gay et al., 2009). There are eight main threats to internal validity, described below:

1. **History**. When experimental treatments extend over longer periods, such as a semester or a year, factors other than the experimental treatment have time to exert influence on the results.

2. **Maturation**. If treatments extend over longer periods, participants may undergo physiological changes that produce differential effects in the dependent variable. For example, they may become stronger, better coordinated, better able to do abstract thinking, or better readers.

3. **Differential selection of participants**. In some studies, selected participants already possess differences that may account for potential variations on a posttest. This is often the case when participants are not selected or assigned randomly.

4. **Testing** (also known as **pretest sensitization**). If pretests and posttests are used, participants may learn enough from the pretest to improve performance on the posttest, even when the experimental treatment has no effect. If equivalent forms of a test are used, despite their being considered equal, one form may in fact be easier than the other.

5. **Instrumentation**. Sometimes the instruments we use to measure performance in experimental studies (e.g., pretests and posttests) are unreliable or lack consistency in their ability to measure variables of interest. Clearly, the result in these cases is inaccurate data.

6. **Statistical regression**. This threat occurs in studies where participants are selected based on their extremely high or extremely low scores on some measure. Statistical regression is the tendency for participants who score very high on one test (e.g., a pretest) to score lower on a second, similar test (e.g., a posttest), or for participants who score very low on a pretest to score much higher on a posttest. In both cases, the

extremely high scorers and extremely low scorers will regress toward the mean, or average score, of the posttest. In essence, they have either "topped out" or "bottomed out," respectively.

7. Attrition (also known as **mortality**). While the experiment is in progress, there may be a loss of participants for reasons such as illness, dropping out, or moving elsewhere. Of course, this is unavoidable, but it may influence the resulting posttest data for a particular group.

8. Selection-maturation interaction (as well as other possible interactive effects). The effects of differential selection of participants may also interact with other threats, such as history, maturation, or testing. Certain intact groups selected to participate in a study may perform better (or worse) or gain a greater (or lesser) advantage from a particular treatment.

Table 7.2 presents these various threats to internal validity and the extent to which they may be controlled in the various types of designs we have discussed in this chapter.

TABLE 7.2 ● Threats to Internal Validity in Various Types of Experimental Designs				
	Type of Research Design			
Threat	**Preexperimental**	**Quasi-Experimental**	**True Experimental**	**Single Subject**
History	Potential threat	Potential threat	Controlled	Potential threat
Maturation	Potential threat	Potential threat	Controlled	Controlled
Differential selection	Potential threat	Potential threat	Controlled	Controlled
Testing	Potential threat	Potential threat if pretest and posttest used	Potential threat if pretest and posttest used	Controlled
Instrumentation	Potential threat	Potential threat if instrument or observational procedures change	Potential threat if instrument or observational procedures change	Potential threat if multiple interventions are used
Statistical regression	Potential threat	Potential threat	Controlled	Controlled
Attrition	Potential threat	Potential threat	Controlled	Controlled
Selection-maturation interaction	Potential threat	Potential threat	Controlled	Controlled

Source: Adapted from Creswell (2005).

External validity of research refers to the extent to which results of a particular study are generalizable, or applicable, to other groups or settings. As you well know, what works in one setting may not work in another. There are three basic types of threats to external validity:

1. **Population validity**. This refers to the degree of similarity among (1) the sample used in a study, (2) the population from which the sample was drawn, and (3) the target population to which results are to be generalized. The greater the degree of similarity among the three, the greater the researcher's confidence can be in generalizing research findings to the broader, target population. This is the reason behind the importance of selecting a representative sample in quantitative studies.

2. **Personological validity**. A given research finding can apply well to some people and poorly to others. Individuals differ in what they find acceptable, comfortable, and useful. Self-directed learning is an example. Some students prefer to work on their own and can do so effectively. Other equally intelligent students require guidance from a teacher and desire the companionship of their peers.

3. **Ecological validity**. This refers to the situation, physical or emotional, that exists during the experiment. An experimental situation may be quite different from a new setting where results are to be applied. For example, some groups of participants, especially when exposed to innovative treatments or conditions, develop a much higher level of motivation to achieve or otherwise perform. Such groups' results may be quite different from results seen in groups that did not experience this heightened level of motivation.

Developmental Activities

1. Brainstorm a potential topic, appropriate for quantitative research. Do you think this topic would be more effectively investigated using a nonexperimental or an experimental approach? Explain your response.

2. Using the topic you brainstormed in Activity 1 above—or perhaps another topic of your choosing—and the general steps for conducting a quantitative research study, briefly sketch out both a nonexperimental and an experimental study to investigate your topic.

3. Based on your responses to Activity 2 above, do you believe that it is possible to *appropriately* and *accurately* investigate the same topic using both experimental and nonexperimental approaches? Why or why not?

4. Consider the following research question: *What is the effect on students' reading comprehension skills of a software program designed to facilitate annotation skills in reading*? Design a true

experimental study to investigate this question, using one of the designs presented in the chapter. Outline several possible threats to the validity of your design and what actions you might take to address those threats.

5. With a topic of your choosing, design a true experimental study to investigate that topic, using one of the designs presented in the chapter. Outline several possible threats to the validity of your design and what actions you might take to address those threats.

Summary

- Quantitative research relies on the collection and analysis of numerical data to describe, explain, predict, or control variables of interest.
- Quantitative research focuses on objectivity that permits the researcher to generalize findings beyond a particular situation or setting.
- Approaches to conducting quantitative research include nonexperimental and experimental designs.
- Nonexperimental research designs comprise techniques where there is no manipulation of any variable in the study. These designs include descriptive research, correlational research, and causal-comparative research.
- Descriptive research focuses on describing and making interpretations about the current status of individuals and settings, and includes observational and survey research.
- In survey research, data are collected from a sample of respondents selected to represent the larger population.

  o There are multiple modes of delivering surveys, including direct administration, mail surveys, telephone surveys, interviews, e-mail surveys, and web-based surveys.

- While electronic surveys have their advantages, they also have numerous technological limitations.
- Three basic types of survey are descriptive surveys, cross-sectional surveys, and longitudinal surveys.
- Three types of longitudinal surveys are trend surveys, panel surveys, and cohort studies.
- Cross-sectional surveys are the most commonly used survey design among educational researchers.
- In survey research, participants are selected so they represent a target population to whom the researcher would like to generalize the results of the study.
- Surveys should be accompanied by a cover letter, which explains the purpose of the study and describes what will be required of participants.
- A strength of survey research is its collection of data from a large number of people. Limitations include potentially low response rates and the time and financial requirements of some modes of data collection.
- Correlational research is designed to discover and possibly measure the relationships between two or more variables.

- Explanatory correlational studies seek to understand and describe related events, conditions, and behaviors.
- Predictive correlational studies predict future conditions or behaviors in one variable from what is known about another variable.

- The basic design for correlational research involves a single group of people who are quantitatively measured on two or more variables that have already happened.
- Relationships are measured by calculating a correlation coefficient, which indicates the direction and strength of the relationship.
- It is critical to remember that "correlation" is not equivalent to "causation."
- Causal-comparative research focuses on exploring the reasons behind existing differences between two or more groups.

  - The presumed cause is the independent variable (also referred to as the grouping variable), and the variable of interest is the dependent variable.
  - Although causal-comparative research cannot explain true cause-and-effect relationships, it is a viable alternative when variables cannot be manipulated due to impracticality or ethics.

- In most quantitative research designs, it is desirable to have a minimum of 30 participants per group.
- The category of experimental research designs includes preexperimental designs, quasi-experimental designs, true experimental designs, and single-subject research designs.
- Generally speaking, all experimental research designs share commonalities, including

participants who are randomly selected and/or randomly assigned to groups, an independent variable that can be manipulated by the researcher, and a common dependent variable that can be measured in all groups in the study.

- Random selection is the process of randomly choosing individuals to participate in a study so that every member of the population has an equal chance of being selected as a member of the sample.
- Random assignment is the process of randomly placing participants in treatment and comparison groups.
- When a study includes random selection *and* random assignment, the study is experimental research; if the study includes *only* random selection, the research is a quasi-experimental study.
- Single-variable designs involve only one manipulated independent variable; factorial designs involve two or more independent variables, at least one of which is manipulated.
- Preexperimental designs are weak and, if used, should be followed by a more stringent research study.
- Quasi-experimental designs come the closest to true experiments, but they still lack random assignment of participants to groups.
- True experimental designs control for nearly all extraneous threats to validity.
- Single-subject research designs are experimental-type studies conducted on individual participants.
- All types of quantitative research designs are subject to threats to validity.
- Internal validity is the degree to which measured differences on the dependent variable are a direct result of the manipulation of the

independent variable and not some other, extraneous condition.

o Threats to internal validity include history, maturation, differential selection of participants, testing effect, instrumentation, statistical regression, attrition, and selection-maturation interaction.

● External validity refers to the extent to which results of a particular study are generalizable to other groups or settings.

o Threats to external validity include population, personological, and ecological validity.

⑤SAGE edge™

Sharpen your skills with SAGE edge!

edge.sagepub.com/mertler

SAGE edge for Students provides a personalized approach to help you accomplish your coursework goals in an easy-to-use learning environment. You'll find action plans, mobile-friendly eFlashcards, and quizzes as well as video, web, and resources and links to SAGE journal articles to support and expand on the concepts presented in this chapter.

8

Mixed-Methods Research

Student Learning Objectives

After studying Chapter 8, students will be able to do the following:

1. List and describe defining characteristics of mixed-methods research

2. Summarize the procedures for conducting mixed-methods research studies

3. List and describe the characteristics of several mixed-methods designs

4. Distinguish between *mixed-methods designs* and *mixed-model designs*

5. Identify and discuss strengths and limitations of mixed-methods research designs

6. Design mixed-methods research studies for a topic of interest

This chapter deals with mixed-methods research, a group of approaches to conducting educational research studies that combines both quantitative and qualitative data. While that description may seem somewhat basic and straightforward, there are many important aspects to the application of mixed-methods designs that the researcher must consider. In this chapter, we will look at the characteristics of mixed-methods research, along with various designs and other important decisions to be made during the process of conducting mixed-methods research studies.

Characteristics of Mixed-Methods Research

The major characteristic of mixed-methods research is that it combines quantitative and qualitative approaches by including both quantitative and qualitative data in a single research study (Gay, Mills, & Airasian, 2009). Creswell and Plano Clark (2011) define mixed-methods research as those studies that include at least one quantitative strand and one qualitative strand. A strand is a component of a study that encompasses the basic process of conducting quantitative or qualitative research: posing a research question, collecting and analyzing data, and interpreting the results. However, these are merely "surface-level" descriptions of the characteristics of mixed-methods research. We will look more closely at specific characteristics in a moment.

Before examining various characteristics of this approach to conducting research, it is important to understand when and how mixed-methods research began. Creswell and Plano Clark (2011) date the beginnings of mixed-methods research back to the mid- to late 1980s. Methodology experts and writers from all around the world seemed to have been simultaneously working on similar ideas regarding the combination of quantitative and qualitative methods. Up to this point in time, many qualitative researchers and quantitative researchers did not see the legitimacy in the *other* approach to doing research. However, members of both research camps began to realize, on a deeper level, the value of the alternate approach. For example, quantitative researchers began to see that qualitative data could play an important role in quantitative research; similarly, qualitative researchers began to see that reporting only qualitative views of the world—and of a few individuals—would not permit generalization of the findings to many other individuals and audiences (Creswell & Plano Clark, 2011). Over the past decade or more, interest in the use of mixed-methods research as a means for studying educational topics and phenomenon has grown substantially.

Between the late 1980s and today, definitions and descriptions of mixed-methods research have shifted and morphed, and they continue to do so. While having a singular definition is desirable for many researchers, Creswell and Plano Clark (2011) have instead offered a definition of *core characteristics* of mixed-methods research. They suggest that their core characteristics provide a broader definition of mixed-methods research, since they combine methods, philosophies, and a research design orientation. These characteristics also highlight the key components that should be considered when designing and conducting a mixed-methods study. These six core characteristics focus on activities of the mixed-methods researcher and include the following actions:

- Collecting and analyzing persuasively and rigorously both qualitative and quantitative data, *based on research questions* [emphasis added]
- Mixing—or integrating or linking—the two forms of data either concurrently by combining or merging them, sequentially by having one build on the other, or embedding one within the other
- Giving priority to one or to both forms of data, *again based on the research questions and the emphasis of the research* [emphasis added]
- Using these procedures in a single research study or in multiple phases of a program of research
- Framing these procedures within philosophical worldviews and theoretical lenses
- Combining the procedures into specific research designs that direct the plan for conducting the study (p. 5)

These core characteristics provide an extremely comprehensive perspective on the critical aspects of engaging in mixed-methods research. You will see them integrated into our discussions as we proceed through this chapter.

Not unlike any other approach to conducting research, when preparing a research study that will use a mixed methodology, the researcher must provide a justification for the use of this approach. Researchers would need to do this even if they were engaged in a study that was purely qualitative or purely quantitative. There are specific situations that would more likely warrant a research approach that capitalizes on the combination of quantitative and qualitative data. Creswell and Plano Clark (2011) have described six scenarios or examples of research problems that are best suited for mixed-methods research:

- *A need exists because one data source may be insufficient.* As you know, qualitative data provide understanding through greater depth, whereas quantitative data provide broader, more general understanding. Each approach has its advantages and limitations. Qualitative data may provide a deep examination of a phenomenon of interest but only with respect to a handful of participants. On the other hand, quantitative data can provide information across a much broader sampling of participants, but the depth of that information is certainly limited. Depending on the goals of a research study—as well as its guiding research questions—one type of data alone may not tell the complete picture or adequately answer the research questions. Additionally, the results from the analysis of qualitative data and those from the collection of quantitative data may be contradictory, which could not have been discovered if only one type or the other was collected and analyzed. Using both types of data in a single research study provides *depth* as well as *breadth*.

- *A need exists to explain initial results.* Sometimes researchers find themselves in situations where the results of the study do not provide complete understanding of the research problem; further explanation is needed. This additional explanation can be provided through the collection and analysis of a *second* set of data that helps explain the results of the *initial* set of data. For example, quantitative data can be used to provide numerical expressions of the relationships among variables or differences between groups, but detailed understanding of what those relationships mean or from where the differences came (i.e., the meanings *behind* the results of the statistical tests) can be provided only by qualitative data collection and analysis, as a follow-up to the initial collection of quantitative data.

- *A need exists to generalize exploratory findings.* As you know from your studies of qualitative research methods, in some research investigations entered into by researchers, the research questions are not known, the variables cannot yet be identified, and the goals of the research cannot be specified at the outset of the study. In these scenarios, an initial phase focused on the collection of qualitative data is necessary simply to *explore* the setting or participants involved. Once there is enhanced general knowledge of the research situation, the qualitative phase can be followed up with a quantitative study to generalize and test what was learned from the initial exploration.

- *A need exists to enhance a study with a second method.* In some research situations, a second method can be added to provide *enhanced* understanding of some phase of research that has been conducted. For example, a researcher could add a qualitative component to enhance an experimental, correlational, or causal-comparative study. Similarly, quantitative data could be added to enhance the findings of an ethnographic, narrative, or grounded theory research study. In these situations, however, the second method is *embedded* or *nested* within the primary method. The design of this approach should not be confused with the one described above, where the second method is used as a *follow-up* to the initial method of data collection.

- *A need exists to best employ a theoretical stance.* There may be a particular research situation where a theoretical perspective dictates the need to collect both quantitative and qualitative data. All data could either be collected simultaneously or sequentially, with one form of data building on the other. The application of a particular theoretical viewpoint may determine this specific need.

- *A need exists to understand a research objective through multiple research phases.* Many research studies require multiple research phases—which may or may not be viewed as individual, separate studies—whereby researchers may need to connect several seemingly independent studies to achieve the overall research goal. This is a common approach used in comprehensive and/or multiyear evaluation or other types of longitudinal studies. As with the previous need, data may be collected simultaneously or sequentially. If the phases of data collection are simultaneous, or occur relatively close in time, we refer to the study as a **multiphase mixed-methods research study**; if the phases of data collection are distinctly separated by substantial periods of time, we might refer to the study as a **multiproject mixed-methods study**.

These scenarios illustrate situations in which mixed-methods research would be an appropriate design for investigating the particular problems. Although this list is not necessarily exhaustive, these cases and explanations can certainly serve as justifications for the researchers' need to use a particular mixed-methods research design. In many cases, researchers may combine some of these six explanations to provide the most accurate justification for the use of mixed-methods designs. As you will also see later in the chapter, these six research problems lay the groundwork for and parallel the various designs of mixed-methods research we will examine shortly.

The Mixed-Methods Research Process

As you might expect, the process for conducting mixed-methods research closely parallels the general process for conducting educational research, presented in Chapter 2. That being said, there are some unique aspects to consider in the process of conducting mixed-methods research. The entire process is outlined and described below (Creswell, 2005; Fraenkel, Wallen, & Hyun, 2012); however, if you compare these steps with those described in Chapter 2, you will notice the additional, unique aspects in the process of conducting mixed-methods research:

1. *Identification of the research problem to be studied.* As we have seen numerous times in this book, the clear identification and specification of a research topic is the first step in any study. Consider that you may want to include both quantitative and qualitative data; however, do not become overly concerned about balancing the two forms of data at this point in the process.

2. *Determination of whether a mixed-methods study is feasible.* If you believe that your study will benefit from the use of quantitative and qualitative data, you must consider what this entails. First and foremost, you must have well-developed skills in gathering both quantitative and qualitative data. Gathering both types of data will also be more time-consuming; so you must factor in the desired timetable for your study. Additionally, you must have the appropriate skills to analyze both types of data. Finally, it is important to consider the make-up of potential audiences for your research—those audiences should be able to understand and have an appreciation for the complexity of mixed-methods designs. If any of the above conditions are not adequately satisfied, a mixed-methods study is likely not feasible.

3. *Development of a clear and sound rationale for doing a mixed-methods study.* Provided the study is feasible, you should consider and be prepared to answer questions of *why* you are collecting both quantitative and qualitative data, *why* both types of data are necessary, and *how* the study will be enhanced as a result of doing so. Again, if you cannot be clear and explicit in providing a rationale, a mixed-methods study may not be appropriate.

4. *Identification of the appropriate mixed-methods design to guide your data collection.* We will discuss mixed-methods designs shortly, but for now you will need to determine the following aspects of your data collection strategy:

- The priority you will give to quantitative and qualitative data
- The sequence of your data collection, if you do not plan to collect both types of data simultaneously
- The specific forms of quantitative and qualitative data you will collect

The determinations you make regarding these three items will typically align with a particular mixed-methods research design, which you should identify for inclusion in your final research report.

5. *Development of research questions for both quantitative and qualitative methods.* In a mixed-methods study, researchers typically delineate research questions that pertain specifically to the analysis of quantitative data and ones that pertain specifically to the analysis of qualitative data. It is possible also to add research questions that can be answered by the *combination* of the interpretations of both kinds of analysis. Depending on the nature of your study, some of the research questions may need to emerge during the course of the study. For example, if you are collecting quantitative data to be followed with collection of qualitative data, those qualitative research questions will likely depend on the outcomes of the quantitative data analysis. (*It is important to note that Steps 4 and 5 may occur in reverse order or concurrently.*)

6. *Review of related literature and development of a written review.* Reviewing related literature provides the same benefits we have discussed in previous chapters—guiding aspects of your study and contextualizing your study. You should develop a thorough written review of the pertinent body of literature to be included in your final research report.

7. *Collection of data.* Qualitative and quantitative procedures for the collection of data, which will be described in full in Chapters 11 and 12, are appropriate for mixed-methods research as well. In fact, there are no differences in data collection procedures—quantitative data in a mixed-methods study are collected just as quantitative data in any study would be, and the same holds true for qualitative data. The only caveat, however, is that care must be taken to ensure that data are collected so they parallel the mixed-methods research design you specified earlier.

8. *Analysis of data.* Similarly, data analysis proceeds just as presented in Chapters 11 and 13. The exception is that you must determine—based on the mixed-methods designed you are using—whether you will analyze quantitative data separately from qualitative data or integrate the two types of data analysis. Again, you must ensure that you are following the particular process outlined by the specific mixed-methods research design you chose.

9. *Development of conclusions and recommendations.* You must draw conclusions, inferences, and recommendations directly from the interpretation of results of the data analysis. Once again, however, you must ensure that you are interpreting the data appropriately; in other words, you must determine if the interpretations of your analytical results will be drawn separately and sequentially, or if they will be done in an integrated, concurrent manner.

10. *Preparation of a final research report.* The final step in conducting a mixed-methods research study is to prepare the final research report. There is some variation in developing a report of mixed-methods research, compared with a report of *just* quantitative or *just* qualitative research. Specifically, the report should parallel your data analysis and interpretation of results. For example, if your study involved separate data collection, analysis, and interpretation for your quantitative data and qualitative data, your report should contain two separate sections for the collection, analysis, and interpretation— one for each type of data. In contrast, if your analysis and interpretation were integrated into one process across both types of data, you should include only one section reporting the combination of quantitative and qualitative data. Thus, the data analysis section is an attempt to converge both types of data into a single set of results and interpretations, relating directly back to the research problem and guiding questions.

Approaches to Conducting Mixed-Methods Research

Numerous mixed-methods design classifications exist in the literature. Creswell and Plano Clark (2011) have identified a minimum of 15 typological schemes for classifying the variety of mixed-methods research designs. Some of these schemes consist of as few as two specific designs, whereas others have as many as 10. For purposes of our discussions here, we will focus our attention on the six prototypical or most common mixed-methods research designs (Creswell & Plano Clark, 2011; Leedy & Ormrod, 2013). These designs include the convergence parallel design, the explanatory sequential design, the exploratory sequential design, the embedded design, the transformative design, and the multiphase design.

Mixed-Methods Research Designs

Mixed-methods research designs are essentially differentiated by (1) the priorities assigned to the two different types of data, (2) the sequence in which the two types of data are collected, and (3) the nature of the analytical procedures (i.e., whether the data will be analyzed individually or in an integrated process). In addition to describing each of the designs in the following sections, I will also present them to you visually, through a common notational system often used to represent mixed-methods research designs (Creswell & Plano Clark, 2011). A listing of the notations and symbols commonly used to describe these designs, along with the meanings of those symbols, is provided in Table 8.1. Knowledge of this notational system is important for the mixed-methods researcher for two reasons: First, it is possible that, within the discussions of models

TABLE 8.1 ● Summary of Notations Used to Describe Mixed-Methods Research Designs

Notation	Example	What the Notation Means
Shorthand: Quan, Qual	Quan	Signifies the quantitative strand of data collection.
All uppercase letters: QUAN, QUAL	QUAL	The qualitative methods are prioritized more heavily in the design.
All lowercase letters: quan, qual	quan	The quantitative methods have a lesser priority in the design.
Plus sign: +	QUAN + QUAL	The quantitative and qualitative methods occur concurrently.
Arrow: →	QUAN → qual	The methods occur in a sequence of QUAN followed by qual.
Parentheses: ( )	QUAN (qual)	A method is embedded within a larger design or procedure, or mixed with a theoretical or program-objective framework.
Double arrows: →←	QUAL →← QUAN	The methods are implemented in a recursive process. (QUAL → QUAN → QUAL → QUAN → etc.)

Notation	Example	What the Notation Means
Brackets: [ ]	QUAL → QUAN → [QUAN + qual]	Mixed-methods [QUAN → qual] is used within a single study or a project within a series of studies.
Equal sign: =	QUAN → qual = Explain results	The purpose for mixing methods is explicated within the notational model.

Source: Adapted from Creswell and Plano Clark (2011).

and designs we will have shortly, variations may be developed to customize the mixed-methods design for a particular purpose. Second, this notational system can be used to convey to various audiences the complexity of mixed-methods designs in a straightforward, easy-to-understand manner.

The first design we will examine is the convergent parallel design. In a **convergent parallel design** (sometimes referred to as a **convergent design**), the researcher collects quantitative and qualitative data at the same time, and typically with perspectives and research questions. The data collection methods are prioritized in an equal manner; that is, one type of data is not given priority, or greater importance, over the other. Quantitative and qualitative data are analyzed independently, but then the results are mixed to achieve an overall interpretation. This is quite similar to a process of *triangulation*, where the researcher hopes that analyses of both data sets will lead to similar and supporting conclusions with respect to the research questions being investigated. The convergent parallel design, along with its notational diagram, is depicted in Figure 8.1.

FIGURE 8.1   ●   Convergent Parallel Mixed-Methods Research Design

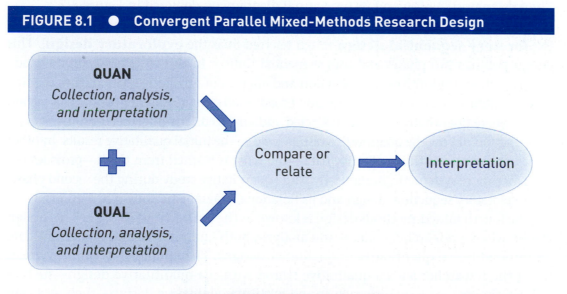

QUAN + QUAL = *Converge results*

Source: Adapted from Creswell and Plano Clark (2011).

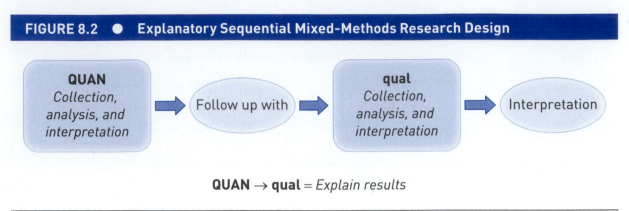

FIGURE 8.2 ●   Explanatory Sequential Mixed-Methods Research Design

QUAN → qual = *Explain results*

Source: Adapted from Creswell and Plano Clark (2011).

The second mixed-methods design is the explanatory sequential design. The **explanatory sequential design** (sometimes simply referred to as the **explanatory design**) occurs in distinct interactive phases. This design begins with the collection and analysis of quantitative data, which is assigned priority by the researcher (remember that this decision is usually guided by the nature of the research questions). The second phase of the study is characterized by the collection of qualitative data. In practice, quantitative data are collected, analyzed, and interpreted first; the nature of those interpretations—along with any unanswered questions or interpretations in need of further explanation—provides guidance for the collection of qualitative data during the second phase. The qualitative data are then analyzed and interpreted in terms of how those results help *explain* the initial quantitative results. In other words, this design allows the researcher to build on the numerical results by digging deeper into the thoughts, beliefs, and perceptions of participants during the second phase. The explanatory design and its procedural diagram are depicted in Figure 8.2.

The third design is essentially a reverse of the explanatory design and is called the **exploratory sequential design** (often referred to as the **exploratory design**). This design also has two phases and uses sequential timing. In this case, however, the study begins with and prioritizes the collection and analysis of qualitative data during the first phase. Building on those exploratory and broad results, the researcher conducts a second phase, where quantitative data are collected and analyzed. The interpretation involves an examination of how the quantitative results *build on* the initial qualitative results. In other words, the nature of the qualitative data—and what is learned from them—provides the basis for a more systematic, numerically based quantitative study during the second phase. The exploratory sequential design and its notational diagram are shown in Figure 8.3.

The fourth mixed-methods design is known as the **embedded design**. This design is used when a researcher collects and analyzes both quantitative and qualitative data within traditional quantitative or qualitative designs. The "embedded" portion comes when the researcher adds a qualitative strand within a quantitative design—such as an experiment—or a quantitative strand within a qualitative design—such as a case study. The embedded design is intended to enhance the overall design in some manner by incorporating the alternative type of data and analysis. The embedded design, along with the notational diagram for both cases, is shown in Figure 8.4.

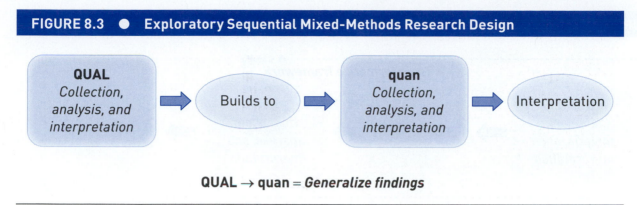

FIGURE 8.3 ● Exploratory Sequential Mixed-Methods Research Design

QUAL → quan = *Generalize findings*

Source: Adapted from Creswell and Plano Clark (2011).

The previous designs represent the four basic mixed-methods research designs. The two additional models we will now discuss are examples of mixed-methods research that brings multiple design elements together within a single study, or within a singular research purpose. The **transformative design** is a mixed-methods design whereby the researcher conducts the entire study within a transformative theoretical framework (Creswell & Plano Clark, 2011). All the researcher's key decisions are made within the context of a transformative framework. In the diagram of this model, shown in Figure 8.5, the focus on a theoretical model is highlighted by the dashed line that surrounds the other components of the model, indicating that the theoretical framework "surrounds" all aspects of the mixed-methods research study.

The sixth and final model we will address is known as the **multiphase design**. The multiphase design combines both sequential and concurrent strands over a period of time in which the researcher is implementing multiple studies, all of which have an overall

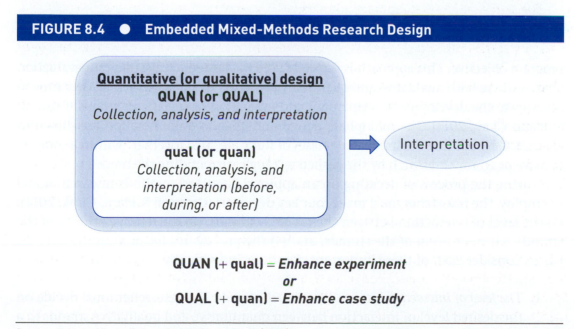

FIGURE 8.4 ● Embedded Mixed-Methods Research Design

QUAN (+ qual) = *Enhance experiment*
or
QUAL (+ quan) = *Enhance case study*

Source: Adapted from Creswell and Plano Clark (2011).

FIGURE 8.5 ● **Transformative Mixed-Methods Research Design**

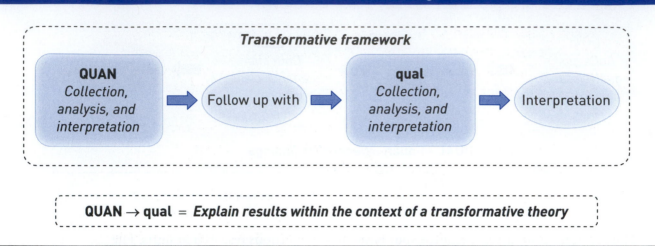

Source: Adapted from Creswell and Plano Clark (2011).

FIGURE 8.6 ● **Multiphase Mixed-Methods Research Design**

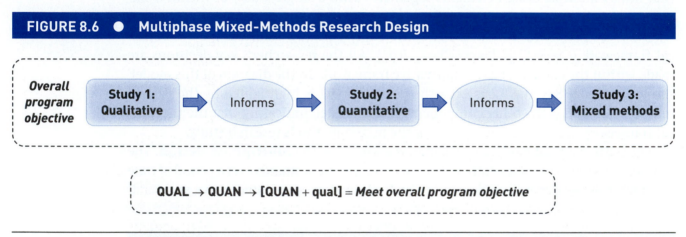

Source: Adapted from Creswell and Plano Clark (2011).

program objective. This approach is typically used in comprehensive program evaluation studies where both qualitative and quantitative approaches are implemented over time to investigate the development, adaptation, and evaluation of specific programs (Creswell & Plano Clark, 2011). The multiphase design and its procedural notation are shown in Figure 8.6. Notice that the individual phases of study are "tied together" within a comprehensive program of research by the dashed rectangle surrounding the model.

During the process of deciding on an appropriate mixed-methods research model to employ, the researcher must make four key decisions (Creswell & Plano Clark, 2011): (1) the level of interaction between the research strands, (2) the relative priority of the strands, (3) the timing of the strands, and (4) the procedures for mixing the strands. Let us consider each of these important questions individually.

1. *The level of interaction between the research strands.* The researcher must decide on the desired level of interaction between quantitative and qualitative strands in a mixed-methods study. The **level of interaction** is the extent to which the two

strands remain independent or interact with each other. Two levels of interaction exist: an independent level and an interactive level.

- When a researcher uses an **independent level of interaction**, the qualitative and quantitative strands—that is, the research questions, data collection, and data analysis—are kept entirely separate. The only "mixing" between the two strands occurs at the end of the study when the researcher draws conclusions from the *overall* interpretation of all data analyses.
- An **interactive level of interaction** occurs when the researcher mixes the two methods, which can occur at different points in the process but must occur prior to the final interpretation of results.

2. *The relative priority of the quantitative and qualitative research strands.* The researcher must make decisions with respect to the relative importance assigned to each strand within the design. **Priority** refers to this relative importance or weighting of quantitative and qualitative methods as a means of answering the guiding research questions. There are three possible prioritization options for any mixed-methods design:

- Quantitative and qualitative methods may receive *equal prioritization* so that each plays an equally important role in addressing the research questions.
- A researcher may assign a *quantitative priority*; that is, greater emphasis is placed on the quantitative data and subsequent analyses, and the qualitative methods fulfill a secondary or supplemental role.
- The reverse scenario occurs when assigning a *qualitative priority*; greater emphasis is placed on qualitative data and analyses, and quantitative methods are used in a supplemental manner.

3. *The timing of the research strands.* **Timing** deals with the temporal relationship between quantitative and qualitative strands in a mixed-methods study. We often discuss timing as it relates to data collection; however, timing actually relates to the entirety of the quantitative and qualitative strands, not just to data collection. There are three methods for classifying timing:

- **Concurrent timing** occurs when a researcher implements both quantitative and qualitative strands simultaneously during the same phase of the study.
- **Sequential timing** occurs when the researcher implements the study in two distinct phases. Collection and analysis of one type of data begins *only after* collection and analysis of the other type of data.
- Finally, **multiphase combination timing** occurs when the researcher implements multiple phases that include sequential and/or concurrent timing. This is typically used in broader programs of research, where there are clearly distinct and separate studies or phases.

4. *The procedures for mixing the two research strands.* **Mixing** is defined as the intentional integration of the study's quantitative and qualitative strands. The stage at which integration occurs is known as the **point of interface**. There are four possible points of interface between quantitative and qualitative strands (Creswell & Plano Clark, 2011):

- *Mixing during interpretation*—Mixing occurs during the final step of the research process after both sets of data have been collected and analyzed independently; it involves a process of drawing conclusions or inferences that reflect both sets of analyses.
- *Mixing during data analysis*—Mixing occurs during the process of analyzing quantitative and qualitative data, where the two sets of results are merged in a process of combined analysis.
- *Mixing during data collection*—Mixing occurs during the stage of a study where the researcher collects a second set of data; the results from the analysis of the first strand build to and guide the collection of the second type of data.
- *Mixing at the level of research design*—Mixing occurs during the larger design stage of the research process; in essence, quantitative and qualitative methods are intertwined throughout the study.

Mixed-methods research designs focus on the duality of data collection, analysis, and interpretation. However, much more complex models for integrating aspects of quantitative and qualitative research also exist. These are known as **mixed-model studies**— as opposed to mixed-*methods* studies—and typically involve the mixing of quantitative and qualitative approaches to research in three areas of the research process: (1) the type of investigation—confirmatory (typically quantitative) versus exploratory (typically qualitative); (2) quantitative data collection and designs versus qualitative data collection and designs; and (3) statistical analysis and inference versus qualitative analysis and inference (Fraenkel et al., 2012). As with mixed-methods research designs, there is also a classification system for mixed-model research designs. However, these models are much more complex—at least some of the designs with combinations of the three phases of research rarely occur in practice (Fraenkel et al., 2012)—and, therefore, those models will not be discussed further in our examination of mixed-methods research.

Validity in Mixed-Methods Research

As with any approach to conducting educational research, the researcher must always ensure that the measurement techniques have resulted in valid indicators of the variables, as well as valid overall research conclusions and inferences. As always, the researcher should be concerned with the study's internal validity, external validity, and credibility and trustworthiness (see Chapters 6 and 7; you will learn more about these qualities of data and research in Chapters 11 and 12).

Leedy and Ormrod (2013) suggest that researchers consider and be able to address several questions whenever they conduct a mixed-methods research study. Many of these questions relate directly to important decisions—discussed in earlier sections of this chapter—that must be made regarding the mixed-methods research design selected for a given study, as well as the integration of quantitative and qualitative methods:

- Are the samples used for the quantitative and qualitative components of the study sufficiently similar in order to justify comparisons between the two types of data?
- Are the quantitative and qualitative data equally relevant to the same or similar topics and research questions?

- Are the two types of data weighted equally in drawing conclusions? If not, what is the justification for prioritization of one type over the other?
- Are you able to use specific qualitative statements or artifacts in the study in order to support or illustrate some of the quantitative results?
- Can obvious discrepancies between the two types of data be resolved? (p. 262)

The researcher must be able to respond positively to these questions; otherwise, the validity and legitimacy of the research and its ultimate findings and inferences may be called into question by the study's intended audiences. This is a big reason for justifying mixed-methods decisions at the outset of the study.

Strengths and Limitations of Mixed-Methods Research

Mixed-methods research has numerous strengths and advantages. First, it can help explain, clarify, and extend results discovered through the use of only one research methodology. Conclusions related to various relationships between variables, group differences, or even group dynamics in a social setting can be enhanced and extended through the collection of the complementary type of data and subsequent analysis. Second, in some instances, research questions may require both types of data to obtain adequate answers. Relying on a single plan for data collection and analysis may limit the researcher in terms of his or her ability to provide such an answer; in this case, the researcher may have no choice but to adapt the research question to fit the data—a practice that is considered unethical and, therefore, is not recommended.

Third, one of the distinct advantages of mixed-methods research is that the strengths of one type of data and analysis can often be used to offset the weaknesses of the other. Qualitative researchers often argue that quantitative research is too objective and does not allow individual participants to share their personal beliefs and perceptions; similarly, quantitative researchers argue that qualitative data can be too easily influenced by one or two participants. Integrating the two types of data allows a researcher to use the strengths of each type while at the same time adequately addressing aspects considered to be weaknesses or limitations. Finally, mixed-methods research is often seen as being more "practical" (Creswell & Plano Clark, 2011). Researchers are not limited to *one* kind of data or *one* form of analysis. The world in which we live typically requires—or at least encourages—multiple perspectives, and mixed-methods research allows for inclusion of those multiple perspectives within a single research study.

Mixed-methods research is not without its limitations. First and foremost, it is much more time-consuming than approaching a research study from a singular methodological perspective. Integrating different types of data collection and analysis, or developing a plan for sequential data collection and analysis, can be an extremely lengthy process. Additionally, many researchers have their own personal limitations in terms of experience and comfort with only one type of research methodology. Even if researchers are "comfortable" in both realms, they typically have a tendency to lean to either the quantitative or qualitative side. This means they will have *some* limitations—even if they are limitations of comfort or experience—that will hinder their ability to successfully design and conduct a mixed-methods research study. Of course, this can be effectively overcome through the use of research teams, where researchers who lean toward the quantitative side can partner with those who lean toward the qualitative side. In this way, they can combine their skills and expertise to design a highly effective mixed-methods study.

Finally, not only because many researchers see mixed-methods research as still growing and developing but also because many researchers possess an apparent "inherent gravitation" toward one form of research or the other, many people still need convincing when it comes to the utility and legitimacy of mixed-methods research (Creswell & Plano Clark, 2011). Some researchers still see it as a new research approach, whereas others may simply have a philosophical dislike for the mixing of methods. Regardless, if you see the value in mixed-methods research and plan to engage in its practice, you should be prepared to defend those decisions among your peers and colleagues.

Developmental Activities

1. What do you see as the greatest strength and the greatest limitation of mixed-methods research? Explain your answers.

2. Locate two to three examples of published mixed-methods research studies. Read and review the studies, and then use the notational system presented in this chapter to diagram the research designs used in these studies.

3. Identify a potential research topic of interest to you. Describe how you could study your topic using the four basic mixed-methods research designs (i.e., convergent, explanatory sequential, exploratory sequential, and embedded designs) as presented in this chapter.

Write a one-paragraph description of the application of each model to your topic. Finally, select one that you think would be the best fit to study your particular topic.

4. In your answer to Activity 3 above, did you struggle with the application of any of the four designs to your topic? Did you feel the need to adapt your topic to fit the designs? Explain your answers.

5. Based on the design you selected as a best fit for your study in Activity 3 above, what challenges do you think you might face in applying that design? Discuss the challenges you anticipate and how you might address them within this design.

Summary

- Mixed-methods research studies combine both quantitative and qualitative data.
- Mixed-methods studies include at least one quantitative strand and one qualitative strand.

- Six core characteristics help define mixed-methods research:

  o Persuasively and rigorously collecting and analyzing both qualitative and quantitative data

- Mixing the two forms of data either simultaneously by combining or merging them, sequentially by having one build on the other, or by embedding one within the other
- Giving priority to one or both forms of data
- Using these procedures in a single research study or in multiple phases of a program of research
- Framing the procedures within philosophical worldviews and theoretical lenses
- Combining the procedures into specific research designs that direct the plan for conducting the study

- When using a mixed-methods approach to conducting a research study, a researcher must provide justification for this choice. Six examples of research problems that are suited for mixed-methods techniques are as follows:

  - A need exists because one data source may be insufficient.
  - A need exists to explain the initial results.
  - A need exists to generalize exploratory findings.
  - A need exists to enhance a study with a second method.
  - A need exists to best employ a theoretical stance.
  - A need exists to understand a research objective through multiple research phases.

- The mixed-methods research process closely parallels the generic research process; however, there are some additional, unique steps:

  - Determining if a mixed-methods study is feasible
  - Developing a clear rationale for doing a mixed-methods study

  - Identifying the appropriate mixed-methods design

- There are numerous typological schemes for classifying mixed-methods research designs.
- Mixed-methods designs are differentiated by

  - the priorities assigned to the two types of data,
  - the sequence in which the two types of data are collected, and
  - the nature of the analytical procedures.

- The four most common and basic mixed-methods research designs are

  - the convergent parallel design, or simply the convergent design;
  - the explanatory sequential design, or simply the explanatory design;
  - the exploratory sequential design, or simply the exploratory design; and
  - the embedded design.

- The researcher must make four key decisions when deciding on an appropriate mixed-methods research design:

  - The level of interaction between the research strands—independent or interactive
  - The relative priority of the quantitative and qualitative research strands—equal prioritization, quantitative prioritization, or qualitative prioritization
  - The timing of the research strands—concurrent, sequential, or multiphase combination timing
  - The procedures for mixing the two strands—defining the point of interface (during interpretation, during data analysis, during data collection, or at the level of research design)

- Mixed-model studies involve the mixing of quantitative and qualitative approaches in all phases of the research process.
- Determining the validity of mixed-methods research parallels the process of determining the validity of both quantitative and qualitative research; however, several additional considerations must be met.
- The strengths of mixed-methods research include that it can help explain, clarify, and extend results of research; it can answer research questions that may require both types of data; one type of data and analysis may be used to offset the weaknesses of the other; and it is seen as more practical.
- Limitations of these approaches include that it is more time-consuming, researchers may be limited by their own comfort and expertise, and mixed-methods research may still need to be justified to some audiences.

$SAGE edge™

Sharpen your skills with SAGE edge!

edge.sagepub.com/mertler

SAGE edge for Students provides a personalized approach to help you accomplish your coursework goals in an easy-to-use learning environment. You'll find action plans, mobile-friendly eFlashcards, and quizzes as well as video, web, and resources and links to SAGE journal articles to support and expand on the concepts presented in this chapter.

Action Research

This chapter deals with the topic of action research—research conducted directly by educational practitioners. While action research typically follows the general process of conducting educational research, all action research studies share some unique qualities. In this chapter, you will learn about the characteristics of action research, the process for conducting this type of research, various approaches to action research, some of its unique qualities, validity in action research, as well as its strengths and limitations.

Characteristics of Action Research

Over the past 10 to 15 years, action research has begun to capture the attention of teachers, administrators, and policymakers around the country (Mills, 2014). *Action research studies* encompass any systematic inquiries conducted by teachers, administrators, counselors, or others with a vested interest in the teaching and learning process or environment, for the purpose of gathering information about how their particular schools operate, how they teach, and how their students learn (Mills, 2014). Further, action research is characterized as research that is done *by* educators *for* themselves. It is truly a systematic inquiry into one's own practice (Johnson, 2008). For example, action research allows teachers to study their own classrooms—that is, their own instructional methods, their own students, and their own assessments—to better understand them and improve their quality or effectiveness. A critical aspect of action research is that it focuses specifically on the unique characteristics of the population with whom a practice is employed or some action must be taken. This, in turn, results in increased utility and effectiveness for the educational practitioner (Parsons & Brown, 2002).

For decades, there has been pressure from both public and governmental sources for improvement in our schools. The public, often provoked by the mass media, have criticized schools for low levels of achievement in math, science, reading, writing, and history (Schmuck, 1997), and for not keeping academic pace with nations around the world. It is not uncommon for school improvement leaders to look toward the enormous body of educational research literature as a means of guiding their improvement efforts. However, many practitioners find that formal academic research is neither helpful nor applicable to their particular setting (Mertler, 2014). This is largely because traditional educational researchers sometimes impose research findings on schools, with little or no attention paid to local variation (i.e., not all schools are the same) and required adaptations (i.e., the extent to which research findings generalize across entire populations; Metz & Page, 2002). Due to this continued imposition of more-traditional research findings, there is a real need for the increased practice of educator-initiated, school- and classroom-based action research (Mertler, 2014).

Action research offers a process by which *current* educational practice can be changed to *better* practice. The overarching goal of action research is to improve practice *immediately* within one or a few classrooms or schools (McMillan, 2012). Because action research is largely about examining one's own practice, reflection is an integral part of the process. **Reflection** is the act of critically exploring what you are doing, why you decided to do it, and what its effects have been. For teachers to be effective, they must become active participants in their classrooms, as well as active observers of the learning process; they must analyze and interpret classroom information—collected in a systematic manner—and then use that information as a basis for future planning and decision making (Parsons & Brown, 2002). **Reflective teaching** is a process of developing lessons or assessing student learning with thoughtful consideration of educational theory, existing research, and practical experience, along with analysis of the lesson's effect on student learning (Parsons & Brown, 2002). This process of systematic collection of information followed by active reflection—all with the aim of improving the teaching process—is the heart of action research (Mertler, 2014).

Even though action research has been practiced for decades, there are still some misconceptions as to what it is and is not. Clarifying these misconceptions is an important component of understanding the uniqueness and appropriateness of action research as an approach to conducting research in education. The following list, compiled from several sources (Johnson, 2008; Mertler, 2014; Mertler & Charles, 2011; Mills, 2014; Schmuck, 1997), is an attempt to provide a description of what action research *is*.

Action research is

- a process that improves education, in general, by incorporating change;
- a process involving educators working together to improve their own practices;
- persuasive and authoritative, since it is done *by* educators *for* themselves;
- collaborative—that is, composed of educators talking and working with other educators in empowering relationships;
- participative, since educators are integral members—not disinterested outsiders—of the research process;
- practical and relevant to classroom teachers and other educators, since it allows them direct access to research findings that are directly applicable;
- about developing critical reflection on one's teaching and the educational process in general;
- a planned, systematic approach to understanding the learning process;
- a process that requires us to "test" our ideas about education;
- open-minded;
- a critical analysis of educational places of work;
- a cyclical process of planning, acting, developing, and reflecting;
- a justification of one's teaching practices.

It is also critical to understand exactly what action research is *not* (Johnson, 2008; Mertler, 2014; Mertler & Charles, 2011; Mills, 2011; Schmuck, 1997):

Action research is not

- the usual thing teachers do when thinking about teaching but, rather, much more systematic and collaborative;
- simply problem solving but, rather, involves the specification of a problem, the development of something new (in many instances), and critical reflection on its effectiveness;
- done *to* or *by* other people but, rather, by particular educators, on their own work, with students and colleagues;
- the simple implementation of predetermined answers to educational questions but, rather, explores, discovers, and works to find creative solutions to educational problems;
- conclusive—the results of action research are neither right nor wrong but, rather, serve as tentative solutions that are based on observations and other data collection and require monitoring and evaluation to identify strengths and limitations;
- a fad—good teaching has always involved the systematic examination of the instructional process and its effects on student learning. Educators are always looking for ways to improve instructional practice, and although teachers seldom have referred to this process of observation, revision, and reflection as *research*, when done systematically and scientifically, that is exactly what it is.

At this point, you may find yourself asking a basic—albeit legitimate—question: *Why would I want to get involved in an action research project, especially with all the demands and responsibilities placed on me as an educator today?* Mertler and Charles (2011) have provided at least some partial answers to this question:

> [First,] action research deals with your problems, not someone else's. Second, action research is very timely; it can start now—or whenever you are ready—and provides immediate results. Third, action research provides educators with opportunities to better understand, and therefore improve, their educational practices. Fourth, as a process, action research can also promote the building of stronger relationships among colleagues with whom we work. Finally, and possibly most importantly, action research provides educators with alternative ways of viewing and approaching educational questions and problems and with new ways of examining our own educational practices. (pp. 339–340)

Unfortunately, the answers to this initial question often prompt another query: *If the benefits are so substantial, why doesn't everyone do action research?* Again, Mertler and Charles (2011) suggest answers to this question:

> First, although its popularity has increased over the past decade, action research is still relatively unknown when compared to more traditional forms of conducting research. Second, although it may not seem the case, action research is more difficult to conduct than traditional approaches to research. Educators themselves are responsible for implementing the resultant changes, but also for conducting the research. Third, action research does not conform to many of the requirements of conventional research with which you may be familiar—it is therefore less structured and more difficult to conduct. Finally, because of the lack of fit between standard research requirements and the process of conducting action research, you may find it more difficult to write up your results. (p. 340)

These responses to sometimes hypothetical—or, in some cases, very real—questions provide compelling reasons for both conducting and not conducting action research projects. It is important to understand how and under what circumstances action research can be implemented effectively and efficiently in educational environments. We now look at five important reasons for using action research in educational settings: to effectively connect theory to practice, to improve educational practice, to foster school improvement, to empower teachers, and as a means for promoting professional growth (Mertler, 2014).

● *Connecting theory to practice.* For decades, we have believed that the best way for research to inform practice is for research findings to filter down from the researchers to the classroom; however, there is typically a disconnect during this process, results do not effectively filter down, and we are left with gaps between what is learned by researchers and what is needed by practicing educators. Action research conducted by educators for themselves can provide one possible mechanism for bridging this gap.

- *Improving educational practice.* A main focus of action research is the improvement of classroom and school practices; however, engaging in these efforts often requires a shift in mind-set for teachers, as well as for other practicing educators. Educators must learn to be reflective and critical of their own practices; once they do this, they open themselves up to the facilitation of better-informed educational decision making. This systematic and critical reflection on one's own professional performance has the potential to result in the direct improvement of educational practice.

- *Fostering school improvement.* As an entity, school improvement is seen as a large-scale, systemic type of improvement. In other words, the goal of school improvement is widespread, far-reaching effort. At first consideration, this seems counterintuitive with the individualized focus of action research; however, if action research is conducted in a *collaborative* manner—across classrooms, departments, grade levels, perhaps even school buildings—it has the potential to lead to the widespread, cohesive, and systemic improvement of instruction and learning.

- *Empowering teachers and other educators.* Action research advances the notion of *teacher empowerment.* When teachers and other educators take the initiative to systematically and critically investigate their own practice by collecting data and making informed decisions, they become much more empowered in the process of educational improvement. They begin to assume leadership roles—at least with respect to informed decision making in their classrooms. This type of leadership and empowerment works in opposition to the traditional top-down administrative model. That is not to say that the decision-making and leadership skills of building- and district-level administrators are not needed—they are most certainly necessary for a school and district to function effectively—but a degree of control is returned to the classroom level when educators become empowered through an action research process.

- *Promoting professional growth.* The focus of action research is on improving practice, finding out what works and does not work in an educational setting. In many respects, it is about growing, developing, and improving as a professional educator. However, it does not subscribe to the more traditional "one-size-fits-all" views of professional development, which typically takes the form of a training session where the focus is the same for every attendee (Mertler, 2013). In this type of professional development, educators are not afforded the opportunity to focus on what they as *individuals* need to improve their professional practice. This model of professional development focuses on *learning* as opposed to *training.* A true benefit of engaging in classroom- or school-based action research is that educators can truly focus on and direct their own professional growth and development in specific areas *they* want to target (Mertler, 2013). Educators see this type of professional development as being much more meaningful and practical. Routine engagement in a process of action research is, perhaps, the epitome of *individualized* and *customizable* professional development for educators.

Approaches to Conducting Action Research

Generally speaking, there are two approaches to—or types of—action research: *participatory action research* and *practical action research*. The purpose of **participatory**

action research is to improve the quality of organizations, communities, and family lives (Creswell, 2005). The broad idea behind this approach to research is to empower individuals and groups to improve their lives and bring about social change at some level (Fraenkel, Wallen, & Hyun, 2012). As you can imagine, to achieve these goals, the research must involve a sizeable number of people who represent diverse experiences and viewpoints, and who are all focused on the same problem. In various sources of literature, you may also see participatory action research referred to as *community-based inquiry*, *collaborative action research*, *emancipatory action research*, or *critical action research* (Creswell, 2005; Fraenkel et al., 2012; Gay, Mills, & Airasian, 2009).

In contrast, **practical action research** is intended to address a specific problem in a classroom, school, or other community (Fraenkel et al., 2012). Its focus is more on the "how-to" approach to the process of conducting action research, and it has much less of a philosophical orientation compared with participatory action research (Gay et al., 2009). Its applications, however, are not limited to educational settings; it has been and continues to be conducted in a variety of settings, including education, social services, and business. Guiding assumptions for the implementation of practical action research include the following (Gay et al., 2009):

- Individual teachers or teams of teachers are able to determine the nature of an action research investigation to be undertaken.
- Action researchers are committed to continuous professional development and school improvement through a process of critical reflection.
- Action researchers are capable of choosing their own areas of focus, determining plans for conducting the research, and developing action plans based on their findings.

For the purposes of this book, our coverage of action research will be restricted to practical action research.

The Action Research Process

One of the most important aspects of action research is that it is a *cyclical*—as opposed to linear—process. In general, the process begins by identifying a central problem or topic, which often requires an examination of current practice. Some observation, monitoring, or other form of data collection and analysis occurs. This results in an action being taken—along with professional reflection—which then serves as the basis for the next stage in the cycle of action research (Mills, 2014). Many research experts have developed models of action research, most of which share common elements. My general model of action research, showing these four elements in a cyclical manner, appears in Figure 9.1. The four stages of this model are

- the *planning* stage,
- the *acting* stage,
- the *developing* stage, and
- the *reflecting* stage.

Notice in Figure 9.1 that the outcome of Stage 4—the reflecting stage—serves as the basis for input into Stage 1—the planning stage—of the next cycle.

To reiterate, the process of conducting action research fairly closely parallels the general process for conducting research in education. There are a couple of unique steps, as you will see in reading through the following outline:

1. *Identifying and limiting the topic.* The first step in any research study is to identify exactly *what* is going to be studied. A primary difference between action research and other types of research studies is that in action research the topic stems from the personal and professional experiences of the educators conducting the research. The topic or problem is central to the educators' lives, such that they have a vested interest in the outcome of the study. Three possible and common topic areas for action research studies are

- trying a new teaching method,
- identifying a problem, or
- examining an area of interest (Johnson, 2008).

2. *Gathering information.* Once the topic has been specified and appropriately limited, the next step in the process is preliminary information gathering, known as **reconnaissance** (Mertler, 2014). This gathering of information may be as simple as engaging in conversations with other teachers, counselors, or administrators in your school or district to gauge their perceptions of your proposed action research topic and

FIGURE 9.1   ●   The Process of Action Research

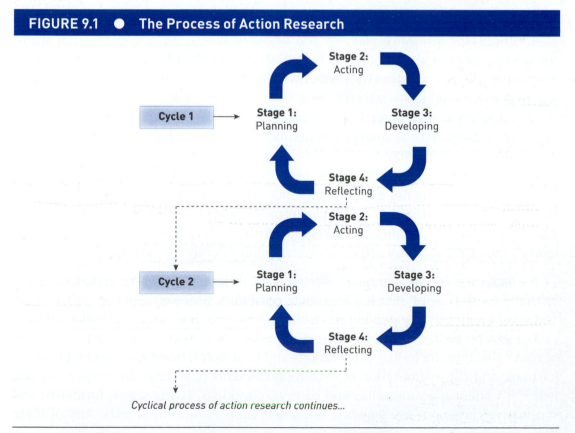

Cyclical process of action research continues...

Source: Mertler (2014).

perhaps to question them for ideas. This can also include reviewing educational materials, such as teacher's manuals or curriculum guides, to look for ideas and suggestions that might inform your study. More formally, reconnaissance involves taking time to reflect on your own beliefs as an educator and to get a better understanding of the nature and context of your research problem (Mills, 2014). Notice that, even in the early stages of action research, reflection is a key component of the process. Reconnaissance can take three forms: self-reflection, description, and explanation. *Self-reflection* is the process of reflecting on your own understanding of things such as educational theories, your values regarding education, and ways your work in schools contributes to the larger context of schooling. The next step is to develop a thorough *description* of the situation or problem you want to change or improve. During this process, you should focus on describing the *who, what, where, when,* and *how* of your problem. The final step in doing reconnaissance is to take this description and provide an *explanation* as to why the problem is occurring. You might even go so far as to develop a hypothesis that will serve to guide your action research study.

3. *Reviewing the related literature.* As in any educational research study, reviewing the existing body of research literature can provide a great deal of guidance in the development of an action research study. Note, however, that this review of existing information is very different from the preliminary information gathering you read about in Step 2 above. A literature review focuses on formally conducted—and, in all likelihood, published—research, as opposed to more informal sources of information. As always, though, the formal review of literature is incredibly important, as it provides a research context for your topic and can help you with methodological decisions along the way.

4. *Developing a research plan.* As you begin to design an action research study, the development of a research plan is critical. One of the distinct benefits of action research is that it is *not* directly aligned with either quantitative or qualitative methods. Any of the qualitative research designs discussed in Chapter 6 or the quantitative designs discussed in Chapter 7 are appropriate for action research studies. That is to say, either quantitative or qualitative methods—or perhaps *both*—are entirely appropriate when designing plans for action research studies. It is for this reason that many people tend to see a close alignment between action research and mixed-methods research. It is certainly not a requirement, but many action research studies will incorporate both quantitative and qualitative forms of data. Of course, as with any research study, the action researcher has a responsibility to behave ethically—especially in light of the fact that many action research studies directly involve students.

5. *Implementing the plan and collecting data.* When it comes to action research, virtually every type of data is a legitimate possibility. Since quantitative, qualitative, and mixed-methods research are all viable designs for action research studies, all sorts of data can be used. In Chapter 11, you will learn about specific qualitative methods of data collection, including observations and field notes, interviews, several types of journals, and the examination of existing documents or records. In Chapter 12, you will learn about questionnaires and surveys, checklists, rating scales, formative and summative classroom assessments, and scores from standardized tests. Any of these data sources are feasible options for the action researcher.

6. *Analyzing the data.* As you will learn in Chapter 11, the analysis of qualitative data resulting from traditional studies begins during data collection and continues throughout the remainder of the study. The analysis of quantitative data resulting from traditional studies typically occurs following the completion of data collection (see Chapter 13). Mixed-methods research data analysis combines these two approaches (see Chapter 8), and this is a typical scenario for action research studies as well. As with any research study, it is critical to ensure that the analytical techniques chosen will match or parallel the research questions being addressed. It is important for the action researcher to know his or her skill sets and comfort level when it comes to dealing with both qualitative and quantitative data. Acknowledgment of these skill levels will enable more appropriate decisions about data sources and analytical techniques. That being said, it is important that the action researcher not become overwhelmed at the prospect of analyzing data. The analysis of action research data is typically much less complex and detailed than for other, more formal types of research studies (Fraenkel et al., 2012).

7. *Developing an action plan.* Once data have been collected and analyzed, the next step in the action research process is development of an action plan. The action plan is the ultimate goal of any action research study—it is the "action" part of action research (Mertler, 2014). The **action plan** is essentially a proposed strategy for implementing the results of an action research project. The plan may focus on a proposed strategy for practical implementation of the findings and/or on recommendations for future cycles of action research. Action plans may be developed at the level of an individual teacher or classroom, for a collaborative group of teachers, or on a schoolwide or even districtwide basis. You will learn more about action planning later in this chapter.

8. *Sharing and communicating the results.* An important part of any research study is the reporting or sharing of results with others in the educational community, and action research is no different. On one level, this seems to be in opposition to what we would expect. If action research is done to benefit an individual teacher's practice, you might be asking yourself what the purpose of sharing or reporting the results might be. Remember, even if the results of an action research study are specific to a particular individual or classroom, other educators may still benefit by learning from the experiences of others who have engaged in action research. Dissemination of the results of action research studies can take many forms. Presentations of a less formal nature may be made to colleagues in a particular grade level or subject area, perhaps during a regularly scheduled faculty meeting. Presentations—which can sometimes also include written summaries (i.e., research reports) of results—may also be made to school boards, principals other administrators, students, and parents. Results of action research studies may also be disseminated to larger audiences, typically in more formal settings. These settings might include professional conferences or other types of teacher or administrator conventions, or even professional journals.

9. *Reflecting on the process.* Since action research is primarily about the critical examination of one's own professional practice, reflection on the process of conducting action research is a critical step. As it pertains to the process of conducting action research, professional reflection must be done at the end of each action research cycle; however, effective educators and action researchers reflect on and critically examine *all aspects* of

the action research process—before, during, and after the study. This is a critical part of systematic inquiry into professional practice, as well as a vitally important component in the action research process.

Earlier, a diagram of the four-stage process of conducting action research was presented (see Figure 9.1). Figure 9.2 integrates this four-stage process with the specific steps involved in conducting action research, which we have just discussed. In this diagram, you can see how the planning stage consists of the first four steps in the action research process—that is, identifying a topic, gathering information, reviewing the literature, and developing a research plan. The acting stage consists of the actual implementation of the study—collecting and analyzing data. Developing an action plan is, in essence, its own stage—the developing stage. Finally, the reflecting stage consists of sharing and communicating the results of action research and reflecting on the overall process.

Action Planning and Reflection

Two characteristics that differentiate action research from other types of formal educational research are (1) the development of action plans and (2) the integration of reflection throughout the process. You will learn a bit more about each of these components in this section. First, let us consider the notion of action planning.

Action research is built on the premise that some type of action will result from your action research project (Johnson, 2008). Action plans resulting from action research studies essentially delineate the researcher's next steps and may be informal or formal (Creswell, 2005), depending on the nature and purpose of the research project (Johnson, 2008). There are no real requirements as to what must or should be included in an action plan. It may consist of brief statements or simple descriptions about the implementation of a new educational practice; a plan to reflect on alternative approaches to addressing the problem; a plan to share what the researcher has learned with others interested in the topic, such as other teachers, administrators, boards of education, or other schools or districts; or any other next steps the researcher might take (Creswell, 2005; Johnson, 2008). The action plan may be more formally written, as an outline for presentation or even a complete report of the research project to submit for publication in a professional journal (Creswell, 2005). The point of developing an action plan is that the researcher has some sort of plan or strategy for trying out, carrying out, or otherwise putting into practice the changes to educational practice that have resulted from the findings of the action research project.

During this phase of the action research process, the researcher is basically trying to answer the following question: *Based on what I have learned from my study, what should I do now?* (Mills, 2014). In most cases, the development of an action plan dictates that something will be done differently in the future. In rare cases, action researchers may discover from their results that everything is fine and nothing needs to change (Johnson, 2008). In such cases, the action plan is to do nothing—other than what they have been doing, because it is working (although, it is important to remember that they would not know this if they had *not* conducted the action research study!). Johnson (2008) has outlined five possible—and common—outcomes of action research studies:

1. A greater understanding of the situation or child under investigation, or of students in general, is developed.

2. A new problem is discovered.

3. A plan, a program, or an instructional method is found to be effective.

4. A plan, a program, or an instructional method is found to need modification.

5. A plan, a program, or an instructional method is found to be ineffective. (pp. 136–137)

Action planning can occur on several different levels, including *individual*, *team*, and *school* or *district levels*. Individual educators who have conducted action research studies in their classrooms or schools—for a wide variety of reasons—typically develop **individual action plans**. The individual educator is usually the target audience for the individual action plan; in other words, an educator may have engaged in action research solely for the purposes of improving some aspect of his or

FIGURE 9.2 ● The Process of Action Research, Showing Specific Research Activities in Each Stage

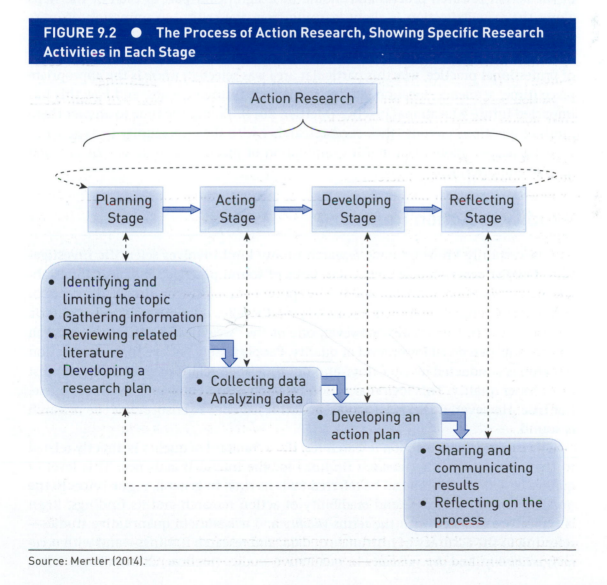

Source: Mertler (2014).

her professional practice. **Team action plans** are developed by collaborative groups of teachers, who have worked together to address an area of common interest to all members of the team. These collaborative teams could comprise teachers at the same grade level or in the same subject area, within a building, across the district, or even through professional networks. Regardless, the members of the collaborative team typically share common characteristics—this becomes the tie that binds the team together. Finally, **school-level** or **district-level action plans** are developed as a result of large-scale, communitywide action research endeavors. These might occur as a result of focused effort across an entire school district, as an example, where there exists a common goal, and focus on improved literacy among early to middle elementary students.

Of course, one cannot do an adequate job of action planning without once again reflecting on the action research process, as well as the overall experience. The second component unique to action research is the integration of reflection throughout the process. At the risk of sounding repetitive, professional reflection is a key component of the action research process and should be a significant part of each of the steps along the way. Reflection is about learning from the critical examination of one's own practice but also about taking the time to critically reexamine exactly *who* was involved in the process, *what* led the action researcher to want to examine this aspect of professional practice, *why* this particular area was selected, *where* is the appropriate place (time, sequence, location, etc.) to implement future changes, and *how* this has impacted future educational practice (Mertler, 2014). Taking the time to answer these kinds of questions provides the action researcher with the opportunity to experience an even deeper, more meaningful examination of practice, as well as a heightened level of empowerment.

Validity in Action Research

As you certainly know by now, research of any kind involves scientific investigation. Quality research must meet standards of sound practice. The basis for establishing the quality of traditional (i.e., experimental) research lies in concepts of validity and reliability. Action research typically relies on a different set of criteria (Stringer, 2007). Historically, however, one of the "weaknesses" of action research has been its perceived lower level of quality. People falsely believe that, since action research is conducted by educators, and not by academicians or researchers, it must be of lesser quality. This idea that action research is somehow inferior is, of course, not true. However, it is critical for the action researcher to ensure that the research is sound.

The extent to which action research reaches a standard of quality is directly related to the usefulness of the research findings for the intended audience. This level of quality in action research can be referred to as its *rigor*. In general, **rigor** refers to the quality, validity, accuracy, and credibility of action research and its findings. Rigor is typically associated with the terms *validity* and *reliability* in quantitative studies—referring to the accuracy of instruments, data, and research findings—and with *accuracy, credibility,* and *dependability* in qualitative studies (Melrose, 2001). (These terms will be discussed further in Chapters 11 and 12.) Many action researchers use the term *rigor* in a much broader sense, encompassing the entire research process, not just its aspects of data collection, data analysis, and findings (Melrose, 2001). Rigor in action research is typically based on procedures of checking to ensure that the results are not biased, or reflective only of the researcher's perspective (Stringer, 2007).

As mentioned, the determination of rigor is often contingent on the intended audience of action research results. Classroom- and school-based action research can be disseminated to a wide variety of audiences—for example, teachers, administrators, counselors, parents, school boards, and professional organizations—and the usefulness of the results of action research often depends on audience members' perceptions of rigor, since it can have different connotations for different audiences (Melrose, 2001). For example, if the research is intended for limited, small-scale dissemination (e.g., among members of the action research group or building staff at a monthly faculty meeting), the necessary level of rigor is much different than if the research is intended for scholarly academic presentation or publication. The broader dissemination needs to be concerned more with generalizability, meaning that the results of the study will extend beyond its scope, to other settings and people (Mertler, 2014).

However, most action research is intended primarily for local-level dissemination and, therefore, has an altogether different focus. It is important to remember that participants in action research studies make mistakes and learn from them (Melrose, 2001); this is inherent to the action research process. The research questions and design are often emergent, changeable, and therefore unpredictable; so there may be no generalizable conclusions at all, as the findings are often context specific and unique to the participants and their setting and situation. The primary concern in action research is typically the improvement of practice—as evidenced by the resulting, visible change—and not the study's rigor—as defined by its ability to be generalized (Mertler, 2014).

Also important to note in our discussion of action research is the concept of objectivity. Objectivity in conducting educational research studies has been discussed in several places in this text. While objectivity and the avoidance of bias are important, bias is unavoidable in virtually any research study. More important than eliminating bias is that the researcher recognizes any limitations in the study that may be influenced or caused by individual or collective bias. Since action research centers on a contextualized and individualized research study—focused on improving practice—this notion of recognizing and disclosing various limitations is extremely important, especially when communicating the results of action research studies.

Numerous methods or techniques can help provide evidence of rigor within the scope of educator-led action research studies. These techniques include repeating the cycle, prolonged engagement in the setting, experience with the action research process, triangulating data, member checking, and participant debriefing (Melrose, 2001; Mills, 2014; Stringer, 2007).

- *Repeating the cycle.* Most action researchers firmly believe that one journey through an action research cycle is not enough. To develop adequate rigor, it is critical to proceed through a number of cycles, where the earlier cycles are used to help inform how to conduct the later cycles (Melrose, 2001). In theory, with each subsequent cycle, more is learned and greater credibility is added to the findings.

- *Prolonged engagement and persistent observation.* To gather enough information to help participants fully understand the outcomes of an action research process, the researcher must provide them with "extended opportunities to explore and express their experience" (Stringer, 2007, p. 58) as it relates to the problem being investigated. However, simply spending more time in the setting is not enough. For example, observations and interviews must be deliberately and carefully conducted (Mills, 2011; Stringer, 2007). These should not be indiscriminate research activities. It is clearly not about the *quantity* of time but, rather, the *quality* of time spent in the setting.

- *Experience with the process.* As with most types of research, rigor and credibility will depend on the experience of the action researcher(s). If a teacher has (or other school personnel have) conducted previous studies, or even previous cycles within the same study, he or she can perform confidently and will have greater credibility with respective audiences (Melrose, 2001). If the action researcher is a novice, however, the entire process may benefit from the use of an experienced facilitator.

- *Triangulating data.* Rigor can be enhanced during the action research process through the inclusion of multiple sources of data and other information (Mills, 2011; Stringer, 2007). This process permits the action researcher to verify the data's accuracy (Mills, 2011) and clarify meanings or misconceptions held by participants (Stringer, 2007). Accuracy of data and credibility of the study findings go hand in hand. You will learn more about *triangulation* in Chapter 11.

- *Member checking.* Depending on the purposes and strategies adopted for a particular study, participants should be provided with opportunities to review the raw data, analyses, and final reports resulting from the action research process (Mills, 2011; Stringer, 2007). This can be a powerful tool for validation of the findings resulting from action research studies, although it may not be appropriate in all action research scenarios. The rigor of the research is enhanced by allowing participants to verify that various aspects of the research process adequately and accurately represent their beliefs, perspectives, and experiences. It also gives them the opportunity to further explain and/or extend the information they have already provided.

- *Participant debriefing.* Similar to member checking, debriefing is another opportunity for participants to provide insight. However, in this case, the focus is on their emotions and feelings, instead of the factual information they have offered (Mills, 2011; Stringer, 2007). They may address emotions that have clouded their interpretations of events or inhibited their memories.

You will read more about many of these techniques—in particular, as they apply to qualitative research—in Chapter 11. As you can see, rigor in action research is very important, even if the reasons for ensuring quality of the research are different from those of more traditional forms of educational research.

Strengths and Limitations of Action Research

Fraenkel and colleagues (2012) have identified five advantages or strengths of action research. First, action research can be conducted by almost any professional in any type of educational setting. Further, it can be conducted by individuals or collaborative teams of educators. Second, action research is focused on the improvement of educational practice. Its purpose is to enable educators at all levels to improve their professional practice, enhance the educational environment, and enrich the teaching–learning process. Third, when educators practice action research, they develop more effective ways to perform as professional educators. Action research has a tendency to lead to more substantial forms of professional development. Fourth, by design, action research can help educators identify problems and issues, and then investigate them in a systematic and scientific manner. Learning how to engage in the action research process requires the clear delineation of a problem, a systematic means of collecting and analyzing data, and the development of a plan for changing future practice—all of which collectively constitutes a systematic and scientific process. Finally, action research can help in the establishment of a community of professional learners within an educational setting. This can reduce a perceived feeling of isolation, while also creating a network of empowered educators.

There are no real limitations to action research, per se. While some researchers claim that action research is a "lesser" approach to conducting research because its findings cannot be generalized to larger populations, action researchers might reply that this is actually a benefit over traditional research. Remember that the purpose of action research is to solve *local-level problems*, not to generalize solutions to larger populations. Sometimes action research solutions will cross over from one setting to another; if that occurs, what we have is a wonderful by-product of action research. Remember that action research is and should be evaluated on a different set of criteria than used for more traditional forms of research. Table 9.1 lists similarities and differences between action research and more formal quantitative and qualitative types of research.

TABLE 9.1 ● Similarities and Differences Between Action Research and Formal Quantitative and Qualitative Research

Action Research	Formal Research
Uses systematic inquiry.	Uses systematic inquiry.
Goal is to solve local-level problems.	Goal is to develop and test theories, and to produce knowledge generalizable to broader populations.
Little formal training is required.	Considerable training is required.
Intent is to identify and correct problems of local concern.	Intent is to investigate larger issues.

(Continued)

TABLE 9.1 ● (Continued)	
Action Research	**Formal Research**
Is conducted by teachers or other educational professionals.	Is conducted by researchers not usually involved in the local setting.
Relies primarily on teacher-developed instruments.	Relies primarily on professionally developed instruments.
Is less rigorous.	Is more rigorous.
Is usually value based (subjective).	Is frequently value neutral (objective).
Uses purposive samples.	Uses random samples (if feasible).
Selective opinions of researcher are often considered as data.	Selective opinions of researcher are never considered as data.
Generalizability is limited (and usually not a goal).	Generalizability is often appropriate (and often a goal).

Source: Adapted from Fraenkel et al. (2012).

Developmental Activities

1. List or describe at least five issues (e.g., problems or possible improvements within your classroom or school) that interest you and that you might want to pursue further. Do you think any of the issues on your list might be appropriate for an action research study? Why or why not?

2. Action research has a fairly specific contextual application. Can you think of any kinds of research questions that could *not* be investigated by means of an action research study? Provide some examples.

3. In your own words, describe why action planning and reflection are such integral components in the action research process.

4. Think of a classroom- or school-based problem you might be interested in solving, or at least investigating. Sketch out a plan for the first four steps in your cycle of action research:

   - Identify your problem or topic.
   - Gather background information.
   - Develop a review of the related literature.
   - Develop a research plan.

5. Suppose students in your school were not achieving at the desired level in the area of mathematics. Using the four-stage procedure for action research—planning, acting, developing, and reflecting—as presented in this chapter, briefly describe how you might *systematically* examine this problem.

Summary

- Action research is a systematic inquiry conducted by educators with a vested interest in the teaching and learning process, for the purpose of gathering information about how their school operates, how they teach, and how their students learn.
- Action research is done *by* educators *for* themselves and is typically characterized as systematic inquiry into one's own practice.
- Action research is a process by which current educational practice can be changed for the better.
- Since action research is largely about examining one's own practice, reflection is an integral component of the research process.
- Reflection is the act of critically exploring what you are doing, why you decided to do it, and what its effects have been.
- Action research is centered on a process of systematic collection of information, followed by active reflection.
- Many aspects of action research characterize it as a unique type of educational research.
- There are at least five important reasons for the use of action research in educational settings:

  o It helps connect theory to practice.
  o It can result in the improvement of educational practice.
  o It can foster widespread school improvement.
  o It empowers teachers and other educators.
  o It can serve as a mechanism for promoting professional growth.

- Action research may be seen as the epitome of customizable professional development for educators.

- Two types of action research are participatory action research and practical action research.

  o The purpose of participatory action research is to improve the quality of organizations, communities, and family lives by empowering individuals and groups.
  o The purpose of practical action research is to address and solve specific problems in classrooms, schools, or other communities; it focuses on the "how-to" approach to the process of conducting action research.

- Guiding assumptions for the implementation of practical action research include the following:

  o Individual teachers or teams of teachers are capable of determining the nature of an action research investigation.
  o Action researchers are committed to continuous professional development and school improvement through the process of critical reflection.
  o Action researchers are capable of choosing their own area of focus, determining plans for conducting research, and developing action plans based on their findings.

- The action research process is cyclical and consists of four stages:

  o Planning stage
  o Acting stage
  o Developing stage
  o Reflecting stage

- Reconnaissance is unique to action research and is the process of gathering preliminary background information.

- Formal reconnaissance can take three forms: self-reflection, description, and explanation.

    o Self-reflection is a process of reflecting on your own understanding of and values regarding education.
    o The second component of reconnaissance is to formally describe the situation or problem that will serve as the focus of action research.
    o The final step is to provide an explanation as to why the problem is occurring, and perhaps to develop a hypothesis about the potential outcome of an action research study.

- An action plan is the ultimate goal of an action research study—the "action" part of action research.
- An action plan is a proposed strategy for implementing the results of an action research project.
- Action planning can occur at the individual educator level, collaborative team level, or school or district level.
- Five possible and common outcomes of action research studies are as follows:

    o A greater understanding of the situation or problem is developed.
    o A new problem is discovered.
    o A plan, program, or instructional method is found to be effective.

    o A plan, program, or instructional method is found to need modification.
    o A plan, program, or instructional method is found to be ineffective.

- Validity of action research is determined by establishing rigor, which refers to the quality, validity, accuracy, and credibility of action research and its findings.
- Techniques used to provide evidence of rigor in action research studies include the following:

    o Repetition of the cycle
    o Prolonged engagement and persistent observation
    o Experience with the action research process
    o Triangulation of data
    o Member checking
    o Peer debriefing

- Some strengths of action research are that it can be conducted by virtually any professional educator or collaborative team of educators, it is focused on the improvement of educational practice, it provides a mechanism for educators to investigate problems in a systematic and scientific manner, and it can aid in the development of communities of professional learners.
- There are no substantial limitations or weaknesses of action research, provided it is used in a suitable context and with an appropriate purpose in mind.

ⓢSAGE edge™

Sharpen your skills with SAGE edge!

edge.sagepub.com/mertler

SAGE edge for Students provides a personalized approach to help you accomplish your coursework goals in an easy-to-use learning environment. You'll find action plans, mobile-friendly eFlashcards, and quizzes as well as video, web, and resources and links to SAGE journal articles to support and expand on the concepts presented in this chapter.

10

Writing a Research Proposal

Student Learning Objectives

After studying Chapter 10, students will be able to do the following:

1. Describe various purposes for developing a research proposal

2. List and describe three sections required in any research proposal

3. Delineate major differences between components of quantitative and qualitative research proposals

4. Develop a complete and accurate research proposal, appropriate for a research topic of interest

In this chapter, you will learn about developing a proposal for conducting a research study. It is important to recognize that you are embarking on a process of *academic* and *scholarly* writing—which likely differs from any other kind of writing you have done. You will learn about the purpose of the research proposal, along with some general components that should be included in it. Finally, we will look at specific aspects of quantitative versus qualitative research proposals.

Purpose of a Research Proposal

A **research proposal** is a written plan for conducting a research study. Generally speaking, it is a detailed plan for what the researcher intends to do—and why—in the course of conducting the research study. All the critical decisions that go into planning a research study should be included in the research proposal. To start, these decisions might include the following aspects of conducting research:

- Specification and limitation of the topic
- Research questions and hypotheses

- Justification for conducting the study
- Existing research that has supported the development of the proposed study
- Proposed methods for sampling
- Proposed methods for data collection
- Proposed methods for data analysis

In other words, many of the things you have learned about in Chapters 3, 5, 6, 7, 8, and 9—and will learn about in Chapters 11 and 12—are important and critical components of the research proposal.

At this point, you might be asking yourself, *Why do I need to do a research proposal?* Development of a research proposal is a critical task in the overall process of conducting a research study in education for several important reasons. First and foremost, a well-thought-out plan can save the researcher—whether novice or experienced—a great deal of time and potential headaches later in the process. Developing a research proposal gives the researcher the chance to think through the process before carrying it out. This can provide opportunities to identify potential pitfalls and problems before they occur.

Second, although developing a research proposal does take time, it will save the researcher time in the long run. Once you are in the middle of conducting a study, rarely will you have ample time to think on your feet and make spur-of-the-moment decisions—although you will still have to do so occasionally. The point here is that you do not want to *plan* to conduct your research by making hurried decisions. Even though factors outside your control may force you to revise your research plan midstream, a well-developed research proposal will not only enable you to make many of these decisions ahead of time but will also help guide any necessary revisions.

A third reason for developing a research proposal is that it will provide a detailed set of procedures for your study, including a timeline for all the major activities. If you run into a stumbling block along the way, referring back to the research proposal can give you an opportunity to see how this "unexpected hurdle" might impact the remainder of the study, since you wrote it all out in detail ahead of time. Fourth, upon completion of your study, you will be expected to write a final research report (see Chapter 14). By taking the time early in the process to develop a research proposal, you will save yourself a great deal of writing time later. Although you will undoubtedly make revisions to areas such as your methods, procedures, and timeline, much of what you write in the research proposal can be used in the final research report.

The fifth reason for developing a thorough research proposal is that, in many situations, a research proposal is required for the study to be approved and for the researcher to get permission to conduct it. In just about any research situation, some sort of research proposal will be required for permission to be granted. Research proposals are necessary for students conducting research related to a master's thesis or doctoral dissertation; they are almost always required for people applying for research grant funding; university faculty who conduct research must have their proposals approved, especially if they are planning to work with human subjects (see Chapters 11 and 12). On the positive side, once your research proposal has been approved, you can feel good that it has passed at least an initial quality-control check.

Finally, the act of engaging in the academic writing process *itself* has important and inherent value in the development of a research study. Formally writing a research proposal helps the researcher specify and clarify ideas. In a manner of speaking, it *forces* the researcher to think through various aspects and decisions involved in the research process and to formalize them in writing. The act of writing necessitates that the researcher articulate thoughts and ideas. Through a process of reflection, editing, and critiquing, the research plan will be strengthened. This process is even more valuable when other researchers and colleagues are invited to review and critique the research proposal. The researcher must ensure that the articulated ideas represented in the research proposal are clear—not only to the researcher but also to outsiders, who will undoubtedly have a different level of interest and background knowledge.

General Aspects of a Research Proposal

Although the titles of the sections may vary, all research proposals share some elements. They all include an introduction section, a methodology section, and a timeline of activities for the study. Depending on the research situation and audience for the proposal, a budget may be required, as well as a brief literature review. The introductory section typically includes the following components:

- An explanation of the phenomenon, topic, or problem for which the investigation is being proposed
- Background information related to the topic or problem
- Purpose of the study
- A rationale or justification for the study
- Specification of the research questions and/or hypotheses

The methodology section is one of the most important parts of a research proposal. It serves as the primary basis for the decision to approve or reject the proposed study. A weak methodology section—with many components missing or not clearly explained—will most certainly result in a negative approval decision. The methodology section typically includes the following:

- A description of the participants, as well as specific processes for selecting them
- A thorough description of the research design
- Methods to be used for data collection, including instruments, protocols, or other data collection materials
- Proposed methods for data analysis

Depending on the type of study being conducted—that is, qualitative, quantitative, mixed methods, or action research—additional information may be required in the proposal. Even if the exact components identified above are required, they may need to be treated or explained differently in the proposal, depending on the type of research to be conducted.

A last key aspect of the research proposal is the writing style. As mentioned in the introduction to this chapter, the researcher is expected to be able to write in an academic and scholarly manner. Numerous conventions of style and format may be required in the research proposal. Further, many of these conventions are implied; in other words, the directions for submitting a grant proposal or thesis/dissertation proposal may not *explicitly instruct* you to follow these requirements of convention, but the expectation is that, as an academic writer, you will. Arguably, these conventions of style and format are less important in a research proposal than in any final research report. Therefore, the specifics related to writing styles and format will be presented in substantial detail in Chapter 14.

Components of a Quantitative Research Proposal

Quantitative research proposals tend to be fairly structured. Most of the components we will discuss are common to nearly all quantitative research proposals. The main sections are (1) introduction, (2) review of related literature, (3) methodology, (4) timeline, (5) budget, (6) references, and (7) appendices. We now consider the specific contents of each of these sections, including some examples from the proposal for a study I recently conducted. The examples throughout this section come from a survey study on the impact of the No Child Left Behind (NCLB) Act on teachers' classroom assessment practices (Mertler, 2010). You will see additional references to this study (e.g., consent letter, survey instrument) in Chapter 12.

1. *Introduction*—Obviously, the introduction section is the first portion of your proposal that reviewers will read. This is where you must grab their attention and set the stage for the sections that follow. Subsections within the introduction include the statement of the problem, the purpose of the study, justification for the study, research questions and hypotheses, and perhaps assumptions and a brief literature review.

   - *The statement of the problem*—This discussion, which may range in length from a paragraph to a few pages, sets the stage for the remainder of the proposal. The **statement of the problem** should provide ample background information and also a thorough description of the context in which the problem is occurring. Here is the statement of the problem from my study:

     Since late in 2001, the No Child Left Behind Act has substantially increased accountability for our nation's K–12 schools. Some research has been done on the impact that NCLB is having on school districts, but very little research has been conducted with teachers. One study looked at their overall knowledge and impressions of the act. Since the act stresses the importance of assessment indicators at the district level, it only makes sense that we begin to look at the impact that NCLB is having on individual teachers' classroom assessment practices.

   - *The purpose of the study*—The **purpose of the study** may be as brief as one sentence or as long as a couple of paragraphs. The idea behind stating the purpose of the study is to clearly explain what the researcher proposes to study, as well as the goals for the research. The purpose of the study from my proposal follows:

The purpose of this study is to gather and describe teachers' perceptions regarding the impact they believe that NCLB has had on their classroom assessment practices.

- *Justification for the study*—Through the **justification for the study**, also referred to as the **rationale for the study**, the researcher's responsibility is to make it clear why this is a topic worthy of investigation. Often, this subsection will, in some respects, address the problems discussed in the earlier subsection. Researchers may also describe the potential benefits of the study. The justification for my study appears below:

In general, the educational community criticizes the NCLB Act quite frequently. These criticisms range from those about its real purpose to issues of NCLB being an unfunded mandate. One thing we know very little about is how NCLB is changing the ways that teachers assess student learning. One would expect that teacher behaviors would have in fact been altered, but we do not know that. It is important that we begin to look at this issue.

- *Research questions/hypotheses*—The research questions and/or hypotheses will guide the conduct of the study. It is important that they be clearly stated and follow logically from the problem statement and the purpose for the study. Recall that the true goal of any research study—to be achieved upon its conclusion—is for the researcher to answer the research questions or pass judgment on the hypotheses. My study had three guiding research questions:

1. *What are K–12 teachers' perceptions of NCLB?*

2. *In what ways do teachers believe that NCLB has influenced their instruction and assessment practices?*

3. *What differences in the perceptions of NCLB's influence on assessment practices exist between groups as determined by gender, school level, education level, teaching experience, and school rating?*

- *(Assumptions)*—**Assumptions** are assertions made by the researcher and assumed to be true but for which no evidence exists. I placed this subsection in parentheses here because it may appear in the introduction section or later in the methodology section of the proposal. My study included one simple, basic assumption:

In this study, it is assumed that teachers have a sense of their perceptions of NCLB and how it impacts their teaching practices. Further, teachers will be able to accurately and honestly describe their perceptions using the instrument provided.

- *(Review of related literature)*—As you know, the review of related literature provides an overview of the existing body of research and what is currently known on the topic. It should support the purpose of the study, as stated in previous chapters. The review of related literature has also been placed in parentheses here because it may appear as part of the introduction section or as a section entirely its own (see below). This often depends on what is required by the individuals or committee who will review the proposal. Some may need very little in the way of a literature review, whereas others may request a three- to four-page literature review. In the interest of brevity, I have not included samples of my study's literature review.

2. *Review of related literature*—As stated above, the literature review provides an overview of the existing research on your topic. If need be, it may represent a separate section within the proposal.

3. *Methodology*—The methodology section is really the meat of your proposal. This section delineates *how you will conduct* the research study and is probably of most interest to those reviewing the proposal, because the information included here is what they are ultimately judging. This section should be brief but extremely clear. Proposal reviewers should not be left with unanswered questions about your proposed methodology.

   - *Research participants/sample*—This subsection of the methodology clearly describes who your participants will be, how they will be selected, and how many you will select. If possible, the population as well as the sample should be described. In some cases, it may not be possible to know the exact number of participants; nonetheless, you should be as clear as possible. As you probably can imagine, this is an incredibly important subsection of the methodology, since reviewers of the proposal will want to be sure you are acting ethically and protecting participants from any potential risks. Here is the description from my proposal:

     Teachers in K–12 schools throughout the state of Ohio will be the participants in the study. Districts will be randomly selected to participate through a cluster sampling procedure (approximately 150 districts from the 614 in the state). Of the 150 sampled districts, some are quite large and others are quite small. Regardless, I would expect the total number of teacher participants to equal several hundred. Initially, superintendents of the randomly selected districts will be contacted in order to ask for their permission to contact their teachers via e-mail (i.e., the cover letter and survey directions will be sent electronically through an e-mail message). Once their permission is secured, the e-mail message containing the cover letter and survey directions will be sent to the superintendents (or other designated individual, such as a district technology coordinator) who will then forward the e-mail message to the entire teaching staff of the particular district. Since the study involves survey methodology, informed consent will be sought through the e-mail cover letter. In addition, this message will contain a hyperlink allowing the participants easy access to the webpage containing the survey. Participants will be informed that their participation in this study is voluntary. By completing and submitting the survey, they are in fact providing their consent to participate. Additionally, they will be instructed that if they do not wish to participate, they should simply disregard the e-mail message.

   - *Research design*—The research design subsection of the proposal clearly describes the plan you will use to conduct the study. It is important to use appropriate terminology when describing your design—for example, "the study will be conducted using a two-group pretest–posttest design." Some designs are much more complex to describe than others. The description of my design appears below:

The proposed study is a survey research study, using a web-based survey. Participants will be asked to click on the hyperlink, which will take them to the website containing the survey. They are simply asked to respond to the questions that appear on the survey and submit those responses electronically.

- *Instrumentation*—In the instrumentation subsection, the researcher clearly describes any tests, tools, protocols, or other instruments that will be used to collect data from participants. As you can imagine, this is also a very important subsection within the methodology. The researcher should clearly describe whether the instrument is an existing, published instrument or a self-developed (i.e., researcher-developed) instrument. Typically, the entire instrument will be included as an appendix to the research proposal. Below is the description of my survey instrument:

An original web-based survey instrument, titled the NCLB∗CAP (Classroom Assessment Practices) Survey, consisting of 22 items, has been developed for purposes of data collection. Teacher respondents will be instructed to respond to each statement on a four-point Likert scale, ranging from "strongly disagree" to "strongly agree." For purposes of addressing Research Question #3, six additional demographic questions have been included on the instrument and asked of respondents. They will be asked to indicate their gender, teaching level, education level, years of teaching experience, and school district and school building rating, as determined by the Ohio Department of Education (ODE).

- *Data collection procedures*—The **data collection procedures** subsection requires the researcher to provide a step-by-step description of all aspects of data collection. This should be done chronologically so reviewers have a sense of the entire data collection process. The procedures section from my proposal follows:

School district participation will be sought through e-mail communications with the superintendents from the randomly selected districts during late summer. Once a superintendent, or an appropriate designee, has agreed to permit the survey to be accessed by the district's teachers, the researcher will send the e-mail "cover letter" to the superintendent and ask that the message be forwarded to the entire teaching staff of that district. Teachers will then be informed that the survey will require only about 10 minutes to complete, that their responses will remain confidential, and that only aggregate results will be reported. This e-mail message will contain an embedded link that will provide direct access for respondents to the NCLB∗CAP Survey. The survey will be administered during a three-week period extending from mid-September through early October. All data will be collected and stored electronically.

- *Data analysis*—The research proposal must also clearly indicate how the collected data will be analyzed. The **data analysis** subsection does not need to be lengthy but does need to clearly describe the proposed procedures.

It is also critical for the researcher to ensure that the proposed analytical techniques parallel the research questions and/or hypotheses, such that the results of the analysis will enable the researcher to answer the questions or address the hypotheses. My data analysis subsection appears below:

All data analyses will be conducted using the Statistical Package for the Social Sciences (SPSS, v. 15). Initial data analyses will include frequencies, percentages, means, and standard deviations to summarize the overall results. An exploratory factor analysis will also be conducted as a data reduction technique in order to reduce the number of items for purposes of group comparisons. Analyses of variance (ANOVAs) will then be used to compare group responses based on gender, teaching level, education level, years of teaching experience, district rating, and school rating. All ANOVA results will be evaluated at an alpha level equal to .05.

- *(Assumptions)*—Again, assumptions may be included either in the methodology section or the introduction section.

- *Limitations and delimitations*—A **limitation** is some aspect of the study that is outside the control of the researcher but may have a potentially adverse effect on the outcomes of the research. In contrast, a **delimitation** is a restriction placed on the study by the researcher to limit its scope. Both limitations and delimitations may inadvertently impact the results of the study and should be acknowledged by the researcher. A brief discussion of the limitations and delimitations of my proposal appears below:

It is important to note a couple of potential limitations and delimitations in this study. The study is seeking to describe teachers' beliefs with respect to specific classroom-based instructional and assessment practices. Since the proposed study will utilize a survey methodology, findings will be based purely on self-reported data, and no efforts will be made within the scope of this study to validate the extent to which these beliefs are consistent with actual classroom practice. In addition, the ultimate findings may be delimited by geographic location (i.e., the sample will comprise teachers who currently work in school districts in Ohio, a state that includes a series of state-mandated achievement tests). External validity of the findings of this study is suggested through the large and broad nature of the sample.

4. *Proposed timeline*—If it is required as a separate section of the proposal, a **proposed timeline** will allow the reviewers to see a detailed plan for all major activities of a given study, as well as when they will occur.

5. *Proposed budget*—A **proposed budget** is not always required in the proposal, but sometimes reviewers want to know if there will be monetary costs involved in the study and what sources will be used to cover those costs.

6. *References*—Any **references** you have cited as part of your introduction or review of related literature should be listed, using the appropriate formatting (see Chapter 14). Every citation in the proposal should be included in the reference list, and every reference on the list must have been cited in the proposal.

7. *Appendices*—Some research proposal submission procedures will require inclusion of **appendices**. These appendices usually include recruitment plans or advertising for the identification of potential research participants, informed consent letters, surveys or other instruments, and interview guides that may be used to collect data.

A generic outline for a quantitative research proposal appears in Figure 10.1. It is also worth mentioning here that these various sections and subsections may sometimes be called by other names, even though they contain the same information about the study. Do not be surprised or frustrated if the guidelines for a research proposal use different section names; just determine what information is required and provide it accordingly.

FIGURE 10.1 ● A Generic Outline for a Quantitative Research Proposal

   I. **Introduction**

      A. The Statement of the Problem

      B. The Purpose of the Study

      C. Justification for the Study

      D. Research Questions/Hypotheses

      E. (*Assumptions*)

      F. (*Review of Related Literature*)

  II. **Review of Related Literature**

 III. **Methodology**

      A. Research Participants/Sample Selection

      B. Research Design

      C. Instrumentation

      D. Data Collection Procedures

      E. Data Analysis

      F. (*Assumptions*)

      G. Limitations and Delimitations

 IV. **Proposed Timeline**

  V. **Proposed Budget**

 VI. **References**

VII. **Appendices**

Components of a Qualitative Research Proposal

Typically, depending on the proposal requirements, a qualitative research proposal is much less structured than a quantitative research proposal (Gay, Mills, & Airasian, 2009) and also much shorter (Bogdan & Biklen, 2007). Often, qualitative researchers are not sure exactly what they will do during the study; therefore, a detailed presentation of the methodology is simply not feasible. Furthermore, a lengthy review of the related literature is typically not included in a qualitative research proposal either (Bogdan & Biklen, 2007). The researcher may not know what body of research is relevant until the study is begun. These points being noted, however, the qualitative researcher must still present a clear vision and *preliminary* articulation of the problem to be investigated, as well as a justification for the proposed study.

Bogdan and Biklen (2007) have suggested that qualitative research proposals may be handled in one of two ways. The first approach involves some level of engagement in fieldwork prior to writing the proposal. This preliminary data collection is then used to guide the development of the proposal. You can likely see how this already conflicts with the quantitative approach to developing a research proposal. Nonetheless, this approach is preferable to the second option, which is to write a proposal without any preliminary data collection. From a qualitative research perspective, such a proposal is highly speculative, at best. It may be nothing more than a rough guess, which could obviously change during the course of the study.

Due to the nature of qualitative research—which tends to be open-ended and emergent—the research proposal itself must be somewhat flexible. This certainly is not meant to imply that there should not be some sort of plan to guide the conduct of the qualitative research study. Gay and colleagues (2009) warn that many institutional review boards, or other approval bodies, may be much more accustomed to dealing with quantitative research proposals. Therefore, the qualitative researcher must exhibit a great deal of skill in developing a proposal that will be clearly understood by a person or persons less comfortable with qualitative methodology.

Although they may not always be used, and may be called by different names, the main sections of a qualitative research proposal include (1) title, (2) introduction, (3) review of related literature, (4) research procedures,(5) potential contributions of the research, (6) limitations, (7) references, and (8) appendices (Gay et al., 2009). We now consider the specific contents of each of these sections, although sample passages will not be included in these discussions.

1. *Title*—The title of a qualitative research proposal carries greater significance than that for a quantitative proposal. It is used to provide a context and a frame of reference for the study, and is the researcher's initial opportunity to convey this perspective to the reviewers of the proposal.
2. *Introduction*—As with any research proposal, this is the section the researcher must use to grab the reader's attention. In a qualitative research proposal, it is vitally important that the introduction provides clarity and contextualization.
   - *The purpose of the study*—The purpose of the study should provide a brief overview of the goals for the proposed research, as it sets the stage for everything that follows in the proposal.

- *Framing the study*—In **framing the study**, the researcher attempts to demonstrate the potential relevance of the proposed study by using a specific context or frame of reference to which the reader will be able to relate. This is also an appropriate subsection for the researcher to indicate—briefly, because this is addressed in greater depth later in the proposal—how the proposed study will contribute positively to this context or frame of reference. This is also a good place for any discussion of a particular theoretical framework to be used in the study.
- *Initial research questions*—As with any research questions, those in a qualitative research proposal should be guided by the purpose of the study and should be tied closely to the body of related literature. Wording of the research questions is critical, albeit for a different reason. Remember that in qualitative research, the questions will likely change and/or emerge during the course of the study; therefore, the initial research questions should allow the researcher room and flexibility for the emergent nature of qualitative research questions.
- (*Review of related literature*)—If the review of related literature is relatively brief—or if the proposal guidelines require—it may be included as part of the introduction section.

3. *Review of related literature*—The review of related literature should present theories and previous research findings that support the initial research questions in the proposed qualitative study. Of course, since the research questions may develop and emerge during the course of the study, additional bodies of literature will need to be explored.

4. *Research procedures*—The research procedures section of the proposal will likely include different levels of specificity, depending on whether or not the researcher conducted any prior fieldwork. Having experience with the designated site and participants would certainly give the researcher greater insight into discussions of the various subsections that appear below.

- *Approach and rationale for the study*—The approach and rationale for the study is the researcher's opportunity to describe the overall approach being used to conduct the qualitative study (e.g., see the various qualitative research designs discussed in Chapter 6).
- *Site and sample selection*—In the site and sample selection subsection of the research procedures, the qualitative researcher clearly describes the site that will be used for fieldwork during the study. Additionally, a description of exactly who will make up the sample, how many individuals will be included, and the procedures used to identify them should be clearly presented. Although the numbers will be drastically different compared with those in a quantitative proposal, it is still critical to indicate and justify the size of the sample to be used.
- *Researcher's role*—The researcher must describe his or her role in various aspects of the study. For example, there will likely be discussions and negotiations regarding access to the site and potential participants. Additionally, the researcher should describe the specific role(s) he or she will play; in other words, and as an example, the researcher may act exclusively as an observer in the process or may be an active participant who is also observing the interactions of a group.

- *Data collection methods*—This section requires the researcher to describe the data collection methods that will be used in the study. This includes the specific fieldwork techniques and instruments to be used, as well as any interview guides, journal prompts, surveys, or other procedures to be used during the course of the study. The researcher should take care to ensure that all initial research questions are appropriately addressed during the discussion of the data collection methods; in other words, discussions of techniques and strategies for each research question should be provided.

- *Strategies for data management*—Since qualitative research has the capability to produce vast amounts of data, it is crucial for the qualitative researcher to describe various strategies for data management. This may include descriptions of how and when handwritten field notes will be recorded and stored, if and when videotaped or audiotaped recordings are planned and where they will be stored, and when interviews might be scheduled and how they will be documented.

- *Data analysis*—The researcher should carefully and systematically describe plans for data analysis. This includes discussions of the processes that will be used to organize, code, and categorize data, likely collected from multiple sources and using various data collection methods. It is important to note if the organization, coding, and categorization will be done by hand or if the researcher will make use of qualitative analysis software programs.

- *Issues of trustworthiness*—Similar to the discussion of data analysis, the researcher should provide a plan for addressing the issue of trustworthiness of the data and ultimate findings during the study. This is typically accomplished by *triangulating* data collected from multiple sources and using a variety of techniques.

- *Ethical considerations*—Ethical considerations are important in any type of research proposal. As researchers, we must always provide assurance that the participants in our studies are not being harmed in any manner, including physically, emotionally, or psychologically. However, because the researcher potentially plays a variety of roles in the research setting, detailed discussions of the ethics involved in those various levels of integration in the site are certainly warranted in the proposal.

5. *Potential contributions of the research*—Even though the researcher addresses this in limited fashion earlier in the proposal, a more detailed discussion of the potential contributions of the research should be included here, now that the reviewers have read how the study will be conducted. Potential implications resulting from the findings of the study should be linked to existing theories and bodies of literature presented earlier in the proposal.

6. *Limitations*—The discussion of limitations in a qualitative research proposal is similar to that in a quantitative proposal. The researcher should discuss any aspect of the study over which he or she has no control but that could affect either ability to conduct the study or ultimate findings of the study. Because of the small number of participants in many qualitative studies, this is a key component of

the proposal. For example, the researcher should discuss the potential problems associated with a lone site—or the majority of participants in a site—deciding to withdraw from the study prior to its completion.

7. *References*—As is the case in a quantitative research proposal, any and all references cited in the introduction or review of related literature should be included in the reference list, and every reference on the list must have appeared somewhere in the proposal.

8. *Appendices*—Appendices included in a qualitative research proposal typically contain informed consent letters, interview guides, and survey instruments. It is not uncommon also to provide a timeline for the study, a list of any associated monetary costs, and a potential outline for the development of the final research report.

Following from the presentation of these components of a qualitative proposal, a generic outline for a qualitative research proposal appears in Figure 10.2. As with

---

FIGURE 10.2 ● A Generic Outline for a Qualitative Research Proposal

 I. Title

 II. Introduction

   A. The Purpose of the Study

   B. Framing the Study

   C. Initial Research Questions

   D. (*Review of Related Literature*)

III. Review of Related Literature

IV. Research Procedures

   A. Approach and Rationale for the Study

   B. Site and Sample Selection

   C. Researcher's Role

   D. Instrumentation

   E. Data Collection Methods

   F. Strategies for Data Management

   G. Data Analysis

   H. Trustworthiness

   I. Ethical Considerations

 V. Potential Contributions of the Research

 VI. Limitations

VII. References

VIII. Appendices

a quantitative research proposal—but even more likely in this case—these various sections and subsections may sometimes be called by other names, even though they contain similar information about a proposed study.

Developmental Activities

1. Are there aspects of either quantitative or qualitative research proposals that you believe are *not* necessary? Why or why not?

2. Which component of a quantitative research proposal do you believe is *the most critical* to a prospective reviewer of the proposal? Why did you select this particular component?

3. Which component of a qualitative research proposal do you believe is *the most critical* to a prospective reviewer of the proposal? Why did you select this particular component?

4. Identify a potential research topic that you believe would be appropriate for quantitative research. In 1 1/2 to 2 pages, develop a brief research proposal for this study, highlighting all the major components.

5. Identify a potential research topic that you believe would be appropriate for qualitative research. In 1 1/2 to 2 pages, develop a brief research proposal for this study, highlighting all the major components.

Summary

- A research proposal is a written plan for conducting a research study.
- Developing a research proposal is important for numerous reasons:

  o A well-thought-out plan can save time and headaches later in the process.
  o It will save the researcher time in the long run.
  o It provides a detailed set of procedures for a research study.
  o It can provide a structure for writing a final research report.
  o It is often required for permission to conduct a study.

- Generally speaking, research proposals share some common elements, including an introduction section, a methodology section, and a proposed timeline for activities within the study.
- The introduction typically consists of a statement of the problem, purpose of the study, justification for the study, and specific research questions.
- The methodology section is one of the most important components of a proposal and consists of a description of the participants, a description of the research design, methods for data collection, and methods for data analysis.

- Quantitative research proposals are fairly structured, with specific components that must be addressed.
- A statement of the problem provides background information and a thorough description of the context in which the problem occurs.
- The purpose of the study clearly explains what the researcher is proposing to investigate.
- The justification or rationale for the study provides an opportunity for the researcher to explain why a given topic is important and worthy of investigation.
- Assumptions are assertions made by the researcher that are believed to be true but not verifiable.
- A limitation is an aspect of a research study that is outside the researcher's control but may have an adverse effect on the outcome of the research.

- A delimitation is a restriction the researcher places on the study to limit its scope.
- Proposed timelines and budgets are often included in research proposals.
- Qualitative research proposals are much less structured and must contain an element of flexibility.
- Qualitative research proposals often benefit from conducting prior fieldwork.
- Titles are often added to qualitative research proposals to provide a context and frame of reference for the study, which is also often included as a separate subsection in the introduction.
- Due to the vast amounts of potential data, strategies for data management should also be included in qualitative research proposals.
- Qualitative researchers should also include a section addressing how they will establish the trustworthiness of their data and findings.

ⓈSAGE edge™

Sharpen your skills with SAGE edge!

edge.sagepub.com/mertler

SAGE edge for Students provides a personalized approach to help you accomplish your coursework goals in an easy-to-use learning environment. You'll find action plans, mobile-friendly eFlashcards, and quizzes as well as video, web, and resources and links to SAGE journal articles to support and expand on the concepts presented in this chapter.

COLLECTING AND ANALYZING DATA

PART III

11

Qualitative Data Collection and Analysis

Student Learning Objectives

After studying Chapter 11, students will be able to do the following:

1. List and describe examples of purposeful sampling techniques

2. Name and describe the major categories of qualitative data collection techniques

3. Explain what is meant by the trustworthiness of qualitative data

4. Identify and define various criteria for determining the validity of qualitative research

5. Describe various strategies that can be used to enhance the validity of qualitative research

6. Describe the general process of inductive analysis

7. Design qualitative data collection procedures and successfully analyze resulting qualitative data for a research topic of interest

In this chapter, we revisit qualitative research methods. This time, however, we focus on procedures for identifying and selecting participants and data collection techniques, as well as techniques for analyzing qualitative data. Several concrete examples are provided to help demonstrate the procedures and techniques discussed.

Sampling Techniques in Qualitative Research

Before we can begin to collect data from participants in a qualitative research study, we must identify and select those participants. One of the more important things to keep in mind about qualitative research is that the goal is not to generalize to a larger population but simply to develop an in-depth description of a specific phenomenon in a particular setting. Therefore, the qualitative researcher *intentionally* selects specific individuals and sites (Creswell, 2005). This constitutes an important distinction between quantitative and qualitative approaches to conducting research. In quantitative research, the focus is on "random sampling"—individuals are selected so they are representative of the larger population, and at the end of the research study, the findings are generalized back to the larger population (you will learn more about sampling techniques used in quantitative studies in Chapter 12). However, in qualitative research, the researcher selects particular people or sites that help best explain and describe the phenomenon being studied.

Because of this targeted approach to selecting participants for a study, Creswell (2005) uses the term *purposeful sampling* when talking about various procedures for selecting samples for qualitative studies. **Purposeful sampling** involves the intentional selection of individuals and sites to learn about or understand the topic at hand (Creswell, 2005). The key in this intentional selection of participants is the researcher's judgment of the degree to which potential participants possess the information needed to address the topic or answer the research questions. The goal is to find participants who are "information rich" (Creswell, 2005). It is important, then, to see that purposeful sampling applies to both individuals and sites.

Numerous purposeful sampling techniques can be used in qualitative research studies. Nine of the more commonly used techniques are described below (Creswell, 2005; Glesne, 2006; Plano Clark & Creswell, 2010) and summarized in Figure 11.1. It is important to note that the first six methods occur prior to starting a qualitative study, whereas the last three occur after a study has already begun.

1. **Maximum variation sampling**—The researcher samples cases or individuals that differ on some important characteristic or trait (e.g., schools with different racial compositions). The goal of this sampling strategy is to build the complexity of our world into the research design. The researcher must first identify the particular characteristic and then purposefully select sites or individuals that display different dimensions or qualities of that characteristic (e.g., selecting one high school that is predominantly African American, a second that is predominantly Hispanic, and a third that is predominantly Caucasian).

2. **Extreme case sampling**—This purposeful sampling strategy focuses on the study of an *outlier* case, or a case that displays extreme characteristics. The outlying characteristics may be deemed positive or negative (e.g., a program that is a unique success or one that is noticeably failing). The goal is to learn more about a case that is particularly bothersome or exceptionally illuminating (e.g., schools that receive persistent funding due to continual academic growth among their students).

3. **Typical sampling**—In opposition to extreme case sampling, this sampling technique focuses on the study of a person or site that is *typical* to outsiders who might be unfamiliar with a particular situation (e.g., an administrator who has been at the same school for many, many years and has become synonymous with the culture in that building).

4. **Theory** or **concept sampling**—Using this technique, the researcher samples individuals or sites because they can help generate or discover a new theory or concept. Obviously, this approach would be useful when conducting grounded theory research studies.

5. **Homogeneous sampling**—This sampling technique operates somewhat in opposition to maximum variation sampling. Here, certain sites or individuals are selected because they possess a *similar* trait or characteristic. The researcher must first carefully identify the characteristic and then find individuals or sites that possess it, such that every person or site included in the sample shares that characteristic.

6. **Critical sampling**—This sampling technique focuses on individuals or sites that represent in dramatic terms the phenomenon being studied. It is critical to sample those individuals or sites because they represent the incident or event in exceptional ways. For example, a researcher would learn much more about teen suicide if the study took place in a high school where there had been six suicides among students in the past 10 years.

7. **Opportunistic sampling**—In some qualitative studies, the focus of the study may emerge during its course. Researchers often find that they need to collect new and different information to answer those emerging questions. This purposeful sampling technique takes place after the research begins, to capitalize on the researcher's realization of new or unfolding events. As the design—and direction—of the study emerges, the researcher may realize that different sites or individuals are needed to better or more appropriately answer the research questions. It should be noted that not all qualitative research is emergent; only experienced qualitative researchers should engage in truly emergent research designs and studies.

8. **Snowball sampling**—In many research situations, it is difficult for the researcher to identify the best individuals to provide data for the study, perhaps because of unfamiliarity with the site or situation. In this case, the researcher may observe or interview participants and then ask them to recommend other individuals who they think would be a benefit to the study. The "snowballing" occurs as a participant recommends another individual, who recommends another individual, and so on.

9. **Confirming and disconfirming sampling**—Once data collection and preliminary analysis have taken place, researchers often look for additional individuals or sites to confirm or disconfirm their initial findings. This method of purposeful sampling is used as a mechanism for following up on previously collected data to verify the accuracy of those findings.

The size of samples used in qualitative research studies can vary greatly from one study to the next and also can depend on several factors. One crucial factor is the choice of qualitative methodology (see Chapter 6). Some methodologies may use only one individual or site, whereas others may use as many as 30 or 40 individuals, possibly located at multiple sites (Creswell, 2005). In most qualitative research studies, however, the number of research sites or participants will be relatively small. An objective of the qualitative

FIGURE 11.1 ● Types of Purposeful Sampling Techniques

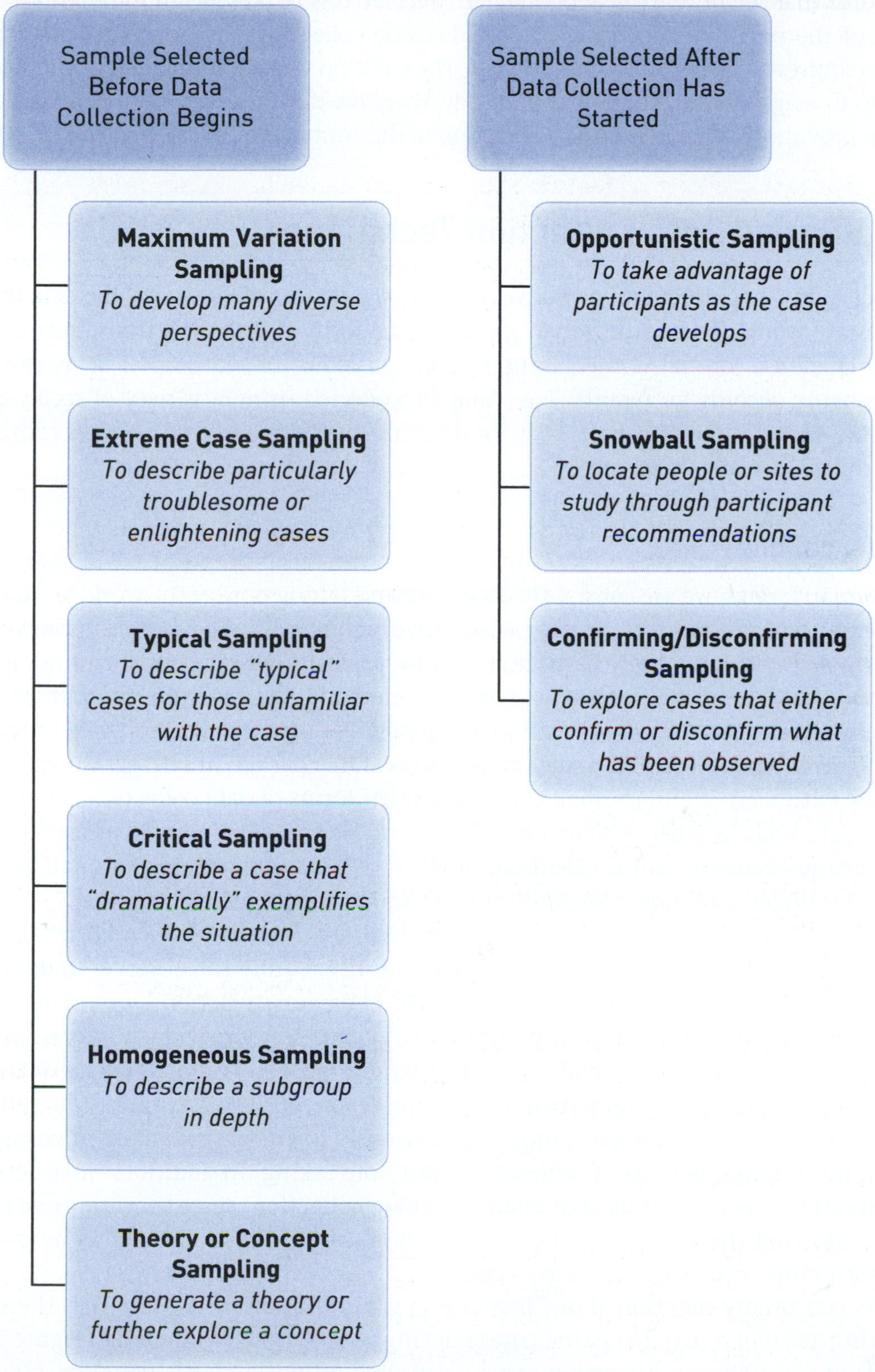

Sample Selected Before Data Collection Begins

- **Maximum Variation Sampling**
  To develop many diverse perspectives

- **Extreme Case Sampling**
  To describe particularly troublesome or enlightening cases

- **Typical Sampling**
  To describe "typical" cases for those unfamiliar with the case

- **Critical Sampling**
  To describe a case that "dramatically" exemplifies the situation

- **Homogeneous Sampling**
  To describe a subgroup in depth

- **Theory or Concept Sampling**
  To generate a theory or further explore a concept

Sample Selected After Data Collection Has Started

- **Opportunistic Sampling**
  To take advantage of participants as the case develops

- **Snowball Sampling**
  To locate people or sites to study through participant recommendations

- **Confirming/Disconfirming Sampling**
  To explore cases that either confirm or disconfirm what has been observed

Source: Adapted from Creswell (2005) and Plano Clark and Creswell (2010).

researcher is to strike a reasonable balance between the number of sites and/or participants and the depth in which he or she can study those individuals or sites—remaining mindful that the primary goal of qualitative research is to provide an in-depth description of the phenomenon being studied. Because collecting and analyzing qualitative data requires a considerable amount time, the addition of each individual or site simply serves to lengthen the duration of the study, therefore diminishing the researcher's ability to provide a deep and holistic description of the entity being studied (Creswell, 2005).

Qualitative Data Collection Techniques

Recall from Chapter 6 that qualitative data are *narrative*; in other words, the data themselves are words. These words may appear in the form of interview transcripts, observational notes, journal entries, transcriptions of audio- or videotapes, or as existing documents, records, or reports. They may be collected using a variety of techniques, but it is important to remember that the resulting qualitative data will always consist of descriptive, narrative accounts.

Observations

As human beings, we are constantly observing and taking note of the world around us. Furthermore, as educators, we are constantly observing our students and others with whom we work. On a daily basis, however, we typically observe our surroundings in a somewhat haphazard manner—something more akin to watching than observing. **Observations,** as a means of collecting qualitative data, involve *carefully* watching and *systematically* recording what you see and hear in a particular setting. Observations can be extremely useful in situations where other forms of data collection simply will not work, such as when teachers want to check for students' nonverbal reactions to something occurring in the classroom or when students are working in small groups, to better understand how they interact and communicate with one another.

Classroom observations can range from highly structured to semistructured to unstructured. **Structured observations** typically require the observer to do nothing but observe, looking usually for specific behaviors, reactions, or interactions. Because so many other things are going on in a given classroom when observations are being made, it is often difficult to conduct structured observations. **Unstructured** or **semistructured observations** allow the researcher the flexibility to attend to other events or activities occurring simultaneously in the classroom or to engage in brief, but intense, periods of observation and note taking. In addition, unstructured observations are more typical of qualitative data collection, since they are "free flowing," allowing the researcher to shift focus from one event to another as new—and perhaps more interesting—events occur.

As was briefly mentioned in Chapter 6, it is also important to note that there are varying levels of researcher participation during observations. As shown in Figure 11.2, levels of researcher participation can range from "primarily participant" on one end of the spectrum to "primarily observer" on the other end (Glesne, 2006). Participant

FIGURE 11.2 ● The Participant–Observer Continuum

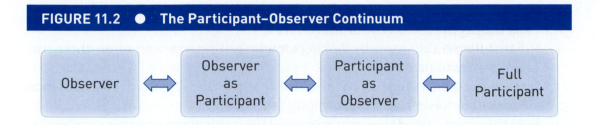

observation may serve as the sole means of data collection, although it is typically supplemented with interviews or other forms of data collection. Participation on the part of the qualitative researcher may fall anywhere along the continuum; there may be times when the researcher finds himself or herself at different points on the continuum during different stages of data collection.

On the extreme left end of the continuum, the researcher acts entirely as an observer. While in this role, the researcher has little or no interaction with the participants being studied (Glesne, 2006). Oftentimes, individual participants who are being observed by a researcher who has assumed the observer role may not even know they are being observed. Moving to the right on the continuum, the next defined point is the observer as participant. An **observer as participant** remains first and foremost an observer but does have some level of interaction with the participants being studied (Glesne, 2006). At a minimum, the participants know they are being observed; so there may be some nonverbal communication or perhaps even casual conversation between the participants and the researcher. While in this role, the researcher is typically seated at the back of the room, observing and taking notes; there is no formal conversation or other interaction with participants.

A much more active role in the setting and context is taken on by the **participant as observer**. In addition to observing and taking notes, the researcher has the opportunity to interact more formally with participants involved in the study. However, the qualitative researcher must be cautious when assuming this role. Glesne (2006) notes that the more you function as a participant in the world you are actively researching, the more you risk losing your objectivity. The obvious trade-off is that the more you participate, the greater your opportunity to learn firsthand what is going on in that setting. The role of the **full participant** is located at the far right end of the continuum. In this role, the researcher is not only the "researcher" but also simultaneously a fully functioning member of the community (Glesne, 2006). In this case, the researcher is first and foremost part of a group—as opposed to being an "outsider"—who also happens to be collecting data on the group members.

Glesne (2006) is quick to point out that the location of the researcher's role along the continuum is not always a conscious decision. Your role as a researcher may depend on several things, including the nature of the research question you are investigating, the context of the study, and the nature of the group and its participants (in other words, how likely or feasible is it that you might be able to "join" them as a participant?).

Creswell (2005) has specified a general process for conducting observations, as outlined in the following steps:

1. Select a site to be observed that can help you best understand the phenomenon serving as the focus of your study.
2. Ease into the site slowly by looking around, getting a general sense of the site, and taking limited notes.
3. Once you gain a sense of the site, identify who or what you will observe, when you will observe it, and for how long.
4. At this point, determine your role along the participant–observer continuum.
5. Conduct multiple observations over an extended period of time to obtain a thorough understanding of the site and participants.
6. Develop a means for recording your observations.
7. Make decisions about what information you will record during an observation.
8. Record both descriptive (factual) and interpretive (commentary) notes (you will read more about these below).
9. When observing, make yourself known but remain as unobtrusive as possible.
10. Upon concluding an observation, slowly remove yourself from the site.

Observations are usually recorded in the form of field notes. **Field notes** are written observations of what you see taking place in a particular setting. Attempting to record everything you see can be overwhelming, especially when trying to determine what is important (and, therefore, worth recording) and what is not. As you observe and record what you see, you will undoubtedly begin to focus on things that are interesting or important. As you make observations over time, patterns will begin to emerge from the data you have collected.

When recording field notes, you may want to consider dividing each page of your notebook into two columns. You should use the left column for recording your actual observations and the right column for noting preliminary interpretations of what has been observed. Bogdan and Biklen (2007) refer to these interpretations as **observer's comments**. Observer's comments often shed light on the emerging patterns in your observational data. Including observer's comments in your observation notes is also one way to integrate *ongoing* analysis into the process of conducting qualitative research. The separation of these two types of commentaries is critical so that *actual* observations are not confused with what you *think* the observed event *means*. As you know, researchers conducting qualitative studies need to remain as objective as possible in the records kept and data collected. As an aside, this need for objectivity also dictates that you not censor what you record. In addition, interpretations of observations may change over time as you collect more data; having a record of these changing interpretations can be invaluable over the course of your study. An example of a page from a book of field notes recorded several years ago during a study of positive reinforcement in a preschool setting, depicting this two-column format of actual observations and associated observer's comments, is provided in Figure 11.3.

Written field notes can become problematic, however. They are often insufficient to depict the richness and details of what one is observing. Videotapes can provide assistance as a tool for recording observations, although they are not without their own limitations. Background noises may prevent you from hearing what you were hoping

FIGURE 11.3 ● Sample Field Note Page, Showing Actual Observation Notes (Left Column) and Preliminary Interpretations (Right Column)

Observation #3 June 10 10:15–11:00	< Observations >	< Observer's Comments (OCs) >
Time →	There were very few forms of interactions between the children and the teachers. The children were playing; behaving, for the most part. One of the teachers was pushing two girls on swings and the other teacher was sitting near the wading pools, watching the children. Carol said several things to certain children. She repeatedly used phrases such as, "Don't do that," "Don't throw water," "Don't throw that in the pool," and "You're gonna break the sprinkler . . . don't do that!"	I don't think that, in the entire time I was there today, I heard one positive comment or saw one positive gesture. It seemed that the teachers were in only a supervisory role. All they appeared to be doing was supervising the behavior and actions of the children in order to prevent accidents or injuries. I'm not saying that this is wrong; on the contrary, it is necessary when conducting an activity of this nature, especially with very young children. I just expected to hear some positive behaviors being praised in addition to the negative being addressed.
	Several children came close to hurting themselves and/or others. One three-year-old girl tried to pour water over the head of a one-year-old. Two boys were throwing beach balls into the pool and inadvertently hitting smaller children who were playing in the pool.	I began to wonder if this type of activity (i.e., supervisory in nature) did not permit the use of many positive comments. Maybe these teachers leave those types of positive reinforcement for classroom activities. Perhaps activities that require quicker thought and action on the part of the teachers—in order to prevent children from being hurt, or worse—don't allow for positive comments or identification of children to model positive behaviors.
	The children continued to play in the pools, the sprinkler, and the swings. I observed very little verbal interaction between the teachers and the children. Initially, most of what I heard came from Carol. She made several comments to the children, such as "Don't do that" and "You need to ride that bike over there." Carol's daughter picked up a garden hose and began playing with it. Twice Carol told the girl to stop playing with the hose and put it down, but to no avail. The third time she spoke to her, she said, "You better put that down or it will turn into a snake and bite you."	Carol's comment was not in jest. She said it with a firm tone in her voice. I didn't like hearing this. I was always taught never to threaten children, regardless of their age and regardless of how idle the threat. I find myself expecting to see and hear this kind of behavior from Carol and not from Marilyn, as I have not yet heard her say something of this nature.

to observe on videotape. Furthermore, video cameras can capture only what is happening in a given direction (i.e., the direction the camera is facing). Prior to beginning any formal observations, researchers should experiment and become familiar with various methods of recording observations to find what works best for the particular setting and situation. It is, however, important to remember that whatever mechanism you use to record your observations, you simply cannot record everything that occurs.

Interviews

An alternative to observing people is to ask them questions directly. This can be accomplished in several ways. **Interviews** are conversations between the researcher and participants in the study. Interviews can be conducted with individuals or groups. It is best to prepare an **interview guide**, containing either specific or general questions to be asked, prior to conducting any interviews.

Similar to observations, interviews are typically classified as structured, semistructured, or open-ended. In a **structured interview**, the researcher begins with an interview guide consisting of a set of predetermined questions. Those questions—and *only* those questions—are asked of each person being interviewed. This is typically done for the sake of consistency. Interestingly, consistency is usually not a concern when collecting qualitative data; it is typically more desirable for the researcher to have some flexibility and to be able to ask clarifying questions (not initially included on the interview guide), to pursue information not initially planned for, and to seek different information from different people.

When gathering truly qualitative data, interviews are probably best conducted following semistructured or open-ended formats. In **semistructured interviews**, the researcher asks several "base" questions but also has the option of following up a given response with additional questions, depending on the situation. When developing interview guides, it is advisable to keep your questions brief, clear, and worded in simple language. For example, if we were interviewing students about their opinions of our school, we might ask the following questions (the bold text represents the base questions asked of everyone, and the italicized text represents the optional, follow-up, probing questions):

- **What do you enjoy most about this school?**

  Why do you enjoy that aspect so much?

  Do you think other schools have this particular benefit?

- **What are your favorite academic subjects?**

  Why is that your favorite subject?

  Do you have any others?

  What about extracurricular activities? Do you participate in any?

  Which are your favorites? Why?

- **What do you like least about this school?**

  Why do you like that so little?

  Is there anything the principal or teachers could do to improve that aspect?

The semistructured interview guide used in the positive reinforcement study referred to earlier (see Figure 11.3) is shown in Figure 11.4, and a portion of the transcript from one interview is shown in Figure 11.5.

Open-ended interviews provide the respondent with only a few questions, very broad in nature. The intent is to gather different kinds of information from various individuals, depending largely on how each person interprets the questions. For example, an open-ended series of interview questions about school climate might include the following:

- What does "school" mean to you?
- What do you like about school?
- What do you dislike?

FIGURE 11.4 ● **Sample Semistructured Interview Guide**

SEMISTRUCTURED INTERVIEW GUIDE

Interview With the Director:

- What type of training and/or certification is held by your classroom teachers?
- Do you have any advice or suggestions for giving positive reinforcement, as discussed with your teachers?

  - How have those suggestions been received by your teachers?
  - Have they attempted to implement them?

- What do you see as acceptable forms of positive reinforcement for children in your school?
- What do you think the meaning of positive reinforcement is for you?

  - Do you think it is the same for your teachers? Why or why not?
  - Do you think it is the same for your students? Why or why not?

Interviews With the Teachers:

- Has your director ever provided you with suggestions for giving positive reinforcement?

  - If so, have you used any of them?
  - To what extent have they been successful?

- What do you see as acceptable forms of positive reinforcement for children?
- What do you think the meaning of positive reinforcement is for you?

  - Do you think it is the same for your students? Why or why not?

FIGURE 11.5 ● Portion of a Semistructured Interview Transcript

CM: How would you describe positive reinforcement? How would you define that, or what does that mean to you?

"Carol": Positive reinforcement means not yelling at the children. It means talking to them in a positive way. Sometimes you can lose your temper. I try not to use time-out a whole lot. I give them choices. If you're going to throw the blocks, then you're going to pick them up. If you're going to hit someone in the head with that toy, then you're going to go apologize to them. And tell them the difference between right and wrong instead of, . . . take for instance E., who likes to throw toys at everybody. Instead of putting him in the corner and my picking up all the toys he's thrown, I make a game out of it. Instead of "E., pick them up, pick them up," we count them as we put them in. So he's still having to do what he did— you know, having to clean up his mess—but we're making a game out of it. Instead of "this was wrong and you're going to sit in the corner for this."

CM: So they don't see it so much as a punishment. Rather, you try to turn it into something constructive?

"Carol": Right. Like this morning, he punched a little girl in the face, and Gail and I both agreed that he needs to sit out of the group for a little while.

CM: So it really depends on the situation? It would be hard to take that situation and turn it into something positive.

"Carol": Right. It depends on what they've done and if they keep doing it all day long. Then they need time away. That's why we have that carpet out there. If the child needs to leave the room and get away from the other children for 5 minutes, they go out and sit on the quiet rug.

As mentioned earlier, interviews are not conducted only with individuals but also with groups. **Focus group** is the name given to simultaneous interviews of people making up a relatively small group, usually no more than 10 to 12 people. This type of interview typically lasts between 1 and 2 hours. Focus groups are especially useful when time is limited and because people often are more comfortable talking in a small group, as opposed to one-on-one interviews. Furthermore, interactions among the focus-group participants may be extremely informative due to people's tendency to feed off others' comments. However, when conducting a focus-group interview, it is important to ensure that *each* participant has the opportunity to speak and share her or his perspective. Sometimes one or two individuals will dominate the discussion; it is the researcher's responsibility to monitor the discussion closely and prevent this from happening. An example of guiding questions used for a study incorporating data collected via a focus group is provided in Figure 11.6.

FIGURE 11.6 ● Sample Guiding Questions Used for a Focus-Group Interview

1. **Perceptions of the process:**

    a) What were your overall perceptions of the process used to gather student feedback on your teaching?

    b) What aspects of the process did you like?

    c) What aspects did you dislike?

2. **Usefulness of feedback:**

    a) How was the feedback you received useful to you?

    b) How was the feedback not useful to you?

3. **Changes to teaching behaviors:**

    a) What changes have you made to any of your teaching behaviors as a result of the student feedback?

    b) What behaviors, if any, are you considering changing in your teaching as a result of the student feedback?

4. **Benefits and consequences:**

    a) What unanticipated benefits did you experience as a result of this process of collecting student feedback?

    b) What negative consequences did you experience as a result of this process of collecting student feedback?

5. **Appropriateness of method:**

    a) Is this method, that of using rating scales, the most appropriate way to collect student feedback?

    b) What method(s) might work better? Why?

6. **Appropriate situations:**

    a) For what specific school situations or student groups would this method of collecting student feedback not be appropriate?

    b) What could be changed in order to make it more suitable in this context or to these students?

7. **Feasibility of process:**

    a) Is this process feasible for teachers to conduct on their own?

    b) If not, what would need to be changed in order to make it more feasible?

(Continued)

FIGURE 11.6 ● (Continued)

8. **Frequency of administration:**

    a) How often should this information be collected from students?

9. **Improvements:**

    a) What specific things could be changed in order to improve this process of collecting student feedback?

10. **Desire to continue:**

    a) Based on your experience, will you continue to collect student feedback in this manner?

    b) If not, will you continue to collect this information but do so by using a different method? Can you describe that method?

---

*Upon completion of the above questions, explain to the participants that the meeting is about to end. Ask them to take a moment and think about what has been discussed. Then, one by one, ask them if they have any additional comments. If necessary, explore relevant or new comments in greater depth.

General steps and guidelines for conducting interviews as part of qualitative research studies appear below (adapted from Creswell, 2005, and Gay, Mills, & Airasian, 2009):

1. Identify the individuals you want to interview.
2. Determine the type of interview you plan to use.
3. Develop your interview protocol, or guiding questions.
4. Locate a quiet, suitable place for conducting the interview.
5. Prior to the interview, seek permission from the interviewee to conduct and audiotape the conversation.
6. In addition to audiotaping, take brief notes during the interview.
7. During the interview, plan to listen more and talk less.
8. Follow your interview guide, but plan to be flexible during the interview.
9. Try not to interrupt the interviewee; let the participant respond fully to your questions.
10. Use probing questions to obtain additional information, but avoid asking leading questions.
11. Avoid judging participants' views, beliefs, or responses; your role is simply to ask the questions and record their responses.
12. Be courteous, professional, and grateful when the interview is complete.

Interviewing, like observing, is a challenging task. It takes some practice to collect meaningful data using either of these techniques. I suggest that, before you use them as part of a real qualitative research study, you practice by observing people in public places (e.g., a shopping mall or sporting event) or by interviewing your friends and family members.

Journals

Teachers, students, and others included in your qualitative research site may keep data **journals**, which can provide valuable insight into the workings of a classroom or school. **Student journals** perform a similar role to that of homework, in that they provide a sense of students' daily thoughts, perceptions, and experiences in the classroom. **Teacher journals** can give teachers the opportunity to maintain narrative accounts of their professional reflections on practice. Class journals are another means of incorporating journaling into qualitative data collection. A **class journal** is a less formal version of a student journal. Students are encouraged to enter their thoughts, ideas, perceptions, feedback, or other forms of response, such as pictures or diagrams, as they wish. Teachers may want to provide some sort of guidelines for making entries in the class journal so it does not become a "quasi-teacher-approved" form of graffiti that may be offensive to other students.

Existing Documents and Records

Often, qualitative research necessitates the gathering of data that already exist. These data are essentially anything collected for a reason *other* than the research study but now being used as data for the study. These **existing documents and records** might take several forms, including (at the individual student level) attendance records, test scores, previous grades, discipline records, and cumulative folders, and (at the school or district level) curriculum materials, textbooks, instructional manipulatives, attendance rates, retention rates, graduation rates, newspaper stories about school events, minutes from faculty or school board meetings, and standardized test scores—perhaps disaggregated by grade level, gender, or ethnicity. However, a word of caution is in order: Whenever using existing data, the researcher must follow the given school district's approved procedures for securing access to these various types of data, and must undertake their use and the ultimate reporting of the results of any analyses in an ethical manner.

Characteristics of Qualitative Data: Accuracy, Credibility, and Dependability

When collecting data for qualitative research studies, it is important for researchers to ensure the data's quality. If data collected for the study are imprecise or if the researcher has actually measured something other than what was intended, at a minimum the data will be inaccurate and misleading; of course, so then will the conclusions of the study (which follow logically from the data collected and analyzed). Validity of research data deals with the extent to which the data collected accurately measure what they purport to measure (i.e., that which the researcher intended to measure). As you will see in Chapter 12, this definition is essentially the same for qualitative data as for quantitative data; however, the methods used to ensure this accuracy differ between the two types of data.

When dealing with the validity of qualitative data, researchers are essentially concerned with the data's *trustworthiness*—for example, their *accuracy* and *believability*.

Trustworthiness is established by examining the *credibility, transferability, dependability*, and *confirmability* of qualitative data, as well as the resultant findings. Gay and colleagues (2009) describe each of these characteristics of qualitative data as follows:

- **Credibility** involves establishing that the results of qualitative research are credible, or believable, from the perspective of the participant(s) in the research. A researcher must factor into data collection and analysis all the complexities of the study, and address issues that are not easily explained.
- **Transferability** involves the provision of descriptive and contextualized statements so that someone reading the study can easily identify with the setting. Remember, in qualitative studies the goal is not to generalize findings to other settings but, rather, to gain a clear, in-depth understanding of this particular setting.
- **Dependability** emphasizes the need for the researcher to account for the ever-changing context within which research occurs. The researcher is responsible for describing the changes that occur in the setting and how these changes affected the way the researcher approached the study; this helps ensure that the data are stable.
- **Confirmability** is a process of establishing the neutrality and objectivity of the data.

Maxwell (as cited in Gay et al., 2009) has provided criteria for establishing the validity of qualitative research through concrete actions to be taken by the researcher. These five criteria, if incorporated into the research study, can contribute to the overall trustworthiness of the data and research.

1. **Descriptive validity**—This is the *factual accuracy* of the account provided in the research. Researchers must be sure not to distort, manipulate, or fabricate events based on inferences.
2. **Interpretive validity**—This refers to the *accuracy of the interpretations* of participants' behaviors and words, and concern that their perspectives are accurately represented.
3. **Theoretical validity**—This concerns the extent to which the study, and its final report, relate the phenomenon being studied to a broader theory.
4. **Evaluative validity**—This refers to the extent to which the researcher behaved objectively enough to report the data and findings in an unbiased manner, without making evaluations or judgments of the collected data.
5. **Generalizability**—This has to do with the extent to which the findings are applicable *within* the community that was studied and can be extended to settings that were *not studied* by the researcher.

The qualitative researcher can use several techniques and strategies to ensure, or at least enhance, the validity of both research data and findings. A key aspect of many of the strategies requires researchers to continually check their perceptions to ensure that they are not being misinformed and that what they *think* they are seeing and hearing is what they *are* seeing and hearing (Fraenkel, Wallen, & Hyun, 2012). These practices include the following strategies (adapted from Gay et al., 2009, and Fraenkel et al., 2012):

- *Use a variety of instruments, methods, and sources to collect data.* The use of multiple methods and sources of data collection will only serve to enhance the validity of research findings. This process of using multiple methods, data collection strategies, data sources—and perhaps even multiple researchers (Glesne, 2006)—is known as *triangulation*. A given finding is supported by showing that independent measures of it tend to agree with or at least do not directly contradict each other. For example, when you observe Susan *doing* something that she *told* you in an interview she does and also indicated on an open-ended questionnaire (see Figure 11.7), you likely will have more confidence in concluding that this is an accurate depiction of Susan's practice. In other words, your interview data have been supported by your observation data and by the questionnaire responses. Had any of the three sources of data contradicted the others, you likely would have arrived at a different conclusion—perhaps that Susan was telling you what she thought you wanted to hear.

- *Engage in persistent and prolonged participation at the study site.* The length of time you spend observing, interviewing, and participating at the site is critical in qualitative research. The idea here is that you spend a substantial amount of time "in the field," so to speak. The more time you spend in the setting, the more likely you will be able to determine what is typical, atypical, and problematic within that setting; the more time spent productively observing participants, and interacting and engaging with them, the more you will be able to develop trust with and get to know them, learn the culture of their setting (whether it be a classroom or school building), and observe patterns of behavior to the point of establishing routine (Glesne, 2006). Observing or interviewing only once or twice will not afford you this luxury.

- *Use peer debriefing and external audits as a means of verifying your processes.* **Peer debriefing** is the act of using other professionals (perhaps colleagues or critical friends) who can help you reflect on the research by reviewing and critiquing your processes of data collection, analysis, and interpretation. An **external audit** involves

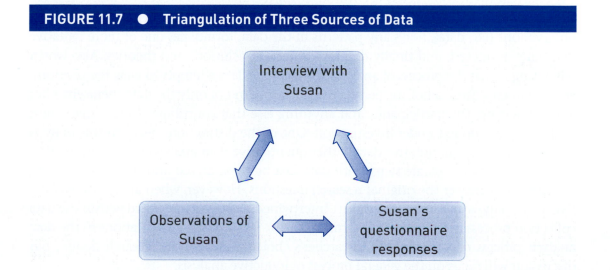

FIGURE 11.7 ● Triangulation of Three Sources of Data

the use of an outside individual (again, a colleague, critical friend, etc.) to review and evaluate the final research report. Both of these strategies provide opportunities for different sets of eyes—as well as additional minds—to review and evaluate the research process, enhancing its overall credibility.

- *Conduct member checks.* **Member checking** is a process of asking participants who were directly involved in the study to review the accuracy of the research report. This is typically done during the draft stage of the report, prior to sharing it in its final form. The purpose of sharing these data sources is to make sure you have represented your participants and their ideas accurately (Glesne, 2006).

- *Develop detailed descriptions and notes, and engage in reflexivity.* All notes from observations and interviews should be as detailed as possible. In addition, making use of observer's comments during data collection to document your initial interpretations, assumptions, or biases will be critical in the latter stages of the research study. This process of intermingling your own preliminary thoughts and interpretations with your notes is known as **reflexivity**.

- *Analyze negative cases.* Sometimes cases (i.e., people or places) do not fit the pattern you have observed up to a certain point in the study. Instead of ignoring these negative cases, you should attempt to eliminate them as *negative* cases by revising the pattern until they fit better or more appropriately. This is sometimes facilitated through prolonged time spent in the setting.

The appropriateness of these strategies as connected to the four criteria for establishing trustworthiness (i.e., credibility, transferability, dependability, and confirmability) is depicted in Table 11.1.

Qualitative Data Analysis Techniques

Recall from earlier chapters that analysis of qualitative data involves the general process of **inductive analysis**. There is no single, widely accepted approach for analyzing qualitative data (Creswell, 2005; Leedy & Ormrod, 2013); it is an eclectic process, at best (Creswell, 2005). When conducting qualitative data analysis, the researcher begins with specific observations (i.e., data), notes any patterns in the data, formulates one or more tentative questions of interest, and finally develops general conclusions and theories. Also worth reiterating is that the process of analyzing qualitative data attempts to view the phenomenon of interest from a holistic perspective, factoring in not only the data themselves but also the setting, the participants, and anything else that contributes to the uniqueness of the specific context under investigation. One of the distinctions between the analysis of qualitative and quantitative data is that quantitative data analysis and interpretation are essentially two separate steps, with data first being analyzed and then results being interpreted to answer the original research questions. However, when analyzing qualitative data, analysis and interpretation are intertwined and often integrated within the data collection process as well (Leedy & Ormrod, 2013). While there are variations to the data analysis process depending on a researcher's choice of qualitative research design, our discussion will focus on the general process of inductive analysis.

TABLE 11.1 ● Criteria and Strategies for Establishing the Validity of Qualitative Data and Research		
Criteria	**Definition**	**Strategies**
Credibility	Researcher's ability to take into account the complexities of the study and address patterns that are not easily explained	• Engage in persistent and prolonged participation at the site. • Use peer debriefing. • Practice triangulation. • Use member checks. • Provide detailed descriptions. • Analyze negative cases.
Transferability	Researcher's ability to portray a highly descriptive account of the setting	• Provide detailed descriptions of the setting. • Collect detailed descriptive data.
Dependability	Stability of the data collected	• Practice triangulation. • Use external audits.
Confirmability	Objectivity of the data collected	• Practice triangulation. • Practice reflexivity.

Source: Adapted from Gay et al. (2009).

Inductive Analysis

After gathering potentially voluminous amounts of qualitative data, the researcher may feel a bit overwhelmed with the task of analysis that lies ahead, as it can seem a monumental undertaking (Parsons & Brown, 2002). The real challenge in conducting an *inductive analysis* of qualitative data is to remember that you are trying to reduce the volume of information you have collected, thereby identifying and organizing the data into important patterns and themes to construct some sort of framework for presenting the key findings of the action research study. But you want to be sure that, during this process of data reduction, you do not minimize, distort, oversimplify, or misinterpret any of your data. Parsons and Brown (2002) describe the process of qualitative analysis as a means of "systematically organizing and presenting the findings . . . in ways that facilitate the understanding of these data" (p. 55). They further describe a three-step process for conducting this analysis: organization, description, and interpretation. Note that these steps are typically iterative, requiring the researcher to collect more data, read and organize it again, attempt to interpret it again . . . and then possibly collect *more* data and begin the cycle all over (Gay et al., 2009).

The organizational step of inductive analysis involves *reduction* of the potentially massive amounts of narrative data in the form of interview transcripts, observational field notes, and any existing documents or records you have collected. This is accomplished through the development of a system of categorization, often referred to as a **coding scheme**, which is used to group data that provide similar types of information (Parsons & Brown, 2002). As you read through your transcripts, field notes, and documents, looking for patterns and themes, categories of narrative information will begin to emerge. You should make note of each category as it appears and code your narrative data accordingly. This is accomplished by searching for words or phrases that reflect specific events or observations and that begin to repeat themselves throughout your data. Some researchers will do this with different-colored markers or by organizing them on index cards; others may use scissors to cut apart the pages of transcripts and field notes and then physically group them together, or use sticky notes for easy reorganization and recategorization. It is important to find some mechanism for coding that works for you.

Additionally, software programs can assist the researcher in organizing the various categories (Creswell, 2005; Leedy & Ormrod, 2013). It is important to keep in mind that these software programs will not analyze the data for you; analysis occurs in the mind of the researcher. The programs will simply aid in organizing, categorizing, and retrieving data. For some qualitative research studies, a simple spreadsheet program such as Excel may be sufficient for data organization (Leedy & Ormrod, 2013). However, for larger data sets, Creswell (2005) stresses that researchers should find a qualitative analysis software program that meets the following requirements:

- It should be relatively easy to use.
- It should accept both text files (i.e., from transcripts) and images (i.e., photographs).
- It should permit you to read and review text and images, and categorize them.
- It should permit easy sorting and searching for text passages and images you may want to include in your report.

Available qualitative analysis software programs include the following (Creswell, 2005; Leedy & Ormrod, 2013):

- Atlas.ti (www.atlasti.de; *for Mac and Windows*)
- Dedoose (app.dedoose.com; *for Mac and Windows*)
- Ethnograph (www.qualisresearch.com; *for Windows*)
- HyperRESEARCH (www.researchware.com/products/hyperresearch.html; *for Mac and Windows*)
- MAXQDA (www.maxqda.com; *for Mac and Windows*)
- QSR N6 and QSR NVivo (www.qsrinternational.com; *for Mac and Windows*)

Some aspects of a study that addressed the use of positive reinforcement in a preschool setting have been shared in this chapter. This study involved numerous field observations and interviews with staff members at the preschool visited throughout the study. Once data collection had been completed, it was necessary to begin wading through field notes, complete with observer's comments, along with interview transcripts. This process included development of the coding scheme that appears in Figure 11.8.

FIGURE 11.8 ● Sample Coding Scheme Resulting From Data Collected as Part of a Study of Positive Reinforcement

Coding Categories Used in the Analysis of the Data

Desc	Description of Sit	**MO**	Missed Opportunity
TChar	Teacher Characteristics	**Modl**	Modeling
TQual	Teacher Qualifications	**TCRel**	Teacher/Child Relationship
Meth	Methodology	**Act**	Academic/Social Activities
CAct	Child Activity	**Sup**	Supervisory Role
TBeh	Teacher Behavior	**PR**	Positive Reinforcement
Pint	Positive Verbal Interactions	**NR**	Negative Reinforcement
NInt	Negative Verbal Interactions	**ChBel**	Child Beliefs/Interpretations
ObsAct	Observer's Actions	**TBel**	Teacher Beliefs
Res	Results of My Presence	**TTrng**	Teacher Training
CBeh	Child Behavior		

Obviously, some categories contained much more data than others; however, at the time, it was important to develop all the categories, since they all had an important connection to the research questions.

After developing the categories, the next step in this study was to reread the data to code the passages contained in field notes and transcripts. Brief passages from one observation session (see Figure 11.9) and one interview transcript (see Figure 11.10) are included here to demonstrate how these samples of data were coded. As you can see from the examples provided, some passages may be coded with one or more of the categories, depending on what is seen or heard, as well as what is *not* seen or heard.

Often, this process of coding data necessitates reading, rereading, and rereading again all your narrative data. You will get to know your qualitative data very well during the process of inductive analysis. Be aware that this process of coding your data is not an easy one; coding schemes are not automatic, nor are they always overtly apparent in your data (Parsons & Brown, 2002). It is truly necessary to spend a good deal of time reviewing the data, both during and following the development of your coding scheme.

The second step in the process of inductive analysis is to *describe* the main features or characteristics of the categories resulting from the coding of data (Parsons & Brown, 2002). This is the stage of the analysis process where the researcher begins to make connections between the data and the original, or emerging, research questions. The researcher needs to reflect on the categories (once again) and describe them in

FIGURE 11.9 ● Sample Page From Field Notes (Passages Coded Using Scheme in Figure 11.8)

One boy asked Carol to push him on the swing and Carol said, "What do you say? What's the magic word?" The boy responded appropriately by saying "Please," and Carol proceeded to push him.

O/C: *Why didn't Carol say anything in response to his correct answer? Especially, when he gave it after being asked only once? What a perfect opportunity to say, "Very good!" or something. She seems to let many "golden opportunities" for giving praise pass her by. I have observed her miss these chances on many occasions.*

MO

Next, I observed Carol's daughter (the girl who has a tendency to misbehave). She wanted to push a bike across the sand, but was having some difficulty. The sand was too deep and the wheels kept getting stuck. She got Marilyn's attention and told her to push the bike for her. Marilyn replied by saying, "Why don't *you* help *me* push it?" The girl quickly agreed and they did it together.

CAct
PR

O/C: *I was very impressed with this brief exchange. Marilyn didn't talk down to the little girl. Instead, she tried to work with her.*

Immediately after this, I noticed Carol playing catch with one of the older boys. They were standing about 15 feet apart. Carol threw the football and the boy made a great catch. Carol turned her attention to other children who were nearby.

CAct
TBeh
CBeh
MO

O/C: *ARGHHH! She didn't even say, "Nice catch." This is frustrating to watch. A short comment like that might have meant a lot to that boy. Yet another apparent missed opportunity.*

terms of their connection to or outright ability to answer the research questions. At this point, qualitative researchers should ask themselves the following question:

How does the information in this particular category help me understand my research topic and answer my research question?

As you address the issues of connectedness of your data to your research questions, it is important also to look for information in your data that *contradicts* or *conflicts with* the patterns or trends that have emerged. These discrepant pieces of information often make your interpretations more difficult, but including them in the process will make your findings more accurate and meaningful.

The final step is to *interpret* that which has been simplified and organized. During this step, the researcher examines events, behaviors, or others' observations—as represented in the coded categories—for relationships, similarities, contradictions, and so on (Parsons & Brown, 2002). The key is to look for aspects of the data that answer your research questions, provide challenges to current or future practice, or may actually

FIGURE 11.10 ● **Sample Excerpt From Interview Transcript (Passages Coded Using Scheme in Figure 11.8)**

CM:	Can you give me some examples of what you think are acceptable forms of positive behavior, at least as far as you're concerned — things that you would think would be acceptable for you to use with your children?	**TBeh**
"Marilyn":	That's a hard one. [laugh] Probably, just talk to them.	
CM:	So, you see positive reinforcement as being mostly a verbal type of thing?	**TBeh PInt**
"Marilyn":	Yeah.	
CM:	Can you give me an example of something that you, like a concrete example of how or when you would use a verbal type of positive reinforcement and what specifically you might say?	**CAct TBeh CBeh**
"Marilyn":	Well, I would talk like what I used all throughout the play period that we're going to. You're always telling them that maybe they shouldn't — well, not exactly shouldn't do something — but, you know . . . I can't explain it. I used to talking to 2-year-olds! [laugh] Like I said, you go through that all day long, you know, telling them what to do and what not to do. Like to pick the toys up, pick this up before you go and get something else.	**TBeh CBeh PInt**
CM:	Well, using that as an example, let's say that you asked the child to do that, to pick up that toy and put it back. Let's take both cases. Let's say first they didn't do it. What would you say in response to that child if they didn't do what you asked them to do?	
"Marilyn":	I would ask them twice, and if they don't do it, I will go and say, "I'm going to pick them up. Why don't you help me do this?"	**TBeh Modl**
CM:	So, you're kind of modeling for them what you want them to do?	
"Marilyn":	Yeah.	

guide future practice. Because the researcher's background, experiences, and expertise will affect how the data are interpreted, descriptions—or, in some cases, concrete examples—should accompany the interpretations offered (Parsons & Brown, 2002). Provided in Figure 11.11 is an excerpt from the final written report of the positive reinforcement study. Notice the discussion of negative comments made by the teachers toward the children and the frequency of missed opportunities for offering the children positive

FIGURE 11.11 ● Excerpt From Final Research Report Documenting "Negative Comments" and "Missed Opportunities" for Positive Reinforcement

Unfortunately, as she became preoccupied with disruptive, off-task behavior, Carol seemed to forget about those children who were on-task. One of the boys finished his painting and held it up to show Carol. He exclaimed, *"Look what I did!"* He seemed very proud of himself. Carol replied, *"What is it?"* The boy looked away and did not answer. She appeared to let opportunities to offer positive reinforcement pass her by — truly a "missed opportunity." For example, she might have responded to the boy's prideful comment by saying something like, *"Oh, that's very nice! Can you tell me what you painted?"* From my own experience, I know that in situations dealing with disruptive behaviors it is often difficult to remember to do the "little things."

Although many of Carol's comments directed at the children were negative, most of the time they were not made with a harsh tone of voice. Sometimes, they were spoken in an almost "pleasant" tone of voice. It was difficult to understand what she meant when she said something negative, but in a positive tone. I found myself wondering if, subconsciously, the children were having the same difficulty (i.e., is she unhappy or not?).

Circle time is an activity where everyone sits on the floor in a circle and discusses daily events, including the day of the week, the month and year, projects they'll be working on that day, and any special events occurring that day. During my observation of Carol's circle time activity, many of the children exhibited negative, off-task behaviors. In nearly every case, Carol responded with negative statements or actions. During the discussion of the day of the week, for example, Carol's daughter began taking things off the calendar. Carol's initial response to the girl was to threaten to send her to time-out. I don't know if Carol would have actually sent her to time-out, but again the situation was dealt with in a negative fashion and with a threat directed toward the child.

It was during circle time that I began to notice something about Carol. She seemed to be focusing only on the negative behaviors exhibited by the children, and doing so consistently. For each one that was misbehaving, there were two or three who were following directions. I expected Carol to identify those who were behaving and complement their actions, perhaps even single them out as models for the others. Unfortunately, I never saw her do this. She only concentrated on the negative displays — more "missed opportunities."

feedback (which you saw earlier in the coded data in Figures 11.9 and 11.10). Also, you should be aware of the way actual data (in the form of interview and observation quotes) that supported the interpretations were incorporated into the written discussion.

Regardless of how you choose to proceed through your data collection, analysis, and interpretation, this process in qualitative research is complex and time-consuming (Leedy & Ormrod, 2013). It is important to be aware that often your analysis and interpretation will not lead you to a single conclusion; multiple interpretations may occur simultaneously. Keep in mind that the researcher is an instrument in the qualitative data collection and analysis process, and all researchers should do as much as possible to minimize the degree to which biases, prior expectations, and personal judgments enter into the final analysis (Leedy & Ormrod, 2013).

Developmental Activities

1. Describe why *you* believe it is important for researchers at any level to take measures to ensure that their collected data are of the highest quality.

2. Briefly describe, in your own words, the general process used to analyze qualitative data. What do you see as the most difficult and/or time-consuming aspect of qualitative analysis?

3. Making good, sound observations typically requires some training, or at least some practice. Find a location with numerous people (e.g., a shopping mall, your student union), decide on some sort of behavior on which you will focus, and spend 30 minutes observing and making field notes on what you see and hear. Include any observer's comments that you feel might be appropriate during your observation. After the 30 minutes of observation, reflect on the experience. What did you think, and how did you feel? How could you improve your observation and note-taking skills for your next qualitative observation session?

4. Brainstorm a topic of interest to you and appropriate for a qualitative research study. Develop a semistructured interview guide for a brief (i.e., roughly 15-minute) interview with an individual. In your guide, be sure to include "optional" probing questions. Next, interview someone using your guide. Afterward, reflect on your experience as an interviewer. What did you think, and how did you feel? How could you improve your skills for your next interview?

5. Qualitative data analysis also requires some practice. Using the interview guide you developed in Activity 4 above, interview two additional people. Using the notes from the three interviews you conducted, take a stab at analyzing those data. Read and reread the transcripts (i.e., your notes), and then try to group or categorize similar responses. Do you see any patterns in your data? Even though you have only three participants, do you see patterns but also negative cases? Finally, reflect on your attempt at conducting qualitative data analysis.

Summary

- Sampling techniques in qualitative research are intentional, as opposed to random.
- This type of sampling is known as purposeful sampling.
- There are several specific types of purposeful sampling:

  ○ In maximum variation sampling, the researcher selects cases that differ on an important characteristic.

  ○ Extreme case sampling focuses on the sampling of an outlying case.

  ○ Typical sampling involves the selection of a person or site that is typical to outsiders.

  ○ Theory or concept sampling helps the researcher generate or discover a new theory or concept.

  ○ In homogeneous sampling, sites or individuals are selected because they possess a similar trait.

○ Critical sampling focuses on individuals or sites that represent in dramatic terms the phenomenon being studied.

○ Opportunistic sampling allows the researcher to sample for new and different information as questions emerge in the study.

○ Snowball sampling relies on participants to recommend other potential participants for the study.

○ Confirming or disconfirming sampling allows the researcher to seek additional data to confirm or disconfirm preliminary findings.

● Qualitative research sample sizes are typically very small, although they may range from a single individual or site to as many as 30 or 40.

○ It is the researcher's responsibility to strike a balance between the amount of data to be collected and the depth of data sought.

● There are numerous ways to collect qualitative research data.

● Observations involve carefully watching and systematically recording what you see and hear in a setting.

● Observations may be structured, unstructured, or semistructured.

● Researchers may assume several roles along the participant–observer continuum.

○ When the researcher is in an *observer* role, participants may not even know they are being observed.

○ An *observer as participant* is primarily an observer but has some interaction in the setting.

○ A *participant as observer* acts as an observer but also interacts more formally with participants.

○ A *full participant* is a researcher who is also a fully functioning member of the community.

● Observations are recorded in the form of field notes.

● When observing and taking field notes, it is good practice to include observer's comments, which are preliminary interpretations of observational data.

● Interviews are formal conversations between the researcher and participants in the study.

● Interviews may be conducted individually or in groups, known as focus groups.

● Before interviewing participants, it is best to prepare an interview guide to be closely followed during data collection.

● Interviews may be structured, semistructured, or open-ended.

● Journals—including student journals, teacher journals, and class journals—can also be used to collect qualitative data at the research site.

● Validity of research data deals with the extent to which the data collected accurately measure what the researcher intended to measure.

● When establishing the validity of qualitative data, researchers are concerned with the data's trustworthiness.

● Trustworthiness is established by examining four criteria: credibility, transferability, dependability, and confirmability.

● Additional criteria that can be used to establish the validity of qualitative research include descriptive validity, interpretive validity, theoretical validity, evaluative validity, and generalizability.

● Triangulation is a process of using multiple methods, data collection strategies, data sources, and sometimes multiple researchers to enhance validity.

- Persistent and prolonged participation in the study site will also enhance the validity of the research.
- Enlisting other professionals to help review and critique your data collection and analysis to enhance the study's validity is known as peer debriefing.
- Having an outsider review the final report is called an external audit, and can also enhance validity.
- Member checking is a process of asking participants to review the accuracy of the research report.
- Reflexivity—the process of documenting and evaluating your interpretations, assumptions,

and biases—also aids in establishing validity.
- Although there is not a single method for analyzing qualitative data, the general approach is a process of inductive analysis.
- Inductive analysis focuses on three main steps: organization of the data, description of coded themes, and interpretation of those themes.
- Numerous software programs are available to assist the researcher in organizing and coding data.
- Qualitative data analysis is complex and time-consuming. Multiple interpretations are a distinct possibility.

⑤SAGE edge™

Sharpen your skills with SAGE edge!

edge.sagepub.com/mertler

SAGE edge for Students provides a personalized approach to help you accomplish your coursework goals in an easy-to-use learning environment. You'll find action plans, mobile-friendly eFlashcards, and quizzes as well as video, web, and resources and links to SAGE journal articles to support and expand on the concepts presented in this chapter.

12

Quantitative Data Collection

Student Learning Objectives

After studying Chapter 12, students will be able to do the following:

1. List and describe various probability sampling techniques for quantitative research

2. List and describe various nonprobability sampling techniques for quantitative research

3. Apply appropriate guidelines for sample sizes in quantitative studies

4. Name, describe, and provide examples of the four scales of measurement

5. Identify and describe major categories of data collection techniques in quantitative research

6. List and describe the types of evidence used to determine the validity of inferences drawn from quantitative data

7. Name and describe various techniques used to determine the reliability of quantitative data

8. Design quantitative data collection procedures for a research topic of interest

In this chapter, we revisit and look more deeply at aspects of collecting quantitative research data. Topics in our examination of quantitative data collection and analysis include sampling techniques, scales of measurement and data collection techniques, and characteristics of quantitative data.

Sampling Techniques in Quantitative Research

As we discussed in Chapter 11, one of the first and most important methodological decisions in the design of a qualitative research study is the selection of an appropriate sample. Quantitative research is no different and also has many of its own unique sampling techniques. Although quantitative researchers do not typically gather data from an entire *population*, their intent is to be able to *generalize* the results of their studies to the entire population. This means that they want to be able to conclude that the results from their research would be applicable to other samples selected from the same population (Gay, Mills, & Airasian, 2009).

Suppose that researchers in a large urban school district want to find out how their teachers feel about a newly implemented national curriculum, along with its associated assessments. Further, suppose that there are more than 12,000 teachers in this school district. Ideally, to discover how *each* teacher feels about the curriculum and assessments, *each* teacher should be interviewed or surveyed. As you can imagine, this would not be feasible, due to the sheer amount of time required for this level of data collection and analysis. Instead, it would be much more practical to collect data from a subset—perhaps 500 teachers—of the entire population of 12,000. If the *sample* of potential respondents is selected correctly and accurately, the conclusions based on *their* data should be applicable to the *entire* group of teachers.

The key is that the sample must be selected *correctly* and *accurately*. To obtain an accurate sample of teachers, the sample must be selected so it is *representative* of the entire population. This means that certain characteristics—those deemed important to the outcome of the study—must be taken into consideration so that members of the sample reflect those characteristics in the same manner as the larger population. For example, the opinions of elementary teachers may differ from those of secondary teachers, male teachers may differ from female teachers, and teachers with more years of experience may differ from those who are relatively new to the profession. Therefore, we would want the sample of teachers to represent *nearly the same proportion* of elementary to secondary teachers, male to female teachers, and more experienced to less experienced teachers as present in the entire population of 12,000 teachers. Following appropriate sampling techniques does not guarantee a representative sample, but it definitely increases the odds of having a representative sample (Gay et al., 2009).

The initial step in this process is to define the population to which the researchers plan to generalize their results. Remember, a population (symbolized in research settings as N) is a group of individuals who share the same *important* characteristics (Creswell, 2005). Members of a population will never share every characteristic, but they do share those characteristics that could influence the outcome of the study. Examples of populations include the following:

- All teachers employed in the same district (these teachers share the same large work environment)
- All advanced-placement high school students in the state (these students share similar curricula and coursework)
- All kindergarten students in a school district who have participated in a behavior modification program (the students share several important characteristics, including grade level, school district, and participation in a particular program)

Keep in mind that populations can be of any size and can cover almost any geographical area (Gay et al., 2009). Because of this potential expanse, rarely is the entire group of interest available to the researcher, which brings us to an important distinction between two terms: *target population* and *accessible population*. A target population (also discussed in Chapter 7) is the group of people to whom the researcher would ideally like to generalize the results of the study. An **accessible population**—sometimes referred to as an **available population** (Gay et al., 2009)—is the group from which the researcher can realistically select subjects. The larger the target population, the more important it is to carefully identify an accessible population. However, in most cases, the population identified for study is a realistic choice (i.e., an accessible population) and not an ideal one (i.e., a target population).

The next step in the process is to select a sample—that is, a subset of the population, symbolized by *n*—for the actual study, such that it is representative of the accessible population so the results can be generalized to the larger group. Quantitative sampling techniques are typically classified into one of two categories: *probability sampling techniques* and *nonprobability sampling techniques*. Specific techniques within each category are shown in Figure 12.1. Each of these categories is described and specific techniques for each explained in the following sections.

Probability Sampling Techniques

As stated above, a good sample for a quantitative research study is representative of the population from which it was drawn. Numerous techniques exist for selecting a sample that is representative; however, not all the techniques provide the same level of assurance concerning representativeness. Gay and colleagues (2009) note that, when it comes to sample selection, we sometimes must compromise the ideal for the feasible. **Probability sampling techniques** are those techniques that permit the researcher to specify the probability, or chance, that each member of the population will be selected for inclusion in the sample. These techniques involve processes of *random selection*—meaning that the sample is chosen in such a way that each member of the population has an equal chance of being selected—and are, consequently, also known as **random sampling techniques**. These are the defining characteristics of probability or random sampling techniques:

1. The chance that each member of the population will be selected for inclusion in the sample can be specified.
2. All members of the population have an equal chance of being selected for inclusion in the sample.

If these two characteristics are not met, the sampling technique will not be a probability or random sampling technique.

There are five basic procedures for selecting a random sample: simple random sampling, stratified sampling, cluster sampling, systematic sampling, and multistage sampling. Each procedure involves the same basic steps: identify the population, determine the appropriate sample size, and select the sample (Gay et al., 2009). However, each technique goes about the sample selection process in a different manner. Although no technique guarantees a perfect representative sample, the most rigorous form of probability sampling and the best way to obtain a representative sample is **simple random sampling** (Creswell, 2005). To obtain a sample that would represent all

FIGURE 12.1 ● Types of Quantitative Sampling Techniques

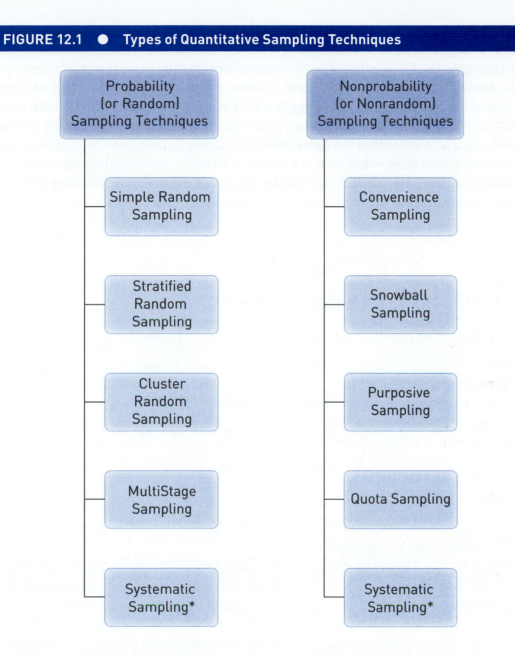

students in a particular school, for example, a process of simple random sampling would be analogous to putting all their names on individual slips of paper, thoroughly mixing them, and blindly drawing out the number desired for the sample. Of course, this procedure is feasible only if the population from which you are selecting a sample is small. Random samples were once hand-selected using tables of random numbers (see Table 12.1). Now, software programs—including the Research Randomizer (www .randomizer.org), which was used to create Table 12.1—greatly facilitate the development of a table of random numbers and the random selection process.

Fraenkel, Wallen, and Hyun (2012) have done a good job of outlining the basic procedures for using a table of random numbers to select a random sample. As a simple example, imagine that we wanted to obtain a sample of 20 participants from a population of 200 individuals, using the random numbers in Table 12.1. First, we would need to obtain a list of all the members of the population, then give each person in the population a unique number; for example, Person 1 would be 001, Person 2 would be 002, and so on. We would begin the selection process by choosing a column of numbers, and then, starting anywhere in that column, we would begin reading three-digit numbers. We would limit ourselves to three-digit numbers because the total number in our population (i.e., 200) is a three-digit number, and we use the same number of digits for each person. Finally, we would write down the first 20 numbers in that column—moving to the next if necessary—that have a value of 200 or less. Say we randomly decided to begin in the third column (i.e., Set 3). Moving down the list, and following the rules we just established, we would identify the following individuals (shaded in Table 12.1):

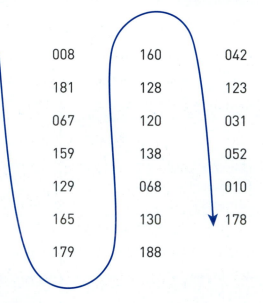

008	160	042
181	128	123
067	120	031
159	138	052
129	068	010
165	130	178
179	188	

We would then return to our population list and identify the 20 people selected above to participate as our sample.

One of the weaknesses of simple random sampling is that representation of specific subgroups is not guaranteed; if it does happen, it is purely by chance. **Stratified random sampling** is a process in which certain subgroups—often referred to as *strata*—are selected for inclusion in the sample. This technique involves the strategic selection of participants from various subgroups and is the best sampling technique when a research goal is to compare participants from different groups within the population (Gay et al., 2009). There are two types of stratified random sampling procedures, depending on the type of representation desired in the study. **Proportional stratified sampling** is a stratified random sampling process where a sample is selected so the identified subgroups in the sample are represented in the exact same proportion in which they exist in the population. **Nonproportional** or **equal stratified sampling** is a similar process; however, the representations of subgroups in the sample are equivalent to one another, as opposed to reflecting the proportions in the population at large. These two stratified random sampling procedures are depicted in Figures 12.2 and 12.3, respectively.

The basic procedures for selecting a stratified random sample are the same as those for selecting a simple random sample, with the exception that the various subgroups (i.e., the strata) must be determined. Furthermore, the researcher must determine

TABLE 12.1 ● Sample Table of Random Numbers

Research Randomizer Results:

10 Sets of 25 Unique Numbers Per Set

Range: From 1 to 99999—Unsorted

Set 1	Set 2	Set 3	Set 4	Set 5	Set 6	Set 7	Set 8	Set 9	Set 10
51312	40448	69822	70553	38996	97480	95571	15295	80619	14314
38629	11574	47697	56326	97764	94949	61800	97790	84012	51597
62187	85233	93275	71247	90593	19661	64460	85867	67967	89876
23735	91887	70008	43067	66739	42216	47068	08031	20014	32795
79048	35387	19845	26396	97436	46670	11206	36494	54613	43726
43735	79194	67209	89543	80288	69524	25601	12368	10388	53897
99235	09751	86399	42848	32662	47224	84228	13267	26981	19250
70535	48705	51364	60669	05904	28739	63130	08347	96644	53732
50312	51020	88207	09820	37264	97128	53823	99436	77334	22039
37967	34454	22425	19159	50556	37457	14188	62052	24266	08745
30659	31660	56250	75466	89877	33405	46929	94010	09665	30392
28765	88336	21889	30384	48853	65711	25042	48178	92886	41202
87424	79963	97882	99482	33713	44533	61350	62056	35457	93935
70640	84206	09444	11636	66281	50120	82222	91250	55089	69155
84846	15817	86817	23954	09895	38449	49585	67119	97641	78011
33199	68640	95942	14870	38160	27498	87245	82158	13282	68493
93888	52898	54181	06585	60452	70538	58439	80132	80652	07466
44396	49291	61753	74820	21333	83664	65123	42575	94002	19727
41595	97764	23417	39129	91694	38265	02851	43774	72129	51620
28760	28318	44540	14165	48625	49138	60632	41887	99883	46891
71973	32039	98651	31565	93683	47272	29493	58681	98169	45387
51635	38725	19685	05179	91547	01350	46886	13658	24282	93859
98454	99462	75427	64941	64210	40298	55574	49773	98860	90145
80602	16639	14972	83941	96595	07352	48930	90686	19983	89140
00042	15440	05410	83419	04864	50980	83417	16921	19520	34524

whether proportional or equal representation is desired and then make appropriate decisions regarding sample size. From there, the process involves the use of a table of random numbers, as described in the previous discussion of simple random sampling.

In some research situations, it is not possible to obtain a list of individual members of the population; such a list may not be available or may not even exist. In these situations, neither simple random sampling nor stratified random sampling can be used as a method of selecting the sample. Even if a list of individual participants is available, it might not be feasible to randomly assign individual students, for example, to experimental conditions. In situations such as these, the best sampling alternative might be to select intact, existing groups (or *clusters*) of participants rather than individuals. This sampling procedure is known as **cluster random sampling**.

The process of cluster random sampling is similar to that of simple random sampling, with the exception of the sampling unit. In simple random sampling, the sampling unit is an individual; however, in cluster random sampling, the sampling unit is an existing group of individuals. For example, if I wanted to survey a representative sample of the 12,000 teachers in an urban district, I could randomly select school buildings—again

FIGURE 12.2 ● Process of Proportional Stratified Random Sampling

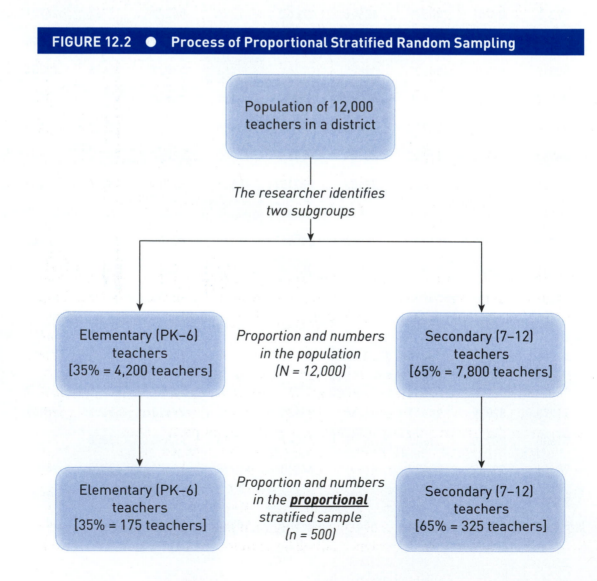

FIGURE 12.3 ● Process of Nonproportional, or Equal, Stratified Random Sampling

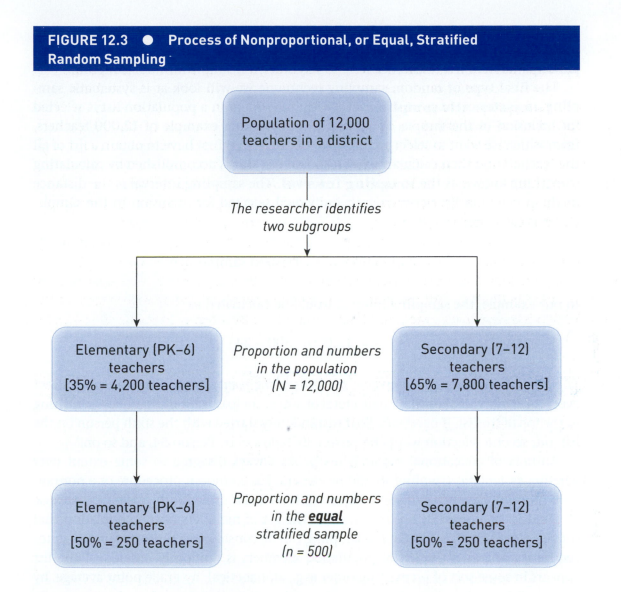

Population of 12,000 teachers in a district

The researcher identifies two subgroups

| Elementary (PK–6) teachers [35% = 4,200 teachers] | *Proportion and numbers in the population (N = 12,000)* | Secondary (7–12) teachers [65% = 7,800 teachers] |

| Elementary (PK–6) teachers [50% = 250 teachers] | *Proportion and numbers in the **equal** stratified sample (n = 500)* | Secondary (7–12) teachers [50% = 250 teachers] |

using the process of randomly assigning numbers to buildings and then selecting from a table of random numbers—and survey every teacher in each of the school buildings selected. In this research scenario, the sampling unit is "school building." The advantage of cluster random sampling is that the population is much smaller, since we are dealing with intact groups instead of individuals. However, as you can imagine, the disadvantage or limitation is that we are less likely to obtain a representative sample of our larger population. Using our example, one school might be made up of teachers that are demographically very different—perhaps in terms of gender or years of experience—from the teachers in another building not selected for participation.

Multistage random sampling, sometimes also referred to as **two-stage random sampling**, is a combination of cluster random sampling and individual random sampling. Rather than randomly selecting 500 teachers from the population of 12,000, a researcher might decide first to cluster sample 10 schools from the population and then randomly select 50 teachers from each school. Essentially, this process involves a random sample of clusters followed by a random sample of individuals from within the selected clusters. Depending on the size and scope of a research study, multistage random sampling can be a more expedient method of randomly selecting participants than if a researcher were to rely solely on simple random sampling.

The final type of random sampling technique we will look at is systematic sampling. In **systematic sampling**, every Kth individual in a population list is selected for inclusion in the sample. Returning to our working example of 12,000 teachers, from which we want to select a sample of 500, we would first have to obtain a list of all the teachers and then calculate what K should be. This is accomplished by calculating something known as the **sampling interval**. The sampling interval is the distance in the population list between each individual selected for inclusion in the sample, and it is calculated as follows:

$$K = \text{Population size} \div \text{Desired sample size}$$

In our example, the sampling interval would be calculated as

$$K = 12{,}000 \div 500 = 24$$

Therefore, beginning at a *randomly selected starting point* on the list, we would select every 24th individual until we had a total of 500 participants for our sample—returning to the top of the list, if necessary. So if we randomly started with the sixth person on the list, our second selection would be Person 30, followed by Person 54, and so on.

Authors of educational research textbooks always disagree to some extent over whether systematic sampling should be classified as a random procedure or a nonrandom procedure. As you can see in Figure 12.1, I listed it under both categories, because its classification depends on the nature of the list of members of the population that the researcher obtains. Systematic sampling can be considered a random sampling procedure *if and only if* the list of population members is randomly ordered. If the list appears in some sort of preexisting order (e.g., alphabetical, by grade point average, by test score) then the process will be a nonrandom sampling procedure. Lists typically appear in some sort of predetermined order; therefore, systematic sampling is rarely a good option when trying to obtain a random, representative sample (Gay et al., 2009). Of course, a researcher could take that list and randomize it, then use the newly randomized list to select a systematic sample, but then the process becomes much more convoluted than if the researcher used a simple random sampling method at the outset.

Nonprobability Sampling Techniques

Although random sampling techniques provide the most appropriate and representative samples for quantitative studies, sometimes randomly selecting people to participate in a study is just not feasible. **Nonprobability sampling techniques**, also known as **nonrandom sampling techniques**, do not permit the researcher to specify the probability that each member of a population will be selected for inclusion in the sample, nor do they create a sampling situation where every member of a population has an equal chance of being selected. In addition to systematic sampling, which we already discussed as a nonrandom sampling technique, we will look at four nonrandom sampling techniques: convenience sampling, snowball sampling, quota sampling, and purposive sampling.

Convenience sampling—which you may also see referred to as *accidental sampling* or *haphazard sampling* (Gay et al., 2009; Leedy & Ormrod, 2013)—is somewhat of a "targeted" sampling technique whereby the researcher simply studies whoever happens to be available at the time and is willing to participate. If you have ever been stopped on the street or in a shopping mall and asked for your opinion on some topic, you have been part of a convenience sample. Due to the nonrandom and nonrepresentative nature of convenience samples, their use should be avoided at all costs. Additionally, when you read articles based on quantitative research studies that use convenience samples, you should question the results and conclusions of those studies. At a minimum, studies that use convenience samples should be replicated to verify the findings of the original study and determine whether or not they were a one-time occurrence (Fraenkel et al., 2012).

You read in Chapter 11 about *snowball sampling* as a qualitative sampling technique. It may also be used as a quantitative sampling technique, often as an alternative to convenience sampling (Creswell, 2005). In snowball sampling, the researcher relies on current participants to identify other people as potential participants in the study. For example, a researcher might survey teachers in a school on a given topic and, after their surveys are completed, might ask those teachers to provide the names of other teachers who they think might also be interested in completing the survey. By using this technique, the researcher essentially gives up any control over who makes up the sample in the study. Especially in a quantitative study, where the goal will be to generalize the results, it should be obvious why snowball sampling is a less-than-desirable sampling technique.

A third nonrandom sampling technique is quota sampling. **Quota sampling** is often seen as a variation of convenience sampling and involves a process of selecting a sample based on precise numbers of individuals or groups with specific characteristics. It is often used in large-scale survey research when obtaining a list of all the members of the population of interest is not possible (Gay et al., 2009). When quota sampling is used, researchers specify exact characteristics as well as the number of people with those characteristics they need to participate in the study. For example, researchers might be interested in interviewing 30 female teachers who have a minimum of 5 years of experience in urban settings and were trained through alternative teacher certification programs, as well as 30 female teachers who have a minimum of 5 years of experience in urban settings and were trained through traditional teacher certification programs. In this example, the similarity of quota sampling to convenience sampling should be obvious. Individuals who meet the desired qualifications must be readily available and accessible; individuals who meet those qualifications but are difficult to locate or contact end up being underrepresented in the sample.

A final type of nonrandom sampling in quantitative studies is **purposive sampling**, whereby people or other sampling units are selected for a particular *purpose*. Purposive sampling is also sometimes referred to as *judgment sampling* because individuals making up the sample are *believed* to be representative of a given population. The difference between purposive sampling and convenience sampling is that in purposive sampling the researcher clearly identifies criteria for selection, whereas in convenience sampling he or she is simply using whoever is available. These clear criteria are the basis for defending the use of purposive samples; however, their use does not eliminate the potential for inaccuracy in the resulting sample selection.

Sample Sizes in Quantitative Studies

A common decision all quantitative researchers must make is what constitutes an appropriate sample size in a quantitative study. Keep in mind that sample sizes in quantitative research are very different from those for qualitative studies. Since the goal of quantitative research is to generalize results to a much larger population, the sample size must be *large enough* to provide *minimally adequate* representation of the larger population. So the question all researchers want answered is, *When is a sample large enough to enable generalization of results?* The answer is never easy or simple. Often, it depends on the nature of the study, the research questions guiding the study, the specific makeup of the population to which the results will be generalized, and many other similar decisions, all of which are unique to individual studies.

Those conditions aside, Gay and colleagues (2009) have provided sound guidelines and rules of thumb for determining sample size, keeping in mind that *the larger the population size, the smaller the percentage of the population required to get a representative sample.* Generally speaking, the minimum sample size depends on the type of research being conducted. Many researchers cite a sample size of 30 as a minimum guideline for correlational, causal-comparative, and true experimental research. In correlational research, a minimum of 30 participants is needed to establish the existence of a statistical relationship. In causal-comparative and experimental research, there should be a minimum of 30 participants in each group (Gay et al., 2009). Larger samples improve the likelihood of detecting differences between groups; however, these group sizes are sometimes difficult to attain. Creswell (2005) recommends a minimum of 15 participants in each group for causal-comparative and experimental studies; with a minimum of two groups, this would give the researcher a total of 30 participants in the study.

When conducting survey research, it is advisable to survey a minimum of 350 individuals (Creswell, 2005) or a minimum of 10% to 20% of the population (Gay et al., 2009). However, these figures can vary greatly depending on several factors within the population being studied. Below, I have summarized specific recommendations regarding sample sizes for survey research studies (Gay et al., 2009):

1. For smaller populations—for example, $N \leqq 100$—there is little point in sampling at all, and the entire population should be studied.
2. If the population size is about 500 (give or take 100)—in other words, $400 \leqq N \leqq 600$—then 50% of the population should be sampled, resulting in an n between roughly 200 and 300 participants.
3. If the population size is around 1,500, then 20% should be sampled, resulting in an n roughly equal to 300.
4. Beyond a certain point (about $N = 5,000$), the population size becomes almost irrelevant and a sample size of 400 will be adequate. Increasing the size of

the sample beyond this point is not critical, but doing so will increase the confidence with which the researcher can generalize results.

Keep in mind that all the numbers and percentages presented here are suggested *minimums*. If obtaining a greater number of participants for the sample is at all possible, then researchers are encouraged to do so.

Other aspects of sampling that may or may not be related to sample size are the issues of sampling error and sampling bias. Even when samples are selected randomly, there is no guarantee that the composition of the sample will be precisely identical to that of the population. In many cases, the differences are the result of chance variations within the population. This chance variation over which the researcher has no control is called **sampling error** and may impact the results of the study. In contrast, **sampling bias** is a *systematic* sampling error that is generally the fault of the researcher. Sampling bias occurs when some aspect of the sampling process creates a bias in the data (Gay et al., 2009). As a simple example, when a survey researcher gets a return rate of 30% of questionnaires sent out, it is important to note that the large number of unreturned surveys may introduce potential bias into the results. In other words, what characteristics were shared by those who did not return the surveys? Since they did not return the surveys, we will never know. This is the potential bias of which we must be aware, and we must decide whether it is severe enough to negatively impact the quality of our data, as well as the resulting conclusions and generalizations we make upon the study's conclusion. If the researcher decides to continue with the study, he or she is obligated to disclose the nature of the bias and contextualize the findings and conclusions within those parameters.

Scales of Measurement

A **measurement scale** is a system used to organize data so they can be reviewed, analyzed, and interpreted appropriately (Gay et al., 2009). In other words, the scale is the set of response options (Creswell, 2005) or the measuring stick used to provide the range of values or scores for each variable (Gay et al., 2009). It is important to understand and recognize the type of *categorical* or *continuous* units—the reader may recall the discussion of these terms for describing variables from Chapter 3—on which each variable is measured, because that information is used to assess the quality of an instrument and to determine the appropriate statistical techniques necessary for analyzing the resulting data (Creswell, 2005). There are four types of measurement scales: nominal, ordinal, interval, and ratio (see Figure 12.4).

A *nominal scale* is the simplest form of measurement and is typically associated with measuring a *categorical variable* (see Chapter 3). Essentially, a nominal scale involves the assignment of labels or names to different categories of a particular variable. Examples of nominal variables include gender (e.g., male and female), marital status (e.g., single, married, and divorced), grade level (e.g., Grade 9, Grade 10, Grade 11, and Grade 12), and school location (e.g., rural, suburban, and urban). Because we are conducting quantitative research and quantitative analyses, numbers are typically assigned to represent the different categories of a variable. This fact sometimes confuses students of research, since we talk about nominal categories being assigned *names* but then we represent them as *numbers*. This is because *all* variables in quantitative analyses must be represented by numerical values. For example, when measuring the variable *gender*, we might assign the male category to be represented by the number 1 and the female category to be represented by the number 2. It is extremely important to remember that the assignment of these particular numbers is *completely arbitrary*; in other words, the numbers do not represent quantities of anything. In our example, females (represented by 2) do not possess twice as much of some characteristic as males do (represented by 1), at least for the purposes of our study. Another researcher studying the same variable *gender* might have reversed the assignment—with females represented by 1 and males by 2—which would be perfectly acceptable, since the assignment of numerical values is arbitrary and without quantitative meaning. The number of statistical analysis techniques that are appropriate for nominal scales is very limited.

Ordinal scales possess the same characteristic as nominal scales in that they classify variables, but ordinal scales also rank variables in order of the degree to which they possess the characteristic being measured. In other words, the assignment of numbers is no longer arbitrary and has some sort of quantitative meaning. Ordinal scales are essentially the equivalent of rank ordering individuals on some characteristic. For example, imagine that we had the average test scores on a statewide assessment of fourth-grade reading comprehension for 10 elementary schools in a district. Those schools, along with their relative ranks and average test scores, appear below:

Rank	School	Average Test Score
1	Eastern Elementary	96
2	Highland Elementary	94
3	Central Elementary	90
4	River Elementary	89
5	Western Elementary	82
6	Lowland Elementary	81
7	Stream Elementary	80
8	Middle Elementary	79
9	Valley Elementary	77
10	Mountains Elementary	75

Notice that the ordinal variable (i.e., *rank*) simply indicates the order in which the average scores fall. This serves as a measure of the amount or size of one elementary school's average test score compared with those of the other elementary schools. Further, notice that the ordinal variable does not indicate the amount of difference between adjacent schools in the rank ordering. For example, the distance between Eastern Elementary (ranked 1) and Highland Elementary (ranked 2) is 2 points, whereas the difference between River Elementary (ranked 4) and Western Elementary (ranked 5) is 7 points. Ordinal scales indicate only *relative standing* among individuals, not the distance between adjacent individuals or the amount of the characteristic they possess. In other words, the intervals between adjacent ranks are not necessarily equivalent. Similar to nominal scales, the number of statistical analysis techniques appropriate for ordinal scales is somewhat limited.

The third-highest scale of measurement is an interval scale. *Interval scales* possess all the characteristics of nominal and ordinal scales, but the subsequent values represent equal intervals. This is a common measurement scale for many tests used in education, including achievement tests, aptitude tests, and attitude tests. If we look again at the example of the average test scores in reading for 10 elementary schools, the variable *average test score* would be classified as an interval scale variable. For example, the distance between Eastern Elementary (with an average score of 96) and Highland Elementary (average score of 94) is 2 points, which is the same

FIGURE 12.4 ● Four Types of Measurement Scales, With Sample Variables

Scale	Sample Variable	Example
Nominal	Gender	 '1' '2'
Ordinal	Class rank	 4th 3rd 2nd 1st
Interval	Test score	 65 75 80 95
Ratio	College tuition	 $0 - - $10,000 - - $20,000 - - $30,000

as the distance between Middle Elementary (with an average score of 79) and Valley Elementary (average score of 77). In both cases, the difference is 2 points. Variables that are measured on equal interval scales may be appropriately subjected to a wide variety of statistical analysis techniques.

The highest level of measurement is a ratio scale. *Ratio scales* possess all the characteristics and properties of the previous three types of measurement scales but have the additional characteristic of a true zero point. This means if someone scores a 0 on a ratio scale variable, he or she lacks *any* of that particular variable. Examples of ratio scale variables include height, weight, time, and distance. For example, the concept of something weighing "nothing" is meaningful and realistic. Because interval variables possess a true zero point, not only can we say that the difference between someone who is 6 feet, 0 inches tall and someone who is 5 feet, 6 inches tall (i.e., 6 inches) is the same as the difference between a person who is 5 feet, 2 inches tall and one who is 4 feet, 8 inches tall (i.e., 6 inches), but we can also claim, for example, that a person who weighs 180 pounds is twice as heavy as someone who weighs 90 pounds (i.e., the *ratio* of their weights is 2:1). It is important to note that we cannot make these kinds of claims with interval scale variables. For example, we could not conclude that a student who scores 90 on a test of reading comprehension has twice as much reading comprehension skill or ability as another student who scores 45 on the same test. Similarly, if a student receives a score of 0 on the reading comprehension test, we know only that he failed to answer any questions correctly; we could not conclude that he has a *complete lack* of reading comprehension skills or ability. Similar to interval scale variables, variables that are measured on ratio scales may be appropriately subjected to a wide variety of statistical analysis techniques.

Quantitative Data Collection Techniques

You will undoubtedly recall from our discussion in Chapter 7 that quantitative data are *numerical*. Generally speaking, just about anything that can be *quantified* (i.e., counted, calculated, tallied, and rated) can be considered quantitative data. This includes not only items that can be counted but also ratings of participants' feelings, attitudes, interests, or perceptions on some sort of numerical scale. Quantitative data collection techniques include surveys, questionnaires, checklists, and rating scales, as well as tests and other more formal types of measurement instruments. For the most part, quantitative data collection techniques are more efficient, in that you can collect data from numerous individuals simultaneously. However, the depth of those data does not begin to compare to that resulting from use of qualitative techniques.

Before we look at specific types of techniques used for the collection of quantitative data, it may be important to note that novice researchers sometimes develop instruments—or use other forms of quantitative data collection strategies—that do not align appropriately with the research questions guiding the study. Further, the proposed means for analyzing the resulting data may not appropriately align with those research questions. One strategy that may help avoid this potential pitfall of research is to develop some sort of matrix that allows the researcher to align research questions, strategies for data collection, and proposed analytical techniques. This should be done at the outset of the study—that is, during the planning stages.

Surveys, Checklists, and Rating Scales

The term **survey** refers to a group of quantitative data collection techniques that involve the administration of a set of questions or statements to a sample of people. Surveys may be administered verbally—which makes them a type of interview, although the resulting data are numerical instead of narrative—or in written form (Mertler, 2014). Surveys administered in written form—specifically known as **questionnaires**—ask participants to answer a series of questions or respond to a series of statements and then return them to the researcher. Surveys and questionnaires permit the researcher to gather a lot of—as well as a variety of—information relatively quickly (Johnson, 2008). Not much limits your use of surveys and questionnaires. You will read more about other specific formats for items on questionnaires—namely, checklists and rating scales—shortly.

Constructing a Survey or Questionnaire When constructing a survey or questionnaire, the researcher must make numerous decisions about the structure and format of the instrument. These decisions involve the type of survey questions to include, the specific format or formats of the questions, as well as specific considerations about the design and administration of the survey instrument. Next, we consider these various aspects of constructing a survey or questionnaire as a means of collecting quantitative data.

Types of Survey Questions. Researchers can choose among several types of survey questions, based on purpose and format. Four categories of survey questions are demographic, knowledge, attitudinal, and behavioral. Demographic questions are those that allow respondents to indicate personal characteristics (e.g., gender, age, level of education). Some examples of demographic questions follow:

What is your gender?

☐ Female
☐ Male

Which of the following is the most appropriate description of the level at which you teach?

☐ Elementary to primary (K–3)
☐ Elementary to intermediate (Grades 4–6)
☐ Elementary (K–6)
☐ Middle (Grades 6–8)
☐ High (Grades 9–12)
☐ Secondary (Grades 6–12)

☐ K–12
☐ Other

Which best describes the educational level you have attained?

☐ BA or BS
☐ MA or MS
☐ Specialist
☐ EdD
☐ PhD

Knowledge questions seek to determine how much an individual knows about a particular subject (Mertens, 2005). This type of question is typified by those found on subject-based tests administered in schools. Although knowledge questions can be used on surveys, their use is typically minimal since respondents could look up the answers.

Questions that ask individual respondents to indicate their attitudes or opinions about some topic are known as **attitudinal questions**. Below are two examples of attitudinal questions from a survey about the No Child Left Behind Act and teachers' assessment practices:

I believe that I know a lot about the No Child Left Behind (NCLB) Act.

☐ Strongly disagree
☐ Disagree
☐ Agree
☐ Strongly agree

I believe that the overall effect of NCLB on my school has been positive.

☐ Strongly disagree
☐ Disagree
☐ Agree
☐ Strongly agree

Finally, **behavioral questions** are survey questions that seek information about actual behaviors of individuals in the sample group. Two sample behavioral questions appear below:

When you use traditional assessments with your students, how often do you use self-developed forms of traditional assessment (e.g., teacher-made chapter tests)?

☐ Never
☐ Not very often
☐ Sometimes
☐ Most of the time
☐ Always

When you use traditional assessments with your students, how often do you use published forms of traditional assessment (e.g., chapter tests from textbooks)?

☐ Never
☐ Not very often
☐ Sometimes
☐ Most of the time
☐ Always

Survey questions can be formatted in a variety of ways, including as closed-ended or open-ended questions. **Closed-ended questions** (also sometimes called **forced-choice questions**) are commonly used in written surveys. These questions typically consist of multiple-choice or other types of items that allow the respondent to select a response from a number of options provided by the researcher directly on the survey. Closed-ended questions may be used to measure opinions, attitudes, knowledge, or behavior. All the preceding examples in this section use a closed-ended format.

Open-ended questions allow for more individualized responses, since respondents are not limited to selecting from a supplied set of options. An example of an open-ended survey question is as follows:

What strategies do you employ when you encounter a struggling reader in your class?

Closed-ended questions provide for greater consistency of responses across respondents, since all individuals are selecting from the same set of options. Responses to such questions are also easier to tabulate and analyze than are responses to open-ended questions, which can vary greatly in length and content across respondents. Because closed-ended questions are quicker to answer than open-ended questions, this format tends to be more popular with respondents. On the other hand, closed-ended questions tend to limit the breadth of responses and take more time to construct (Fraenkel et al., 2012).

There are several common types of closed-ended survey questions. The most commonly used types are checklists, Likert questions, and Likert-type questions. **Checklists** are questions that consist of a list of behaviors, characteristics, skills, or other criteria that the researcher is interested in studying. A checklist provides only a dichotomous set of response options. Typically, survey respondents indicate that they *do* or *do not* possess something, or *have* or *have not* observed something, for example. These questions are characteristically quick and easy to respond to, and not too difficult to construct; however, the researcher is limited with respect to the statistical techniques he or she can use to analyze responses. An example of a checklist appears below:

In which content areas are advanced placement courses offered in your school (please check all that apply)?

☐ English
☐ Foreign languages
☐ Mathematics

☐ Social studies
☐ Science

A **Likert** (pronounced "lick-ert") **question** begins with a statement and then asks individuals to respond on an agree–disagree continuum. The Likert scale typically ranges from "strongly disagree" to "strongly agree." There is no specific rule about the number of points you must have on a Likert scale, but 5 points, as shown below, is quite common.

1 = Strongly disagree

2 = Disagree

3 = No opinion

4 = Agree

5 = Strongly agree

Quite a bit of disagreement exists among experts regarding the appropriateness of including a neutral point on a scale (Mertler, 2014). By including a neutral point as a response option, the researcher allows respondents to indicate that they *truly* are neutral or have *no opinion* if in fact that is the case. However, when provided with a neutral option, people sometimes *avoid* thinking about how they truly feel; they simply select the neutral option, which may not represent their actual belief (i.e., the data they provide is inaccurate). On the other hand, if individuals *truly* are indifferent or have no opinion and you do not provide this option—because you are operating under the assumption that no one is truly neutral about anything—you "force" them to choose something they do not really believe, which also results in inaccurate data. There is no right or wrong answer when it comes to deciding on inclusion of a neutral point on a rating scale, but researchers should consider the implications of including or excluding such an option (Mertler, 2014). Several Likert questions appear below. Notice the format of the Likert items and that a higher number corresponds to a higher level of agreement with a given statement.

1	2	3	4	5
Strongly disagree	Disagree	No opinion	Agree	Strongly agree

1.	My teacher tells me when I do good work.	1	2	3	4	5
2.	My teacher encourages me to ask questions when I don't understand what's going on in class.	1	2	3	4	5
3.	My teacher tells us why the things we are learning are important.	1	2	3	4	5

4.	My teacher makes it clear how grades are determined.	1	2	3	4	5
5.	I really pay attention in this class.	1	2	3	4	5
6.	My teacher is fair when students misbehave.	1	2	3	4	5
7.	My teacher teaches things in an order that makes sense.	1	2	3	4	5
8.	My teacher takes time in class to help students.	1	2	3	4	5
9.	This class is challenging to me.	1	2	3	4	5
10.	My teacher gives fair tests.	1	2	3	4	5

A similar category of question is a **Likert-type question**. This type of scale also exists on a continuum, but it measures something other than extent of agreement. For example, a Likert-type item might require participants to respond on a scale that examines quality (from "excellent" to "poor"), frequency of occurrence (from "always" to "never"), or degree of benefit (from "very beneficial" to "not at all beneficial"). Two examples of Likert-type scales are provided below:

1. How would you describe your level of preparation, in terms of assessing student performance, that resulted from your undergraduate teacher education program?
   - ☐ Not at all prepared
   - ☐ Not very well prepared
   - ☐ Slightly prepared
   - ☐ Somewhat prepared
   - ☐ Well prepared

2.

1	2	3	4	5
Not at all		Some of the time		All the time

	Adjustment Indicators						
Student Name	Fearful	Relates Well to Peers	Complains of Illness	Cries Easily	Exhibits Self-Confidence	Frustrated	Intimidated	Appears Happy

Survey Design Considerations. The process of designing a survey should not be taken lightly. Failure to follow some general guidelines for survey development can result in inaccurate data, which will then be followed by inaccurate inferences drawn about the population of interest. Whenever possible, it is imperative to follow the guidelines listed below (Creswell, 2005; Fraenkel et al., 2012; Gay et al., 2009; McMillan, 2012; Mertens, 2005):

- *Provide directions that make the respondents' task clear.* For example, indicate whether you want your respondents to circle their responses, mark checkboxes, or write their responses in the blanks provided.
- *Include only items that relate to the purpose and research questions of the study.* Do not try to collect too much information. Generally speaking, the longer the survey, the lower the response rate will be.
- *If you plan to make comparisons between subgroups, you <u>must</u> remember to include the pertinent demographic questions.* For example, you cannot compare the responses of males with those of females unless you ask the respondents to indicate their gender. Once your data have been collected, it will be too late to go back and attempt to get this information.
- *Survey questions should be clear and unambiguous.* Avoid using words that are subject to interpretation. For example, the question, "Do you spend a lot of time doing homework?" (where individuals are likely to have different interpretations of "a lot") should be reworded to ask, "How much time do you spend doing homework?"
- *Avoid asking leading questions, which might suggest that one answer is preferable to another.* For example, the question that begins, "Would you agree with most people that . . . ?" could more appropriately be stated as, "Do you believe that . . . ?"
- *Keep your questions short, with a straightforward focus.* This makes the task of providing an answer easier for respondents.
- *Avoid double negatives and negative wording in general.* Negatives tend to confuse people, especially when they are reading quickly. For example, consider the following question: "Which of the following are not rules that you would not be opposed to in your classroom?" As worded, this question is very confusing. Rewording the question as follows would undoubtedly clarify the task for respondents: "Which of the following rules do you believe would be appropriate for your classroom?"
- *Emphasize critical words in the question by formatting them in italic, bold, or underlined print.* This forces potential respondents to read the question more carefully, while also helping them focus on what the researcher has deemed important or critical.
- *Avoid the use of double-barreled questions.* A **double-barreled question** is one that essentially asks two different things. Consider the following prompt: "My principal is approachable and responsive." Since it is possible to be approachable and not responsive (or vice versa), this could be a difficult prompt to answer. If both components are important in your study, separate them into two separate prompts.

- *Use correct grammar and spelling.* Many people will get "turned off" if incorrect grammar is used or if words are misspelled. This will only serve to lower your response rate and credibility.
- *Include a cover letter with the survey.* The cover letter serves as a type of consent form for individuals who may respond to a survey or questionnaire. It essentially serves the same purpose as a consent form, accurately disclosing the potential involvement of participants in the survey study. An example of a cover letter is provided in Figure 12.5, and the survey that accompanied the letter is provided in Figure 12.6. Notice that the majority of the items on the survey are Likert items, followed by several demographic-type checklist items.

At this point, it is important to note several factors related to the use of surveys and rating scales with students and, in particular, younger children. Researchers must ensure that the various aspects—not just the reading level—of the instrument are appropriate for the age or grade level of students. Earlier, we discussed the advantages and limitations of using a 5-point scale, where the midpoint represents "no opinion" or "neutral." You can see how this might create difficulties for younger children, as they might not be able to discriminate between adjacent points on the scale. However, I do not believe that researchers should be apprehensive about using such data collection instruments with younger children. You would likely provide fewer options on the scale and perhaps even use graphics for the children to indicate their responses.

To illustrate my point, several years ago, I was part of a research team that attempted to "survey" kindergarten students as part of the prekindergarten-to-kindergarten transitions study. We had the teachers read various statements to the children and then asked them to put an X through the face that represented how they felt (see Figure 12.7 on p. 249).

Unfortunately, the children had no idea—and our explanations did not help at all—what purpose the numbers were to serve. They were instructed to locate the number 1 on their response sheet, as the teacher read the first statement number, and then place their X on the appropriate face. After the first few statements—and as we walked around the room to monitor data collection—we realized that they were simply placing the X over the same faces in the first row. Yikes—not good data! Several of the children had response sheets that looked like this:

Even the novice researcher can see the problems this created with respect to the accuracy of our data! On the spur of the moment, we decided to revise the nature of the response sheet by swapping out the numbers for icons (e.g., ✐, ✂, ✇, ✈) that we believed the children could identify more easily. Using this format, we could direct the children's attention to the box with a certain image in it and have them place their response only in that box.

FIGURE 12.5 ● Sample Cover Letter for a Web-Based Survey

RE: NCLB & TEACHERS' ASSESSMENT PRACTICES

Dear Ohio Teacher,

I am currently conducting a Web-based survey research study titled **"The Impact of NCLB on Teachers' Classroom Assessment Practices,"** the purpose of which is examine how (or if) NCLB has affected the ways in which teachers assess the academic learning of their students.

Your superintendent has granted approval for teachers in your district to participate in the study as one of 150 randomly selected school districts in Ohio. The purpose of this e-mail message is to ask for your participation in the study. I am asking you to participate in the study by simply completing the survey as honestly and openly as you can. The survey should only take about 10–15 minutes to complete. When you have completed the survey, simply click on the **SUBMIT** button located at the bottom of the page to send your responses to me. Please make sure you submit your responses only once! Additionally, please complete the survey by **September 30, 20XX.**

Please be assured that your responses will be anonymous. There will be no way for me to determine the origin of your responses. You will not be contacted for any further information. No one other than you will know if you have or have not participated in this study. Additionally, no individual information will be shared; only aggregate results will be reported. Finally, due to the Web-based nature of the survey, there exists a minimal chance that your responses could be intercepted, by individuals not involved with this study, while being transmitted.

Your participation in this study is voluntary. By completing and submitting the survey, you are giving your consent to participate. Please be assured that your decision to participate or not participate in this study will have no impact on your relationship with your respective school district. If you do not wish to participate, simply disregard this message. If you have any questions regarding this survey study, I may be contacted at *mertler@ bgsu.edu.* You may also contact the Chair, Human Subjects Review Board, Bowling Green State University, (419) 372-7716 (*hsrb@bgsu.edu*) if any problems or concerns arise during the course of the study.

I would like very much for you to participate in the study by completing the brief survey which can be found by clicking on the following link:

http://edhd.bgsu.edu/mertler/nclbsurveya.php

It is important to note that the survey is best viewed with Internet Explorer (version 5 or higher) or Netscape Navigator/Communicator (version 4.5 or higher).

In advance, thank you very much for your participation in this research endeavor and best of luck in the remainder of your school year!

Best Regards,

Craig A. Mertler, Ph.D.
Associate Professor of Assessment and Research Methodologies

APPROVED – BGSU HSRB
EFFECTIVE 8/22/20XX
EXPIRES 8/14/20XX

FIGURE 12.6 ● Sample Web-Based Survey

Survey of Ohio Teachers' Perceptions of NCLB and Its Impact on Their Classroom Assessment Practices

The purpose of this survey is to explore the impact that the No Child Left Behind Act (NCLB) has had on the ways that classroom teachers assess the academic learning of their students. This survey should take no more than 10 minutes of your time. Your participation in this brief survey is greatly appreciated!

SECTION 1

Please respond to each of the statements below, indicating the extent to which you agree or disagree with each one, using the following scale:

SD = Strongly Disagree
D = Disagree
A = Agree
SA = Strongly Agree

1.	I believe that I know a lot about the No Child Left Behind (NCLB) Act.	SD ☐	D ☐	A ☐	SA ☐
2.	NCLB has forced me to change the focus of my classroom instruction.	SD ☐	D ☐	A ☐	SA ☐
3.	NCLB has changed the nature of academic motivation for students and has placed more stress on students.	SD ☐	D ☐	A ☐	SA ☐
4.	NCLB has changed the nature of instructional motivation for teachers and has placed more stress on teachers.	SD ☐	D ☐	A ☐	SA ☐
5.	The importance placed on Ohio's achievement tests and the Ohio Graduation Test (OGT) have led to instruction that violates the standards of good educational practice.	SD ☐	D ☐	A ☐	SA ☐
6.	I feel more pressure and stress as a result of the increased testing mandates in Ohio and the related need to improve student performance.	SD ☐	D ☐	A ☐	SA ☐
7.	My students feel more stress as a result of the increased testing mandates in Ohio.	SD ☐	D ☐	A ☐	SA ☐
8.	NCLB has forced me to change the ways in which I assess my students' academic performance.	SD ☐	D ☐	A ☐	SA ☐

(Continued)

(Continued)

		SD	D	A	SA
9.	As a result of NCLB, I create a greater number of my classroom tests such that they mirror the same format and types of questions on the state's achievements tests and/or the OGT.	☐	☐	☐	☐
10.	I use multiple-choice classroom tests more frequently than I have in the past.	☐	☐	☐	☐
11.	I have substantially DECREASED the amount of time spent on instruction of content NOT tested on the state-mandated tests.	☐	☐	☐	☐
12.	I have NOT let NCLB or the state-mandated testing program in Ohio influence what or how I provide instruction to my students.	☐	☐	☐	☐
13.	I have substantially INCREASED the amount of time spent on instruction of content that I know is covered on the state-mandated tests.	☐	☐	☐	☐
14.	I have NOT let NCLB affect how I assess the academic achievement and progress of my students.	☐	☐	☐	☐
15.	I spend much more time throughout the year preparing my students for the state-mandated tests.	☐	☐	☐	☐
16.	As a result of NCLB, I now spend more time teaching test-taking skills to my students.	☐	☐	☐	☐
17.	I have used sample test items from the state tests, approved by the Ohio Department of Education, to help prepare my students to take the tests.	☐	☐	☐	☐
18.	As a result of NCLB, I use standardized test data to help guide and improve my instruction.	☐	☐	☐	☐
19.	In my school, I believe that most teachers are carrying on their work much as they did before NCLB.	☐	☐	☐	☐
20.	In my school, I believe that NCLB has forced teachers to divert their attention away from more important issues that can better improve teaching and learning.	☐	☐	☐	☐
21.	I do not care to know any more about NCLB and its effect on my work as a classroom teacher than I do right now.	☐	☐	☐	☐
22.	I believe that the overall effect of NCLB on my school has been positive.	☐	☐	☐	☐

SECTION 2

Please respond to each of the following questions:

23. What is your gender?

- ☐ female
- ☐ male

24. Which of the following is the <u>most appropriate</u> description of the level at which you teach?

- ☐ elementary–primary (K–grade 3)
- ☐ elementary–intermediate (grades 4–6)
- ☐ elementary (K–6)
- ☐ middle (grades 6–8)
- ☐ high (grades 9–12)
- ☐ secondary (grades 6–12)
- ☐ K–12
- ☐ other

25. Which <u>best</u> describes the educational level you have attained?

- ☐ B.A. or B.S.
- ☐ M.A. or M.S.
- ☐ Specialist
- ☐ Ed.D.
- ☐ Ph.D.

26. <u>Including the current year</u>, how many years of experience do you have as a classroom teacher?

- ☐ 1–5 years
- ☐ 6–10 years
- ☐ 11–15 years
- ☐ 16–20 years
- ☐ 21–25 years
- ☐ 26–30 years
- ☐ more than 30 years

27. What is the current Ohio Department of Education rating for your <u>school district</u>?

- ☐ Excellent
- ☐ Effective
- ☐ Continuous Improvement
- ☐ Academic Watch
- ☐ Academic Emergency
- ☐ Don't Know

(Continued)

(Continued)

28. What is the current Ohio Department of Education rating for your school building?

☐   Excellent
☐   Effective
☐   Continuous Improvement
☐   Academic Watch
☐   Academic Emergency
☐   Don't Know

Click here to submit your responses

Thank you for your assistance!!!

If you have any questions about this survey, please feel free to contact me:

Dr. Craig A. Mertler

Bowling Green State University

Bowling Green, Ohio

Formative and Summative Classroom Assessments

In many cases, the focus of educational research studies is on student learning. In these research scenarios, multiple sources of data can be—and probably should be—used to help answer the guiding research questions. Many of these data sources are routinely used in the day-to-day process of providing instruction to students and then assessing their mastery of those instructional objectives or units (Mertler, 2014). **Formative classroom assessments** are administered *during* instruction to determine what sorts of adjustments should be made to that instruction while it is ongoing (Mertler, 2003). Formative assessments are primarily informal and often administered spontaneously, including observations, oral questioning, and student reflections. Based on your knowledge of various methods for data collection, it should be obvious how informal assessments such as observations, questions, and reflections can be used as legitimate sources of research data.

Summative classroom assessments are administered *after* a substantial period of instruction (e.g., following completion of an instructional unit, at the end of a semester or course) to inform administrative decisions, such as assigning final grades, or simply to provide a broader overview of student achievement (Mertler, 2003). Generally speaking, summative assessments are more formal, and their administration is usually scheduled in advance. This category of summative assessments that could be used as sources of research data includes chapter tests, unit tests, end-of-course tests, major performance-based projects (e.g., research reports, research-based presentations)—typically any assessment that would measure student achievement and span numerous instructional objectives and/or skills. Other formal assessment

FIGURE 12.7 ● Sample Rating Scale Used With Young Children

Student Self-Assessment Survey

Directions:

1. Ask your students to think back to the very first day of Kindergarten.

2. Read item to your students and instruct them to respond in the appropriate space on the Student Self-Assessment Response Form.

1.	☺	☹
2.	☺	☹
3.	☺	☹
4.	☺	☹
5.	☺	☹
6.	☺	☹
7.	☺	☹
8.	☺	☹
9.	☺	☹
10.	☺	☹

instruments that might be included here are scores on homework assignments and quizzes, and final semester or course grades.

The advantage of using formative and summative assessments as sources of data in educational research studies is that they are typically another type of "existing" data—not at the school or district level but, rather, at the teacher or classroom level—in that they are routinely administered during the teaching–learning process. Therefore, depending on the nature of the study and the research questions, incorporating these sources of data can facilitate conducting the study and make it somewhat more practical, since designing data collection instruments *specifically* and *only* for a given research study is not always necessary. However, one disadvantage of using these data is the potential mismatch with the goals of the research study. Researchers must ensure that these instruments will provide the data specifically required to answer the research questions stated at the outset of the study. Otherwise, these data—*from the perspective of the research study*—are potentially meaningless. This—along with other, similar issues— is central in establishing the *validity* and *reliability* (which we will discuss shortly) of the instruments used to collect data, as well as of the resulting data themselves.

Standardized Test Scores

Standardized test scores are also routinely used as quantitative data sources in research studies. It is important to realize that these formal data collection instruments may also be considered existing records, since they are administered to students as a regular part of classroom instruction and district-level accountability. If these types of data are to be included in a quantitative educational research study, however, they should not be the only source of data; they can be supplemented with more local data sources, such as observations, self-developed surveys, or other existing data forms. This may be important in terms of helping contextualize the study and its findings; however, reliance on sources that are more local in nature (i.e., self-developed) may potentially limit the generalizability of the study to other settings and to the population at large.

Standardized tests exist in a wide variety, ranging in type, purpose, and resulting data (i.e., scores). Categories of standardized tests include performance measures, attitudinal measures, and behavioral measures (Creswell, 2005). Examples of standardized tests within these categories include, but are certainly not limited to, the following (Creswell, 2005):

- **Performance measures**—These measures are used to assess an individual's ability to *perform* on some sort of test or inventory.

  - ✓ **Norm-referenced tests**—Scores from these tests indicate how well an individual performed in relation to a large group of test takers. Examples include the California Achievement Test, the Comprehensive Test of Basic Skills, the Iowa Test of Basic Skills, the Metropolitan Achievement Test, and the Stanford Achievement Test, as well as tests that measure IQ, cognitive ability, and school readiness.

  - ✓ **Criterion-referenced tests**—Scores from these tests indicate how well an individual performed in comparison with preestablished criteria. Examples include the General Educational Development test, and statewide and national tests of achievement. (Note that many of the tests listed as norm-referenced tests above will also provide criterion-referenced scores, although their main purpose is the comparison of performance to a larger group.)

  - ✓ **Intelligence tests**—These tests measure an individual's intellectual ability. Arguably the best-known example is the Wechsler Intelligence Scale for Children. Others include the Wechsler Adult Intelligence Scale and the Stanford-Binet Intelligence Scale.

  - ✓ **Aptitude tests**—These provide an estimate of a person's ability to perform at some time in the future or in a different situation. Examples include the American College Test, Graduate Management Admission Test, Graduate Record Examination, Law School Admission Test, Medical School Admission Test, SAT, and Test of English as a Foreign Language.

  - ✓ **Interest inventories**—These inventories provide information about an individual's interests to help that individual make career choices. An example is the Strong Interest Inventory.

✓ **Personality inventories**—These tests identify and measure human characteristics in an attempt to predict or explain behavior over time and across situations. A prime example is the Minnesota Multiphasic Personality Inventory.

- **Attitudinal measures**—These instruments assess people's *attitudes* or *feelings* toward topics of an educational nature.

    ✓ *Affective scales*—These instruments measure various positive or negative *affects*, or feelings, related to a given topic. Examples include the Attitudes Toward Self Scale and the Rosenberg Self-Esteem Scale.

- **Behavioral measures**—These measures are essentially used to record *behavioral observations* on a checklist for some other sort of instrumentation.

    ✓ *Behavioral checklist*—Examples include the Measurement of Inappropriate and Disruptive Interactions, Flanders Interaction Analysis, and Behavioral Checklist in Reading.

When trying to identify an instrument for use in a research study, you essentially have three choices: develop your own, use an existing instrument, or adapt an existing instrument. We have already discussed techniques for constructing your own instrument. Should you choose to use or adapt an existing instrument, there are some things you should know. First, most existing instruments have been published and copyrighted; so you will need permission to use them, in any form, in a study you might be conducting. This permission may be sought from the publisher or the author of the instrument. When requesting permission to use someone else's data collection instrument, the researcher must clearly explain the purpose of the study, who will serve as the participants, why this instrument is appropriate for the study, and whether or not any modifications will be made to the instrument.

Second, researchers should take advantage of certain resources when trying to locate existing instruments. Existing instruments are sometimes quite advantageous because, as the old saying goes, there is no need to reinvent the wheel. If an instrument already exists to measure exactly what you want to measure, developing your own is unnecessary. A list of some strategies that can help the researcher locate existing instruments is provided below (Creswell, 2005):

- *Review published research articles*. Often, the same articles you read for a literature review will provide information about the instruments used in related studies. Many of these instruments may be commercially available. Even if an instrument is not commercially available, you can contact the author of the article to seek permission to use the instrument.
- *Conduct a search in the ERIC database*. Searching ERIC is certainly a benefit when reviewing related literature, but ERIC can also be a useful repository for instrumentation for research studies. The process is similar to that outlined above: Once you have identified an instrument as having been used in a relevant research study, contacting the author is often an appropriate way to gain access to the instrument.

- *Use the ERIC Clearinghouse on Assessment and Evaluation.* This website (ericae.net), affiliated with ERIC, contains a wealth of information regarding educational assessment, evaluation, and research methodology. Additionally, by clicking on the "Test Locator" link (ericae.net/testcol.htm) at the top of the home page, researchers can gain access to several databases of existing instruments. These databases include instruments that are free to use, tests in the Educational Testing Service (ETS) Test Collection database, and the Buros Center for Testing measurements (buros.org). For example, the ETS Test Collection database (www.ets.org/test_link/about) is a searchable database of more than 25,000 tests and other measurement instruments.
- *Review publications specifically listing instruments that are commercially available.* Guides developed over the years can help researchers identify instruments that are commercially available to individuals and institutions, primarily for research purposes. These guides include the *Mental Measurements Yearbook* and *Tests in Print*, both of which are available through the Buros Center for Testing website (buros.org).

Characteristics of Quantitative Data: Validity and Reliability

Validity and reliability are essential characteristics of quantitative research. The researcher has an ethical obligation to engage in practices focused on assessing and ensuring that the data, results of analyses of those data, and conclusions and inferences drawn from those analyses are both valid and reliable. Next, we look at validity and reliability, and the methods and techniques for determining them.

Validity in Quantitative Research

Validity is an essential quality in quantitative research and has to do with whether the data are, in fact, what they are believed or purported to be; in other words, did we *actually* measure what we intended to measure, based on the focus of our research (Mertler, 2014)? Though any data you might collect may be entirely accurate, the critical factor is whether or not they are appropriate and accurate *for your purposes* (i.e., do they enable you to accurately answer your research questions?). For example, imagine that a reading teacher uses the results from the reading portion of a standardized test to group her students into above-average, average, and below-average reading groups. Now imagine that a social studies teacher uses *those same reading scores* to identify students who he believes would be successful in an advanced-placement history course. The first interpretation and use of the scores is valid; the second is not. In terms of the social studies teacher's use of the data, they were invalid for his purposes (Mertler, 2014). The critical point to remember is that validity refers to the degree to which evidence supports the *inferences* a researcher makes based on the data he or she has collected using a particular instrument; the *inferences* are validated, *not* the instrument itself (Fraenkel et al., 2012). Determination of the validity of data ultimately has a substantial effect on the interpretation of those data, once they have been analyzed, and the subsequent conclusions drawn from those results (Mertler & Charles, 2011).

Determining the Validity of Inferences Drawn From Quantitative Data Presently, validity is seen as a unitary concept (American Educational Research Association, American Psychological Association, & National Council on Measurement in Education, 1999), combining what were previously described as four distinct types of validity: content, concurrent, predictive, and construct. Validity is defined as the "degree to which all the accumulated evidence supports the intended interpretation of test scores for the proposed purpose" (p. 11). Validity of data obtained from the administration of tests (usually quantitative data) can be determined through the examination of various sources of *evidence of validity*. Although similar to the four "outdated" types of validity, the five sources of validity evidence are unique in their own right (Mertler & Charles, 2011).

Evidence of Validity Based on Test Content. This source of evidence is based on the relationship between the *content* addressed on a test—or other instrument used for data collection—and the underlying *construct* (or characteristic) it is trying to measure. In other words, it is the degree to which the test measures an intended content area. This type of evidence often includes logical analysis of content coverage on the test, as well as the judgments of experts in the particular content field. This type of evidence was formerly referred to as *content validity*. Evidence of content validity requires both *item validity* and *sampling validity* (Gay et al., 2009). Item validity is concerned with the extent to which the items that appear on a test are *relevant* to the content area being tested. Sampling validity has to do with how well the items that appear on the test *represent* the total content area being tested.

Evidence of Validity Based on Response Processes. This source of validity evidence often results from the analysis of individual *sets of responses* from a test. Examining patterns of response or questioning respondents about the performance or strategies they used on a particular test can provide insight into the specific characteristics actually being measured by a set of test items. Patterns of response—for example, a tendency to agree with certain types of statements and disagree with others—can reveal underlying characteristics of individual participants or groups of participants (e.g., females). Gathering and processing this type of evidence typically requires the use of advanced statistical analyses.

Evidence of Validity Based on Internal Structure. Analysis of the internal structure of a given test involves an examination of the extent to which the *relationships among the test items* conform to or parallel the construct—that is, the underlying characteristic—being measured. Often, subsets of test items that on the surface appear to be measuring the construct of interest may actually be measuring something slightly, or even drastically, different. This source of evidence is somewhat analogous to the evidence of validity based on test content; however, in this case, the focus is on how the items on the test relate to one another, as opposed to considering them individually. This form of evidence is similar to the former category known as *construct validity*. It also requires the use of advanced statistical analyses.

Evidence of Validity Based on Relations to Other Variables. Analyses of the relationships between test scores and other measures of the same or similar constructs can provide evidence of the validity of the scores resulting from the instrument of interest. For example, one might investigate the relationship between college entrance exam scores and eventual college grade point averages. Similar measures might include other tests or inventories, or performance (e.g., "hands-on") criteria that purport to measure the same thing. This type of evidence, formerly known as *criterion validity*, involves computations of correlation coefficients (known in this specific application as *validity coefficients*). Two types of validity coefficients can serve as measures of the evidence of validity based on relationships to other variables: *concurrent validity coefficients* and *predictive validity coefficients*. **Concurrent validity coefficients** are correlation coefficients that measure the relationship between scores on the instrument of interest and scores on a similar instrument, administered at roughly the same time (i.e., concurrently). In contrast, **predictive validity coefficients** are measures of the relationship between scores on the instrument of interest and scores on some measure taken quite some time (e.g., several years) later.

Evidence of Validity Based on Consequences of Testing. Testing, as well as any other type of data collection, is done with the expectation that some benefit will be realized from the intended and appropriate use of the scores. The process of validation should indicate whether these specific benefits are likely to be realized. Examples of such benefits include improved academic achievement, increased self-esteem, and boosted motivation. At a minimum, testing (as well as other forms of data collection) should not have a detrimental effect. If this is the case, then data collection using that particular instrument had negative consequences on the participants in the study. Obviously, this is not something we want to occur when conducting research studies in education.

Reliability in Quantitative Research

Reliability, a second essential characteristic of quantitative data, refers not to the accuracy of data and subsequent inferences but to the *consistency* of those data. For example, if a researcher administers a certain test repeatedly under identical circumstances but obtains different results each time, the researcher must conclude that the test is unreliable. If, however, the researcher obtains similar results each time the test is administered, the results can be considered reliable and, therefore, potentially useful for the purposes of that particular research study.

Determining the Reliability of Quantitative Data Reliability of quantitative data is typically established by correlating the test results with themselves, or with scores from similar measures. Therefore, determining reliability is a purely statistical process. Further, reliability is expressed numerically as a reliability coefficient (i.e., a correlation coefficient specifically used to provide a quantitative measure of the degree of reliability). Reliability coefficients can range from a minimum of 0.00 to a maximum of +1.00. The closer a reliability coefficient is to +1.00, the closer we are to having perfect reliability—although no test or instrument will guarantee perfect reliability. Extending the notion of perfect reliability, high reliability—in other words, a coefficient close to +1.00—indicates that the instrument has minimal error. Again, as error is inherent in all measures of human behavior and performance, it is incredibly unlikely—although not impossible—to obtain perfect reliability. Three different methods are used: *test–retest*, *equivalent-forms*, and *internal consistency reliabilities*.

Determining **test–retest reliability** (also referred to as **stability**) involves administering a given test to a group of participants and then, perhaps a week later, readministering the same test to the same people. The scores from the first and second administrations are correlated, and the resultant coefficient of correlation provides an index of reliability; the higher the correlation coefficient (i.e., as it approaches 1.00), the more reliable the test. The procedure used for determining test–retest reliability is as follows:

1. Administer the test to a group of participants.
2. After a relatively minimal amount of time has passed—often 1 to 2 weeks— administer the *same* instrument to the *same* group of participants.
3. Calculate a reliability (i.e., correlation) coefficient between the two sets of scores.
4. Evaluate the resulting reliability coefficient, often referred to as the **coefficient of stability**.

Equivalent-forms reliability (often referred to as **equivalence**) is similar to the test–retest method of determining reliability, except that in this case two different forms of the test are used for measuring the same thing, as opposed to using an identical form on two occasions. This process is very similar to the previous one:

1. Administer Form A of the test to a group of individuals.
2. Shortly thereafter, administer Form B of the test to the same group of individuals.
3. Calculate a reliability (i.e., correlation) coefficient between the two sets of scores.
4. Evaluate the resulting reliability coefficient, referred to here as the **coefficient of equivalence**.

In the two techniques for calculating reliability presented above, two administrations of the instrument are required. In many cases and research scenarios, this is not practical or feasible. **Internal consistency reliability** is the extent to which items in a single test are consistent among themselves and with the test as a whole. There are three techniques for determining internal consistency reliability: *split-half, Kuder-Richardson,* and *Cronbach's alpha reliabilities.*

Split-half reliability is appropriate when testing a single group on two occasions is not feasible or when an alternate form of a test is not available. Further, it is appropriate when a test or measurement instrument is very long. The procedure for determining split-half reliability is as follows:

1. Administer the total test to a group of participants.
2. Divide the test into two comparable halves, or subtests. The most common practice for doing this is to separate the odd-numbered items (which will form Subtest 1) from the even-numbered items (forming Subtest 2).
3. Correlate the two sets of scores.
4. Apply the Spearman-Brown correction formula.
5. Evaluate the resulting reliability coefficient.

Note that there is an extra step in the calculation of a split-half reliability coefficient. This extra step—applying the *Spearman-Brown correction formula* (which you may sometimes see called the *Spearman-Brown prophecy formula*)—is necessary to correct for the length of the test. Since longer tests tend to be more reliable than shorter tests, the correction formula must be applied because we have calculated a reliability coefficient on a test only *half as long* as the *actual* test. For example, if our original test contained 100 items, our split-half reliability would actually be a correlation between two 50-item tests. In this scenario, the Spearman-Brown correction formula would provide an estimate of the reliability for the 100-item test, thus increasing the estimate of reliability. The formula is simple:

$$r_{total\ test} = \frac{2r_{split-half}}{1 + r_{split-half}}$$

So, if we had obtained a split-half reliability equal to .70, our correction would be calculated as follows:

$$r_{total\ test} = \frac{2(.70)}{1 + .70} = \frac{1.40}{1.70} = .82$$

You may come across other measures of internal consistency reliability in the research literature. Two commonly reported measures are **Kuder-Richardson (KR-20) reliability** and **Cronbach's alpha reliability**. Without going into great detail, these two measures are both basically *averages of all possible split-half reliabilities.* Their interpretations are similar to the split-half reliability coefficient; a high KR-20 reliability or high alpha reliability both indicate good reliability. Cronbach's alpha reliability is a general formula, of which the KR-20 formula is a special case (Gay et al., 2009).

The KR-20 formula is a highly respected method for assessing reliability, but it is useful only for items that are scored dichotomously (i.e., either "right" or "wrong"). For example, multiple-choice and true–false items are scored dichotomously. When items have more than two possible outcomes—for example, when using a 4-point Likert or Likert-type scale—Cronbach's alpha should be used to calculate the reliability. While the KR-20 formula is well respected, the authors provided an alternative, more easily computed formula, known as KR-21. It requires less time than any other method of estimating reliability, although it tends to provide a more conservative estimate (Gay et al., 2009). The KR-21 formula is as follows:

$$r_{total\ test} = \frac{(K)\left(SD^2\right) - \overline{X}(K - \overline{X})}{(SD^2)(K - 1)}$$

where

K = the number of items on the test

SD = the standard deviation of the scores

$\overline{X}$ = the mean of the scores

In Chapter 13, you will learn how to calculate the mean and standard deviation for a set of scores, but for now, let us consider an example where a researcher has administered a 100-item test and has calculated the mean to be 82 ($\overline{X} = 82$) and standard deviation to be 8 ($SD = 8$). The internal consistency reliability would be calculated as follows:

$$r_{total\ test} = \frac{(100)\left(8^2\right) - 82(100 - 82)}{\left(8^2\right)(100 - 1)}.$$

$$= \frac{(100)(64) - 82(18)}{(64)(99)}$$

$$= \frac{6400 - 1476}{6336} = \frac{4924}{6336} = .78$$

The resulting internal consistency reliability coefficient for our test is .78—not too bad!

Relationship Between Validity and Reliability

We often think of validity and reliability as two distinct concepts, but in fact they share an important relationship. It is possible for scores obtained from an instrument to be reliable (consistent) but not valid (measuring something other than what was intended). In contrast, scores cannot be both valid *and* unreliable; if scores measure what was intended to be measured, it is implied that they will do so consistently. Therefore, reliability is a necessary but not sufficient condition for validity. When establishing the validity and reliability of your research data, always remember the following adage: *A valid test is always reliable, but a reliable test is not necessarily valid.*

Developmental Activities

1. Think of a possible research topic and study that would require you to select a random sample of participants. Draft a step-by-step plan for selecting a sample using any two of the five possible random sampling techniques presented in this chapter.

2. Think of a possible research study you might want to conduct (perhaps using the same topic as in Activity 1 above). Develop a list of possible variables for inclusion in your study at each of the four levels of measurement. Try to come up with three to four variables each at the nominal, ordinal, interval, and ratio levels.

3. Contrary to popular belief, developing a quality survey instrument is not easy; it often requires some practice to write good, quality survey items. Identify a research area of interest to you, and develop a 15- to 20-item survey, containing different types of items (e.g., Likert items, Likert-type items, checklists, etc.). Pay close attention to the survey design considerations outlined in the chapter.

4. Consider various pros and cons of using standardized test data in research studies. Present a case either for or against the use of standardized test scores as research data.

5. Consider pros and cons of using existing published or unpublished instruments as a means to collect data in research studies. Present a case either for or against the use of existing instrumentation to collect research data.

Summary

- Clearly identifying the target population and the accessible population is important in the sampling process.
- Random sampling techniques share two important characteristics:
  - The chance that each member of the population will be selected can be specified.
  - All members of the population have an equal chance of being selected.

- Simple random sampling is the best way to obtain a representative sample, although no method guarantees perfect representation of the population.
- Stratified random sampling is a process whereby certain subgroups are selected for inclusion in the sample.
  - Proportional stratified sampling involves a process where the identified subgroups

in the sample are represented in the same proportion in which they exist in the population.

○ Equal stratified sampling is a process where the representation of subgroups is equal.

- Cluster random sampling involves the random sampling of existing groups, or clusters.
- Multistage random sampling is a combination of cluster random sampling and individual random sampling.
- Systematic sampling involves selecting the *K*th individual from a population list.

  ○ Depending on the organization of the list, systematic sampling may be a random sampling technique or a nonrandom technique.

- Nonrandom sampling techniques do not permit specification of the probability of inclusion in the population, nor do they guarantee that every member of the population has an equal chance of being selected.
- Convenience sampling involves a selection of whoever happens to be available.
- In snowball sampling, current participants identify other individuals to act as participants in the study.
- Quota sampling involves the selection of the sample based on precise numbers of individuals with specific characteristics.
- Purposive or judgment sampling identifies individuals who are believed to be representative of a given population.
- Generally speaking, the larger the population size, the smaller the percentage of the population required to get a representative sample.
- When samples are selected randomly, there is still a chance that differences will exist between the population and the sample; this is known as sampling error.

- Sampling bias is a systematic error and is usually the fault of the researcher.
- A measurement scale is a system used to organize data so they can be reviewed, analyzed, and interpreted appropriately.

  ○ Nominal scales are associated with measuring a categorical variable.
  ○ Ordinal scales possess the same characteristics as nominal scales but also rank order variables based on the degree to which they possess a given characteristic.
  ○ Interval scales possess all the characteristics of nominal and ordinal scales, but the values represent equal intervals.
  ○ Ratio scales are the highest level of measurement and possess all the characteristics of the other scales but also have a true zero point.

- Quantitative data collection techniques vary greatly.
- Surveys are a group of quantitative data collection techniques that involve the administration of a set of questions or statements to a sample of respondents.
- Questionnaires are specific types of surveys that are administered in written form.
- Four types of survey questions are demographic, knowledge, attitudinal, and behavioral questions.
- Closed-ended, or forced-choice, questions resemble multiple-choice or other types of items where respondents select from a number of given options.
- Open-ended questions allow for more individualized responses.
- Checklists are closed-ended items that provide only a dichotomous response option.

- Likert items begin with a statement and then ask individuals to respond on an agree–disagree continuum.
- Likert-type items also exist on a continuum but measure something other than agreement.
- Developing quality survey instruments is not an easy task; researchers should follow the design guidelines.
- Formative and summative classroom assessments can be used as sources for quantitative data.
- Standardized test scores can also be used as sources of data.
- Validity and reliability are essential qualities in quantitative research.
- Validity has to do with whether we actually measured what we intended to measure, and whether the inferences follow logically from our interpretations.
- Evidence of validity must be collected during research studies to determine the validity of research inferences.

  o Evidence of validity comes from the following sources: test content, response processes, internal structure, relations to other variables, and consequences of testing.
  o Determination of the validity of inferences from collected data is based on judgment or the calculation of validity coefficients.

- Reliability has to do with the consistency of the data that are collected.

  o Reliability of quantitative data is determined through several statistical procedures, including test–retest reliability (stability), equivalent-forms reliability (equivalence), and internal consistency methods.
  o Methods for determining internal consistency reliability include split-half, Kuder-Richardson, and Cronbach's alpha reliabilities.

- Reliability is a necessary but not sufficient condition for validity.

$SAGE edge™

Sharpen your skills with SAGE edge!

edge.sagepub.com/mertler

SAGE edge for Students provides a personalized approach to help you accomplish your coursework goals in an easy-to-use learning environment. You'll find action plans, mobile-friendly eFlashcards, and quizzes as well as video, web, and resources and links to SAGE journal articles to support and expand on the concepts presented in this chapter.

13

Quantitative Data Analysis

In this chapter, we look much more deeply at aspects of analyzing quantitative research data. Topics in our examination of quantitative data analysis will include the preparation of data for analysis, statistical analysis software, common descriptive and inferential statistical analysis techniques, and cautions in the use of statistics.

Quantitative Data Analysis Techniques

You should recall from earlier chapters that analysis of quantitative data involves the application of statistical analysis procedures to data collected during an educational research study. The term *statistics* has multiple meanings. One meaning refers to summary indices resulting from data analysis—indices such as a mean, median, standard deviation, and coefficient of correlation. Another meaning refers to the *procedures* by which data are analyzed mathematically. The procedural aspects of statistics are used to describe and analyze data in various ways, to accomplish certain research-related tasks. The following list summarizes the most common purposes behind various statistical procedures:

- *To summarize data and reveal what is typical and atypical within a group.* Research often yields hundreds or thousands of items of numerical data that, until summarized, cannot be interpreted meaningfully. Suppose you had the raw measurements of heights, weights, and intelligence quotient (IQ) scores for all of last year's high school graduates in the state of Florida. That would give you thousands of pages of numerical data that, if you tried to make sense of them, might leave you scratching your head. Statistics are used to reduce masses of data into information more easily understood by showing what is average, how much difference exists between highest and lowest values, what the most commonly occurring value is, and how spread out the values are. Knowing those things, you would have a much clearer picture of various characteristics of recent high school graduates in Florida.

- *To show relative standing of individuals in a group.* Statistics are frequently used to show where an individual stands for a given measurement in relation to all other individuals in the sample. Such standings are shown through percentile rankings, grade-equivalent scores, age-equivalent scores, and stanine scores—concepts discussed later in this chapter.

- *To show relationships among variables.* Investigators are often interested in determining whether correlations exist among variables—for instance, between people's ages and the amount of time they spend watching television or between students' self-concept and their academic achievement. Relationships such as these are described by means of statistical correlations.

- *To show similarities and differences among groups.* Researchers are often interested in ascertaining whether groups are similar to or different from each other. For example, they need to make sure, particularly for experimental research, that the two or more groups involved at the beginning of the experiment are about equal in the specific characteristic (i.e., dependent variable) being investigated. They then check to see whether the treatment condition given to one of the groups has changed that characteristic in some way, compared with the group(s) that did not receive the treatment.

- *To identify error that is inherent in sample selection.* Samples almost always differ to some degree from the population from which they are drawn. This introduces a degree of error—referred to as *sampling error* or simply *error*—into research so that we can never be sure a statistical finding would occur in the exact same manner, proportion, or degree in the population. Error refers to the disparity between what is measured in a sample and what exists in the population. Statistical procedures enable researchers to determine the amount of error associated with measurements, means, correlations, and differences between means. Once this error is known, researchers can specify the *confidence levels* for a particular value or finding. For example, if we find a sample mean of 6.2 and then determine its *standard error*—a quantitative measure of sampling error, defined as the average distance of the sample mean from the population mean—we can conclude, with a specified degree of confidence (e.g., 95%), that the population mean lies somewhere within a given range, such as between 5.30 and 7.10.

- *To test for significance of findings.* When researchers discover apparent correlations between variables or differences between group means, they apply statistical tests of significance. They do this to determine whether their findings might be due to the researchers' having, *by chance*, selected a sample that did not reflect the population or if, in fact, the findings represent *real* differences or relationships that exist in the population. If the likelihood that the sample accurately reflects the population turns out to be high, the researcher will call the finding "significant," meaning that a particular finding resulting from sample data is probably also real for the population, rather than one that occurred only in the sample because of chance errors. However, if the test suggests that the finding might not be of sufficient magnitude to overcome any errors in the selection of the sample, the researcher will deem the finding "not significant," meaning that it is likely not real for the population.

- *To make other inferences about the population.* As noted, researchers are seldom able to investigate an entire population and must, therefore, work with samples; yet one of the goals of most quantitative research is to show that the resultant findings for the sample are true also for the population. Thus, when we determine a mean score for the sample, for instance, we want to be able to say that the same, or similar, mean score exists in the population as a whole. Of course, since we have not investigated the entire population, we can only make inferences about the population mean. In doing this, we assign probability levels that allow us to say that the sample finding is "likely to be the same" for the population, within specified limits.

Before proceeding further, let us take a moment to discuss how populations, samples, parameters, and statistics are related. As we discussed in Chapter 12, a *population* is all the individuals who make up a designated group, whom we are ultimately interested in studying, and, therefore, about whom we are interested in drawing conclusions. If we want to know about sixth-grade students in California, the population referred to consists of all sixth-grade students in California. A *sample* comprises a smaller group, or subset, drawn from a population and carefully selected to closely reflect the characteristics of the population. Samples are used in research because it is often impossible and almost always inconvenient—due to financial constraints, time factors, and so on—to study an entire population. For researchers to be able to suggest that what they have learned from the sample also applies to the population, samples need to be selected so they are representative of the population, at least as closely as possible.

Parameters are numerical indices that describe a population, such as the number of individuals included, the measurements made of them, and descriptions that indicate average, dispersion, or relationships among those measurements. Parameter indices are usually symbolized by Greek letters, while their sample counterparts are usually symbolized by English or Roman letters. To illustrate, the population mean (or average) is symbolized by the Greek letter µ, pronounced *mew*, while the sample mean is symbolized by M or $\overline{X}$. In contrast, **statistics** are numerical indices and procedures that describe the sample and help the researcher make inferences about the population. Statistics (which apply to the sample) are directly analogous to parameters (which apply to the population). Because samples almost never *exactly* reflect populations, statistics almost never exactly equal the parameters to which they correspond. *Sampling error* is the term applied to this discrepancy between a sample statistic and a population parameter.

Preparing Data for Analysis

Once data have been collected, they must be appropriately prepared to be analyzed using statistical procedures. (*On a side note, the word* data *is always plural. Its singular form is* datum, *but we do not often use that form because researchers usually discuss a collection of data points, as opposed to a single data point. When you write and talk about data, be sure to use the plural form.*) First of all, data must be *scored*, meaning that a number must be assigned to every value for every variable. This is straightforward if the variable is being measured as a quantitative score on an instrument. For example, suppose a student scores 82 out of 100 points on a measure of scientific literacy. That student's value on the variable "scientific literacy" would be equal to a score of 82. However, numerical values must also be assigned to categorical or nominal variables. In Chapter 12, in our discussion of scales of measurement, we addressed the fact that demographic variables such as "gender"—to be subjected to and included in statistical analyses—must be assigned a numerical value. In this case, the assignment of the number is arbitrary, so it lacks quantitative meaning. Nonetheless, numerical values must be assigned to all values of all variables. Similarly, scaled items, such as Likert and Likert-type items, must also be assigned numerical values. The scale may consist of the points "strongly agree," "disagree," "agree," and "strongly agree"; however, to be included in statistical analyses, numerical values must be assigned to each of these points—for example, 1, 2, 3, and 4.

Several procedures can be used to facilitate the coding of responses (Creswell, 2005). The process might be as simple as including the assigned numerical values directly on the instrument. For example, you might see the following scale on a questionnaire:

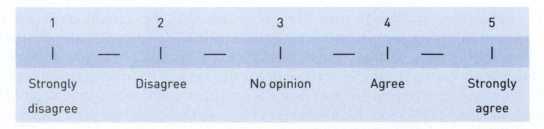

Notice that the five categories of response for the Likert items are included and have also been assigned numerical values directly on the survey instrument. You might also provide the assigned values in a format such as this:

In which content areas are advanced placement courses offered in your school? (Please check all that apply.)

□ (1) English

□ (2) Foreign languages

□ (3) Mathematics

□ (4) Social studies

□ (5) Science

Again, notice how numerical values have been placed directly on the instrument. In this case, we see another example of arbitrarily assigned numerical values, where the value does not have a quantitative meaning but is assigned purely for identification purposes. Another alternative is to create a **codebook**, which is a list of variables or questions indicating how the responses for each item will be coded (see Figure 13.1).

FIGURE 13.1 ● Example of a Codebook

Variable Name	Variable Label or Description	Measure	Values
age	Age of respondent	Ratio	
educ		Ratio	97 = not applicable; 98 = don't know; 99 = no answer
sex	Respondent's sex	Nominal	1 = male; 2 = female
degree	Respondent's highest degree	Ordinal	0 = less than HS; 1 = high school; 2 = junior college; 3 = bachelor's; 4 = graduate; 7 = not applicable; 8 = don't know; 9 = no answer
satjob	Job satisfaction	Ordinal	0 = not applicable; 1 = very satisfied; 2 = mod satisfied; 3 = a little dissatisfied; 4 = very dissatisfied; 8 = don't know; 9 = no answer
satjob2	Job satisfaction	Nominal	1 = very satisfied; 2 = not very satisfied
income4	Total family income in quartiles	Ordinal	1 = 24,999 or less; 2 = 25,000 to 39,999; 3 = 40,000 to 59,999; 4 = 60,000 or more
rincom91	Respondent's income	Ratio	0 = not applicable; 1 = LT $1000; 2 = $1000-2999; 3 = $3000-3999; 4 = $4000-4999; 5 = $5000-5999; 6 = $6000-6999; 7 = $7000-7999; 8 = $8000-9999; 9 = $10000-12499; 10 = $12500-14999; 11 = $15000-17499; 12 = $17500-19999; 13 = $20000-22499; 14 = $22500–24999; 15 = $25000-29999; 16 = $30000-34999; 17 = $35000-39999; 18 = $40000-49999; 19 = $50000-59999; 20 = $60000-74999; 21 = $75000+; 22 = refused; 98 = don't know; 99 = no answer
hrs1	Number of hours worked last week	Ratio	98 = don't know; 99 = no answer; -1 = not applicable

(Continued)

FIGURE 13.1 ● (Continued)

Variable Name	Variable Label or Description	Measure	Values
wrkstat	Labor force status	Nominal	0 = not applicable; 1 = working full time; 2 = working part time; 3 = temp not working; 4 = unempl, laid off; 5 = retired; 6 = school; 7 = keeping house; 8 = other; 9 = no answer
jobinc	Importance of high income	Ordinal	0 = not applicable; 1 = most impt; 2 = second; 3 = third; 4 = fourth; 5 = fifth; 8 = don't know; 9 = no answer
impjob	Importance to Respondent of having a fulfilling job	Ordinal	0 = not applicable; 1 = one of the most important; 2 = very important; 3 = somewhat important; 4 = not too important; 5 = not at all important; 8 = don't know; 9 = no answer
bothft	Both spouses work full time	Nominal	0 = no; 1 = yes
husbft	Husband employed full time	Nominal	0 = no; 1 = yes
husbhr	Hrs worked last week by husband	Ratio	
wifeft	Wife employed full time	Nominal	0 = no; 1 = yes
wifehr	Hrs worked last week by wife	Ratio	
id		Nominal	
agecat4	4 categories of age	Ordinal	1 = 18-29; 2 = 30-39; 3 = 40-49; 4 = 50+

Source: Adapted from Mertler and Vannatta (2013).

An alternative to this kind of codebook is developed by taking a blank copy of the survey instrument and handwriting the codes directly on it. An example of this technique is shown in Figure 13.2.

The benefit of preparing a codebook is that it provides invaluable guidance to the researcher. I have witnessed too many novice researchers begin to enter data into a spreadsheet only to forget the system they were using to code the responses. Midway through data entry, responses might begin to be coded in an opposite manner—what was originally coded and entered as a 1 is now entered as a 5 and vice versa. In other words, the coding is reversed. As you can imagine, this leads to erroneous conclusions at the end of the study. Investing the time on the front end to prepare and code your data will pay off later, as your data to be analyzed will be as clean and accurate as possible.

FIGURE 13.2 ● Example of a Codebook Created Directly on a Survey Instrument

		1	2	3	4
1.	I believe that I know a lot about the No Child Left Behind (NCLB) Act.	SD ☐	D ☐	A ☐	SA ☐
2.	NCLB has forced me to change the focus of my classroom instruction.	SD ☐	D ☐	A ☐	SA ☐
3.	NCLB has changed the nature of academic motivation for students and has placed more stress on students.	SD ☐	D ☐	A ☐	SA ☐
4.	NCLB has changed the nature of instructional motivation for teachers and has placed more stress on teachers	SD ☐	D ☐	A ☐	SA ☐
5.	The importance placed on Ohio's achievement tests and the Ohio Graduation Test (OGT) have led to instruction that violates the standards of good educational practice.	SD ☐	D ☐	A ☐	SA ☐

SECTION 2
Please respond to each of the following questions:

23. What is your gender?
    1 ☐ female
    2 ☐ male

24. Which of the following is the most appropriate description of the level at which you teach?
    1 ☐ elementary–primary (K–grade 3)
    2 ☐ elementary–intermediate (grades 4–6)
    3 ☐ elementary (K–6)
    4 ☐ middle (grades 6–8)
    5 ☐ high (grades 9–12)
    6 ☐ secondary (grades 6–12)
    7 ☐ K–12
    8 ☐ other

25. Which best describes the educational level you have attained?
    1 ☐ B.A. or B.S.
    2 ☐ M.A. or M.S.
    3 ☐ Specialist
    4 ☐ Ed.D.
    5 ☐ Ph.D.

26. Including the current year, how many years of experience do you have as a classroom teacher?
    1 ☐ 1–5 years
    2 ☐ 6–10 years
    3 ☐ 11–15 years
    4 ☐ 16–20 years
    5 ☐ 21–25 years
    6 ☐ 26–30 years
    7 ☐ more than 30 years

27. What is the current Ohio Department of Education rating for your school district?
    1 ☐ Excellent
    2 ☐ Effective
    3 ☐ Continuous Improvement
    4 ☐ Academic Watch
    5 ☐ Academic Emergency
    6 ☐ Don't Know

Selecting a Statistical Analysis Software Program

Numerous software programs are available to assist with the analysis of quantitative data. Some of them can be quite expensive, although most provide free, downloadable trial versions through their websites, as well as less-expensive student versions. Some of the more popular statistical packages include the following:

- Excel (office.microsoft.com/excel)
- Minitab (www.minitab.com)
- SAS Statistics (www.sas.com)
- Statistical Package for the Social Sciences (www.spss.com)
- StatCrunch (www.statcrunch.com)
- SYSTAT (www.systat.com)

Arguably the most popular program in the broad field of education is Statistical Package for the Social Sciences (SPSS). SPSS is a complete statistical analysis package, able to easily analyze your data with both descriptive and inferential techniques, including advanced and multivariate analyses. The program can also generate high-quality and detailed graphs and charts. Another relatively accessible program for quantitative analysis is Microsoft Excel. As most people are aware, Excel is part of the Microsoft Office suite of products (along with Word and PowerPoint). Excel is a powerful tool you can use to create and format spreadsheets, and analyze and share information. It is an excellent program for database management and spreadsheet applications, as well as for statistical analysis and the generation of professional-looking charts.

The only limitation for many of the programs listed above is that they can be expensive. At the time of this writing, SPSS retailed for more than $1,000, although student versions were available for 6-month (at $37.00 + a $4.99 download fee) and 12-month (at $69.00 + a $4.99 download fee) rentals through a third-party site (www.onthehub.com/spss/). Excel is typically sold as part of the Microsoft Office suite of products, although it can be purchased separately for $109.99.

If you plan on doing a lot of research and data analysis over the next several years, I recommend either of the above analytical programs. In addition, it is not uncommon for colleges and universities to have site licenses to programs such as SPSS. In those instances, users can access the program either from a computer on campus or from an off-campus location by logging in through a VPN (i.e., virtual private network). However, for most novice researchers who will not be doing extensive data analysis—and who might also like to do their analyses from home—StatCrunch is a wonderful alternative. StatCrunch is a *web-based* data analysis software system that works in similar fashion to any statistical software you might purchase and install on your home or office computer, although there is nothing to download or install. You must purchase a subscription—student subscriptions are $13.20 for 6 months and $22.00 for 12 months; instructor subscriptions are free—and create a login name and password to access any data or results you wish to save on the StatCrunch server—a nice, additional benefit of your subscription. The main login screen for StatCrunch is shown in Figure 13.3.

FIGURE 13.3 ● Main Login Screen for StatCrunch

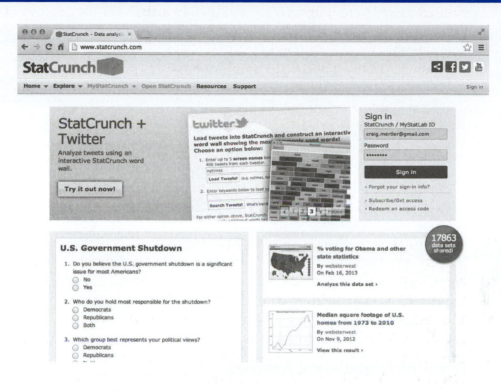

Periodically throughout the remainder of our discussions of statistical analyses, demonstrations of analyses conducted in StatCrunch will be included. To begin, you must log in through the main screen. Once you have logged in, you simply click on *Open StatCrunch* to begin the program. The resulting window—an interactive Java window—is shown in Figure 13.4. Analyses are run on StatCrunch by first entering data directly into this window. As with most any statistical analysis program, the columns represent variables and the rows represent cases, subjects, or participants. By clicking on the column headings, you can name the variables in your data set.

Before we examine specific statistical techniques, let us quickly recap the primary differences between descriptive and inferential statistical techniques. *Descriptive statistics* simplify, summarize, and—as the name implies—describe data. Most procedures are relatively straightforward, with little or no mathematical calculations involved. *Inferential statistics*, on the other hand, are used to determine the likelihood that the results obtained from collecting data from a sample are similar to the results that would have been obtained if the entire population had been studied. Generally speaking, inferential statistics are much more complex and involve statistical formulas and calculations. In addition, use of inferential statistics involves numerous conceptual aspects, which we will discuss momentarily. We begin our specific examination of statistical analysis techniques with descriptive analyses, followed by inferential analyses.

FIGURE 13.4 ● Data Entry Screen in StatCrunch

Columns represent variables

Rows represent participants

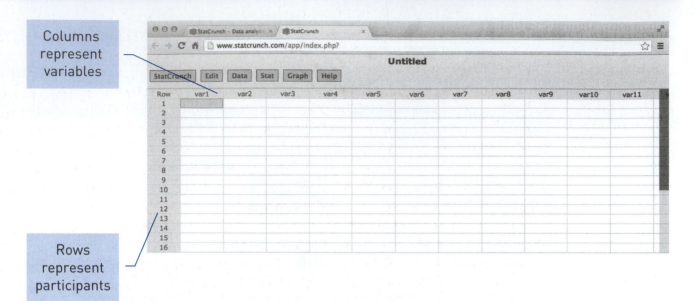

Descriptive Statistical Analysis

Some studies rely solely on the use of descriptive statistics, whereas others use descriptive statistics as the initial analyses to describe the samples before submitting the data to inferential statistical analyses. Regardless of the focus of the study and the guiding research questions, descriptive statistical analyses are extremely important when it comes to simplifying and summarizing data in any type of study. There are categories of descriptive statistical analysis techniques appropriate for all four scales of measurement. Those categories include the following:

- Frequency distributions
- Measures of central tendency
- Measures of dispersion or variability
- Measures of relationship
- Measures of relative position

Frequency Distributions A **frequency distribution** is a tabulation of the number of times each value of a variable occurs. This is particularly useful for variables that are measured on nominal or ordinal scales. Subjecting your data to a frequency analysis serves several important purposes. First, it is an extremely efficient way to simplify and summarize your data. For example, imagine that you surveyed more than 1,200 individuals and asked them to indicate their gender, which you coded as follows: 1 = female and 2 = male. Looking at a spreadsheet consisting of more than 1,200 1s and 2s, you would never be able to surmise how many females and how many males responded to the survey; however, the frequency distribution could reveal the following very quickly:

1	2
Females	Males
785	465

Second, a frequency distribution can give you a mechanism for checking the accuracy of your data. Imagine that when entering all those 1s and 2s in your spreadsheet, you inadvertently entered the value 22 on several occasions. Perhaps your fingers were typing faster than your mind was thinking or your eyes were reading. Regardless of the reason, your frequency distribution might appear as follows:

1	2	22
Females	Males	???
785	465	4

This would serve as a quick indication that you made errors in data entry and have four participants coded incorrectly. Without the frequency distribution, you might never spot the four 22s in your enormous spreadsheet of data.

As mentioned above, frequency distributions are useful and meaningful for variables that are measured on nominal and ordinal scales; however, they tend not to be as useful or succinct in summarizing data with interval or ratio variables. Imagine a situation where you had 15 students complete an exam that was scored on a scale of 0 to 100 points. It is entirely possible that no two students received the same score. Therefore, your frequency distribution would consist of 15 values, each with a frequency of one student. You can see how this would do nothing to simplify and summarize your data; after computing a frequency distribution, you would be right back where you started. Therefore, other descriptive techniques must be used to summarize variables that have been measured on interval or ratio scales.

Measures of Central Tendency **Measures of central tendency** consist of a single score that represents what is typical among a group of scores. They provide an extremely efficient means of summarizing variables with lots of data into a single value. Generally speaking, the single value represents the "middle" or "central" value in the data set. The three measures of central tendency are the mean, median, and mode. The **mean** is the most commonly used measure of central tendency and is appropriate for variables measured on interval or ratio scales. Understand that you cannot calculate an average score for a nominal variable, such as "gender"; actually, you *could* calculate it, but it would have no meaning (e.g., how meaningful is the knowledge that the "average gender" among our more than 1,200 survey respondents is 1.72?).

The mean is calculated as the arithmetic average of all the scores on a single variable—by adding all the scores and then dividing by the total number of scores:

$$\bar{X} = \frac{\Sigma X}{n}$$

where

$\overline{X}$ = the mean, or average, of the scores

ΣX = the sum (Σ) of all the scores

n = the number of scores on the particular variable

For example, imagine that we had the following set of scores:

$$1, 4, 4, 5, 5, 5, 5, 6, 7, 8$$

The mean would be calculated as follows:

$$\overline{X} = \frac{\Sigma X}{n} = \frac{50}{10} = 5$$

The **median** is the midpoint of all the scores in the distribution; it is the point at which 50% of the scores are located above and 50% fall below. Before you attempt to find the median, all scores must be ordered from lowest to highest. If there is an odd number of scores, the median is the middle score in the order. If the number of scores for the variable is an even number, the median is the midway point between the two middle scores. For example, imagine that we had the following set of scores:

$$3, 4, 4, 4, 4, 5, 5, 6, 7, 8$$

Since there is an even number of scores in the set (i.e., 10 scores), the median for these scores would be the midpoint between 4 and 5, or 4.5. Notice that there is no mathematical calculation involved in determining the median. The median is typically an appropriate measure of central tendency when data represent an ordinal scale.

The **mode** is defined as the score that is obtained by more participants than any other score; in other words, it is the most frequently occurring score in the data set. Again, there is no calculation involved in determining the mode; it is found by simply looking at a set of scores and seeing which one occurs most often. Consider the following data set:

$$3, 4, 4, 4, 4, 5, 5, 6, 7, 8$$

The mode would be 4, since it occurs more often (i.e., four times) than any other score in the data set. Sometimes, two scores may have the same maximum frequency of occurrence. In these situations, the data set is described as *bimodal*. If there are more than two modes, the data set is *multimodal*. While the mode is certainly not the most accurate measure of central tendency, it is the only appropriate measure of central tendency when data are measured on a nominal scale.

When trying to determine which measure of central tendency to use or report for a given variable, it is often best to determine all three measures of central tendency, compare them against the entire data set, and determine which measure *best represents* the typical score. When used in isolation, any of the three measures may result in potentially misleading interpretations. For example, imagine that we obtained the following set of IQ scores:

$$90, 90, 95, 96, 100, 101, 103, 104, 105, 195$$

The three measures of central tendency for the scores would be as follows:

$$\text{Mode} = 90$$

$$\text{Median} = 100.5$$

$$\text{Mean} = 107.9$$

In this situation, the median is clearly the best representation of what is typical in this group. If we reported only the mode as representing the most typical value, we would be estimating far too low. Similarly, the single, extreme high score of 195 (known as an *outlier*, due to its marked difference from the rest of the scores) acted to "inflate" the mean value. Each and every data set is different, and all three measures of central tendency should be evaluated to determine which provides the most appropriate index of typicality.

Measures of Dispersion or Variability While measures of central tendency indicate what is *typical* about the set of scores, **measures of dispersion** or **variability** indicate what is *atypical* about those scores. Essentially, these are measures of the amount of spread in a set of scores. Typically, measures of variability are reported alongside measures of central tendency to give a more complete picture of what an entire set of scores looks like. There are four basic measures of variability—range, quartile deviation, variance, and standard deviation.

The simplest measure of variability is the **range**, which is the difference between the highest score and the lowest score in a distribution. Calculation of range involves a basic subtraction problem. For example, consider the data set we examined earlier:

$$90, 90, 95, 96, 100, 101, 103, 104, 105, 195$$

The range would be calculated as follows:

$$X_{high} - X_{low} = 195 - 90 = 105$$

Similar to the mode, the range does not provide a great deal of information in terms of the variability of a set of scores; however, it does give a rough, quick indication of the amount of variability in a set of data.

A **quartile deviation** is defined as half the difference between the third or upper quartile (i.e., the top 25%, also known as the 75th percentile) and the first or lower quartile (i.e., the bottom 25%, also known as the 25th percentile) in a distribution of scores. More specifically, it is half the difference between the score that separates the top 25% from the bottom 75% and the score that separates the bottom 25% from the top 75%. The calculation of a quartile deviation is similar to that of a median, which can also be defined as the second quartile or the 50th percentile.

Calculation of a quartile deviation first requires that all scores be ordered from lowest to highest:

$$88, 89, 90, 90, 90, 95, 96, 98, 100, 101, 102, 103, 103,$$
$$104, 105, 106, 106, 108, 110, 195$$

In the above set of 20 scores, the score of 105 defines the third quartile, or 75th percentile (i.e., 25% or 5 of the 20 scores are greater than the score of 105). Similarly, the score of 95 defines the first quartile, or 25th percentile, as 25% or 5 of the 20 scores fall below this score. The quartile deviation is then calculated as follows:

$$QD = \frac{Q_3 - Q_1}{2} = \frac{105 - 95}{2} = \frac{10}{2} = 5$$

When a quartile deviation score is small, the scores in the distribution are closer together; if it is large, the scores are more spread out. The quartile deviation is a more accurate measure of variability, especially compared with the range, and is appropriate for variables where the median is the most appropriate measure of central tendency—in other words, for variables that are measured on an ordinal scale.

The **variance** is a third measure of variability, defined as the average distance of all the scores from the mean. It is the measure of variability appropriate for variables measured on interval and ratio scales. Calculating the variance is fairly straightforward; it is essentially the average of the differences between each of the scores and the mean. For example, consider the following small data set:

$$90, 90, 95, 96, 100, 101, 103, 104, 106, 195$$

The mean (i.e., $\Sigma X/n$) for this data set is 108. The difference between each score and the mean is determined as follows:

$$90 - 108 = -18$$
$$90 - 108 = -18$$
$$95 - 108 = -13$$
$$96 - 108 = -12$$
$$100 - 108 = -8$$
$$101 - 108 = -7$$
$$103 - 108 = -5$$
$$104 - 108 = -4$$
$$106 - 108 = -2$$
$$195 - 108 = 87$$

However, now we encounter a slight problem. Since we want to calculate the *average* distance from the mean, we next need to sum these differences and then divide by 10.

Unfortunately, with any data set, summing the different scores will always result in a value equal to zero. This should make some logical sense; since the mean represents the "arithmetic middle" of the data set, the distances greater than the mean and those less than the mean should cancel each other out (i.e., sum to zero). One mathematical method to work around this is to square each difference so we have only positive numbers:

$$90 - 108 = -18 \rightarrow -18^2 = 324$$
$$90 - 108 = -18 \rightarrow -18^2 = 324$$
$$95 - 108 = -13 \rightarrow -13^2 = 169$$
$$96 - 108 = -12 \rightarrow -12^2 = 144$$
$$100 - 108 = -8 \rightarrow -8^2 = 64$$
$$101 - 108 = -7 \rightarrow -7^2 = 49$$
$$103 - 108 = -5 \rightarrow -5^2 = 25$$
$$104 - 108 = -4 \rightarrow -4^2 = 16$$
$$106 - 108 = -2 \rightarrow -2^2 = 4$$
$$195 - 108 = 87 \rightarrow 87^2 = 7569$$

We then calculate the variance (symbolized by SD^2) by summing the squared scores and dividing by the number of scores:

$$Variance = SD^2 = \frac{\sum(X - \bar{X})^2}{n} = \frac{8688}{10} = 868.8$$

The essential problem with this calculation is that the resulting value has very little meaning to us in a given research context. In our example above, it does not make much sense to talk about the "average distance of scores from the mean being equal to 868.8 points" when we do not even have a single score that large. This issue results from having squared each of the differences. Because of this mathematical calculation, variance is seldom reported in research studies; however, it is a necessary calculation to obtain the final measure of variability.

The **standard deviation** is formally defined as the average distance of the scores from the mean and is calculated by finding the square root of the variance of a set of scores. This mathematical manipulation returns the variance to the same scale on which the variable was originally measured. Now the standard deviation as a measure of variability has *meaning* with respect to the originally measured variable. Once the variance has been calculated, finding the square root of the variance will determine the standard deviation. The formula for calculating the standard deviation (SD) is as follows:

$$SD = \sqrt{SD^2} = \sqrt{\frac{\sum(X - \bar{X})^2}{n}}$$

Continuing with our example above, the standard deviation would be equal to the square root of 868.8, or 29.48. Considering all the scores that composed our small data set, this number seems to make sense with respect to the observed variability among those scores.

The standard deviation is the most frequently used measure of variability and is used appropriately with interval and ratio data. Similar to the mean—which is typically seen as the central tendency counterpart to the standard deviation—the standard deviation is considered the most stable measure of variability, since it includes every score in its calculation (Gay, Mills, & Airasian, 2009). Using both the mean and standard deviation to describe a set of scores provides a great deal of information about those scores.

Measures of Relationship The fourth category of descriptive statistical analyses includes those techniques that measure relationships. There are numerous types of *correlation coefficients*, which is the name given to these measures of the direction and degree of relationship between two variables. Obviously, correlation coefficients are calculated when analyzing data from studies using correlational research designs. You should remember from our discussion of correlational research in Chapter 7 that correlation coefficients report the *direction* and the *strength* of the relationship between two variables. Most correlation coefficients range in value from –1.00 to +1.00 (although some can range from .00 to +1.00). The direction is indicated as either a positive or a negative value on the scale. If it is a **negative correlation**, a minus sign is used (e.g., –.48); if it is a **positive correlation**, either a plus sign or no sign is used (e.g., +.48 or .48). Positive and negative correlations are of equal magnitude; that is, positive .48 (.48) is not larger or stronger than negative .48 (–.48). Positive and negative simply show the direction of the relationship. In a positive relationship, high scores on one variable tend to be associated with high scores on the second variable, while low scores are associated with low scores. In a negative relationship, high scores on one variable tend to be associated with low scores on the other variable. For example, quality of diet is *positively* correlated with overall health—the better the diet, the better the health. Quality of diet is *negatively* correlated with incidence of disease—the better the diet, the less frequent or serious the incidence of disease.

The strength of the relationship is indicated by the magnitude of the numerical value of the coefficient, where strong correlations are typically considered as those whose values exceed ±.70, and weak correlations are those whose values tend to fall between –.30 and .00 and between +.30 and .00. A general rule of thumb for interpreting correlation coefficients is presented in Figure 13.5; however, it is critical to remember that this is a *general* rule of thumb. Correlation coefficients must *always* be interpreted within the context of existing research on a given topic or with specific variables. For example, if you conducted a correlational research study and obtained a correlation coefficient of +.30, using Figure 13.5, you would conclude that this was a weak, positive relationship. However, if you reported that all previous research investigating these two particular variables resulted in correlation coefficients between .00 and +.10, your conclusion and interpretation should change dramatically. In this case, the correlation coefficient you obtained (i.e., +.30) was *substantially stronger* than those found previously. One might interpret the correlation coefficient of +.30—in this particular research context—to be a somewhat *strong* relationship.

It is worth reiterating an important characteristic of any measure of relationship: Correlation does *not* imply causation (see Chapter 7). Therefore, researchers must exercise caution when interpreting the results of correlational analyses and drawing conclusions based on them. As with previous descriptive statistical techniques up to this point, correlation coefficients can also be computed by hand, but statistical software makes this calculation fairly painless; so from this point forward in our discussion of statistical analyses, formulas for calculating various statistical measures will be used sparingly.

Several kinds of variable data can be correlated, although the following list is just a sampling of the more frequently used types of correlations. Some experts in educational research methods and statistical analysis have reported more than 30 different types of correlation coefficients. The first type we will look at is **bivariate correlations**—that is, correlations that involve only two sets of scores or two variables. As we have discussed, the researcher must have, at a minimum, two measures or ratings for each individual in a given sample. Most commonly, correlational studies explore the relationship between variables that are measured on an interval or ratio scale, such as numerical test scores or numerical measures of physical performance. The **Pearson product-moment correlation**—often called Pearson's *r* or simply *r*—is used to correlate data such as these.

FIGURE 13.5 ● General Rule of Thumb for Interpreting Correlation Coefficients

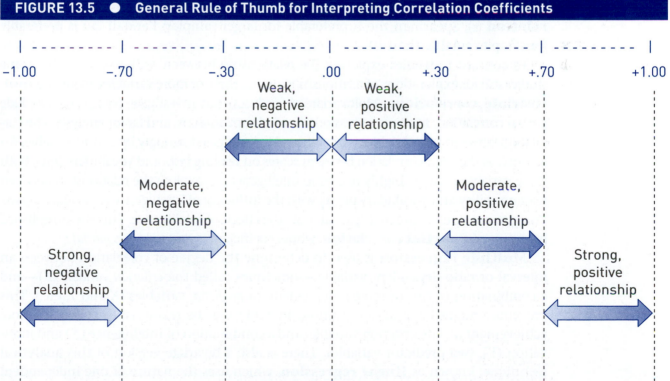

In some research situations, it may be desirable to measure the relationship between an interval or ratio variable and a nominal variable. In many instances, nominal variables are typically expressed as *dichotomies*—either an **artificial dichotomy** (one to which participants are arbitrarily assigned, such as "happy–sad") or a **natural dichotomy** (one that occurs naturally, such as "left-handed–right-handed"). A **biserial correlation** (symbolized by r_{bis}) is used to explore the relationship between an interval or ratio variable and an artificial dichotomy. For example, "school achievement," an interval variable, could be correlated with "family income" (measured as "above the poverty line" and "below the poverty line"). Notice that this is an artificial dichotomy, because the dollar figure that separates "poverty" from "nonpoverty" is arbitrary. A **point-biserial correlation** (symbolized by r_{pb}) is used when one variable is interval or ratio and the other is a natural dichotomy. For example, "school achievement," an interval variable, could be correlated with the "number of parents living in the home" (either 1 or 2, a natural dichotomy).

Some research explores relationships in which both variables are expressed as dichotomous nominal variables. If the dichotomies are both natural—for example, "handedness" ("left" or "right") and "varsity sports participation" ("yes" or "no")—a **phi correlation** (symbolized by ϕ) is used. If both variables are artificial dichotomies—for example, "class participation" ("high" or "low") and "family income" ("poverty" or "nonpoverty")—a **tetrachoric correlation** (r_{tet}) is the appropriate correlational statistical procedure.

Data organized into rankings (i.e., ordinal data), such as "best to worst," "quietest to loudest," or rankings based on grades received, can be correlated through two different procedures—the **Spearman rho correlation** (r_s) and the **Kendall tau correlation** (τ). Spearman rho is preferable for larger samples; Kendall tau is preferable for samples smaller than 10.

In contrast to studies exploring the relationship between only two variables, some studies call for explorations of relationships among three or more variables, requiring **multivariate correlations**. Multivariate procedures that investigate correlations include partial correlation, multiple regression, discriminant analysis, and factor analysis. The correlation between two variables is often found to be affected strongly by a third variable. An example is the high correlation between scores on reading tests and vocabulary tests; both these variables may be highly related to intelligence. To explore the relationship between reading ability and vocabulary per se, with the influence of intelligence removed, it is necessary to use a procedure that "partials out" the effects of intelligence. This is accomplished by means of a **partial correlation**, whose coefficient is referred to as *partial r*.

Multiple regression is used to determine the degree of correlation between an interval or ratio dependent variable—sometimes called the *criterion variable* (Z)—and a combination of two or more independent, or *predictor*, variables (X and Y, etc.). This procedure might be used, for example, in exploring the relationship between school achievement (Z, the criterion variable) and a combination of intelligence (X) and motivation (Y), two predictor variables. There is also a bivariate version of this analytical technique, known as **linear regression**, which uses the nature of one independent variable as a means of predicting scores on a single dependent variable.

Discriminant analysis is analogous to multiple regression, except that the Z or criterion (dependent) variable consists of two or more categories, rather than a continuous range of values. An example might be an exploration of the relationship between class participation (Z, categorized as "above average" and "below average") and a combination of self-concept (X) and grade point average (Y). A final multivariate correlational procedure—called **factor analysis**—is often used when a large number of correlations have been explored in a given study; it is a means of grouping into clusters, or *factors*, certain variables that are moderately to highly correlated with one another. In studies of intelligence, for example, numerous variables may be explored, and those that are found to be highly correlated with one another are clustered into factors such as verbal ability, numerical ability, spatial orientation, and problem solving. Factor analysis is also frequently used to analyze data resulting from the administration of a test or survey that contains many items.

Measures of Relative Standing Measures that indicate where a given score falls in a distribution, in relation to all other scores in that distribution, are known as **measures of relative standing**. These types of statistics are typically used to compare the performance of an individual on one or more measures or tests with the entire population of individuals who took the same test, which is why these measures are also referred to as *norm-referenced scores*. Measures of relative standing are determined by the position of scores in relation to the mean within a common distribution, known as a **normal distribution** (see Figure 13.6).

Normal distributions have three main characteristics (Mertler, 2003):

- The distribution is symmetrical (i.e., the left and right halves are mirror images of each other).
- The *mean* (or arithmetic average), *median* (the score that separates the upper 50% of scores from the lower 50% of scores), and the *mode* (the most frequently occurring score) are the same and are located at the exact center of the distribution.
- The percentage of cases in each *standard deviation* (or the average distance of individual scores away from the mean) is known precisely.

When the normal distribution was first developed, it was based on the belief that nearly all physical characteristics in humans are, by nature, distributed randomly around an average value (Mertler, 2007). Furthermore, the vast majority of cases are located in the middle of the distribution (indicating that most people are, roughly speaking, "average"). A very small proportion of individuals can be found at the extreme ends of the distribution. This serves as an indication that, with respect to most characteristics, the majority of people are relatively similar to one another (e.g., about-average height), with a minority of people at the high (i.e., very tall) and low (i.e., very short) ends.

As shown in Figure 13.6, each standard deviation in a normal distribution contains a fixed percentage of cases. The mean score plus and minus one standard

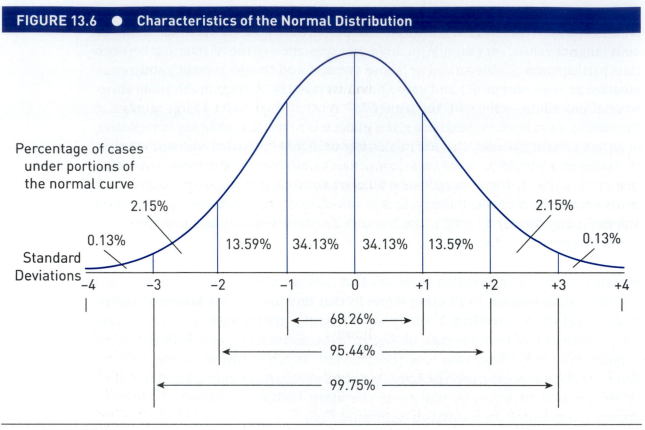

FIGURE 13.6 ● Characteristics of the Normal Distribution

Percentage of cases under portions of the normal curve

2.15%

0.13%

Standard Deviations

13.59%   34.13%   34.13%   13.59%

2.15%

0.13%

−4   −3   −2   −1   0   +1   +2   +3   +4

68.26%

95.44%

99.75%

Source: Mertler (2007).

deviation contains about 68% of the individuals making up the distribution; 95% of the cases are within two standard deviations of the mean; and more than 99% of the cases are within three standard deviations. From the figure, it should be clear that 50% of the cases, or scores, are located above the mean (i.e., the right half of the distribution) and 50% are located below the mean (i.e., the left half); this should also make intuitive sense, because in a normal distribution, the mean and median are the same score.

Raw scores are frequently converted or transformed into comparable scores to make them more understandable and more easily comparable. Remember, how-ever, that once raw scores have been converted, they cannot be treated as if they are still raw scores. For example, converted scores cannot be averaged in an effort to obtain a composite (i.e., overall) converted score. Two of the most frequently used measures of relative standing are percentile ranks and standard scores. **Percentile ranks** (symbolized by *%ile* or *PR*) are scores that indicate one's relative standing in comparison with percentages of others who have taken the same test or have been included in the same measurement. Percentiles are commonly misinterpreted; they have nothing to do with percentage correct but, instead, indicate relative position. Suppose you were informed that your raw score on a graduate aptitude test was 89. That would tell you virtually nothing. But if you were also informed that your score placed you in the 73rd percentile, you would understand that you did as well as or better than 73% of all people who had taken the test. Percentile ranks are appropriately used to report relative standing for variables measured on ordinal and interval scales.

There are numerous different types of standard scores. A **standard score** is a calculation that expresses how far an individual score is from the mean, typically in standard deviation units (Gay et al., 2009). Several examples of standard scores that serve as measures of relative standing are provided in Figure 13.7.

A **z-score** is the most basic type of standard score, where 99% of the scores range between –3.00 and +3.00. The sign indicates whether the score is above or below the mean; the numerical value indicates the distance—in standard deviation units—from the score to the mean. It is calculated with a simple formula, where the difference between an individual's score and the mean score is divided by the standard deviation:

$$z = \frac{X - \bar{X}}{SD}$$

A **T-score** is very similar to a z-score; however, it has been transformed to a scale that is easier to understand. A T-score scale does not contain any negative values, which sometimes creates confusion when interpreting z-score values. T-scores exist on a scale where the mean is equal to 50 and the standard deviation is equal to 10; therefore, 99% of the scores on a T-score scale will fall between 20 (i.e., the mean minus three standard deviations) and 80 (i.e., the mean plus three standard deviations). The formula for converting a z-score to a T-score is as follows:

$$T = 10z + 50$$

As shown in Figure 13.7, many of these measures of relative standing are analogous to one another—they are simply reported on scales with different means and standard deviations. For example, the College Entrance Exam Board (CEEB) scale—which used to report scores for tests such as the SAT entrance examination and the Graduate Record Exam—has a mean of 500 and a standard deviation of 100. Its conversion from a z-score scale is as follows:

$$CEEB = 100z = 500$$

Notice the similarity between this formula and the one used to calculate a T-score. One of the advantages of these measures of relative standing is that they permit researchers to convert scores on one scale to scores on a corresponding scale with relative ease. By closely examining Figure 13.7, one can see that a z-score of +1.50 is equivalent to a T-score of 65 and a CEEB score of 650.

Visual Depictions of Descriptive Analyses A final category of techniques for describing data does not really contain any statistical procedures; however, these techniques can be an effective means of *visually describing* your research data. In addition to true

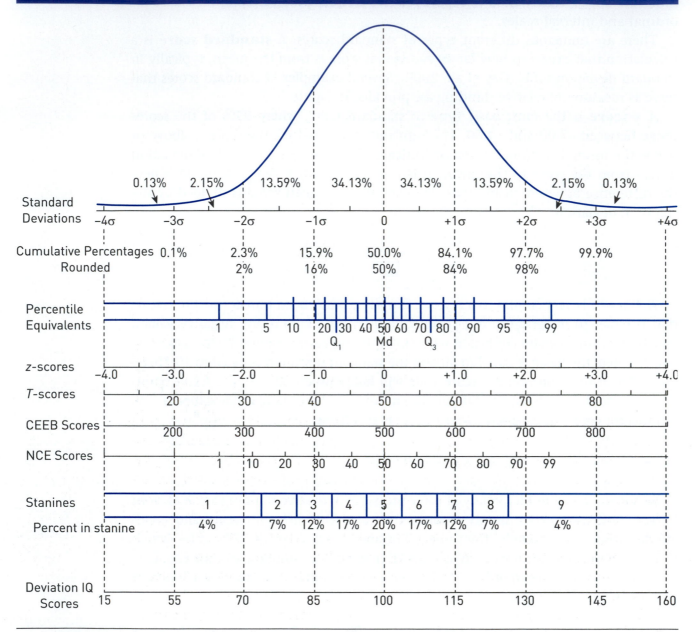

FIGURE 13.7   ●   Types of Standard Scores and Their Relations to the Normal Distribution

Source: Mertler (2007)

statistical analysis procedures, data can also be displayed visually through the use of frequency distribution tables or graphs, such as histograms, bar charts, or pie charts. In a **frequency distribution table**, scores are arranged from highest to lowest, moving down the table. In a second column, labeled "Frequency," the number of individuals who received each score is listed; this is known as the frequency with which each score was earned. Finally, a third column presents the frequency value in terms of the percentage or total number of individuals at each score value. An excerpt from a frequency distribution table is shown below:

Total Score	Frequency	Percentage
8	4	1.1
11	1	.3
12	3	.8
13	2	.5
14	6	1.6
15	9	2.4
16	15	4.0
17	16	4.3
18	17	4.6
19	21	5.6
20	22	5.9

Histograms can present the same frequency distribution information in a more visual manner. Figure 13.8 displays the same data shown in the table above but as a histogram. Notice that the height of each bar indicates the frequency of each score category.

When data appear in categories (as when Likert scales are used) as opposed to falling on a continuous scale (e.g., test scores), bar graphs and pie charts may be used. **Bar charts** are quite similar to histograms, except that adjacent bars do not touch (since the scale is not continuous). **Pie charts** can also be used to visually present categorical data. Figures 13.9 and 13.10 show a bar graph and a pie chart, respectively, for the same set of data.

Finally, relationships can also be depicted visually, through the use of a scatterplot. A **scatterplot** is a visual representation of the relationship between two interval or ratio variables. The requirements for scatterplots are similar to those for calculating a correlation coefficient: You must have scores on *each* variable for *each* member of the sample. If an individual is missing a score on one of the variables, that individual will be excluded from the calculation of the correlation coefficient, as well as from the scatterplot. A sample scatterplot comparing "hours spent studying" and "test score" is shown in Figure 13.11.

An Example of Descriptive Analysis Let us now take a look at simple examples of some of the above-mentioned descriptive analyses using StatCrunch (www.statcrunch.com). Once you have logged in with your username and password, click on *Open StatCrunch* at the top of the screen. You can then either begin typing data into the spreadsheet, or you can load from an existing data file by clicking

(text continues on p. 286)

FIGURE 13.8 ● Sample Histogram Showing the Frequency for Various Test Scores

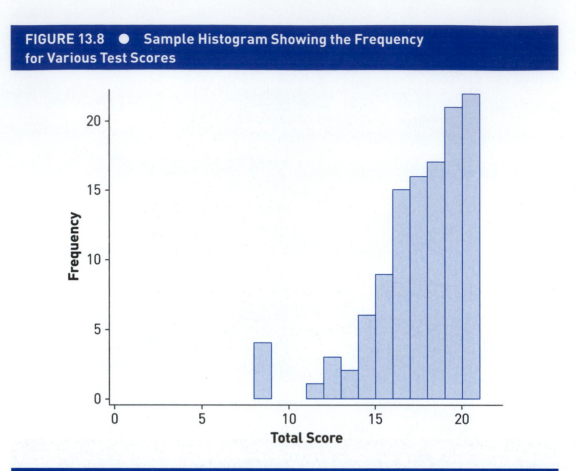

FIGURE 13.9 ● Sample Bar Graph Showing the Frequency for Females and Males

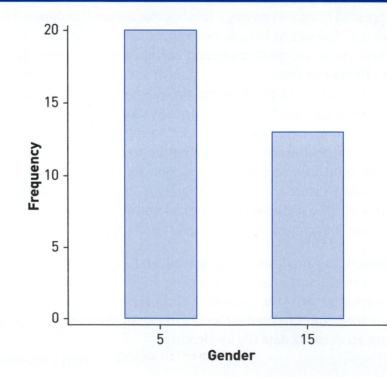

FIGURE 13.10   ●   Sample Pie Chart Showing the Frequency for Females and Males

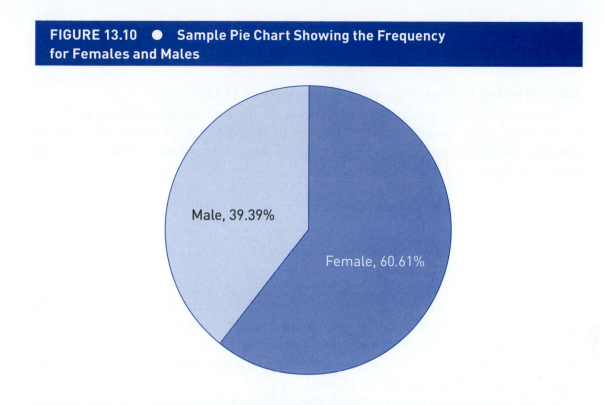

FIGURE 13.11   ●   Sample Scatterplot Showing the Relationship Between Time Spent Studying and Test Score

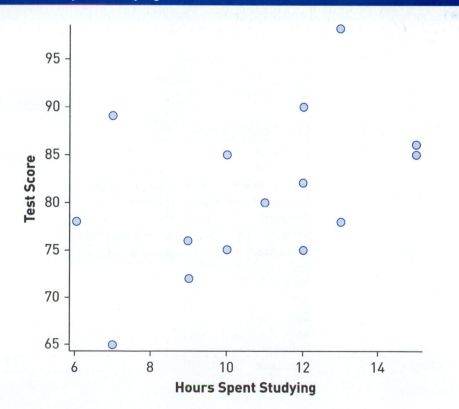

Data

> **⇥ Load Data**

followed by the location of the source file (see Figure 13.12).

For our descriptive analysis examples, I loaded the data file that appears in Figure 13.13. There were several nominal variables in this data set on which I wanted to obtain a frequency distribution. To accomplish this, I selected the following options (shown in Figure 13.14):

Stat

> **⇥ Tables**

> > **⇥ Frequency**

In the resulting dialog box that now opens (see Figure 13.15), I specify the variables and statistical analyses I wish to conduct. Under *Select Columns*, I choose the variables *Group*, *Gender*, and *Age*. Under *Type*, I select *Frequency*, and then I click the *Compute!* button. A new output window will open, providing the results of my analyses (see Figure 13.16).

Finally, I also want to run some descriptive analyses on the questions appearing on the instrument. To do this, I select the following (see Figure 13.17):

FIGURE 13.12 ● Dialog Box for Opening a Data File in StatCrunch

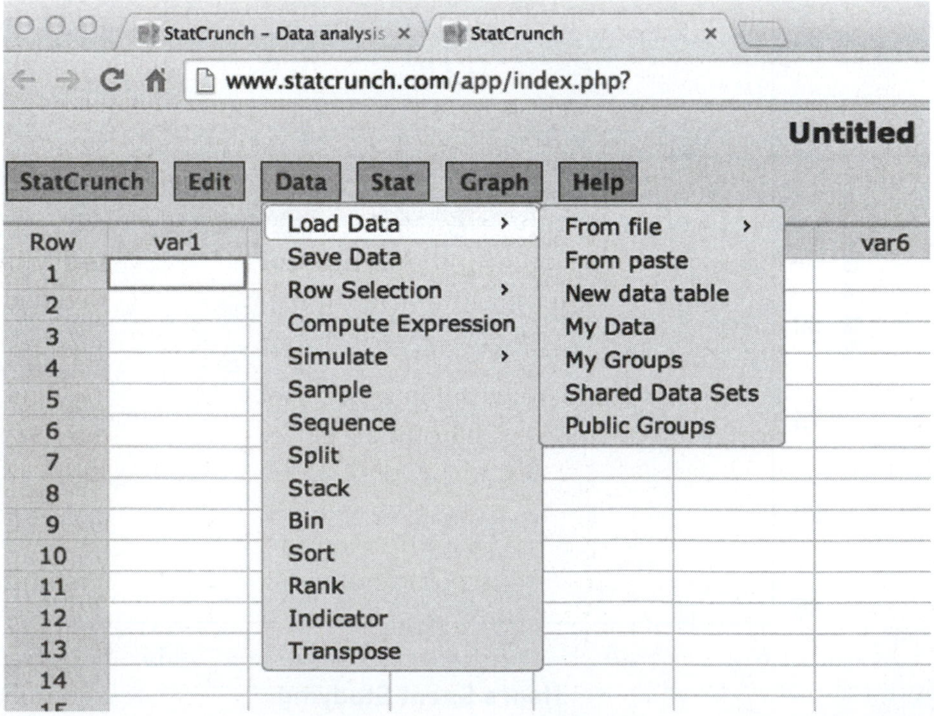

FIGURE 13.13 ● Data File for the Working StatCrunch Example

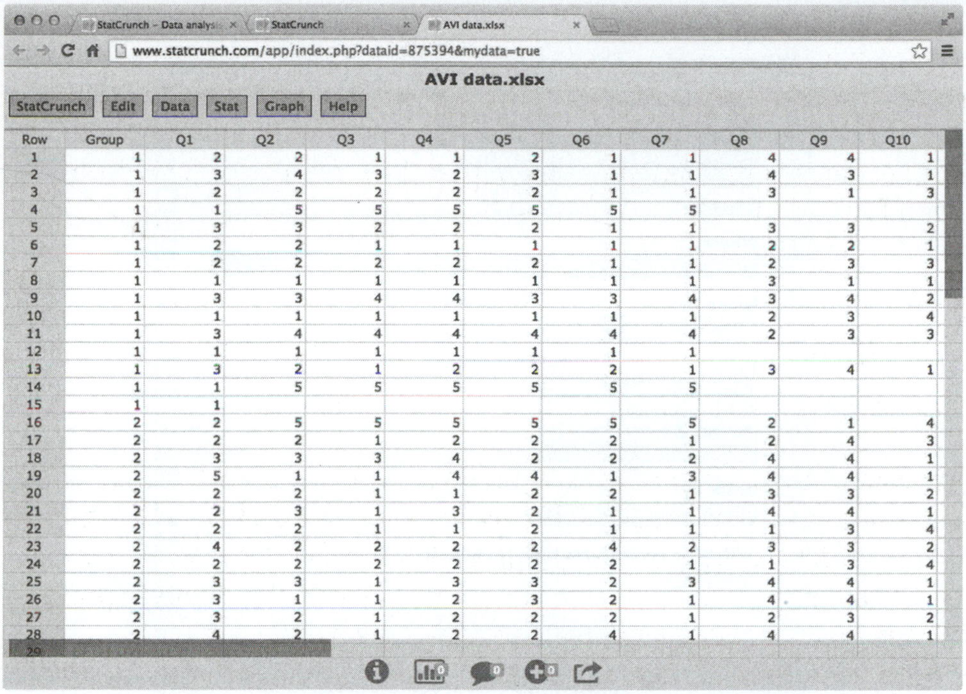

FIGURE 13.14 ● Dialog Box for Creating a Frequency Distribution Table in StatCrunch

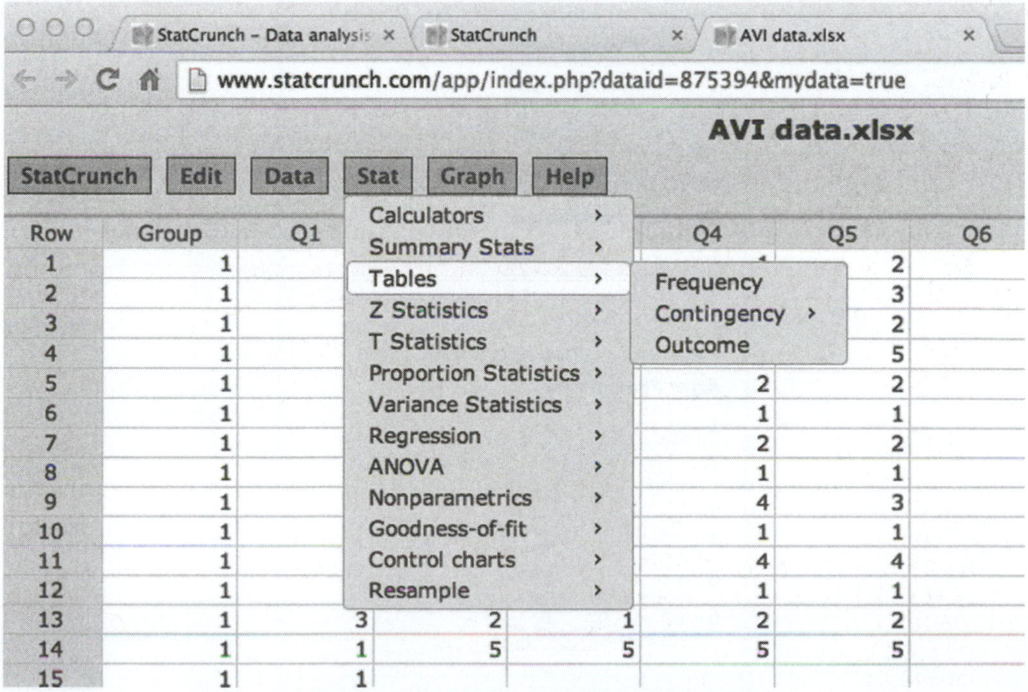

FIGURE 13.15 ●   Dialog Box for Specifications of a Frequency Analysis in StatCrunch

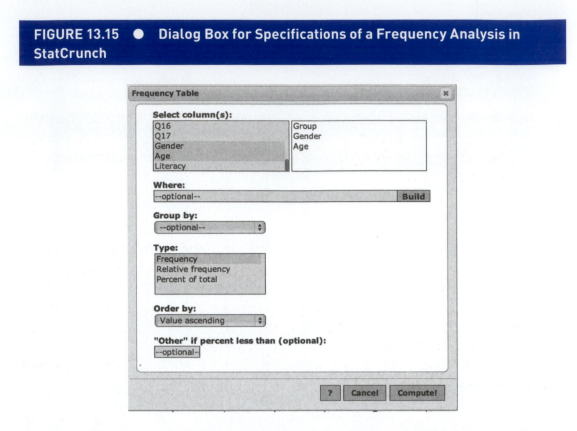

FIGURE 13.16 ●   Statistical Output for a Frequency Analysis in StatCrunch

Options

Frequency table results for Group:

Group	Frequency
1	15
2	13

Frequency table results for Gender:

Gender	Frequency
1	16
2	11

Frequency table results for Age:

Age	Frequency
1	6
2	11
3	4
4	2
5	2
6	1

Stat

↪ **Summary Stats**

↪ **Columns**

Under *Select Columns*, I choose the variables *Q1*, *Q2*, *Q3*, *Q4*, and *Q5*. Under *Statistics*, I select *n*, *Mean*, *Std. dev.*, *Median*, and *Range*, and then I click the *Compute!* button (see Figure 13.18). A new output window opens, containing the results of my analyses for these five items (see Figure 13.19).

Inferential Statistical Analysis

Because their purpose goes beyond simply summarizing and describing data, inferential statistics are subject to much more stringent requirements. We will talk about several of those requirements and characteristics in a moment. However, one distinction between inferential and descriptive statistics is the assumption that the data represent at least an interval or ratio scale of measurement, although in some cases, inferential statistics can be used to analyze ordinal data, such as those that result from the use of Likert or Likert-type items. As was mentioned earlier, inferential statistics are used specifically to test hypotheses about the following categories of analyses:

- Tests of relationships
- Tests of differences between groups
- Tests for prediction of group membership
- Tests for underlying structure

FIGURE 13.17 ● Dialog Box for Creating a Descriptive Analysis in StatCrunch

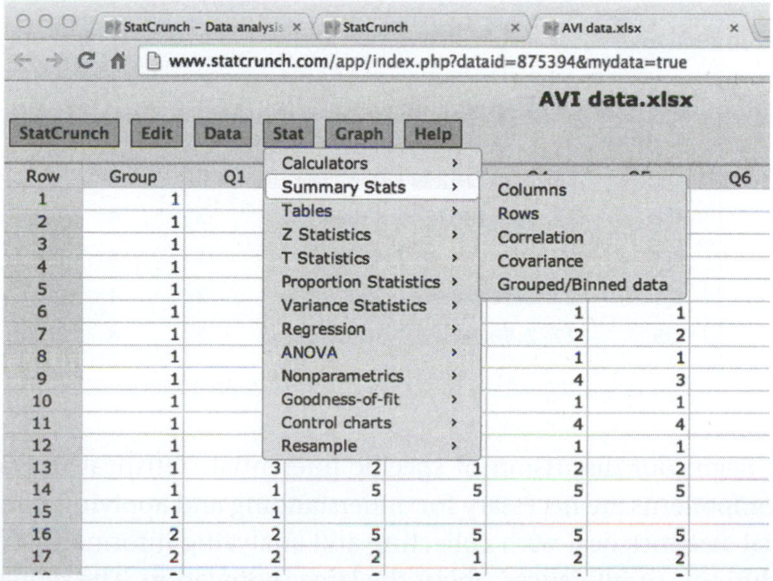

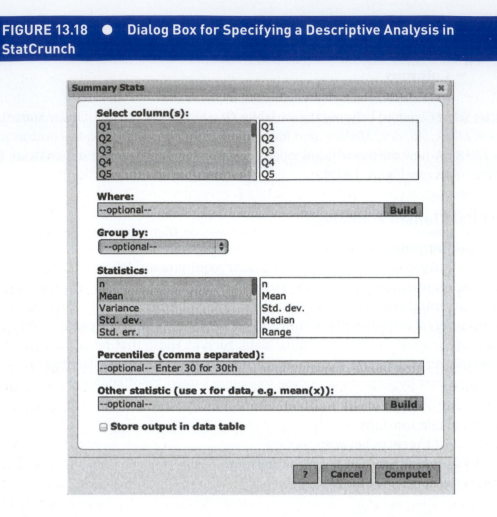

FIGURE 13.18 ● Dialog Box for Specifying a Descriptive Analysis in StatCrunch

FIGURE 13.19 ● Statistical Output for a Descriptive Analysis in StatCrunch

Summary statistics:

Column	n	Mean	Std. dev.	Median	Range
Q1	28	2.3571429	1.0261141	2	4
Q2	27	2.4814815	1.2206672	2	4
Q3	27	2	1.4142136	1	4
Q4	27	2.4444444	1.3397283	2	4
Q5	27	2.4814815	1.1887411	2	4

Before we begin our discussion of specific inferential statistical techniques, many conceptual components are necessary for understanding and applying inferential statistics. Inferential statistics deal with collecting and analyzing information from samples to draw conclusions, or inferences, about the larger population. The representativeness of the sample is a critical factor in the validity of the inferences drawn from the analyses; the more representative the sample, the more generalizable the results will be to the population from which the sample was selected (Mertler & Vannatta, 2013).

For example, assume we are interested in determining whether or not two groups differ from each other on some dependent variable. If we use a random sampling technique to increase the likelihood that we have a representative sample and we find a difference between the means for the two groups at the end of our study, the ultimate question in which we are interested is *whether a similar difference exists in the population from which the samples were selected*. Different scenarios might have played out in our study. It is possible that no real difference exists in the population—that the one we found between our samples was simply due to chance. Perhaps if we had randomly selected two *different* samples, we would not have discovered a difference.

However, if we do find a difference between our samples and we conclude that it is large enough to infer that a real difference exists in the population (i.e., the difference was *statistically significant*), then what we really want to know is, "How likely is it that our inference is incorrect?" This idea of "how likely is it" is *the* central concept in inferential statistics (Mertler & Vannatta, 2013). In other words, if we inferred that a true difference exists in the population, how many times out of 100 would we be wrong? Another way of looking at this concept is to think of selecting 100 random samples, testing each of them, and then determining for how many of the 100 samples our inference would be wrong.

Several key concepts underlie the application of inferential statistics. One of those—eluded to above—is the concept of *standard error*. In all likelihood, no sample will ever perfectly represent the population. In fact, if we selected several random samples from the same population, each sample mean would probably be different from the other sample means, and probably none of them would be equal to the population mean. This expected chance variation among sample means is known as *sampling error*. Sampling error is inevitable and unavoidable, and cannot be eliminated by the researcher.

Even though sampling errors are random, they behave in an orderly fashion. If enough samples are selected and means are calculated for each sample, all samples will not have the same mean, but those means will be normally distributed around the population mean; this is called the **distribution of sample means** (Mertler & Vannatta, 2013). A mean of this distribution of sample means can be calculated and will provide a good estimate of the population mean.

Furthermore, as with any distribution of scores, we can calculate a mean (as described above), but we can also calculate a measure of variability for the distribution. The standard deviation of the sample means is referred to as the **standard error**. The standard error of the mean tells us by how much we would expect our sample means to differ if we used other samples from the same population. This value, then, indicates how well our sample represents the population from which it was selected; obviously, the smaller the standard error, the better. With a smaller standard error, we can have more confidence in the inferences we draw about the population based on sample data. In reality, we certainly do not have the time or resources to select countless random samples, nor do we need to. Only the sample size and the sample standard deviation are required to calculate a good estimate of the standard error (SEM or $SE_{\bar{x}}$):

$$SEM = SE_{\bar{x}} = \frac{SD}{\sqrt{N-1}}$$

where

SEM or $SE_{\bar{x}}$ = the estimated standard error of the mean

SD = the standard deviation of the scores

N = the sample size

The main goal of inferential statistics is to draw inferences about populations based on sample data, through a process of *hypothesis testing*. In **hypothesis testing**, researchers test predictions they have made based on data collected from the sample. Again, suppose the difference between the means for two groups was being examined to determine if it was statistically significant. The *null hypothesis* (H_0) predicts that the only differences that exist in the population are chance differences that represent *only* random sampling error. In other words, the null hypothesis states that there is no true difference to be found in the population. In contrast, the *research* or *alternative hypothesis* (H_1) states that one method is expected to be better than the other or, in other words, that the two group means are not equal—therefore representing a true difference in the population. In inferential statistics, we are testing the null hypothesis, since it is easier to disprove the null than to prove the alternative (Mertler & Vannatta, 2013).

Null hypotheses are tested through the application of specific statistical criteria known as **significance tests**. Significance tests are the procedures the researcher uses to determine if the difference between sample means is large enough to rule out sampling error as an explanation for the difference. A test of significance is made at a predetermined—also known as a priori—**probability level** (i.e., the probability that the null hypothesis is correct). This provides the criteria that allow the researcher to pass judgment on the null hypothesis. For example, if the difference between two sample means is not large enough to convince us that a real difference exists in the population, the statistical decision will be to *"fail to reject the null hypothesis."* In other words, we are *not rejecting* the null hypothesis—I know . . . the double negatives are difficult!—which stated that there was no real difference, other than a difference due to chance, between the two population means. On the other hand, if the difference between sample means was substantially large (i.e., large enough to surpass the statistical criteria), we would *"reject the null hypothesis"* in favor of the alternative hypothesis and conclude that a real difference, beyond chance, exists in the population. A number of tests of significance can be used to test hypotheses, including the *t*-test, analysis of variance, chi-square test, and tests of correlation—all of which we will consider momentarily.

Based on the results of these tests of significance, the researcher must decide whether to (1) reject or (2) fail to reject the null hypothesis. The researcher can never know with 100% certainty whether the statistical decision was correct, only that he or she was *probably* correct. Remember that, in inferential statistical analyses, we talk exclusively in terms of probabilities and likelihoods. There are four possibilities with respect to statistical decisions—two that reflect correct decisions and two that reflect erroneous conclusions:

1. The null hypothesis is actually true (i.e., there is no difference in the population), and the researcher concludes that it is true (*fail to reject H₀*)—a *correct* decision.
2. The null hypothesis is actually false (i.e., a real difference exists), and the researcher concludes that it is false (*reject H₀*)—a *correct* decision.
3. The null hypothesis is actually true, and the researcher concludes that it is false (*reject H₀*)—an *incorrect* decision.
4. The null hypothesis is actually false, and the researcher concludes that it is true (*fail to reject H₀*)—an *incorrect* decision.

If a researcher concludes that a null hypothesis is false when it is *actually* true (Scenario 3 above), he or she has committed a **Type I error**; if a null hypothesis is *actually* false when it is concluded to be true (Scenario 4 above), a **Type II error** has been made (see Figure 13.20). Type I errors are typically seen as being more serious, compared with Type II errors (Gay et al., 2009).

When researchers make a decision regarding the status of a null hypothesis, they do so with a preestablished (a priori) probability of being incorrect. This probability level is referred to as the **level of significance** or **alpha (α) level**. This value is the criterion for statistical significance; in other words, it determines how large the difference between means must be to be declared significantly different, thus resulting in a decision to reject the null hypothesis. The most common probability levels used in educational settings are $\alpha = .05$ and $\alpha = .01$. The selected significance level (α) determines the probability of committing a Type I error; in other words, it specifies the researcher's risk of being wrong. The probability of committing a Type II error is symbolized by β (beta) but is not arbitrarily set as alpha (α) is. To determine the value for β, a complex series of calculations is required. Many beginning researchers assume that it is best to set the alpha level as small as possible (thus reducing the risk of a

FIGURE 13.20 ● Table for Possible Outcomes of Statistical Decisions

		Researcher's Conclusion	
		Ho True	Ho False
Actual	Ho True	Correct Decision	Type I Error
Condition	Ho False	Type II Error	Correct Decision

Type I error to almost zero). However, the probability levels of committing Type I and Type II errors have a complementary relationship (Mertler & Vannatta, 2013). If one reduces the probability of committing a Type I error, the probability of committing a Type II error increases (Gay et al., 2009). These factors must be weighed, and levels established, prior to the implementation of a research study.

The **power** of a statistical test is the probability of rejecting H_0 when H_0 is, in fact, false—in other words, making a correct decision (Scenario 2 above). Power is appropriately named, since this is exactly what the researcher hopes to accomplish during hypothesis testing. Therefore, it is desirable for a test to have high power (Mertler & Vannatta, 2013). Power is calculated in the following manner:

$$Power = 1 - \beta$$

Like α, power is established arbitrarily but should be set at a high level, since the researcher is hoping to reject a null hypothesis that is not true and wants to have a high probability of doing so (Brewer, 1978).

At this point, you might be asking yourself how researchers *actually* determine if a difference or relationship is statistically significant. As a result of conducting the analysis, we obtain a numerical index known as a *p*-value. The **p-value** we obtain from our analysis indicates the probability of chance occurrences in our actual study. The *p*-value must be compared with the alpha level (which is set prior to data collection), typically set at .05 in educational research studies. An α level of .05 indicates that we can be reasonably certain that the differences we obtain will only 5% of the time be due to chance, thus representing no real difference between the two groups. The rule of thumb for comparing the obtained *p*-value with the α level and thus determining statistical significance is as follows:

If $p < \alpha$, then the difference or relationship is statistically significant.

If $p \geq \alpha$, then the difference or relationship is not statistically significant.

Another factor related to hypothesis testing is *effect size*. **Effect size** (often symbolized by *ES* or h^2) is defined as the size of the treatment effect the researcher wishes to detect with respect to a given level of power. In an experimental study, *ES* is equal to the difference between the population means of the experimental and control groups divided by the population standard deviation for the control group (note that there are numerous formulas for estimating effect size; this is a commonly used formula):

$$ES = \eta^2 = \frac{\overline{X_1} - \overline{X_2}}{SD_2}$$

In other words, effect size is a measure of the amount of difference between the two groups, reported in standard deviation units. Effect sizes can also be calculated for correlation coefficients or for mean differences resulting from nonexperimental studies (Mertler & Vannatta, 2013). Remember that, whenever reporting *p*-values, one should also calculate and report a measure of effect size.

An important relationship exists between tests of statistical significance and effect size: A more powerful statistical test will be able to detect a smaller effect size. Cohen (1988) established a rule of thumb for evaluating effect sizes: An *ES* of .2 is considered small, one of .5 is considered medium, and one of .8 is considered large. A researcher would want to design a study and statistical analysis procedures powerful enough to detect the smallest effect size that is of interest and nontrivial (Harris, 1998).

Now that we have a basic conceptual understanding of inferential statistical analysis, we will look at techniques that fall into four categories—analytical techniques for relationships, for group differences, for prediction of group membership, and for underlying structure (Mertler & Vannatta, 2013). The goal of the following sections is not to provide thorough coverage of various inferential statistical techniques but merely to expose the reader to the variety of techniques that exist, along with their respective purposes and goals.

Tests of Relationships The general goal of the following group of inferential statistical tests is to measure the relationships between variables. However, some techniques do not stop there; they may have a broader goal of predicting or explaining an organizational structure that might underlie a group of variables, but they accomplish this by capitalizing on the nature and degree of the relationships among the variables. We will first look at **bivariate analyses**—those that involve only two variables.

The first bivariate statistical test of the relationships between variables is the chi-square test, which actually has two versions. The **chi-square goodness-of-fit test** is used to analyze categorical data to determine if observed frequency counts are significantly different from those that would be expected in the population. The **chi-square test of independence**—also used appropriately with nominal, or categorical, data—is used to test the significance of a relationship between two categorical variables. The name is appropriate in that the goal of this analysis is to determine if the two variables are independent or not—in which case they would be related. The following would be an appropriate research question for a chi-square test of independence:

What is the nature of the relationship between the gender of middle school students and whether each is right- or left-handed? Is that relationship statistically significant?

By far the most commonly used bivariate correlational analysis technique is the calculation of a *Pearson correlation coefficient* (*r*). As we discussed previously, the correlation coefficient describes the strength and direction of the relationship between two interval or ratio variables. In this particular analysis, there is no distinction between the independent and dependent variable; it is simply a bivariate analysis where the two variables are treated equally. A research question appropriate for a bivariate correlational analysis would be:

What is the nature of the relationship between SAT scores and freshman GPA in college? Is that relationship statistically significant?

A simple example of a correlational analysis appears in Figure 13.21. Although you can see that the obtained correlation coefficient is relatively weak (i.e., rounded to two decimal places, $r = .27$), it is nonetheless a statistically significant relationship, since $p < .0001$ (which makes it less than an α level of .05).

Remember that, earlier in this chapter, we also considered several other measures of relationship. Although the scales of measurement appropriate for those analyses differ, the logic and application behind the correlational analysis are the same. A related correlational analysis technique is known as *linear regression* (also known as *bivariate regression*, or simply *regression*). In bivariate regression, the relationship between an independent variable and a dependent variable is used for the purposes of developing an equation so that, in the future, if we have scores on the independent variable, we can predict values on the dependent variable. A research question appropriate for bivariate regression might be the following:

To what degree do SAT scores predict college freshman GPA?

The remaining tests of relationships are types of **multivariate analysis**—meaning that they involve more than two variables. The first of these is *multiple regression*, which is a logical extension of bivariate regression. The purpose of multiple regression is to identify the best combination of predictor variables for a single dependent variable. It is used appropriately in a research scenario that features several independent variables (measured, at least, on an interval scale) and one dependent variable (also measured on an interval scale). Although the specific regression procedure may vary, the general procedure focuses on producing the best combination of predictor variables for the dependent variable. The analytical procedure selects independent variables, one at a time, by their ability to account for the most variance in the dependent variable. As each variable is selected and entered into the group of predictors, the *overall* relationship between the *group* of

FIGURE 13.21 ● Sample Results From a Correlational Analysis Conducted in StatCrunch

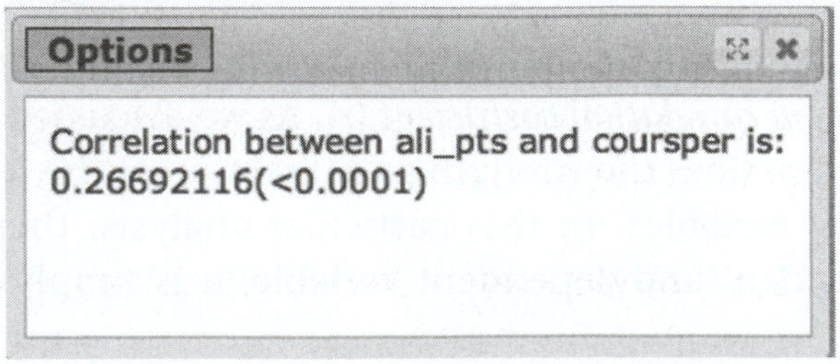

Options

Correlation between ali_pts and coursper is:
0.26692116(<0.0001)

predictors and the dependent variable is reassessed. When no variables remain that explain a significant amount of variance in the dependent variable, the regression model is complete. An appropriate question for a multiple regression analysis might be the following:

Which combination of risk-taking behaviors (amount of alcohol use, drug use, sexual activity, and violence) best predicts the incidence of depression among adolescents?

A further extension of multiple regression is multivariate multiple regression. In **multivariate multiple regression**, a group of independent variables is identified as the best set of predictors for a group of dependent variables.

Two final—and substantially advanced—statistical techniques for analyzing relationships are path analysis and structural equation modeling. **Path analysis** is another technique focused on testing relationships that uses multiple applications of multiple regression to estimate causal relationships, both direct and indirect, among several variables. In addition, path analysis tests the acceptability of a causal model hypothesized by the researcher. An example of a path analysis research question is as follows:

What are the direct and indirect effects of reading ability, family income, and parental involvement on students' GPA?

Finally, **structural equation modeling** is a substantially advanced technique that can be thought of as a combination of path analysis and factor analysis (Gay et al., 2009), which you will learn more about later in this chapter. Its goal is to build a model that explains the interactive relationships among a large number of variables.

Tests of Group Differences The primary purpose of testing for group differences—especially in experimental studies—is to determine a cause or relationship between independent and dependent variables. In nonexperimental studies, testing for differences allows the researcher to determine if statistically significant differences exist between groups on some dependent variable. The appropriate test is typically based on the number of categories in the independent variable, the number of variables, and the number of dependent variables.

The first type of test of group differences is a *t*-test. An **independent samples *t*-test** (sometimes known as an **independent measures *t*-test**) is an appropriate analysis technique in research designs where two groups are being compared on a common dependent variable, such as a test score. The two groups are defined as levels of the independent variable—for example, an experimental group that receives a treatment condition and a comparison group that does not—or the levels could be defined as existing groups. In other words, this design requires *two* groups, each measured *once*. The mean scores are then calculated for each group and statistically compared. An example of an appropriate research question for this type of test is as follows:

Do boys and girls have significantly different scores on a test of problem-solving ability?

A second example of a *t*-test is a **repeated samples *t*-test**. You may see this referred to as a **repeated measures *t*-test** or a **paired samples *t*-test**. The fundamental difference in a research study appropriate for this test is that now we have *one* group being measured *twice*. This is a common statistical analysis technique in research designs where groups are pretested and posttested. Similar to the process for an independent samples *t*-test, group means are obtained—in this case, one for the pretest and one for the posttest—and then statistically compared. An example of an appropriate research question for this type of test is as follows:

Does the exposure of students to hands-on laboratory activities result in significantly different academic achievement?

An example of the results of an independent samples *t*-test conducted in StatCrunch appears in Figure 13.22. Notice that School 1 outscored School 2 by more than 3 points (under the heading "Sample Diff."). Also, in this analysis, the difference between the mean scores for the two schools was statistically significant.

Analysis of variance—also known as **ANOVA**—is actually a family of group comparison techniques. A basic **one-way ANOVA** is an extension of an independent samples *t*-test, with one important difference: Groups must be measured on the same dependent variable, but this technique is appropriate when there are *more than two groups* being compared. For example, we might have a situation where we have three or four groups, each being measured once. A sample research question is as follows:

Do urban, suburban, and rural schools have significantly different scores on the statewide reading test?

The designs appropriate for the three preceding types of analysis for comparing groups—that is, independent samples *t*-test, repeated measures *t*-test, and one-way ANOVA—are outlined in Figure 13.23.

FIGURE 13.22 ● Sample Results From an Independent Samples *t*-Test Conducted in StatCrunch

Hypothesis test results:
μ_1 : Mean of ali_pts where school=1
μ_2 : Mean of ali_pts where school=2
$\mu_1 - \mu_2$: Difference between two means
$H_0 : \mu_1 - \mu_2 = 0$
$H_A : \mu_1 - \mu_2 \neq 0$
(with pooled variances)

Difference	Sample Diff.	Std. Err.	DF	T-Stat	P-value
$\mu_1 - \mu_2$	3.0944243	0.54631231	273	5.6642038	<0.0001

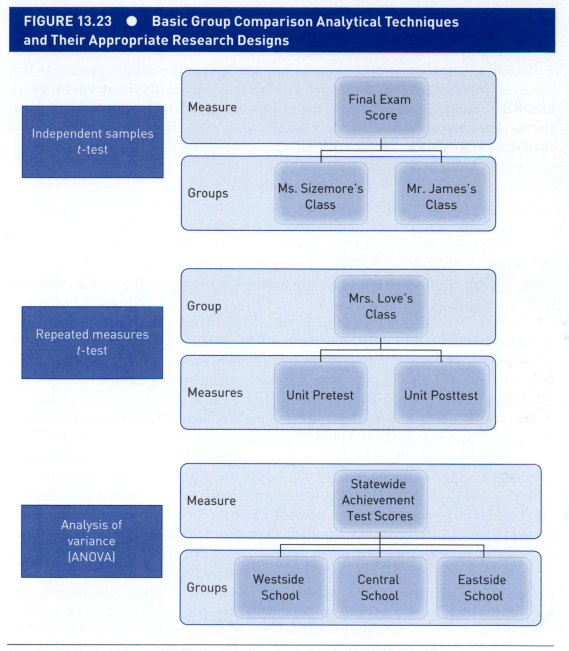

FIGURE 13.23 ● Basic Group Comparison Analytical Techniques and Their Appropriate Research Designs

Source: Adapted from Mertler (2014).

The family of ANOVA techniques builds on the basic design of a one-way ANOVA. A **factorial ANOVA** is a simple extension of the one-way ANOVA, where two (or more) independent variables are included. When there are two independent variables, the appropriate analysis technique is known as a **two-way ANOVA**; for three independent variables and beyond, the correct term is *factorial ANOVA*.

Sometimes additional variables can be included in the design, acting as controls for a variable that may influence the dependent variable. These control variables are known as **covariates**, and the appropriate analytical technique for this design is an

analysis of covariance, or **ANCOVA**. The basic design with one independent variable is a **one-way ANCOVA**; however, researchers can also have designs appropriate for a **two-way ANCOVA** or **factorial ANCOVA**.

Finally, multiple dependent variables can be added to the designs as well. In this situation, we have a technique known as **multivariate analysis of variance**, or **MANOVA**. Similarly, we can extend multivariate designs to include variations such as **factorial MANOVA**, **multivariate analysis of covariance (MANCOVA)**, and **factorial MANCOVA**. A sample research question appropriate for multivariate analysis of covariance is as follows:

> *Does school location (urban, suburban, and rural) significantly affect reading achievement, math achievement, and science achievement, after controlling for family income?*

Notice how the design builds from previous ANOVA research questions with the addition of appropriate variables.

Tests for Prediction of Group Membership The overarching purpose of this group of analytical techniques is to identify specific independent variables that, in combination, will best protect group membership as defined by a categorical (nominal) dependent variable. The two techniques here include discriminant analysis and logistic regression. *Discriminant analysis* is sometimes seen as the reverse of MANOVA (Mertler & Vannatta, 2013). In MANOVA, a researcher begins with a categorical independent variable (which defines group membership) and seeks to identify group differences based on a combination of dependent variables. In contrast, discriminant analysis seeks to identify the combination of quantitative independent variables that best predicts group membership as defined by a single dependent variable with two or more categories. Essentially, discriminant analysis attempts to interpret the patterns of differences among the predictor, or independent, variables. Therefore, the analysis often produces several sets or combinations of independent predictor variables. Each independent variable set is referred to as a *discriminant function*. Significance tests serve as the basis for the development of the variable sets contributing to each discriminant function, as well as the overall assessment of the predictability of each function. A sample research question appropriate for discriminant analysis is as follows:

> *Which high school variables (i.e., reading achievement, math achievement, science achievement, extracurricular activities, leadership roles) best predict college success?*

Logistic regression is similar to discriminant analysis in that they both attempt to identify a set of independent variables that best predicts group membership on a categorical dependent variable. The basic form of logistic regression involves a dependent variable that is dichotomous. Further, the independent variables may be categorical (i.e., nominal scale) and/or quantitative (i.e., interval or ratio scale). The analysis estimates the probability of group membership on the dependent variable occurring as

FIGURE 13.24 ● Decision-Making Tree for Statistical Tests

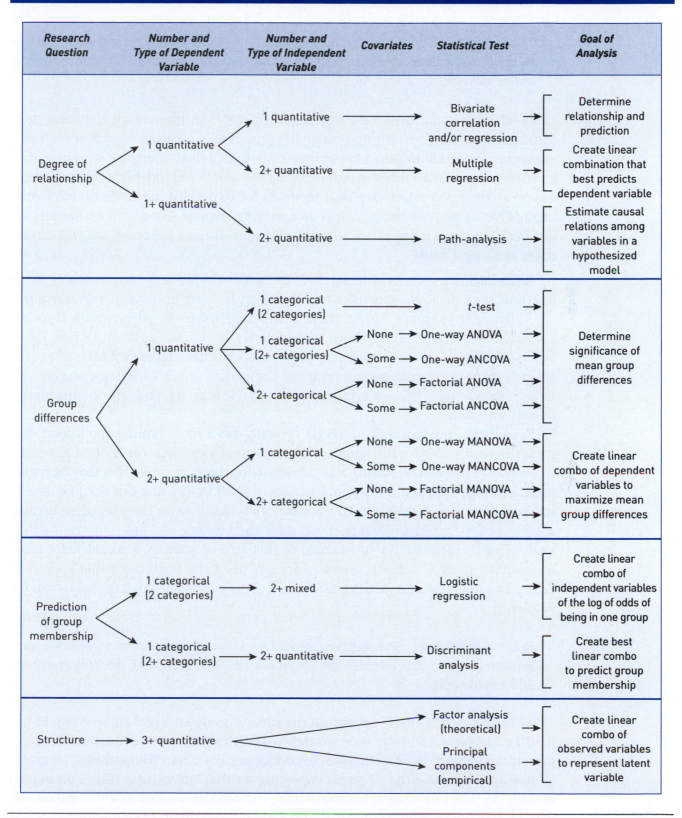

Source: Mertler and Vannatta (2013).

the values of the independent variables change. A sample research question appropriate for logistic regression is as follows:

To what extent do certain high school variables (i.e., reading achievement, math achievement, science achievement, extracurricular activities, leadership roles) increase the odds of college success?

Tests of Underlying Structure The final category of inferential statistical tests includes those that investigate underlying structure. In some research scenarios, a researcher may want to gain a better understanding of the underlying structure of an instrument, or may be interested in reducing the number of independent variables in a large study. Appropriate statistical methods for accomplishing these types of goals include factor analysis and principal components analysis. These two techniques are different but share many characteristics; therefore, for our purposes, we will discuss them as a single entity.

Factor analysis permits a researcher to explore the underlying structures of an instrument or data set, structures that can then be used to develop and test a theory (Mertler & Vannatta, 2013). These underlying structures, which result from the reduction of the number of independent variables, are known as latent factors. *Latent factors* are essentially unobservable variables, traits, or characteristics. This is one of the advantages of factor analysis and principal components analysis: Researchers are able to measure variables that are typically unobservable (e.g., IQ, problem-solving ability, or cognitive skills).

Principal components analysis typically has a more limited application. It is generally used to reduce the number of independent variables; this is often the desire of a researcher when conducting analyses involving many variables that may be highly correlated (e.g., reducing a 100-item instrument to 10 factors that can then be used in subsequent statistical analyses). This is much more desirable for the researcher, because analysis of 100 variables would be much more cumbersome and time-consuming than analysis of 10 variables. As an example of this type of analysis, I conducted a large-scale survey study ($n = 1,531$) several years ago, using the instrument that appears in Figure 12.6 in Chapter 12 (Mertler, 2010). One of my guiding research questions was the following:

What differences in the perceptions of NCLB's influence on assessment practices exist between groups as determined by gender, school level, education level, teaching experience, and school rating?

Although only 22 items appear on the survey, doing all these group comparisons for 22 variables would have been unwieldy. Therefore, I subjected the final data to a principal components analysis, prior to conducting my group comparisons. I was able to statistically reduce the 22 items appearing on that survey to a three-component underlying structure: *student test preparation*, *instructional changes*, and *stressful motivation*. I then conducted my comparisons based on those three components.

Cautions in Using Statistics

Researchers should try not to go overboard in using statistics. In your research, specify exactly what you want to know—what questions you wish to answer or which hypotheses you intend to test; then select the statistics that are appropriate for describing your data and for performing the analyses those decisions require. Make sure the statistical analyses contribute directly to the purposes you have in mind. Remember, too, that statistics do not *prove* anything; in the results of all educational research, there will remain a degree of uncertainty. Significance levels help only by showing the *chances* of one making an error in judgment.

One area where novice researchers seem to struggle is in the decision of an appropriate statistical test for the analysis of their data. Mertler and Vannatta (2013) have developed a decision-making tree for statistical tests (see Figure 13.24) to help with some of these choices. The following steps serve as a guide to using this device (p. 18):

1. Identify the variables in the research question.
2. Indicate which variables are the independent and dependent variables and covariates (if any).
3. Determine the type (categorical or quantitative) of all variables. If a variable is categorical, determine the number of categories.
4. Determine the purpose of the research question: degree of relationship, group differences, prediction of group membership, or structure. Here are a few helpful hints for using the variable information to determine the research question purpose:

    *   When the independent variables and dependent variables are all quantitative, the purpose is "degree of relationship."
    *   When the independent variables are categorical and the dependent variables are quantitative, the purpose is "group differences."
    *   When the dependent variables are categorical, the purpose is "predicting group membership."

5. Apply the information from the preceding steps to the decision-making tree, following the process of decisions—research question, number and type of dependent variables, number and type of independent variables, and covariates—to determine the appropriate test.

As for significance, it is possible to determine that a particular finding is significant, statistically speaking, when in fact the magnitude of the finding is so small that it makes no practical difference whatsoever. These types of results can occur when a researcher uses very large samples. This constitutes the crucial distinction between *statistical significance* and **practical significance**. For example, it might be discovered that in a particular high school population, students born in May have a mean IQ that is 1 point higher than that of students born in October and, further, that the difference is statistically significant. But what possible importance could that minuscule difference have? Conversely, it might be found, in a small sample of 10 students, that mathematics taught through a new method produced a 30% higher achievement gain than did the traditional teaching method. But because the sample is so small, the finding may not have achieved a level of *statistical* significance. Rather than reject that finding, which might have very important implications, one might wish to report the *practical* significance of the finding and then repeat the research using a larger sample.

Statistics *assist* logical thought processes; they cannot *replace* logic. They help investigators interpret data, answer research questions, and test hypotheses. They do not make interpretations, nor can they be offered up as the final word in research on any topic. So, regardless of how impressive statistics might appear, remember that the researcher's thought processes—and how they "make sense" of statistical results—are valued most in quality research.

Developmental Activities

1. Think of a possible research topic, and develop several research questions for investigating that topic. Based on the nature of your stated research questions, identify appropriate statistical techniques you would use to analyze your resulting data.

2. Think of a possible research study you might want to conduct (perhaps on the same topic as in Activity 1 above). Develop a list of possible research questions that would appropriately use only *descriptive* statistical analysis techniques.

3. Think of a possible research study you might want to conduct (perhaps on the same topic as in Activity 1 above). Develop a list of possible research questions that would appropriately use only *inferential* statistical analysis techniques.

4. Develop a list of pros and cons for the use of statistical analysis software to analyze research data.

5. Access to statistical analysis programs has certainly made the analysis of quantitative data much easier for researchers; however, their relative ease of use still involves a bit of a learning curve. Develop a fictitious database, consisting of 10 to 15 variables and 25 to 30 participants. At a minimum, be sure to include variables that are measured at the nominal and interval scales of measurement. Using StatCrunch, conduct several types of descriptive analyses (e.g., frequency distribution, correlation, summary statistics, and/or bar charts and histograms) and inferential analyses (e.g., significance tests of correlations and group differences, such as a *t*-test).

Summary

- Analysis of quantitative data involves the application of statistical techniques. There are several purposes behind the use of statistical analysis procedures:

  - To summarize data and reveal what is typical and atypical
  - To show relative standing of individuals in a group

- To show relationships among variables
- To show similarities and differences among groups
- To identify error inherent in sample selection
- To test for significance of statistical findings
- To make inferences about the population

- Parameters are numerical indices that describe a population; statistics are numerical indices that describe a sample.
- Data must be prepared for analysis by being numerically coded, using a codebook, and entered into a database.
- Descriptive statistics are those techniques that simplify, summarize, and describe data.
- Inferential statistics are techniques used to determine the likelihood that the results obtained from a sample are similar to those that would have been obtained from an entire population.
- Descriptive statistical techniques include the following categories: frequency distributions, measures of central tendency, measures of dispersion or variability, measures of relationship, and measures of relative position.

  - Arguably, the most commonly used descriptive techniques are measures of central tendency (i.e., mean, median, and mode) and measures of variability (i.e., range, variance, and standard deviation).

- Numerous types of correlational analyses are available, depending on the scale of measurement used with each variable in the analysis.
- Measures of relative standing are based on the location of an individual with a common distribution, based on the normal distribution.

- The normal distribution has three important characteristics: The distribution is symmetrical; the mean, median, and mode are the same score and located at the exact center of the distribution; and the percentage of cases in each standard deviation is known precisely.

- Visual representations are also a way to describe quantitative data.
- Inferential statistical techniques include tests of relationships and tests of differences between groups.
- Determining statistical significance is the process of concluding that the sample difference is large enough to infer that a real difference also exists in the population.
- The standard error is a measure of the variability of sample means in a distribution.
- Inferential statistics is based largely on the idea of hypothesis testing, where the null hypothesis is tested to determine statistical significance.
- The level of significance, or alpha (α) level, is the value used as the criterion to determine statistical significance. In educational research studies, alpha is typically set at .05 or .01.
- Four possible outcomes can result from a test of statistical significance; two represent correct decisions, and two represent errors.

  - A Type I error has been committed when a researcher concludes that a null hypothesis is false when it is actually true.
  - A Type II error has been committed when a researcher concludes that a null hypothesis is true when it is actually false.

- The p-value obtained from the analysis is compared with the α level to determine significance. If p is less than α, then the difference or relationship is statistically significant.

- Effect size is important in hypothesis testing and is defined as the amount of difference between two groups (i.e., the treatment effect) in standard deviation units.

- Bivariate tests of relationships include the chi-square test for independence, Pearson correlation coefficient, and linear or simple regression.

- Multivariate tests of relationship include multiple regression, multivariate multiple regression, path analysis, and structural equation modeling.

- There are numerous tests of group differences, including independent samples *t*-test, repeated samples *t*-test, and analysis of variance (ANOVA).

- Several variations of analysis of variance include designs with multiple independent variables, covariates, and multiple dependent variables.

- Tests for prediction of group membership include discriminant analysis and logistic regression.

- Tests underlying structure include factor analysis and principal components analysis.

- Researchers should be cautious not to go overboard when using statistical analysis techniques and to stay focused on their research questions and purposes for their studies.

- Researchers should consider practical significance, as well as statistical significance.

$SAGE edge™

Sharpen your skills with SAGE edge!

edge.sagepub.com/mertler

SAGE edge for Students provides a personalized approach to help you accomplish your coursework goals in an easy-to-use learning environment. You'll find action plans, mobile-friendly eFlashcards, and quizzes as well as video, web, and resources and links to SAGE journal articles to support and expand on the concepts presented in this chapter.

THE RESEARCH REPORT

PART IV

14

Writing a Final Research Report

Student Learning Objectives

After studying Chapter 14, students will be able to do the following:

1. Provide a rationale for the importance of identifying your audience prior to writing a final research report

2. Explain the importance of maintaining anonymity and confidentiality in a research report

3. Discuss appropriate ways to report the results in qualitative studies

4. Discuss appropriate ways to report results in quantitative studies

5. Outline various practical guidelines for writing and why they are important to the writing process

6. Develop a well-written final research report

This chapter introduces all the various aspects involved in development of a written research report. You will learn about general guidelines—including style guides, conventions of academic writing, and conventions of format—as well as practical guidelines for writing. However, we begin our discussion by examining the importance of knowing exactly who forms the audience for your research report.

Importance of the Audience

Upon completing a research study, the goal for most researchers is to disseminate the research so it can be useful and beneficial to others. In most cases, dissemination occurs in the form of a final research report. However, for the report—and, therefore, the findings of the research—to be useful to others, it must be written so it is acceptable to and understandable by the target audience. This means that the researcher has to *know* who forms the audience for the results of a particular study. There are numerous potential audiences for research reports, including college and university faculty, journal editors and reviewers, reviewers of conference papers, policymakers, practitioners, and other researchers.

Each of these audiences has its own unique criteria, expectations, and standards for written research reports. For example, college and university faculty must follow specific guidelines—as set forth by a graduate school, college, or perhaps even academic department—and must write reports so they follow these criteria and standards. In contrast, editors and reviewers for academic journals look for different qualities when reading written research reports. Sometimes the criteria emphasize simplicity and readability of a research report; in other circumstances, the expectation is that a great deal of detail and attention be paid to the technical aspects of the research process. Regardless, it is the researcher's responsibility to know who the intended audience is, as well as what their criteria and expectations are. Table 14.1 provides a listing of potential audiences for written research reports in education, along with their expectations and criteria.

TABLE 14.1 ● Potential Audiences for Research Reports, Along With Their Expectations	
Audience for Research	**Criteria and Expectations**
University faculty (advisors or committee members)	• Standards as set forth by the graduate school/college/department • Standards traditionally used by an individual
Journal reviewers and editors	• Published standards (which may vary from journal to journal) • Differential standards, based on the use of quantitative or qualitative research methods • Standards set forth by a specific style guide • Adherence to the submission requirements
Educational practitioners	• Relevance of the research problem and/or results of the study • Ease of identifying results • Practicality and applicability of research findings
Conference paper reviewers	• Alignment of the topic and report to the theme of the conference • Appropriateness of the topic for the conference's audience • Adherence to the submission requirements
Policymakers	• Ease of identifying and understanding results • Immediate application of results • Clarity and brevity of ideas communicated

Source: Adapted from Creswell (2005).

General Guidelines for Writing a Research Report

While the purpose for writing a research report, as well as the intended audience for that report, may vary, there are numerous qualities shared by most all forms of academic writing. Academic writing is not creative writing; it tends to be factual and interpretive. In my opinion, it resembles scientific writing more closely than it does any other form of writing. In this section, you will learn about style guides for academic writing, as well as conventions of style and format.

The research process adheres to certain **conventions**, which are agreed-on procedures that help ensure the accuracy of data and findings. These conventions contribute to the validity of research and increase our confidence in the research results. When research conventions are not followed, the credibility of the research—and perhaps of the researcher—can be called into question. The same is true for research reports. They, too, are prepared according to conventions that promote both readability and credibility. It is important that you recognize these conventions and follow them when preparing any type of research report. Failure to comply with conventions does not render research invalid (per se), but a researcher's credibility can be damaged by unconventional report styles and formats.

Style Guides

When preparing written reports, researchers are expected to follow the **style guide** used in the institution where the research was conducted or by a particular journal. Some colleges and universities have prepared their own guides, while most have adopted existing style guides. The following is a list of well-known and commonly used style guides:

American Psychological Association. (2010). *Publication manual of the American Psychological Association* (6th ed.). Washington, DC: American Psychological Association. (*Note: This is frequently called APA style.*)

Campbell, W., Ballou, S., & Slade, C. (1990). *Form and style: Theses, reports, term papers* (8th ed.). Boston, MA: Houghton Mifflin. (*Note: This is often referred to as Campbell.*)

Modern Language Association. (2009). *MLA handbook for writers of research papers* (7th ed.). New York: Modern Language Association of America. (*Note: This is frequently called MLA style.*)

Turabian, K. (2014). *A manual for writers of term papers, theses, and dissertations* (8th ed.). Chicago, IL: University of Chicago Press. (*Note: This is often referred to as Turabian.*)

University of Chicago Press. (2011). *The Chicago manual of style: The essential guide for authors, editors, and publishers* (16th ed.). Chicago, IL: University of Chicago Press. (*Note: This is frequently called Chicago style.*)

The APA manual is arguably the most commonly used style guide in the broad field of education. For years, many researchers have relied on the APA manual for providing the wide variety of formats used for citing references. However, this manual provides much more in the way of stylistic information for researchers. It includes aspects of writing research reports such as

- organization and format of a manuscript;
- expressing ideas and reducing bias in written language;
- editorial style (e.g., punctuation, capitalization, abbreviations, headings, quotations, and expression of numbers, including statistical information within the text);
- formatting tables, figures, and footnotes; and
- reference formats.

Each university graduate school or professional journal has adopted a style it prefers; it is important for you to familiarize yourself with the appropriate, preferred style. Scholarly journals also have styles they prefer, and when you submit an article for publication, you are expected to use that journal's style. Journals typically inform prospective authors of the required style in their requirements for manuscript submission. Style guides, especially the APA manual, are invaluable resources for the educational researcher.

Conventions of Academic-Style Writing

Conventions of academic-style writing are simply agreed-on procedures that help ensure the readability and credibility of research reports (Mertler & Charles, 2011). As we discussed earlier, readers of journals and other outlets for research reports have certain expectations regarding format and style. When writing reports of the results of any type of research, it is important for researchers to follow these conventions. The conventions of style we will examine are as follows:

- Titles of reports
- Person and voice
- Tense
- Anonymity and confidentiality
- Tentative versus definitive statements
- Clarity
- Consistency
- Simplicity of language

Titles of Reports For most readers of your research report, the title will be the first thing they read. The title is the initial screening mechanism for anyone considering reading the report (Mertler, 2014). The title should act as an attention grabber but must indicate clearly what the study and the report are about. Sometimes researchers are inclined to develop cute, clever titles that pose riddles or are extremely vague (Mertler, 2014). Catchy, clever titles should be avoided unless they also happen to describe the topic accurately. There is nothing inherently wrong with a clever title, provided it clearly describes the topic in the study at hand (Mertler & Charles, 2011).

Readers of research rely on titles to indicate whether reports deal with topics they specifically want to read about. For that reason, titles of research reports are sometimes rather long, though writers generally try to limit them to 15 words or fewer.

Person and Voice   Generally speaking, qualitative research reports are written in the *first person*. This is done in an attempt to capture individuals' thoughts, feelings, or interpretations of meaning and process, and this approach includes the thoughts and feelings of the researcher/author (Mertler & Charles, 2011). Furthermore, qualitative—as well as quantitative—research reports tend to be written using *active voice*, as opposed to passive voice. In a sentence using active voice, the subject of the sentence performs the action expressed by the verb: *The student gave her book report to the class.* On the other hand, in a sentence using passive voice, the subject is acted on; he or she receives the action expressed by the verb: *A book report was given by the student to the class.*

In contrast, quantitative research reports are typically written in the third person, although this convention is beginning to change a bit (Mertler & Charles, 2011). Usually, the authors do not refer to themselves as *I* or *we* but, rather, as *the author* or *the researchers*. This is done deliberately to serve as an indication of the objectivity incorporated into quantitative studies. As mentioned above, quantitative research reports should use active voice rather than passive voice. Researchers should write, "The writer found . . ." or "The investigator reached the following conclusions . . ." (both active voice), rather than "It was found that . . ." or "The following conclusions were reached . . ." (both passive voice). The active voice tends to be a more reader-friendly form of writing. You can clearly see this fundamental difference between the two voices in the following two versions of the same statement:

> It was expected by the researcher that some positive behaviors would be heard being praised in addition to the negatives being addressed. (*Passive voice*)

> I just expected to hear some positive behaviors being praised in addition to the negatives being addressed. (*Active voice*)

The APA manual (Section 3.18, p. 77) also states that authors of research reports should use the active voice rather than the passive voice.

Tense   Research reports are generally written in the *past tense* (Mertler & Charles, 2011). The main reason for this is that the research has already been conducted and, in some cases, completed. The review of related literature is almost exclusively written in the past tense, since you are summarizing research that has already occurred and been published or otherwise disseminated. Your methodology, results, and conclusions sections are also written in the past tense for the same reason, in that they have already occurred. However, some sections may be written in the *present* tense. Introductory sections of reports—where the topic is introduced and the research questions and hypotheses are stated—are typically written in the present tense. This is because the researcher is describing a *current* situation, problem, or concern. Since the situation or concern is ongoing—and likely was not resolved as a result of the study—it remains a current issue and should be described in that manner. Also, any recommendations for the future, including your action plan, are probably most appropriately written in present or future tense (Mertler, 2014).

The specific advice offered in the APA manual (Section 3.18, p. 78) is that the past tense should be used to express an action or a condition that already occurred and did so at a specific time in the past, such as when you report the results of another researcher's work (e.g., "Jones (2006) *presented* similar results . . ."). When presenting a past action or condition that did *not* occur at a specific, definite point in time, the present-perfect tense should be used (e.g., "Since 2000, several researchers have arrived at similar conclusions").

Anonymity and Confidentiality In Chapter 4, you read about the importance of maintaining anonymity and confidentiality with respect to participants in any research study. This ethical consideration also most certainly extends to the writing process. When developing a final research report, it is crucial that the researcher keep the identities of participants involved in the study confidential. This can be accomplished through the use of pseudonyms or simply by not providing identifiable details. This not only pertains to individual participants but also to participating schools or districts.

Tentative Versus Definitive Statements When reporting the results of research studies, researchers must be careful to avoid making statements with too much confidence or certainty (Mertler, 2014). In some sections of your report, you can be definitive, while in others it is essential that you remain at least somewhat tentative (Mertler & Charles, 2011). When describing your methodology (i.e., your research design, data collection), you should be *quite* definitive and precise. You are trying to create for your readers a clear picture of your study and of the procedures you followed. You can also be definitive when reporting the results of descriptive statistical analyses. If you report the number of students involved in your study, the mean and standard deviation for a set of test scores, or the percentage of students who indicated that they prefer the current class schedule in a particular school building, you can provide specific numbers, even to exact decimal places if you desire. Since there are customary and *objective* methods of calculating the mean, standard deviation, and percentages, there will be no question (i.e., nothing left to individual interpretation) regarding the values you obtain and ultimately report (Mertler, 2014). In other words, two individuals cannot take the same set of data, independently calculate the mean, and obtain different values. Thus, it is acceptable to write such statements as the following:

The mean for the sample was equal to 29.11, and the standard deviation was 2.45.

Of all the students surveyed, 68% indicated that they liked the current class schedule.

The coefficient of correlation was equal to +.54.

In contrast, when reporting your conclusions and any subsequent implications of your research, you must be more tentative. It is unethical to present any type of research conclusions with absolute certainty. In contrast to descriptive statistical analyses, your inferential analyses (in the case of quantitative data) or inductive analyses (in the case of qualitative data) inherently contain *subjective interpretations* (Mertler, 2014). These results, conclusions, interpretations, or implications may, in fact, differ from individual to individual. Therefore, when stating conclusions or implications, they might read as follows:

> There seem to be different contexts, or situations, within the preschool setting where positive reinforcement is more appropriately used.

> As these results suggest, it may be critical for instruction on this topic to be presented by experts in the field who are also knowledgeable about the reality of K–12 classrooms.

In the case of these two sample statements, notice the tentative nature of each as typified by "There *seem to be* . . ." and "it *may be* critical for . . ." Note that the findings have *not* been presented as absolutes.

Clarity and Consistency   The clarity of any written research report is a crucial aspect for its potential audience. Your final written report should be clear enough for another person to read and duplicate with relative ease the methodological steps you employed (Johnson, 2008). One factor that contributes to enhanced clarity is the use of as few words as possible. It seems like a straightforward tactic, but it is not always *that* straightforward. The simple result of being concise is that your report becomes more readable for your audience. Another technique for achieving clarity in your report is assuming that your readers know nothing about your topic, or your procedures, and you must explain everything to them, in the simplest terms possible. Finally, organizing your report in a logical format can improve its clarity and readability (Johnson, 2008). The use of headings and subheadings enables the reader to follow the same sort of outline you used to write the report, and creates a nice flow. Additional information about formatting research reports is presented later in this chapter.

Striving for consistency in your writing style will also enhance the clarity of your written research report. Your stylistic decisions, word usage, meanings, special symbols, abbreviations, and acronyms should remain as consistent as possible (Mertler & Charles, 2011). For example, if you symbolize the mean with an italicized uppercase *M* early in your report, do so throughout the remainder of your report. The same can be said for formatting, such as indentations, quotes, spacing, and headings; however you format them the first time (ideally in APA style), you should do so the same way *each and every time*. This will let your readers know what to expect as they maneuver through your report. You should also format sections, tables, charts, figures, and references in a consistent manner throughout your research report. All these efforts enable you to create a report that is easier and less cumbersome for your readers to comprehend. The APA manual similarly stresses the importance of continuity in your writing (Section 3.05, p. 65). It states that readers will have a better understanding of your ideas if you strive for continuity in your words, concepts, and development of themes throughout your report.

Simplicity of Language I always remind students in my graduate research methods courses that when writing their research reports, they are not trying to create a novel for the best-seller list! Research reports should be written in straightforward and simple (rather than elaborate and flowery) language (Mertler & Charles, 2011). The APA manual refers to this as the "economy of expression" (Section 3.06, p. 67). It stresses using shorter sentences, eliminating redundancy and wordiness, and avoiding the use of overly detailed descriptions. Failure to follow these guidelines will not impress your readers; rather, they will likely be turned off to reading the rest of your report.

Remember that you are trying to get straight to the point, without adopting a literary style. A key for this is to avoid the *overuse* of adjectives and adverbs (Mertler, 2014). Excessive use of these descriptive terms makes your report more difficult to read. Believe it or not, people will choose to read your report not for entertainment (as they would a novel) but, rather, to become better informed about the topic you investigated—probably because they share your interest in that topic. Do not try to impress your readers with your mastery of a dictionary or the thesaurus tool in your word processor. You need to explain your research procedures, your results, and your conclusions clearly enough for readers to understand them, but you also need to keep your message short and simple. After all, their time is limited—you do not want them to give up or to avoid your report simply because they find it difficult to read (Mertler, 2014).

Conventions of Format

Research reports, regardless of the type of research they stem from, tend to follow a general structure—although those structures can differ for qualitative versus quantitative reports. This structure is based on several **conventions of format**, which essentially provide a generic outline, or at least suggested components, for a typical research report. Most traditional reports contain four to six sections, depending on the type of research conducted (Mertler & Charles, 2011). As you read in Chapter 10, in our discussion of research proposals, reports have standard components. For a proposal, these components include an introduction, a review of literature, and a description of the methodological procedures followed. For a final research report, we add a couple of standard sections—a presentation of the findings and a summary of the conclusions. The organizational outline, as indicated by various headings and subheadings, typically used in traditional quantitative research reports follows this format (Mertler & Charles, 2011):

Introduction

    Statement of the Problem

    Purpose of the Study

Justification of the Study

Research Questions or Hypotheses

Assumptions

Review of Related Literature

Methodology

Participants

Research Design

Instrumentation

Data Collection Procedures

Data Analysis Procedures

Limitations and Delimitations

Results

Conclusions and Recommendations

References

Notice that there are six main sections, in bold type above. These six sections are fairly standard, at least in a quantitative research report. In fact, if you decide at some point to conduct a quantitative thesis or dissertation study, the first five sections—excluding the references—usually correspond to the five chapters that make up the final product. Subheadings can be added wherever appropriate. For example, subheadings are normally added into the literature review section—which can be anywhere from 30 to 100 pages in a thesis or dissertation—to make it more readable. Imagine how difficult it would be to read a 100-page review of literature that does not appear to have any structural organization—each paragraph simply leading to the next (I have had to read such literature reviews, and it is not easy!).

In contrast, qualitative research reports do not have what could be considered a standard template to follow. These reports do not lack structure; in fact, they tend to be well structured and organized. The difference is that each qualitative study is so unique and individualized that it would be nearly impossible to generate a standard outline of headings and subheadings for qualitative research reports.

A final formatting issue that needs to be addressed is the length of the final research report. This is another one of those questions my graduate students commonly ask: *How long does our report have to be?* The easy answer to that question is, *As long as it needs to be to tell your story thoroughly and accurately.* They do not usually like that answer, but it is often the most appropriate one I can offer. There are, of course, more formal guidelines for the length of research reports that depend largely on their purpose. If you are presenting your study to fellow practitioners, I suggest keeping your write-up brief, perhaps between a few and several pages. You might consider starting with just your main headings—they really provide a strong structure, in outline form, to anything you write—and then writing a brief paragraph summary for each one. An alternative would be to start with your main headings but list only bulleted highlights for each section.

If you are submitting a research report for possible presentation at a professional conference, you will need to provide a much greater level of detail for all aspects of your research study. Most papers I present at professional conferences range from 20 to 30 double-spaced pages, although no limit is typically specified for this type of report. Ultimately, you are the best judge of the length of your research reports because you must decide if you have included enough context and detail to give your audience a clear understanding of your study (Mills, 2014). Similarly, if you are submitting your paper for possible publication in an academic journal, that journal will typically provide prospective authors with guidelines for the length of their reports. Submission guidelines will vary, but *average* length for a manuscript submitted to a journal is about 25 to 30 double-spaced pages. In their guidelines for contributors, journal editors typically provide the desired report length in terms of total words. This can seem a bit overwhelming when you see that you have to write several thousand words! To facilitate this process, I use a general conversion rate to determine the approximate—and I emphasize *approximate*—number of typed pages and the corresponding number of formatted pages: *Roughly 2 1/2 pages of double-spaced type will equal 1 page of final, laid-out print.*

Also realize that if and when your article is accepted for publication, the journal will reformat it to meet its publication style. At a minimum, this usually means that your double-spaced report will be reformatted in a different font style and font size, and will probably be single-spaced. For example, an article of mine recently published in a journal was 28 double-spaced pages when I sent the final version to the editor. When it appeared in print, it spanned only 16 of the journal's pages.

Findings or Results   In Chapter 10, we discussed various subsections of the introduction and methodology portions of the research proposal. For the most part, guidelines for the contents of those subsections remain the same, or very similar, in a final research report. The additional sections needed in a final research report are (1) findings and (2) conclusions and recommendations. Because these components can be unique and often pose difficulties for researchers, they warrant further discussion here. First, we will look separately at the presentation of qualitative and quantitative results.

Presentation of Qualitative Results.   One of the aspects of writing research reports that tends to frustrate novice and experienced researchers alike—and perhaps even impede their writing productivity—is how to present the results of their analyses most efficiently and effectively (Mertler, 2014). Depending on the type of data you have collected, the results section may form the majority of your research report. When reporting the results of the analysis of qualitative data, it is important to realize that you are attempting to create for your readers a picture of what you have discovered (Johnson, 2008). You must try to take all you have collected in the form of field notes, interview transcripts, journal entries, and so on, and convert them into something your readers can easily digest (Johnson, 2008). Of primary importance is that you not try to report every bit of data collected; this will only overwhelm your readers. Instead, your goal is to describe the most meaningful trends or patterns you saw emerge from your analyses (Mertler, 2014).

In addition to the suggestions presented earlier, specifically pertaining to conventions of academic-style writing, Johnson (2008) has suggested several more guidelines for reporting the results of qualitative data analyses. Following these five guidelines can help make your research report clearer and more effective for your audience.

1. *Make every effort to be impartial in your write-up.* As we have discussed numerous times throughout this book, it is not possible to be *totally* impartial and objective; human nature simply does not allow it. However, it is essential that qualitative researchers represent all aspects of their research studies as fairly, accurately, and objectively as *possible* (Leedy & Ormrod, 2013). Johnson (2008) stresses that you should try to steer clear of the "letter-to-the-editor syndrome" (p. 198). You are trying to describe your study and what you discovered while conducting it. It is critical that you avoid the inclusion of value-laden statements in your research report. Your audience will likely view frequent expressions of your biases or partiality in a negative light. Consider the following statement:

It was clear that the teachers involved in this study did not value in any way the professional development opportunities presented to them, as they consciously chose not to participate in them.

That statement might be better written as follows:

Observations of the teachers indicated that they did not participate in the professional development opportunities, perhaps because they did not see their value.

Phrases such as "it was clear" and "consciously chose not to participate" have negative connotations and imply value judgments on the part of the researcher. These types of statements should be avoided, whenever feasible.

2. *Include references to yourself where they are warranted.* In research reports, it is completely acceptable to use first-person pronouns—such as *I*, *my*, and *me*—when describing something you did in the context of your qualitative research study. For example, it would be appropriate to write the following:

During this study, I collected data by observing and interviewing 14 students.

You played an active role in the study—likely as a participant on some level—and it would be awkward to refer to yourself using less personal forms of reference, such as *the researcher* or *the author*. In addition, such labels become more cumbersome for the readers of a qualitative research report. With this in mind, however, try not to overuse these types of references. You are still writing a scientific research report; you do not want it to read like a personal journal or diary.

3. *Take your readers through all aspects of your study.* Allow your readers to see the study through your eyes. Do not leave out any details of what you did and why you did it. You should follow—as closely as possible, allowing yourself some degree of personalization—the formatting for outlines of research proposals (as presented in Chapter 10) and for research reports (as presented earlier in this chapter). Even if you decide not to label your sections using these particular headings, you should still include all the integral aspects of your study. The basic rule of thumb is that someone reading your research report should be able to replicate what you did (i.e., your exact procedures) simply by reading your account of the study.

4. *Include representative samples when they enhance your presentation.* Anytime you incorporate samples of verbatim quotes from oral interviews or word-for-word excerpts from a participant's journal, your data are much more likely to come alive for the reader (Johnson, 2008). Your data, as well as your analyses and interpretations of those data, will become much more interesting. From the reader's perspective, these samples create a true sense of being there, as if the reader is observing the participants interacting within their setting, for example. The following is a passage from the discussion section of my report on a study of positive reinforcement in a preschool setting:

> *Initially, Carol stated that positive reinforcement means not yelling at children. It means talking to them in a positive way. She revealed that giving children choices is central to her beliefs. Instead of punishing them (e.g., by placing them in time-out), she tries to turn displays of negative behavior into something constructive. As an example, Carol mentioned Ethan, who "likes to throw toys at everybody. Instead of putting him in the corner and me picking up all the toys he's thrown, I make a game out of it. Instead of 'Ethan, pick them up, pick them up,' we count them as we put them in. So he's still having to do what he did, you know, having to clean up his mess, but we're making a game out of it, instead of 'this was wrong and you're going to sit in the corner for this.'"*

Notice how the inclusion of Carol's verbatim account reads in a much more interesting fashion than if I had summarized what she said in my own words.

5. *Include interesting but nonessential information in appendices, whenever appropriate.* Often, you will have information that you think might be interesting to your readers but that would interrupt the flow of the report or make it incredibly lengthy. Readers might get bogged down with the details—and perhaps the volume—of this information. For example, members of your audience might appreciate and enjoy reading the transcripts from your interviews or your complete field notes from observation sessions *but* as an aspect of the research *outside* of the report itself. Such information would most certainly be too lengthy to include in the body of your research report; however, if you believe that your readers might be interested in seeing it, you can include it in *appendices*

at the end of your report. These sections are appropriate for research reports presented in local venues or at professional conferences, where there is typically not a set page limit. Conversely, they would likely be inappropriate for inclusion in reports submitted to journals, because they may make a document too lengthy to publish. For example, the complete, final report from my positive reinforcement study was 88 double-spaced pages—36 pages made up the body of the report, and 52 pages formed the appendices (i.e., observation field notes and interview transcripts).

Presentation of Quantitative Results. Although there are more options for reporting the results of quantitative data analyses, the task is not necessarily simpler. You can present the results of analyses of numerical data in narrative form or in graphical, visual form. Similar to the presentation of qualitative data analyses, many of the general suggestions for writing up research also apply to the reporting of quantitative analyses. However, Johnson (2008) has also provided several additional guidelines for reporting the results of quantitative data analyses. The following six guidelines will help make the presentation of quantitative results clearer and more understandable for a research audience.

1. *Suggestions for expressing quantifiable data using numerals.* There are specific guidelines for presenting numerical data, according to the APA manual. Numerals (e.g., 1, 14, 251) should be used to express quantifiable information in the following cases:

- For any value greater than or equal to 10 (e.g., *a total of 24 interviews were conducted*)
- When specifying dates, ages, or time (e.g., *the study began on September 10, 2004, and lasted 12 weeks*)
- When reporting the number of participants in a study (e.g., *there were 57 students who participated in the program*)
- When indicating grade level (e.g., *most children learn how to read in Grades 1 and 2*)
- When reporting scores or ratings (e.g., *Thomas received a score of 25 out of a possible 35 points on the instrument*)

2. *Suggestions for expressing quantifiable data using words.* The APA manual also provides guidelines for presenting numerical information using words (e.g., *one, fourteen, two hundred fifty-one*). Words should be used to represent numerical data in the following situations:

- For values less than 10 (e.g., *for the collection of data, six observations and three interviews were conducted*)
- For numbers that begin sentences (e.g., *Fifty-seven students participated in the program*) [Note: Due to the awkward nature of this sentence structure, my general suggestion is to try to avoid starting any sentence with a number.]

3. *Numerical data should be reported in descending order (from greatest to least).* Numerical data presented in quantifiable order make more sense and are easier for most people to read and understand. While I prefer presenting data from greatest value to least, the reverse order is equally acceptable. Consider the following statement:

When asked to indicate their favorite subject, 65 students preferred science, 35 preferred language arts, 28 preferred social studies, and 19 preferred math.

This seems to be more easily understood than a variation organized alphabetically, for example:

When asked to indicate their favorite subject, 35 students preferred language arts, 19 preferred math, 65 preferred science, and 28 preferred social studies.

4. *Report the total number involved before reporting numbers in categories.* In an effort to improve the clarity of the previous example, researchers should always report the total number of participants prior to reporting the numbers in individual categories:

Students were asked to indicate their favorite subject. Of the 147 responses, 65 students preferred science, 35 preferred language arts, 28 preferred social studies, and 19 preferred math.

5. *Use tables to organize larger amounts of numerical data.* Tables are efficient tools to organize lots of numerical data in a nonrepetitive, condensed manner. Tables are *not* meant to take the place of information written in the text of a report but, rather, to *complement* that information. That being said, a table can stand on its own—for example, during a conference presentation. Often, when making formal presentations of research at a conference, researchers will show tables to the audience and use them as the basis for discussing the results. An example of this complementary relationship between a narrative presentation of results and a table of data, from a paper I presented a few years ago, appears in Figure 14.1. Notice how some, but not all, of the same information is provided in both the text and the table; they do not present identical information. Also, the table could be used as a visual aid and a mechanism for discussing the results during a presentation of the study. Note the stylistic formatting of the table, which closely follows APA style.

6. *Figures can also be used to organize and present numerical data, largely without numbers.* Figures can depict the results of data analysis visually and graphically. Various types of visuals that can be used as figures were presented in Chapter 13. Figures are not labeled in the same manner as tables, per APA style. The word *figure* is capitalized but also italicized, and the figure number appears below the figure itself. The title of the figure appears on the same line as the figure number. Shown in Figure 14.2 is an example of a histogram, along with its complementary text, from the same research paper as the previous example of the table.

FIGURE 14.1   ●   Example of the Complementary Relationship Between the Text and a Table in a Research Report

A second phase of pilot testing with the revised ALI was conducted during spring 2004 with 250 preservice teachers. It is important to note that similarity between the two institutions was established by examining the means, standard deviations, and reliability coefficients, as well as statistically comparing the total scores on the ALI across the two groups (see Table X). After deleting outliers with standardized total scores (i.e., z-scores) exceeding ±3.00 (of which there was only one case), the total scores were compared for the first ($M = 24.50$, $SD = 4.92$) and second ($M = 22.98$, $SD = 4.05$). No significant difference was found between total ALI scores for the two institutions, $t(247) = 2.558$, $p > .01$, two-tailed.

Table X.

Descriptive Statistics for the Total ALI Scores for the Two Institutions Studied

Institution	N	Mean	Standard Deviation	r_{KR20}
Institution #1	150	24.50	4.92	.78
Institution #2	99	22.98	4.05	.62
Total	249	23.90	4.64	.74

Since figures are not treated the same as tables, each is numbered sequentially, in the order in which it is referenced in the research report. In other words, tables are numbered sequentially, beginning with Table 1, and figures are also numbered sequentially, beginning with Figure 1. Imagine you had both tables and figures in your report, appearing in this order: a table—a table—a figure—a table—a figure. The sequence of tables and figures would be numbered in the following manner:

Table 1

Table 2

Figure 1

Table 3

Figure 2

Conclusions, Discussion, and Recommendations   In the fifth section of most research reports, the researcher presents and discusses the conclusions reached during the investigation. Sometimes, especially in theses and dissertations, this section is called "Conclusions and Recommendations." In shorter reports, it may be labeled "Findings" or "Findings and Implications." In this final section, the researcher—at last!—has the

FIGURE 14.2 ● Example of the Complementary Relationship Between the Text and a Figure in a Research Report

Examination of the item analysis results from this phase revealed a value similar to that resulting from the first phase for instrument reliability, $r_{KR20} = 0.74$. Across the 35 items appearing on the ALI, item difficulty values range from a low of 0.212 to a high of 0.992; the mean item difficulty was equal to 0.681. The entire distribution of difficulty values is presented in Figure X.

Figure X.

Distribution of ALI item difficulty values

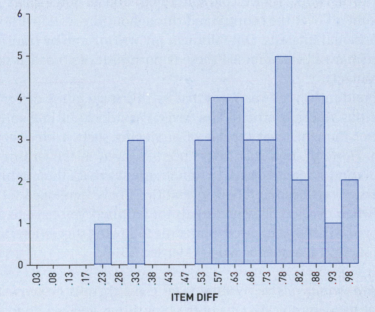

ITEM DIFF

opportunity to interpret and otherwise discuss the conclusions from the study. This portion is often quite meaningful because, to a large degree, it is the researcher's first opportunity in the report to let the audience know what he or she thinks about the results of the study. However, it is important to note that this section should not be used purely for speculation. This is not a place to talk about things that really do not "fit" anywhere else in the report. The researcher can speculate and interpret, but those discussions should be based only on the actual research findings and also should be tied back to the literature review. It is critical to show how the findings of the research study either support or contradict the existing body of literature. If the research study was undertaken to fill a gap in that body of research literature, to what degree has that gap been filled by the present research? More than anything else, the conclusions, discussions, and recommendations section is the portion of the report that allows you to tell what you believe the findings mean, how you have interpreted them, what they imply for education, or what they suggest for further research. Admittedly, this is the one place in the report where you are allowed to speculate a bit, to move a little beyond hard evidence and strict logic—but only within reason.

Practical Guidelines for Writing

Writing—some people love it; others detest it. Regardless of which side of that fence you fall on, it is important to recognize that writing of an academic nature is arguably the one aspect of any profession that keeps that profession changing, growing, and expanding (Mertler, 2014). Communication—especially of research and research findings—among the members of any given profession allows those members to stay abreast of new ideas, innovations, and opportunities. Writing is the primary mechanism through which we can learn more about a given topic, share with others what we know about a topic, and gather ideas for new things to try in our profession. In addition, professional communication about a specific topic can provide exceptional opportunities to network. I have communicated, and in some cases actually met, with people from all over the country and throughout the world with whom I share common professional interests. Only through my writing and by reading the written works of others have I been afforded these opportunities to broaden my network of professional contacts.

If you had told me several years ago that by this stage in my career I would have written numerous research articles and several textbooks, I probably would have laughed. I never thought I was capable of producing such written works related to my profession. However, now that I have been engaged in the writing process for a number of years and several projects, I can honestly say that I thoroughly enjoy it! For me, the key has always been to follow several tips I have developed for myself. Keep in mind that when developing your "rituals for writing," you have to find out what works best for *you*. With that in mind, I offer the following suggestions to help each of you become a successful academic writer (Mertler, 2014):

1. *Establish a writing routine.* Writing takes time; there is no sense thinking it is something that happens quickly. One of the best things you can do to facilitate your writing is to make it part of your professional life. Find time where it falls, or make time if necessary. In this way, writing becomes just another one of our important professional activities. In addition, find a comfortable place to write—perhaps at your home computer or with a legal pad and a pencil at your kitchen table. Find a place that works for you, and make it part of your routine.

2. *Try to write at the same time every day.* Along with establishing a writing routine, try to build into your daily schedule some time for writing. Perhaps it will be 30 minutes or an hour. Regardless of the amount of time, make it a regular part of your daily routine. For example, you might decide that 30 minutes before school is the best time for you to write, or maybe after school or after dinner will be best.

3. *Write as if you are talking to a friend.* Remember that you are trying to communicate your study and the results as clearly as possible. When you write, imagine that you are telling a friend about your study. This friend knows nothing about the topic, so you must communicate all aspects of the study in understandable, simple terms.

4. *Begin with an outline and organize your thoughts accordingly.* When I write, I begin by developing a thorough outline. Then all I have to do is fill in the blanks of the outline. The outline helps keep me on track and focused; plus, it creates a series of checkpoints for my finished product.

5. *Do not worry initially about spelling, grammar, and how your report reads.* When developing the first draft of a research report, do not focus too much on how your report reads. I believe that many people who are new to academic writing fall victim to this—they try to make their reports read "perfectly" the first time out. Do not concern yourself with finding the ideal phrase or the correct spelling of a given word. At this point in the writing process, you should be focused only on getting your thoughts, ideas, and information on paper. At this stage, Mills (2011) advises researchers to "look for progress, not perfection" (p. 181). You will have ample opportunities to refine your writing at a later stage.

6. *Remember that writing a first draft is only the first step in the writing process.* When you begin to write, it is important to realize that you are writing a first draft. You will have opportunities to edit and revise . . . and then edit and revise again. This part of the process enables you to further refine and clarify your thoughts and ideas; each time, they become a little more coherent, clear, and cohesive, bringing an improved sense of flow to your report.

7. *Develop a commitment to writing throughout all phases of the research study.* Writing should not be treated as merely the final step in the process. By making an ongoing commitment to writing, the researcher is able to continuously generate thoughts, provoke additional ideas, and make sense of the overall writing process. In addition, this discipline makes the development of the final research report somewhat easier, since writing has been occurring all along.

8. *Last, but in my mind most important, develop a realistic writing schedule.* If you begin writing with no clear sense of schedule, you essentially lack the incentive to continue making progress on your report. Developing a realistic—and I stress the word *realistic*—schedule for your writing is the first thing you should do, before ever putting your first word on paper. A writing schedule—along with the detailed outline you develop in Suggestion 4 above—really provides the skeletal framework for your completed research report.

These suggestions—especially Suggestion 8—have helped me throughout my various writing projects. The closer I can stick to my writing schedule, the more successful my writing project will be. In addition, there is something to be said for being able to check off sections of your report as you complete them; it creates a sense of accomplishment, provides you with repeated opportunities to pat yourself on the back, and provides the necessary encouragement to keep going, because you can see the light at the end of the proverbial tunnel! As an example, the photo that appears in Figure 14.3 is a page from my writing calendar for this book. Notice how I crossed days off and checked chapters off as I completed them. Just remember to find what works for you, and stick with it.

FIGURE 14.3 ● Sample Page From the Author's Writing Calendar

An Example of a Research Report

Several times throughout this book, I have alluded to the research study I conducted on the influence of No Child Left Behind on teachers' assessment and instructional practices, including excerpts from the research proposal (see Chapter 10) and data collection instrumentation (see Chapter 12). Appendix A contains the complete research report resulting from this study; this report was presented at two professional conferences and was also published in a peer-reviewed journal (Mertler, 2010).

Developmental Activities

1. Do you believe that writing a research report is an important, culminating activity in the research process? Why or why not? Provide justifications for your responses.

2. Identify and obtain a copy of a published research article, or another research report, on a topic of interest to you. Based on the various guidelines and suggestions presented in this

chapter (i.e., conventions of style, conventions of format, and guidelines for presenting the results of analyses), write a brief critique of the research report, highlighting those aspects of the written report that the author(s) did well and those aspects that you believe could be improved.

3. Find a report of qualitative research related to an area of interest to you. What types of things do you notice about the writing style? Which of the suggestions presented in the chapter did the author(s) follow? Which suggestions did the author(s) not follow?

4. Find a report of quantitative research related to an area of interest to you. What types of things do you notice about the writing style? Which

of the suggestions presented in the chapter did the author(s) follow? Which suggestions did the author(s) not follow?

5. Conduct a quick survey of at least 20 people, asking them to indicate their favorite color. Once you have collected your data, analyze them using both qualitative and quantitative techniques. First, use inductive analysis to develop groups—based on color preference—and numbers of people within each group. Report your results in narrative fashion. Second, analyze your data quantitatively by counting the number of responses for each color identified. Report your results three ways: narratively, using a table, and using an appropriate graph or figure.

Summary

- When writing a research report, it is important to have knowledge of your audience and their expectations.
- Conventions are agreed-on procedures that help ensure the accuracy of data and findings in written research reports.
- Several style guides exist, but the most commonly used and well-known guide in the field of education is the *Publication Manual of the American Psychological Association*, or APA manual.
- Most universities have adopted a style that they prefer for written research reports.
- Conventions of academic-style writing are agreed-on procedures that help ensure the readability and credibility of research reports. They require attention to the following:

  ○ Titles
  ○ Person and voice
  ○ Tense
  ○ Tentative versus definitive statements
  ○ Clarity
  ○ Consistency
  ○ Simplicity of language

- Generally speaking, qualitative research reports are written in the first person and quantitative reports are written in the third person.
- Most research reports are written in the past tense, although some sections may be written in the present tense.
- Conventions of format are agreed-on procedures that provide a general structure for a typical research report.

- The six main sections of any research report are as follows:

  - Introduction
  - Review of related literature
  - Methodology
  - Results
  - Conclusions and recommendations
  - References

- The length of a research report will vary based on its purpose and intended audience.
- Qualitative results should be presented in an unbiased manner, may appropriately include references to the researcher, should walk readers through all aspects of the study, include representative samples, and should incorporate nonessential information in appendices.
- Quantitative results include the appropriate expression of quantifiable data according to guidelines in the APA manual, should report numerical data in descending order, and should use tables and figures to support results presented in the text.
- The conclusions and recommendations section of a report is an opportunity for the researcher to share personal opinions and insights about the study.
- Academic writing is not an easy task for everyone. Practical guidelines that can help researchers achieve their goals include the following:

  - Establishing a writing routine
  - Writing at the same time each day
  - Writing as if you are talking to a friend who knows nothing about your topic
  - Beginning with an outline and organizing your thoughts
  - Not worrying about spelling, grammar, and readability during the drafting stages
  - Remembering that a rough draft is just the first step of the writing process
  - Developing a realistic writing schedule

$SAGE edge™

Sharpen your skills with SAGE edge!

edge.sagepub.com/mertler

SAGE edge for Students provides a personalized approach to help you accomplish your coursework goals in an easy-to-use learning environment. You'll find action plans, mobile-friendly eFlashcards, and quizzes as well as video, web, and resources and links to SAGE journal articles to support and expand on the concepts presented in this chapter.

Teachers' Perceptions of the Influence of *No Child Left Behind* on Classroom Practices

Abstract

Due to the magnitude of *NCLB*, the pressure on teachers has increased to perhaps immeasurable proportions. One could argue that *NCLB* has ramifications for nearly all aspects of the teaching–learning process, including classroom-based assessment. The purpose of this study was to describe the extent to which K–12 teachers perceive that *NCLB* has influenced their instructional and assessment practices. Differences based on several demographic variables were also examined. An original instrument was administered to teachers and 1,534 responses were received. Salient findings revealed that teachers believe *NCLB* is having negative impacts on instructional and curricular practices, including higher levels of stress related to improving student performance. Teachers reported several changes in how they assess students. Significant group differences were found, particularly on the resultant components of *Student Test Preparation* and *Instructional Changes*.

Background

The *No Child Left Behind Act of 2001* (*NCLB*) requires all states in the nation to set standards for grade-level achievement and to develop a system to measure the progress of all students and subgroups of students in meeting those state-determined grade-level standards (U.S. Department of Education, 2004). This act represents a marked departure from the efforts of the Clinton administration to develop a single national test. *NCLB* provides a mandate for national testing, but leaves the format and design of the test up to individual states (Sloane & Kelly, 2003). Furthermore, because of the inconsistencies in the implementation of the mandate, students in some states will

Adapted from Mertler, C. A. (2010). Teachers' perceptions of the influence of No Child Left Behind on classroom practices. *Current Issues in Education, 13*(3). Available online: http://cie.asu.edu/ojs/index.php/cieatasu/article/viewFile/392/31

not graduate or be promoted unless they are able to pass their respective state's test (Kober, 2002). In this most recent era of high-stakes testing, the amount of pressure and stress imposed upon students—and teachers, as well—has increased immensely. Many leaders believe that this push for increased test scores, with little regard for how those improvements are attained, have created an accountability system that tends to cultivate inappropriate and sometimes unethical behaviors on the part of educators. Additionally, research has cited the fact that large-scale, high-stakes standardized testing movements actually result in decreases in student learning. For example, in their study of high-stakes test data from 18 states, Amrein and Berliner (2002) concluded that student learning is indeterminate, remains at the same level it was before the policy was implemented, or actually *decreases* [emphasis added] when high-stakes testing policies are instituted. They further concluded that a transformation of current high-stakes testing policies is warranted due largely to this lack of improvement to student learning, as well as unintended consequences associated with high-stakes testing policies (e.g., increased drop-out rates, teachers' and schools' cheating on exams, teachers' defection from the profession).

Due to the magnitude of the *NCLB* testing mandates, the extent of this "pressure to perform" and its impact on teachers and their classroom practices has increased to perhaps immeasurable proportions. Nonetheless, it is imperative for the educational community at large to better understand the degree to which teachers have altered their instructional and assessment practices based primarily on their knowledge, understanding, and implementation of *NCLB*. The purpose of this study was to describe the extent to which K–12 teachers perceive that *NCLB* has influenced their instructional and assessment practices. Additionally, the study sought to determine if any differences in these perceptions existed based on gender, school level, education level, teaching experience, and school and district rating.

The Impact of *No Child Left Behind*

The *No Child Left Behind Act* has been the topic of substantial debate since its enactment in early 2002. Arguably, its most crucial component is the heightened requirement for—as well as its greater importance placed on—accountability and high-stakes testing. Few people would disagree with the notion that high-stakes testing can be a driving force behind fundamental change in schools. However, there is little agreement as to whether this change is for better or for worse (Abrams, Pedulla, & Madaus, 2003). Whereas, some have argued that the guarantee of rewards and the threats of sanctions will promote higher quality teaching and, therefore, higher student achievement, others have argued that focusing instruction on the ultimate goal of performance on high-stakes tests only limits the scope of classroom instruction and student learning. Research studies have revealed somewhat mixed findings regarding the impact of *NCLB*, depending on whether one examines its effects on student achievement or its effects on motivation and stress.

In comparing student achievement and growth in achievement prior to the implementation of *NCLB* (school year 2001–2002) and following its implementation (school year 2003–2004), researchers at the Northwest Evaluation Association found mixed results in their analyses of mathematics and reading assessment data from over 320,000 students in more than 200 school districts in over 22 states. The main finding reported by Cronin, Kingsbury, McCall, and Bowe (2005) was that mathematics and reading scores had improved over the initial two-year period of *NCLB*. However, they also found that student growth scores had decreased, that students in grade levels tested by state assessments have higher achievement and growth than students who are in non-tested grades, and that student growth in every ethnic group had decreased slightly since *NCLB* was implemented. The researchers concluded that there is evidence that *NCLB* has improved student achievement, but if the change in achievement continues at roughly the same magnitude, *NCLB* will not bring schools anywhere near the requirement of 100 percent proficiency by 2014.

Research has not been limited to examinations of the effects of *NCLB* and its testing requirements on student achievement, but has also investigated the effects on student and teacher motivation. Abrams et al. (2003) and Stecher (2002) delineate several positive and negative effects on both students and teachers. The positive effects on students include that high-stakes tests motivate them to work harder in school, provide them with better information about their own knowledge and skills, and send clearer signals to students about what to study. Frustration, discouragement from trying, increased competition, and a general devaluation of grades and school assessments are the primary negative student effects.

Positive effects on teachers include improvements in the diagnosis of individual student needs and the identification of strengths and weaknesses in the curriculum, as well as increased motivation to work harder and smarter, to align instruction with standards, and to identify content not mastered by students, thus allowing for redirected instruction. These positive effects are countered by the facts that high-stakes tests increase stress and decrease morale among teachers, encourage teachers to focus more on specific test content rather than on standards, lead teachers to engage in inappropriate and unethical test preparation practices, and entice teachers to cheat when preparing or administering tests (Abrams et al., 2003; Stecher, 2002). According to teachers, much of this pressure comes from district administrators, building administrators, and the media (Herman & Golan, n.d.).

That being said, there is certainly a lack of agreement regarding the effects of testing on student motivation. Some believe that high-stakes accountability testing is unfairly criticized for these effects (Sloane & Kelly, 2002). The authors discuss that it is not clear if the anxiety experienced by students in high-stakes testing situations is due to the tests themselves—as well as the consequences of the resulting test scores—or to generally ineffective preparation for learning, which may be attributable to numerous causes, which could possibly include poor instruction.

Teachers' Perceptions of *No Child Left Behind*

Since the implementation of *NCLB*, research has shown that, generally speaking, teachers do not have favorable perceptions of the law. In 2004, researchers at The Civil Rights Project at Harvard surveyed over 1,400 teachers regarding their knowledge of *NCLB* and how they were responding to its mandates (Sunderman, Tracey, Kim, & Orfield, 2004). Among the key findings from the study, teachers confirmed that the accountability system created by *NCLB* is influencing the instructional and curricular practices of teachers, but is also producing unintended and possibly negative consequences. Specifically, teachers reported that they ignored important aspects of the curriculum, de-emphasized or completely neglected untested topics, and tended to focus their instruction on tested subjects, sometimes excessively. Additionally, these teachers rejected the idea that *NCLB*'s testing requirements would ultimately focus teachers' instruction and/or improve the curriculum. Finally, teachers who were teaching in schools that had been identified as needing improvement reported that they did not plan to be teaching in those same schools five years in the future. Generally, teachers believed that *NCLB* sanctions would cause teachers to transfer out of schools not making adequate progress (Sunderman et al., 2004).

In a survey conducted by the *NCLB* Task Force of the National Staff Development Council, nearly half of the 2,000 educators responding to the survey believed that the impact of *NCLB* on professional development has had "no discernable effect." These teachers reported that professional development activities were more of an obligation, as opposed to being meaningful, useful professional learning opportunities. Only a small percentage (14%) believed the *NCLB*-funded professional development is "improving the quality of teaching" (National Staff Development Council [NSDC], 2004).

Furthermore, and perhaps more pertinent to this study, the results of the NSDC survey revealed that nearly 60% of teachers believed that the law is having a negative impact on their work settings. Forty percent reported that they experience *NCLB* implementation pressures that negatively impact teacher morale and performance (NSDC, 2004). One-tenth reported that one effect of the law is that teachers are being forced to divert their attention away from more important educational issues that could improve teaching and learning. Approximately the same proportion believed that educators are carrying on their work much as they did prior to the implementation of *NCLB*. In contrast, over one-fourth of responding teachers indicated that the law is having a more positive effect, as evidenced by the fact that many educators were beginning to think, talk, and act in new ways that could ultimately result in higher levels of student performance (NSDC, 2004).

No Child Left Behind and Classroom Assessment

Since *NCLB* places such high-stakes consequences on its mandated standardized testing, teachers must do a more thorough job of teaching to their respective curricular standards. They must also engage in meaningful and valid classroom assessment in order to accurately determine the knowledge and skills that have been mastered by their students, as well as those content areas that may require redirected instruction to entire classes or individualized student reinforcement. One could make the argument that *NCLB* has far-reaching ramifications for nearly all aspects of the teaching–learning process, of which classroom-based student assessment is a part. Unfortunately, at this point in time, very little research exists regarding the relationship between *NCLB* and teachers' classroom assessment practices.

In a statewide survey conducted with teachers in Virginia, McMillan, Myran, and Workman (1999) found that more than three-fourths of elementary teachers and one-third of secondary teachers believed that their statewide testing program had a "somewhat" or "extensive" impact on their teaching and assessment. Specifically, teachers reported that they did not cover untested areas of the curriculum nearly as much as those areas that were tested, and that they tended to emphasize breadth rather than depth of content coverage. Teachers also reported greater use of multiple-choice formats on their self-developed classroom tests. Many teachers identified accountability and increased pressures as the driving forces behind these changes in assessment and instruction (McMillan et al., 1999). These results have been supported by a more recent, nationwide survey of more than 4,000 teachers (Abrams et al., 2003).

With respect to a smaller, yet important, aspect of this relationship, there is research that has examined the arena of test preparation practices. Researchers have identified five types of legitimate test preparation practices that help students demonstrate more completely their knowledge and skills. These strategies include teaching the entire content domain, using a variety of assessment and test item formats, teaching time management skills, fostering student motivation, and reducing test anxiety (Gulek, 2003; Miyasaka, 2000). These practices are considered by the measurement community to be ethical strategies for helping students prepare to take high-stakes tests, largely because they produce student learning that is robust; that is to say, the learning is generalizable to contexts beyond student performance on the test (Gulek, 2003).

However, inappropriate test preparation practices also abound. The basic problem with these practices is that they focus only on raising scores on a given test without also increasing students' knowledge and skills in the broader subject being tested (Kober, 2002; Gulek, 2003). These practices include such teacher behaviors as limiting content instruction to a particular item format, teaching of those objectives from the domain that are sampled on the test, using instructional guides that review actual items from a recent issue of a test, and limiting instruction to actual test items (Gulek, 2003; Mehrens, 1991). Abrams, Pedulla, and Madaus (2003) summarized research in which teachers reported giving greater attention, with regard to instruction and assessment, to content areas they knew would appear on a state test. Some teachers reported de-emphasizing or completely neglecting untested subjects or content. These types of practices are arguably a result of the stress and pressure experienced by teachers to raise test scores (Stecher, 2002; Mehrens, 1991).

Purpose of the Study

The purpose of this study was to describe the extent to which K–12 teachers perceive that *NCLB* has influenced their instructional and assessment practices. Additionally, the study sought to determine if any differences in these perceptions existed based on gender, school level, education level, teaching experience, and school and district rating. The specific research questions addressed in this study were:

1. What are K–12 teachers' perceptions of *NCLB*?
2. In what ways do teachers believe that *NCLB* has influenced their instruction and assessment practices?
3. What differences in the perceptions of *NCLB*'s influence on assessment practices exist between groups as determined by gender, school level, education level, teaching experience, and school rating?

Methods

Participants

The population for this study included all K–12 teachers in the state of Ohio during the 2005–2006 school year. Participation was sought through initial contact with superintendents from 156 school districts (roughly 25% of the total 614 school districts in the state). This initial list was randomly selected from the Ohio Department of Education's online database of school districts (http://www.ode.state.oh.us/data/extract_oed_addgrades.asp). Email communications with the superintendents provided them with an explanation of the study and asked for their agreement to allow their teachers to participate. By using this procedure, the researcher was not required to have access to individual teachers' email addresses. Once a superintendent agreed to allow the district's teachers to participate, he or she was asked to simply forward an email "cover letter" to respective teachers via email. Thirty-eight of the 156 districts (24%) agreed to participate. The researcher sought an additional random sample of 105 districts. From the second random sample, 15 districts agreed to participate. Completed surveys were submitted from 1,534 teachers representing 53 school districts (more than 20% of those districts randomly sampled) across the state.

Instrumentation

An original Web-based survey instrument, titled the *NCLB * CAP (Classroom Assessment Practices) Survey*, consisting of 22 items, was developed for purposes of data collection. Teacher respondents were instructed to respond to each statement on a four-point Likert scale, ranging from "strongly disagree" to "strongly agree." For purposes of addressing Research Question #3, six additional demographic questions were asked of respondents. They were asked to indicate their gender, teaching level, education level, years of teaching experience, and school district and school building rating, as determined by the Ohio Department of Education (ODE).

With respect to these last two questions, some explanation of this rating system is in order. Each year, ODE provides local report cards for each school district and building in the state of Ohio. Both districts and individual buildings are provided with a rating based on multiple measures, including the results from statewide assessments, graduation rates, and attendance as the input variables (Ohio Department of Education [ODE], 2004). Specifically, the three measures are:

- the school's or district's *Adequate Yearly Progress* (AYP) for students in 10 student groups;
- a series of *state indicators*, defined as a minimum percentage of students at or above the proficient level on grade-level achievement tests (at grades 3, 4, 5, 6, 7. and 8) and on the Ohio Graduation Test; and
- a *performance index score*, ranging from 0 to 120, and defined as the average of performance level scores (i.e., below basic, basic, proficient, and advanced) received by students on each of five subjects tested in grades 4 and 6 (ODE, 2004).
- School district ratings and their descriptions are as follows:
- *Excellent*—district meets 22 or 23 (of 23) indicators, or has a score of 100 or more on the Performance Index (PI);
- *Effective*—meets 17 to 21 indicators, or has a score of 90 to 99.9 on the PI;
- *Continuous Improvement*—meets 11 to 16 indicators, or has a score of 80 to 89.9 on the PI, or meets AYP (the lowest a district can be rated is they meet AYP is Continuous Improvement);
- *Academic Watch*—meets 8 to 10 indicators, or has a score of 70 to 79.9 on the PI and has missed AYP; and
- *Academic Emergency*—meets 7 or fewer indicators, has a score less than 70 on the PI and missed AYP (ODE, 2004).

The rating for an individual school is based, in part, on the percentage of indicators that apply directly to that school (rather than out of a total of 23 for the entire district). These school-level ratings are as follows:

- *Excellent*—school meets 94% or more of applicable indicators, or has a score of 100 or more on the Performance Index (PI);
- *Effective*—meets 75% to 93.9% of applicable indicators, or has a score of 90 to 99.9 on the PI;
- *Continuous Improvement*—meets 50% to 74.9% of applicable indicators, or has a score of 80 to 89.9 on the PI, or meets AYP (the lowest a district can be rated is they meet AYP is Continuous Improvement);
- *Academic Watch*—meets 31% to 49.9% of applicable indicators, or has a score of 70 to 79.9 on the PI and missed AYP; and
- *Academic Emergency*—meets 30.9% or fewer indicators, has a score less than 70 on the PI and missed AYP (ODE, 2004).

The initial set of content-based items were adapted from a handful of existing instruments (i.e., Abrams et al., 2003; NSDC, 2004; Sunderman et al., 2004). The *NCLB * CAP Survey* underwent pilot-testing (with data collected from a randomly-selected sample from the population previously described) and revision prior to its implementation. Content-evidence of validity was also collected during the pilot-testing phase, based on reviews from survey research experts, as well as from classroom teachers. An alpha coefficient value equal to .76 was obtained for instrument's overall reliability.

Procedures

School district participation was sought through email communications with the superintendents from the randomly selected districts during late summer. Once a superintendent, or an appropriate designee, agreed to permit the survey to be accessed by the district's teachers, the researcher sent the email "cover letter" to the superintendent and asked that the message be forwarded to the entire teaching staff of that district. Teachers were informed that the survey would require only about 10 minutes to complete, that their responses would remain confidential, and that only aggregate results would be reported. This email message contained an embedded link which provided direct access for respondents to the *NCLB * CAP Survey*. The survey was administered during a three-week period extending from mid-September through early-October. All data were collected and stored electronically.

Data Analyses

All data analyses were conducted using the Statistical Package for the Social Sciences (SPSS, v. 15). Initial data analyses included frequencies, percentages, means, and standard deviations to summarize the overall results. An exploratory factor analysis was conducted as a data reduction technique in order to reduce the number of items for purposes of group comparisons. Analyses of variance were then used to compare group responses based on gender, teaching level, education level, years of teaching experience, district rating, and school rating. All ANOVA results were evaluated at an alpha level equal to .05.

Results

The descriptive, overall results of the analyses are presented first. These results are followed by a discussion of the data reduction procedure and the subsequent group comparisons. Provided in Table 1 is a summary of the demographic characteristics of the sample.

Overall Results

The descriptive results for the 22 items appearing on the survey, including the percentages of response for each point on the scale, means, and standard deviations, are presented in Table 2. With respect to teachers' knowledge of *NCLB*, nearly three-fourths (72%) of teachers responding to the survey indicated that they believed that they knew a lot about *NCLB* and nearly half (43%) specified that they did not care to know anything more about it and its effects on their work as classroom teachers. Nearly three-fourths (73%) of teachers believe that *NCLB* has forced teachers to divert their attention away from the types of issues that can actually improve teaching and learning. Only 31% believed that the overall effect of *NCLB* on their schools has been positive, and only 24% believed that most teachers are carrying on their work much as they did prior to the law.

TABLE 1 ● Demographic Characteristics of Teachers as Represented by Frequencies and Percentages

Demographic Characteristic	Frequency	Percentage
Gender		
Female	1186	78.8
Male	319	21.2
School Level		
Elementary	697	50.4
Secondary	687	49.6
Education Level		
B.A./B.S.	408	26.8
M.A./M.S.	1039	68.2
Doctoral/Specialist	76	5.0
Years of Teaching Experience		
1–5 years	228	15.0
6–10 years	316	20.8
11–15 years	238	15.7
16–20 years	194	12.8
21–25 years	166	10.9
25–30 years	199	13.1
More than 30 years	179	11.8
District Rating		
Excellent	84	5.7
Effective	808	54.5
Continuous Improvement	248	16.7
Academic Watch	298	20.1
Academic Emergency	44	3.0
School Rating		
Excellent	280	19.5
Effective	657	45.8
Continuous Improvement	326	22.7
Academic Watch	122	8.5
Academic Emergency	49	3.4

	TABLE 2 ● *Percentages of Teachers' Responses, Means, and Standard Deviations for Items Appearing on NCLB * CAP Survey (n = 1,531)*				
	Frequencies (Percentages) of Response				
Item	**1** **SD**	**2** **D**	**3** **A**	**4** **SA**	**Mean** **(SD)**
I believe that I know a lot about the No Child Left Behind (*NCLB*) Act.	35 (2%)	392 (26%)	931 (61%)	167 (11%)	2.81 (.65)
NCLB has forced me to change the focus of my classroom instruction.	68 (5%)	441 (29%)	748 (49%)	260 (17%)	2.79 (.77)
NCLB has changed the nature of academic motivation for students and has placed more stress on students.	68 (5%)	338 (22%)	579 (38%)	530 (35%)	3.04 (.87)
NCLB has changed the nature of instructional motivation for teachers and has placed more stress on teachers.	12 (1%)	98 (7%)	599 (40%)	805 (53%)	3.45 (.65)
The importance placed on Ohio's achievement tests and the Ohio Graduation Test (OGT) have led to instruction that violates the standards of good educational practice.	36(2%)	380 (25%)	613 (40%)	488 (32%)	3.02 (.82)
I feel more pressure and stress as a result of the increased testing mandates in Ohio and the related need to improve student performance.	26 (2%)	166 (11%)	629 (42%)	696 (46%)	3.32 (.73)
My students feel more stress as a result of the increased testing mandates in Ohio.	16 (1%)	201 (13%)	642 (42%)	655 (43%)	3.28 (.73)
NCLB has forced me to change the ways in which I assess my students' academic performance.	21 (1%)	356 (24%)	806 (53%)	325 (22%)	2.95 (.71)
As a result of *NCLB*, I create a greater number of my classroom tests such that they mirror the same format and types of questions on the state's achievements tests and/or the OGT.	37 (3%)	284 (19%)	743 (49%)	439 (29%)	3.05 (.76)
I use multiple-choice classroom tests more frequently than I have in the past.	139 (9%)	837 (56%)	398 (27%)	119 (8%)	2.33 (.75)
I have substantially DECREASED the amount of time spent on instruction of content NOT tested on the state-mandated tests.	49 (3%)	345 (23%)	635 (42%)	476 (32%)	3.02 (.82)

Item	Frequencies (Percentages) of Response				Mean (SD)
	1 SD	2 D	3 A	4 SA	
I have NOT let *NCLB* or the state-mandated testing program in Ohio influence what or how I provide instruction to my students.	424 (28%)	842 (56%)	213 (14%)	33 (2%)	1.90 (.71)
I have substantially INCREASED the amount of time spent on instruction of content that I know is covered on the state-mandated tests.	28 (2%)	240 (16%)	742 (49%)	491 (33%)	3.13 (.74)
I have NOT let *NCLB* affect how I assess the academic achievement and progress of my students.	283 (19%)	849 (57%)	322 (22%)	42 (3%)	2.08 (.71)
I spend much more time throughout the year preparing my students for the state-mandated tests.	28 (2%)	272 (18%)	721 (48%)	472 (32%)	3.10 (.75)
As a result of *NCLB*, I now spend more time teaching test-taking skills to my students.	28 (2%)	291 (20%)	817 (55%)	358 (24%)	3.01 (.71)
I have used sample test items from the state tests, approved by the Ohio Department of Education, to help prepare my students to take the tests.	49 (3%)	268 (18%)	699 (47%)	477 (32%)	3.07 (.79)
As a result of *NCLB*, I use standardized test data to help guide and improve my instruction.	46 (3%)	394 (26%)	835 (56%)	219 (15%)	2.82 (.71)
In my school, I believe that most teachers are carrying on their work much as they did before *NCLB*.	311 (21%)	831 (55%)	315 (21%)	46 (3%)	2.06 (.73)
In my school, I believe that *NCLB* has forced teachers to divert their attention away from more important issues that can better improve teaching and learning.	38 (3%)	375 (25%)	674 (45%)	418 (28%)	2.98 (.79)
I do not care to know any more about *NCLB* and its effect on my work as a classroom teacher than I do right now.	148 (10%)	704 (47%)	495 (33%)	153 (10%)	2.44 (.81)
I believe that the overall effect of *NCLB* on my school has been positive.	331 (22%)	698 (47%)	436 (29%)	34 (2%)	2.12 (.77)

The majority of the survey items dealt with the impact of *NCLB* on classroom practice. Some of the more prominent individual item results were found with statements that addressed increased amounts of pressure and stress that are being caused by *NCLB*. An overwhelming majority ($n = 1,404$, 93%) of teachers indicated that *NCLB* has changed the nature of instructional motivation for teachers and has placed more stress on teachers, although a slightly smaller number of teachers ($n = 1,325$, 88%) believed that they *personally* were feeling more pressure and stress. A smaller, but meaningful, number ($n = 1,109$, 73%) of teachers believed that *NCLB*, in general, has changed the nature of academic motivation for and has placed more stress on students; however, more teachers ($n = 1,297$, 85%) felt that *their* students were feeling additional stress, as compared to students in general. Two-thirds ($n = 1,008$, 66%) of teachers agreed that *NCLB* has forced them to change the focus of their classroom instruction. An even greater amount ($n = 1,101$, 72%) indicated that the law and its required testing mandates have led to instruction that violates standards of good educational practice.

According to these teachers, *NCLB* has had a major impact on their instruction of content. The vast majority ($n = 1,266$, 84%) of teachers agreed that *NCLB* had influenced what or how instruction is provided to students. Additionally, 74% ($n = 1,111$) indicated that they have substantially decreased the amount of time spent on content that they knew was *not* tested on the state-mandated tests. Similarly, 82% ($n = 1,233$) responded that they had substantially increased the amount of time spent on content that they knew would appear on the state tests.

Finally, with respect to the assessment of student learning, teachers clearly indicated several prominent impacts of *NCLB*. Three-fourths ($n = 1,131$, 75%) of teachers indicated that *NCLB* had forced them to change the ways in which they assess their students' academic performance. A substantial majority ($n = 1,193$, 80%) indicated that they spent much more time throughout the school year preparing students for the state-mandated tests. Many teachers engaged in this type of preparation by teaching test-taking skills ($n = 1,175$, 79%), by using sample items from previous versions of the state tests to help prepare students to take the tests ($n = 1,176$, 79%), and by creating a greater number of classroom tests so that they mirror the format and item types which appear on the state's tests ($n = 1,182$, 78%). Interestingly, 65% ($n = 976$) disagreed with the statement that they use multiple-choice classroom tests more frequently than in the past.

Factor Analysis Results

In an effort to reduce the number of items into more meaningful clusters of items for purposes of group comparisons, the data were subjected to an exploratory factor analysis. Principal components extraction with varimax rotation was used in order to reduce the number of items to a smaller set of uncorrelated variables for use in analysis of variance procedures. Using the criterion of eigenvalues equal to 1, the analysis returned four components. However, items composing two of the components were so diverse that naming those components proved quite difficult. Therefore, the researcher requested the extraction of three components, which lent themselves nicely to interpretation. This three-component solution explained 52% of the variability across the items. The loadings for this resultant three-component solution are shown in Table 3. Based on the relationships between items within components, it

TABLE 3 ● Loadings, Eigenvalues, Percent of Variance Accounted For, and Reliability Coefficients for Resulting Components			
	Component		
Item	**1**	**2**	**3**
I spend much more time throughout the year preparing my students for the state-mandated tests.	.79	.23	.13
I have used sample test items from the state tests, approved by the Ohio Department of Education, to help prepare my students to take the tests.	.78	.03	.01
I have substantially INCREASED the amount of time spent on instruction of content that I know is covered on the state-mandated tests.	.77	.13	.14
As a result of *NCLB*, I create a greater number of my classroom tests such that they mirror the same format and types of questions on the state's achievements tests and/or the OGT.	.71	.08	.17
As a result of *NCLB*, I now spend more time teaching test-taking skills to my students.	.70	.24	.12
I have substantially DECREASED the amount of time spent on instruction of content NOT tested on the state-mandated tests.	.69	.32	.15
I have NOT let *NCLB* or the state-mandated testing program in Ohio influence what or how I provide instruction to my students.	−.68	−.01	−.25
I have NOT let *NCLB* affect how I assess the academic achievement and progress of my students.	−.66	−.02	−.27
As a result of *NCLB*, I use standardized test data to help guide and improve my instruction.	.63	−.20	.18
I use multiple-choice classroom tests more frequently than I have in the past.	.40	.24	.01
In my school, I believe that most teachers are carrying on their work much as they did before *NCLB*.	−.31	−.20	−.29
I believe that the overall effect of *NCLB* on my school has been positive.	−.11	−.80	.06
In my school, I believe that *NCLB* has forced teachers to divert their attention away from more important issues that can better improve teaching and learning.	.15	.77	.08
The importance placed on Ohio's achievement tests and the Ohio Graduation Test (OGT) have led to instruction that violates the standards of good educational practice.	.11	.76	.14
My students feel more stress as a result of the increased testing mandates in Ohio.	.32	.57	.29

(Continued)

	Component		
Item	1	2	3
NCLB has changed the nature of instructional motivation for teachers and has placed more stress on teachers.	.19	.54	.50
I do not care to know any more about NCLB and its effect on my work as a classroom teacher than I do right now.	−.09	.50	−.04
I feel more pressure and stress as a result of the increased testing mandates in Ohio and the related need to improve student performance.	.41	.49	.36
NCLB has forced me to change the focus of my classroom instruction.	.32	.14	.68
NCLB has changed the nature of academic motivation for students and has placed more stress on students.	.17	.45	.60
I believe that I know a lot about the No Child Left Behind (NCLB) Act.	.01	-.19	.58
NCLB has forced me to change the ways in which I assess my students' academic performance.	.46	.21	.52
Eigenvalue	5.57	3.59	2.27
Percent of variance accounted for [a]	25.33	16.31	10.34
Alpha reliability coefficient [b]	.57	.53	.64

TABLE 3 ● (Continued)

[a]Total percent of variance accounted for by three components = 51.98

[b]Overall alpha reliability = .76

was feasible to attach conceptual labels to each. Following an interpretation of these loadings, Component 1 was labeled *Student Test Preparation*, Component 2 was labeled *Stressful Motivation*, and Component 3 was labeled *Instructional Changes*.

Group Comparisons

The responses (as the three component scores) from teachers were compared across the various demographic data collected (i.e., gender, teaching level, education level, years of teaching experience, district rating, and school rating). These results are summarized in Table 4.

Females scored higher (i.e., they had a higher level of agreement) on each of the three component scores than their male counterparts. However, the differences between females and males were significant only for *Student Test Preparation*, $F(1, 1298) = 5.58$, $p = .02$, $\eta^2 = .004$, and for *Instructional Changes*, $F(1, 1298) = 32.14$, $p < .01$, $\eta^2 = .024$. The difference for *Stressful Motivation* was not significant, $F(1, 1298) = 1.54$, $p = .216$, $\eta^2 = .001$. These results indicate that female teachers are doing more to prepare students to take the state-mandated tests and that they are making more *NCLB*-induced instructional changes

TABLE 4 ● *Summary of Significant Group Comparison Results*

Demographic Factor	Dependent Variable (Component)	F-ratio	P-value	Eta Squared
Gender	Student Test Preparation	5.58	.02	.004
	Instructional Changes	32.14	<.01	.024
School Level	Student Test Preparation	34.40	<.01	.031
	Instructional Changes	53.10	<.01	.042
Years of Teaching Experience	Student Test Preparation	2.80	.01	.013
District Rating	Student Test Preparation	7.03	<.01	.022
School Rating	Student Test Preparation	6.61	<.01	.021

than are male teachers. However, it is important to note that the discrepancy in sample sizes between females ($n = 1{,}186$) and males ($n = 319$) certainly could have impacted these statistical results.

A similar pattern of differences was apparent for the comparisons between elementary and secondary teachers in the sample. Elementary teachers scored higher on all three components than did secondary teachers. However, only two of these differences were significant. The difference for *Student Test Preparation* was significant, $F(1, 1198) = 34.40$, $p < .01$, $\eta^2 = .031$, as was the difference for *Instructional Changes*, $F(1, 1198) = 53.10$, $p < .01$, $\eta^2 = .042$. The difference for *Stressful Motivation* was not significant, $F(1, 1198) = .57$, $p = .45$, $\eta^2 = .000$. These results indicate that elementary teachers are doing more to prepare students to take the state tests and that they are making more instructional changes than are secondary teachers.

Although none of the education level comparisons were significant, teachers with masters degrees scored higher than both those with bachelors or doctoral/specialist degrees on *Student Test Preparation*, $F(2, 1313) = 1.11$, $p = .33$, $\eta^2 = .002$. Those teachers with bachelor's degrees scored higher than the other two groups on *Stressful Motivation*, $F(2, 1313) = 3.03$, $p = .05$, $\eta^2 = .005$. Finally, those with doctoral/specialist degrees scored highest on *Instructional Changes*, $F(2, 1313) = .458, p = 63$, $\eta^2 = .001$.

Those with 6–10 years of teaching experience scored highest on *Student Test Preparation*, where there was a significant difference, $F(6, 1309) = 2.80$, $p = .01$, $\eta^2 = .013$. Scheffé *post hoc* tests revealed the only significant difference to be between those with 6–10 years of experience and those with more than 30 years of experience. There were no significant differences based on years of teaching experience for *Stressful Motivation*, $F(6, 1309) = .77$, $p = .59$, $\eta^2 = .004$, or for *Instructional Changes*, $F(6, 1309) = .74$, $p = .62$, $\eta^2 = .003$.

With respect to the current school district rating, a significant difference was found for the *Student Test Preparation* component, $F(4, 1279) = 7.03$, $p < .01$, $\eta^2 = .022$. Teachers from districts rated as "Academic Emergency" scored significantly higher (indicating that they were engaged in more of these practices) than those rated "Excellent" or "Effective." Additionally, "Academic Emergency" and "Academic Watch" were both significantly different from those rated "Continuous Improvement." Although there were no significant differences for *Stressful Motivation*, $F(4, 1279) = .70$, $p = .59$, $\eta^2 = .002$, those from "Academic Watch" districts scored highest. Similarly, there were no significant differences for *Instructional Changes*, $F(4, 1279) = 1.18$, $p = .32$, $\eta^2 = .004$, those from "Effective" and from "Academic Watch" districts scored highest.

Finally, with regard to the current school building rating, a similar pattern of results was found. There was again a significant difference for *Student Test Preparation*, $F(4, 1241) = 6.61$, $p < .01$, $\eta^2 = .021$, with teachers from "Academic Emergency" and "Academic Watch" schools scoring significantly higher than those from "Excellent" and "Effective" schools. Again, although there were no significant differences for *Stressful Motivation*, $F(4, 1241) = 1.55$, $p = .19$, $\eta^2 = .005$, those from "Academic Emergency" schools scored highest. Similarly, there were no significant differences for *Instructional Changes*, $F(4, 1241) = 1.96$, $p = .10$, $\eta^2 = .006$, those from "Academic Emergency" schools scored highest.

Discussion

The results of this study support those of the limited studies previously conducted on the topic of the impact of *NCLB* on teachers' classroom practices. Consistent with recent studies (Abrams et al., 2003; McMillan et al., 1999; NSDC, 2004; Sunderman et al., 2004), this study found that teachers do not have favorable perceptions of *NCLB*. Specifically, teachers believe that *NCLB* is having negative impacts on both instructional and curricular practices of teachers. The vast majority of teachers in the large sample employed in this study also reported that they have substantially reduced the amount of time spent teaching content that they know is *not* tested on the state-mandated tests and substantially increased time spent on tested content. Previously, 60% of teachers surveyed indicated that *NCLB* was having a negative impact on their work settings (NSDC, 2004); in the present study, 69% of teachers believed that its impact on their work, as well as on their school setting, was negative. Teachers in this study also reported experiencing much greater levels of pressure and stress related to the need to improve student performance as a result of *NCLB* and its associated testing mandates. This stress has also "trickled down" to the students of these teachers. This study has provided empirical evidence of assertions made by Abrams et al. (2003) and Stecher (2002).

Specifically, with respect to classroom assessment practices, the results of this study have strongly supported previous research (Abrams et al., 2003; McMillan et al., 1999). A substantial majority of teachers in this study reported that they had changed the ways in which they assess students, spent more time teaching test-taking skills, used sample items from previous tests, and created a greater number of classroom tests that paralleled the format of state tests. The lone finding from this study that seems to contradict previous research (e.g., McMillan et al., 1999) is that well over half of the teachers reported that they did not use multiple-choice classroom tests more frequently than in the past.

This study found that teachers have experienced a substantial increase in stress and pressure as a result of its testing mandates, as well as the push to improve student performance on those tests. Teachers in this study have reported altering numerous aspects of their instruction, including content coverage and methods of assessing student performance. Teachers believe that these types of changes have forced them to take time away from more important aspects of the teaching–learning process. These results seem to support an assertion made by Abrams et al. (2003) that these state tests are the more powerful influence on teaching practices, as opposed to the content standards themselves.

While it is important to remember that the ultimate purpose of any test is to improve teaching and learning (Kober, 2002), this study strongly supports previous research (e.g., Abrams et al., 2003) that *NCLB*, with its emphasis on and pressure to improve student performance as measured by standardized assessments, has quite possibly led to an increased level of teacher-led student test preparation in our schools. While this appears to be an ethical and admirable effort on the part of teachers, Abrams et al. (2003) are quick to point out that these "highly consequential tests encourage teachers to employ test preparation strategies that may result in improved test scores . . . but may not represent an actual improvement in achievement" (p. 25).

The group comparisons from this study revealed some interesting findings. The fact that there were no significant differences between any subgroups on the *Stressful Motivation* component suggests that all teachers—regardless of gender, school setting, education level, years of teaching experience, or effectiveness ratings—are feeling the stress of this increased accountability and the need to improve student performance. Although the effect sizes were not large, the two largest group differences were obtained for comparisons between elementary and secondary teachers on the *Student Test Preparation* and *Instructional Changes* components. Elementary teachers indicated significantly more time spent on test preparation and that they had made more instructional changes than secondary teachers. This is not surprising when one takes into consideration the nature of state-mandated testing in Ohio. There is substantially more testing that occurs during the elementary years of school. In addition to diagnostic testing in grades 1 and 2, students in elementary grades are required to take achievement tests in the following grade levels and subjects:

- Grade 3—mathematics and reading
- Grade 4—mathematics, reading, and writing
- Grade 5—mathematics and reading (science and social studies will be added in 2006–2007)
- Grade 6—mathematics and reading (ODE, 2005).

At the secondary level, students are tested in mathematics and reading in grades 7 and 8. Additionally, students begin taking the Ohio Graduation Test (OGT) in grade 10. Arguably, there is more pressure at the elementary level for students to demonstrate academic achievement on these tests since they are being tested every year in grades 1 through 6. However, at the secondary level, students are tested only three times between grades 7 and 12. Elementary teachers in Ohio may feel it necessary to spend more time preparing students to take the state tests and may engage more frequently in making changes to their instruction.

Similarly, more pressure to demonstrate improvements in student achievement may be felt by those districts or individual schools that are currently rated low (i.e., "Academic Watch" and "Academic Emergency") on the state's effectiveness scale. These districts and schools are on a much shorter timeline, so to speak, to show improvements and to demonstrate adequate yearly progress than those that are rated as being more effective. Teachers, as well as administrators, in these districts and buildings undoubtedly feel that they must do more, and do it sooner rather than later, to improve student performance. However, this fact raises an interesting set of questions. In light of greater pressure to perform, are these teachers preparing students for these tests by using only those practices that are generally agreed-upon as being acceptable by the greater measurement community? If not, they may be engaging in practices that are truly, and only, artificially inflating test scores (Urdan & Paris, 1994). Examples of these unacceptable test preparation practices include

- acquiring actual test questions from a current test form and teaching students the answers;
- giving students actual test questions for drill, review, or homework; and
- copying, distributing, or keeping past versions of a test that have not been officially released as practice exams (Kober, 2002).

A second question relates to teachers' knowledge of these practices. If teachers are using any of these practices, are they aware of their ethical "violations?" We might assume and take for granted that teachers would know what is and is not appropriate practice in this arena. For example, however, it is possible that a given teacher may not be aware that the state may reuse some of the same test questions, or the same entire test version, from year to year (Kober, 2002). A final question of interest is that if these teachers are engaged in unethical test preparation practices, have they taken this initiative on their own, or are they feeling increased pressure to do so from district or school-level administrators? Again, it is possible that this is happening without realizing that certain practices are considered unacceptable.

It is important to note a couple of limitations of the results of this study. Although the findings are limited by geographic location (all teachers currently work in school districts in Ohio, a state which includes a series of state-mandated achievement tests), external validity of the findings of this study is suggested through the large and broad nature of the sample. The study sought to describe teachers' beliefs with respect to specific classroom-based instructional and assessment practices. Of course, the findings are based purely on self-reported data, and no efforts were made within the scope of this study to validate the extent to which these beliefs are consistent with actual classroom practice. Worthy of reiteration is the fact that this was a study of teachers' *perceptions* of the impact of *NCLB*, and not one of scientifically studying the extent to which *actual* classroom practices have changed as a direct result of *NCLB*.

In light of the findings from this study of teacher perceptions, it is imperative for various groups to be aware of any unintended effects of *NCLB*. For example, policymakers need to be aware of how the law is affecting teachers. The increased pressure that has been placed on teachers to raise levels of student academic achievement has made their daily work much more stressful. Furthermore, teachers have been forced to change the ways that they provide instruction to students and assess their resultant academic performance. They have substantially altered the amount of time spent on specific content, which sometimes conflicts with their respective academic content standards and violates sound educational practice. Additionally, teachers have resorted to spending much more time teaching students how to take standardized achievement tests, perhaps turning to unethical practices in order to achieve higher test scores. Similarly, administrators need to be mindful of these issues as well. They should be aware of these unintended consequences of *NCLB* and should look for ways to address increased stress levels, perhaps through professional development activities. They should definitely be cognizant of the potential for their teachers to utilize unethical test preparation practices. Closely examining how teachers are instructing students in the skills of test-taking may be a critical first step.

In light of the earlier discussion of unacceptable test preparation practices, it is recommended that teachers gain a better understanding of not only these *un*acceptable practices, but also activities whose practice would be more acceptable. Some students do not perform to the best of their abilities because they lack skills in test taking (Hogan, 2007; Linn & Miller, 2005). Specifically, students can be taught "testwiseness" skills (i.e., test-taking strategies) in order to prevent this type of inadequacy from lowering their test scores. These skills can be mastered by most students, but they need practice in order to develop them (Linn & Miller, 2005). Testwiseness skills that students should be taught, and given the opportunity to practice, include

- listening to and/or reading test directions carefully (including following proper procedures for marking responses on the answer sheet);
- listening to and/or reading test items carefully;
- establishing a pace that will permit completion of the test or subtest;
- skipping difficult items (instead of wasting valuable testing time) and returning to them later;
- making informed guesses, as opposed to just omitting items that appear too difficult;
- eliminating possible options (in the case of multiple-choice items), by identifying options that are clearly incorrect based on knowledge of content, prior to making informed guesses;
- checking to be sure that an answer number matches the item number when marking an answer; and
- checking answers, as well as the accuracy of marking those answers, if time permits (Linn & Miller, 2005).

The importance of engaging in these types of practices with students in advance of the administration of standardized tests is not only that they are seen as acceptable and ethical, but that they likely will result in test scores that demonstrate real student learning (Mertler, 2007).

Since there were so many group differences on the *Student Test Preparation* component, it is imperative that we shed light on the phenomenon. In order to understand this potential "problem" more completely, it is recommended that researchers look more closely at how teachers engage in student test preparation, focusing perhaps on particular test preparation strategies used by teachers. We need to better understand what specific techniques are used, why those techniques are used (i.e., what teachers are hoping to accomplish by using them), and the nature of their overall effectiveness. If they fail to improve actual student learning, their use should be strongly discouraged.

References

Abrams, L. M., Pedulla, J. J., & Madaus, G. F. (2003). Views from the classroom: Teachers' opinions of statewide testing programs. *Theory Into Practice, 42*(1), 18–29.

Amrein, A. L. & Berliner, D. C. (2002, March 28). High-stakes testing, uncertainty, and student learning *Education Policy Analysis Archives, 10*(18). Retrieved February 19, 2010 from http://epaa.asu.edu/epaa/v10n18/.

Cronin, J., Kingsbury, G. G., McCall, M. S., & Bowe, B. (2005, April). *The impact of the No Child Left Behind Act on student achievement and growth: 2005 edition.* Retrieved February 14, 2006, from the Northwest Evaluation Association Web site: http://www.nwea.org/research/NCLBstudy.asp

Gulek, C. (2003). Preparing for high-stakes testing. *Theory Into Practice, 42*(1), 42–50.

Herman, J. L., & Golan, S. (n.d.). *Effects of standardized testing on teachers and learning: Another look.* (CSE Technical Report 334). Los Angeles, CA: University of California, National Center for Research on Evaluation, Standards, and Student Testing.

Hogan, T. P. (2007). *Educational assessment: A practical approach.* Hoboken, NJ: John Wiley & Sons.

Kober, N. (2002). *Teaching to the test: The good, the bad, and who's responsible* (Test-Talk for Leaders, Issue No. 1). Washington, D.C.: Center on Education Policy.

Linn, R. L., & Miller, M. D. (2005). *Measurement and assessment in teaching* (9th ed.). Upper Saddle River, NJ: Merrill/Prentice Hall.

McMillan, J. H., Myran, S., & Workman, D. (1999). *The impact of mandated statewide testing on teachers' classroom assessment and instructional practices.* Paper presented at the annual meeting of the American Educational Research Association, Montreal, Canada.

Mehrens, W. A. (1991, April). *Defensible/indefensible instructional preparation for high stakes achievement tests: An exploratory trialogue.* Paper presented at the annual meeting of the American Educational Research Association, Chicago, IL.

Mertler, C. A. (2007). *Interpreting standardized test scores: Strategies for data-driven instructional decision making.* Thousand Oaks, CA: Sage.

Miyasaka, J. R. (2000, April). *A framework for evaluating the validity of test preparation practices*. Paper presented at the annual meeting of the American Educational Research Association, New Orleans, LA.

National Staff Development Council. (2004). *NCLB: Survey finds many educators experience little positive NCLB impact on professional development*. Retrieved May 20, 2005, from http://www.nsdc.org/library/policy/NCLBsurvey2_04.cfm

Ohio Department of Education. (2004). *2004–05 Ohio school district rating definitions*. Retrieved July 15, 2005, from http://www.ode.state.oh.us/reportcard/definitions/rating.asp

Ohio Department of Education. (2005). *Implementation schedule of Ohio statewide assessments*. Retrieved March 2, 2006, from http://www.ode.state.oh.us/proficiency/PDF/IMPLEMENTATION_SCHEDULE_OHIO_STATEWIDE_ASSESSMENTS083005.pdf

Sloane, F. C., & Kelly, A. E. (2003). Issues in high-stakes testing programs. *Theory Into Practice, 42*(1), 12–17.

Stecher, B. (2002). Consequences of large-scale, high-stakes testing on school and classroom practice. In L. S. Hamilton, B. M. Stecher, & S. P. Klein (Eds.), *Making sense of test-based accountability in education.* (pp. 79–100). Santa Monica, CA: RAND.

Sunderman, G. L., Tracey, C. A., Kim, J., & Orfield, G. (2004). *Listening to teachers: Classroom realities and No Child Left Behind*. Cambridge, MA: The Civil Rights Project at Harvard University.

Urdan, T. C., & Paris, S. G. (1994). Teachers' perceptions of standardized achievement tests. *Educational Policy, 8*(2), 137–156.

U.S. Department of Education. (2004). *A guide to education and "No Child Left Behind."* Retrieved September 10, 2005, from http://www.ed.gov/NCLB/overview/intro/guide/guide.pdf

• Glossary •

A-B design. Single-subject design where baseline measures (A) are obtained over time and then a treatment (B) is implemented, during which time additional measures are recorded

A-B-A design. Single-subject design where baseline measures (A) are obtained over time and a treatment (B) is implemented, then the treatment is reversed or removed and additional measures (A) are recorded; also known as *reversal design*

accessible population. The group from which the researcher can realistically select subjects; also known as an *available population*

accurate disclosure. Obligation on the part of the researcher to accurately inform participants about the general topic of the research, the nature of their participation, and any unusual tasks in which they may engage

action plan. Proposed strategy for implementing the results of an action research project

action research studies. Applied educational research studies that address local-level problems with the anticipation of finding immediate solutions; conducted by educational practitioners

alpha (α) level. See *level of significance*

alternating-treatment design. Single-subject design where two treatments are alternated in quick succession and changes in the participant's behavior are plotted on a graph to facilitate informal comparisons

alternative hypothesis. See *research hypothesis*

analysis of covariance (ANCOVA). Analysis of variance designs that incorporate the use of covariates

analysis of variance (ANOVA). A family of group comparison statistical techniques

anonymity. Protection offered to research participants when their identities are kept hidden from the researcher

appendices. Additional information not included in the body of a research proposal or written report but added at the end for the benefit of reviewers/ readers

aptitude tests. Standardized tests that provide an estimate of a person's ability to perform at some time in the future or in a different situation

artificial dichotomy. A dichotomy to which participants are arbitrarily assigned

assent. Agreement to participate in a research study, when the participant is a minor (under the age of 18)

assumptions. Assertions made by the researcher and assumed to be true but for which no evidence exists

attitudinal measures. Standardized instruments used to assess people's attitudes or feelings toward topics of an educational nature

attitudinal questions. Survey questions that ask individual respondents to indicate their attitudes or opinions about some topic

attrition. Threat to internal validity occurring when there may be a loss of participants for reasons such as illness, dropping out, or moving elsewhere; also known as *mortality*

autobiographical study. A form of narrative research where the information is written and recorded by the individual who is the subject of the study

available population. See *accessible population*

bar charts. Similar to histograms, except that adjacent bars do not touch; visual depiction used for categorical data

behavioral measures. Standardized measures used to record behavioral observations on a checklist for some other sort of instrumentation

behavioral questions. Survey questions that seek information about individuals' actual behaviors

biographical study. A form of narrative research where the researcher writes and records the experiences of another person's life

biserial correlation. Used to measure the relationship between an interval or ratio variable and an artificial dichotomy

bivariate analyses. Statistical analyses that involve only two variables

bivariate correlations. Correlations that involve only two sets of scores or two variables

bivariate regression. See *linear regression*

Boolean operators. Keywords—most commonly *and* and *or*—that enable the retrieval of terms and specific combinations

case studies. In-depth qualitative studies of specifically identified programs, activities, people, or groups

causal-comparative studies. Nonexperimental research studies that compare groups—where group membership is determined by something that occurred in the past—on subsequent data on another variable in such a way that it makes possible drawing potential causal relationships between the two variables; also referred to as *ex post facto studies*

census. A cross-sectional survey conducted for an entire population, as opposed to a sample drawn from the population

checklists. Questions that consist of a list of behaviors, characteristics, skills, or other criteria that the researcher is interested in studying, where respondents indicate that they do or do not possess something, or have or have not observed something, for example

chi-square goodness-of-fit test. Used to analyze categorical data to determine if observed frequency counts are significantly different from those that would be expected in the population

chi-square test of independence. Used to test the significance of a relationship between two categorical variables

class journal. Less formal version of a student journal, where students are encouraged to enter thoughts, ideas, perceptions, feedback, or other forms of response, such as pictures or diagrams

closed-ended questions. Survey questions that consist of multiple-choice or other types of items that allow the respondent to select a response from a number of options provided by the researcher directly on the survey; also known as *forced-choice questions*

cluster random sampling. Randomly sampling intact, existing groups (or clusters) of participants rather than individuals

codebook. A list of variables or questions indicating how the responses for each item will be coded for statistical analysis

coding scheme. Development of a system of categorization for coding qualitative data

coefficient of equivalence. Correlation coefficient resulting from the determination of equivalent-forms reliability

coefficient of stability. Correlation coefficient resulting from the determination of test–retest reliability

cohort study. Type of survey study where the researcher studies within a specified population a subgroup (called the "cohort") whose members share some common characteristic

comparative studies. Nonexperimental research studies that compare two or more groups on one or more measured variables

comparison group. More appropriate term for a *control group*, since the nontreatment group may not be receiving the standard conditions but may receive something else, or even nothing at all

concept sampling. See *theory sampling*

concurrent timing. Occurs when a researcher implements both quantitative and qualitative strands simultaneously during the same phase of a mixed-methods study

concurrent validity coefficients. Correlation coefficients that measure the relationship between scores on the instrument of interest and scores on a similar instrument, administered at roughly the same time

confidentiality. Protection offered to research participants when the researchers know the identities of the participants but do not disclose that information to people outside of the research study

confirmability. Technique for assessing trustworthiness in qualitative studies; process of establishing the neutrality and objectivity of the data

confirming and disconfirming sampling. Technique researchers use to look for additional individuals or sites to confirm or disconfirm their preliminary findings; used in qualitative research

confounding variables. Traits or conditions whose presence is likely not recognized or considered by the researcher, and that may influence the outcome of the research study

consent. Agreement to participate in a research study, when the participant is age 18 or older

contextualization. In ethnographic research, where research findings are interpreted with reference to the particular group, setting, or event being observed

continuous variables. Variables that measure gradational differences along some continuum

control group. The group of study participants who receive the standard condition, as determined by the level of the independent variable

convenience sampling. A "targeted" sampling technique whereby the researcher simply studies whoever happens to be available at the time and is willing to participate

conventions. Agreed-on procedures that help ensure the accuracy of research data and findings

conventions of academic-style writing. Agreed-on procedures that help ensure the readability and credibility of research reports

conventions of format. Procedures that provide a generic outline, or at least suggested components, for a typical research report

convergent design. See *convergent parallel design*

convergent parallel design. Mixed-methods research design where the researcher collects quantitative and qualitative data at the same time, and typically with separate perspectives and research questions; also referred to as a *convergent design*

correlational studies. Nonexperimental research studies that measure the degree and nature of the relationship between two or more variables

counterbalanced design. Quasi-experimental design where each group is exposed to each treatment—however many there may be—but in a different order than are the other groups

covariates. Additional variables included in designs that can act as controls for a variable that may influence the dependent variable

cover letter. Letter that accompanies a written survey or precedes the interview process; explains the purpose of the study and describes what will be asked of participants

credibility. Strategy for assessing trustworthiness in qualitative studies; involves establishing that the results of qualitative research are credible, or believable, from the perspective of the participant(s) in the research

criterion-referenced tests. Standardized tests that result in scores that indicate how well an individual performed in comparison with preestablished criteria

critical sampling. Sampling technique focused on individuals or sites that represent in dramatic terms the phenomenon being studied; used in qualitative research

Cronbach's alpha reliability. Type of internal consistency reliability that is essentially an average of all possible split-half reliabilities; used appropriately when items have more than two possible outcomes

cross-sectional survey. Survey involving the examination of the characteristics of—and possibly differences among—several samples or populations measured at one point in time

data analysis. Thorough description of techniques used to analyze data collected as part of a research study

data collection procedures. Step-by-step description of all aspects of data collection for a given study

deductive reasoning. A process of reasoning that works from more general, broad-based ideas, concepts, observations, or experiences to the more specific, in a "top-down" manner

delimitation. Restriction placed on the study by the researcher to limit its scope

demographic questions. Survey questions that allow respondents to indicate personal characteristics (e.g., gender, age, level of education)

dependability. Technique assessing trustworthiness in qualitative studies; emphasizes the need for the researcher to account for the ever-changing context within which research occurs

dependent variable. The variable of ultimate interest in a research study

descriptive statistics. The group of statistical analysis techniques that enable researchers to summarize, organize, and simplify data

descriptive studies. Nonexperimental research studies that report information about the frequency or amount of something

descriptive survey. A one-shot survey for the purpose of simply describing the characteristics of a sample at one point in time

descriptive validity. The factual accuracy of the account provided in qualitative research

dichotomous variables. Special cases of discrete variables with only two possible categories

differential selection of participants. Threat to internal validity where participants who are selected for a study already possess differences that may account for potential variations on a posttest

direct administration. Method of administering a survey in person to all members of a given group, usually at the same time

directional research hypothesis. Research hypothesis that indicates the direction of the results

discrete variables. Variables that are categorical in nature, meaning that they are divided into separate categories

discriminant analysis. Statistical technique analogous to multiple regression, except that the dependent variable consists of two or more categories, rather than a continuous range of values

distribution of sample means. Distribution created by drawing numerous random samples from a population and calculating means for each sample; all samples will not have the same mean, but those means will be normally distributed around the population mean

district-level action plans. Action plans developed and implemented by an entire school district

double-barreled question. A single survey question that essentially asks two different things within the same statement or question

ecological validity. Threat to external validity that occurs when an experimental situation is quite different from a new setting where results are to be applied

Education Resources Information Center (ERIC). The largest database for locating research in education

educational research. Research studies that involve the application of the scientific method to educational topics, phenomena, or questions

effect size. Size of the treatment effect the researcher wishes to detect with respect to a given level of power

e-mail surveys. Surveys delivered to potential respondents via e-mail that require an e-mailed set of responses in return

embedded design. Mixed-methods research design where the researcher collects and analyzes both quantitative and qualitative data within traditional quantitative or qualitative designs; the "embedded" portion comes when the researcher adds a qualitative strand within a quantitative design, or vice versa

empirical research studies. Well-researched articles and reports that are based on the collection of original data

epiphanies. Key turning points in the lives of participants and perhaps in the life of the researcher as well; may be experienced during narrative research studies

equal stratified sampling. See *nonproportional stratified sampling*

equivalence. See *equivalent-forms reliability*

equivalent-forms reliability. Method of determining reliability whereby two different forms of the test are used for measuring the same thing; also referred to as *equivalence*

ethnographic research. Type of qualitative research that describes social interactions between people in group settings

evaluative validity. Extent to which the researcher behaved objectively enough to report the data and findings in an unbiased manner, without making evaluations or judgments of the collected data

***ex post facto* studies.** See *causal-comparative studies*

existing documents and records. Any sort of qualitative data that already exists in the school setting, prior to the study taking place

experimental group. The group of study participants who are exposed to the new or innovative condition under investigation in the study, as determined by the level of the independent variable; also known as the *treatment group*

experimental research. A type of research where the researcher has control over one or more of the variables included in the study that may somehow influence (or cause) the participants' behavior

explanatory correlational studies. Correlational studies that try to understand and describe certain related events, conditions, and behaviors

explanatory design. See *explanatory sequential design*

explanatory sequential design. Mixed-methods design where the collection and analysis of quantitative data receives priority and is conducted first, followed by the collection and analysis of qualitative data; also referred to as the *explanatory design*

exploratory design. See *exploratory sequential design*

exploratory sequential design. Mixed-methods design where the collection and analysis of qualitative data receive priority and are conducted first, followed by the collection and analysis of quantitative data; also referred to as the *exploratory design*

external audit. Use of an outside individual (a colleague, critical friend, etc.) to review and evaluate a final research report

external validity. The extent to which results of a particular study are generalizable, or applicable, to other groups or settings

extreme case sampling. Purposeful sampling strategy that focuses on the study of an *outlier* case, or a case that displays extreme characteristics; used in qualitative research

factor analysis. Correlational technique used when a large number of correlations have been explored in a given study; it is a means of grouping into clusters, or factors, certain variables that are moderately to highly correlated with one another

factorial ANCOVA. Extension of the one-way ANCOVA, where two (or more) independent variables are included

factorial ANOVA. Extension of the one-way ANOVA, where two (or more) independent variables are included

factorial designs. Research designs that involve two or more independent variables, at least one of which is manipulated

factorial MANCOVA. Extension of one-way ANCOVA, where two (or more) independent variables and more than one dependent variable are included

factorial MANOVA. Extension of one-way ANOVA, where two (or more) independent variables and more than one dependent variable are included

field notes. Written observations of what you see taking place in a particular setting

focus group. Simultaneous interviews of people making up a relatively small group, usually no more than 10 to 12 people

forced-choice questions. See *closed-ended questions*

formative classroom assessments. Assessments that are administered during instruction to determine what sorts of adjustments should be made to that instruction while it is ongoing

framing the study. A researcher's attempt to demonstrate the potential relevance of the proposed study by using a specific context or frame of reference to which the reader will be able to relate

frequency distribution. Descriptive analysis technique; a tabulation of the number of times each value of a variable occurs

frequency distribution table. Table presenting scores in a distribution that are arranged from highest to lowest, moving down the table

full participant. Researcher role where the researcher is not only the "researcher" but also simultaneously a fully functioning member of the community

generalizability. Extent to which the findings of a given study are applicable within the community that was studied (in quantitative studies) and can be extended to settings that were not studied by the researcher (in qualitative studies)

Google Scholar. A searchable Internet database of scholarly literature

grounded theory research. Qualitative research studies that attempt to discover a theory that relates to a particular environment

histograms. Present the same information as a frequency distribution but in graph form; the height of each bar indicates the frequency of each score category

historical research. Qualitative research that describes events, occurrences, or settings of the past in an attempt to better understand them, learn from past failures and successes, and see if they might apply to present-day problems and issues

history. Threat to internal validity that occurs when experimental treatments extend over longer periods and factors other than the experimental treatment have time to exert influence on the results

homogeneous sampling. Sampling technique whereby certain sites or individuals are selected because they possess a similar trait or characteristic; used in qualitative research

hypotheses. Predicted outcomes of a research study

hypothesis testing. Statistical procedures whereby researchers test predictions they have made based on data collected from the sample

independent level of interaction. Level of interaction in a mixed-methods study where the qualitative and quantitative strands—that is, the research questions, data collection, and data analysis—are kept entirely separate

independent measures *t*-test. See *independent samples* t-*test*

independent samples *t*-test. Appropriate analysis technique in research designs where two groups are being compared on a common dependent variable, such as a test score; also known as an *independent measures* t-*test*

independent variables. Any variables over which the researcher has control in a study, meaning that the researcher determines which participants in the study will receive which condition

individual action plans. Action plans resulting from action research studies where the individual educator is the target audience

inductive analysis. Eclectic analytic process for conducting qualitative data analysis, where the researcher begins with specific observations (i.e., data), notes any patterns in the data, formulates one or more tentative questions of interest, and finally develops general conclusions and theories

inductive reasoning. A process of reasoning that works in a "bottom-up" manner and involves the development of broad, general conclusions from observations of a very limited number of events or experiences

inferential statistics. Techniques that are used to determine the likelihood that the results obtained from collecting data from a sample are similar to the results that would have been obtained if the entire population had been studied

informed consent. The act of participants—or their parents or legal guardians, in the case of children and other sensitive or vulnerable populations—agreeing to participate in a study once they know its nature and what their involvement will include

institutional review boards (IRBs). Mandated boards at colleges and universities that review and approve both student and faculty research

instrumentation. Tests, tools, protocols, or other instruments that will be used to collect data from participants; also, a threat to internal validity where the instruments used to measure performance in experimental studies (e.g., pretests and posttests) are unreliable or lack consistency in their ability to measure variables of interest

intelligence tests. Standardized tests that measure an individual's intellectual ability

interactive level of interaction. Level of interaction in a mixed-methods study that occurs when the researcher mixes the two methods, which can occur at different points in the process but must occur prior to the final interpretation of results

interest inventories. Standardized inventories that provide information about an individual's interests to help that individual make career choices

internal consistency reliability. Extent to which items in a single test are consistent among themselves and with the test as a whole; require only one administration of an instrument

internal validity. Degree to which measured differences on the dependent variable are a direct result of the manipulation of the independent variable, and not some other variable or extraneous condition or influence

interpretive validity. The accuracy of the interpretations of participants' behaviors and words, and concern that their perspectives are accurately represented

interval. Measurement scale that possesses all characteristics of both nominal and ordinal scales, but the subsequent values represent equal intervals

interview guide. Delineation of either specific or general questions to be asked of participants

interviews (in qualitative research). Qualitative data collection technique consisting of conversations between the researcher and participants in the study

interviews (in survey research). Most costly type of data collection in survey research because surveys must be administered individually and face-to-face

item validity. Extent to which the items that appear on a test are *relevant* to the content area being tested

journals. Technique for qualitative data collection; may be kept by teachers, students, and others included in a qualitative research site; can provide valuable insight into the workings of a classroom or school

justification for the study. Statement of why a particular research topic is important and worthy of investigation; also referred to as *rationale for the study*

Kendall tau correlation. Measure of the relationships between two ordinal variables; used with samples smaller than 10

key informants. Individual members of a research participant group who typically can provide better quality information and insights

knowledge questions. Survey questions that seek to determine how much an individual knows about a particular subject

Kuder-Richardson (KR-20) reliability. Type of internal consistency reliability that is essentially an average of all possible split-half reliabilities; used appropriately when items are scored dichotomously

level of interaction. Extent to which the two strands of a mixed-methods research study remain independent or interact with each other

level of significance. The preestablished (a priori) probability of making an incorrect hypothesis-testing decision; also known as *alpha (α) level*

life history. Narrative research that portrays an individual's entire life

Likert question. Survey question that begins with a statement and then asks individuals to respond on an agree–disagree continuum

Likert-type question. Survey question that exists on a continuum, similar to a Likert question, but measures something other than extent of agreement

limitation. Some aspect of the study that is outside the control of the researcher but may have a potentially adverse effect on the outcomes of the research

linear regression. Bivariate version of multiple regression; uses the nature of one independent variable as a means of predicting scores on a single dependent variable; also known as *bivariate regression* or *regression*

literature review. A comprehensive examination of the information and knowledge base related to a given research topic

logico-inductive analysis. A thought process that uses logic to make sense of patterns and trends in qualitative data

logistic regression. Similar to discriminant analysis in that both attempt to identify a set of independent variables that best predicts group membership on a categorical dependent variable; here, the dependent variable is dichotomous

longitudinal survey. Survey where individuals in one group or cohort are studied at different points in time

mail surveys. Administering or distributing the survey instrument to the sample by sending a hard copy to each individual and requesting that it be returned by mail before a certain date

matching posttest-only control group design. Quasi-experimental design using two groups of participants from the same population; members of the groups are matched, one group is exposed to the experimental treatment or condition, both groups are given a posttest, and then those scores are compared to see if the groups differ on the dependent variable

matching pretest–posttest control group design. Quasi-experimental design where a pretest is administered to all participants and, based on the results of the pretest, each participant is matched with another participant who has a relatively similar pretest score; groups are then created by putting each person from the pair into a separate group (i.e., one into the experimental group and one into the comparison group)

maturation. Threat to internal validity that occurs when treatments extend over longer periods of time and participants may undergo physiological changes that produce differential effects in the dependent variable

maximum variation sampling. Sampling technique whereby the researcher samples cases or individuals that differ on some important characteristic or trait; used in qualitative research

mean. The arithmetic average of all the scores on a single variable; most commonly used measure of central tendency and appropriate for variables measured on interval or ratio scales

measurement scale. System used to organize data so they can be reviewed, analyzed, and interpreted appropriately

measures of central tendency. Measures that consist of a single score that represents what is typical among a group of scores

measures of dispersion. Measures that indicate what is *atypical* about a set of scores; also known as *measures of variability*

measures of relative standing. Statistics that indicate where a given score falls in a distribution, in relation to all other scores in that distribution

measures of variability. See *measures of dispersion*

median. The midpoint of all the scores in the distribution; it is the point at which 50% of the scores are located above and 50% fall below

member checking. Process of asking participants who were directly involved in the study to review the accuracy of the research report

mixed-methods research designs. Research studies that use both qualitative and quantitative approaches and data within a single study

mixed-model studies. Extension of mixed-methods research designs that involves the mixing of quantitative and qualitative approaches to research in three distinct areas of the research process

mixing. The intentional integration of a mixed-methods study's quantitative and qualitative strands

mode. The most frequently occurring score in a data set

mortality. See *attrition*

multiphase combination timing. In a mixed-methods study, implementation of multiple phases that include sequential and/or concurrent timing

multiphase design. Mixed-methods design that combines both sequential and concurrent strands over a period of time in which the researcher is implementing multiple studies, all of which have an overall program objective

multiphase mixed-methods research study. Mixed-methods study where the phases of qualitative and quantitative data collection are simultaneous, or occur relatively close in time

multiple-baseline design. Single-subject design where two or more (often three) behaviors, people, or settings are plotted in a staggered graph, where a change is made to one but not the other two, and then to the second but not the third behavior, person, or setting

multiple regression. Statistical technique used to determine the degree of correlation between an interval or ratio dependent variable and a combination of two or more independent variables

multiproject mixed-methods study. Mixed-methods study where the phases of qualitative and quantitative data collection are distinctly separated by substantial periods of time

multistage random sampling. Combination of cluster random sampling and individual random sampling; also known as *two-stage random sampling*

multivariate analysis. Statistical analyses that involve more than two variables

multivariate analysis of covariance (MANCOVA). Extension of ANCOVA with more than one dependent variable

multivariate analysis of variance (MANOVA). Extension of ANOVA with more than one dependent variable

multivariate correlations. Measures of the relationships among three or more variables

multivariate multiple regression. An extension of multiple regression where a group of independent variables is identified as the best set of predictors for a group of dependent variables

narrative research. Qualitative research that conveys experiences as they are expressed in the lived and told stories of individuals

natural dichotomy. A dichotomy that occurs naturally

naturalistic observation. In qualitative research, the researcher's role is to watch and listen attentively and to record as accurately as possible all pertinent information as it occurs naturally

negative correlation. Measure of the relationship between two variables, where high scores on one variable tend to be associated with low scores on the other variable

nominal. Scale of measurement that involves the assignment of a label or name to a category; these variables are typically analogous to discrete or categorical variables

nondirectional research hypothesis. Research hypothesis that states that there is a difference but will not specify the direction of that difference

nonexperimental research. A type of research where the researcher does not have direct control over any variable in the study, either because it has already occurred or because it is not possible (or, perhaps, ethical) for it to be influenced

nonprobability sampling techniques. Sampling techniques that do not permit the researcher to specify the probability that each member of a population will be selected for inclusion in the sample, nor do they create a sampling situation where every member of a population has an equal chance of being selected; also known as *nonrandom sampling techniques*

nonproportional stratified sampling. Stratified random sampling process where the representations of subgroups in the sample are equivalent to one another; also known as *equal stratified sampling*

nonrandom sampling techniques. See *nonprobability sampling techniques*

normal distribution. Bell-shaped distribution of scores; positions of individual scores in the distribution serve as the basis for determining measures of relative standing

norm-referenced tests. Standardized tests that result in scores that indicate how well an individual performed in relation to a large group of test takers

null hypothesis. Hypothesis that states that no effect will occur, no relationships exist between variables, or no differences will be found between groups; symbolized as H_0

observations (in qualitative data collection). Carefully watching and systematically recording what you see and hear in a particular setting

observer as participant. Role of a researcher during data collection where he or she remains first and foremost an observer but does have some level of interaction with the participants being studied

observer's comments. On-the-spot interpretations of field notes as a way to integrate ongoing analysis into the process of conducting qualitative research

one-group pretest–posttest design. Preexperimental research design involving a single group that is pretested, exposed to a treatment condition, and then posttested

one-shot case study. Preexperimental research design involving a single group that is exposed to a treatment condition and then posttested

one-way ANCOVA. Extension of a one-way ANOVA design that includes a covariate

one-way ANOVA. Extension of an independent samples *t*-test but appropriate when more than two groups are being compared

open-ended interviews. Interviews that provide the respondent with only a few questions, intended to gather different kinds of information from various individuals, depending largely on how each person interprets the questions

open-ended questions. Survey questions that allow for more individualized responses, since respondents are not limited to selecting from a supplied set of options

opportunistic sampling. Purposeful sampling technique that takes place after the research begins, to capitalize on the researcher's realization of new or unfolding events; used in qualitative research

oral history. A type of narrative research conducted by gathering the personal reflections of events, as well as implications of those events, from one or several individuals

ordinal. Measurement scale that builds on the characteristics of nominal scales by also ranking individuals in order of the degree to which they possess a certain characteristic

paired samples *t*-test. See *repeated samples* t-test

panel study. Survey study where the researcher examines the exact same people over a specified length of time

parameters. Numerical indices that describe a population

partial correlation. Measure of the relationship between two variables that "partials out" or removes the effects of a third variable that strongly affects them both

participant observer. Role of qualitative researcher in which the researcher engages actively in all group activities as a regular member of the group being studied, in addition to observing and taking notes; also known as *participant as observer*

participant as observer. See *participant observer*

participatory action research. Action research focused on improving the quality of organizations, communities, and family lives

path analysis. Analytical technique focused on testing relationships that uses multiple applications of multiple regression to estimate causal relationships, both direct and indirect, among several variables

Pearson product-moment correlation. Measure of the relationship between two variables on an interval or ratio scale; also known simply as *Pearson's correlation*

Pearson's correlation. See *Pearson product-moment correlation*

peer debriefing. Practice of using other professionals (perhaps colleagues or critical friends) who help a researcher reflect on the research by reviewing and critiquing the processes of data collection, analysis, and interpretation

percentile ranks. Scores that indicate one's relative standing in comparison with percentages of others who have taken the same test or have been included in the same measurement

performance measures. Standardized assessments used to assess an individual's ability to perform on some sort of test or inventory

personal experience story. A narrative study of an individual's personal experience as related to a single or multiple incidents or private situations

personality inventories. Standardized tests that identify and measure human characteristics in an attempt to predict or explain behavior over time and across situations

personological validity. Threat to external validity occurring when a given research finding applies well to some people and poorly to others, for no obvious reason

phenomenological studies. Qualitative research that engages the researcher in a process of individual interviews in an attempt to fully understand a specific phenomenon

phi correlation. Measure of the relationships between two variables when both are natural dichotomous variables

pie charts. Charts used to visually present categorical data

pilot test. A trial run of the data collection process to determine if any revisions should be made before actual data collection occurs

point-biserial correlation. Used to measure the relationship between two variables when one is interval or ratio and the other is a natural dichotomy

point of interface. The stage at which integration of qualitative and quantitative strands occurs in a mixed-methods study

population. A group of individuals who share the same important characteristics

population validity. Threat to external validity as determined by the degree of similarity among (1) the sample used in a study, (2) the population from which the sample was drawn, and (3) the target population to which results are to be generalized

positive correlation. Measure of the relationship between two variables where high scores on one variable tend to be associated with high scores on the second variable, while low scores are associated with low scores

posttest-only control group design. Experimental design that is similar to the static-group comparison design but where participants have been randomly assigned to the experimental and comparison groups

power. In significance testing, the probability of rejecting H_0 when H_0 is, in fact, false—a correct decision

practical action research. Action research that is intended to address a specific problem in a classroom, school, or other community

practical significance. Results of statistical tests that have practical and applied importance in a particular setting

predictive correlational studies. Correlational studies that try to predict future conditions or behaviors in one variable from what we presently know of another variable

predictive validity coefficients. Measures of the relationship between scores on the instrument of interest and scores on some measure taken quite some time (e.g., several years) later

pretest–posttest control group design. Experimental design with two groups whose members have been randomly assigned, are administered a pretest, receive some sort of treatment condition (or, perhaps, the absence of a treatment condition), and are posttested at the end of the study

pretest sensitization. See *testing*

primary sources. Firsthand accounts of original research, such as journal articles, monographs, and papers presented at professional research conferences

principal components analysis. Advanced analytical technique used to reduce the number of independent variables, usually when conducting analyses involving many variables that may be highly correlated

priority. Relative importance or weighting of quantitative and qualitative methods as a means of answering the guiding research questions in a mixed-methods study; prioritization may be quantitative, qualitative, or equal

privileged observer. Role of a qualitative researcher in which the researcher does not participate in the activities of the group being studied

probability level. The predetermined (i.e., at the outset of the study) probability that the null hypothesis is correct

probability sampling techniques. Sampling techniques that permit the researcher to specify the probability, or chance, that each member of the population will be selected for inclusion in the sample; also known as *random sampling techniques*

problem statement. A reiteration of the research problem as a complete sentence

proportional stratified sampling. Stratified random sampling process where a sample is selected so the identified subgroups in the sample are represented in the exact same proportion in which they exist in the population

proposed budget. Tentative listing of financial costs for all major aspects of a given study

proposed timeline. Tentative detailed schedule for all major activities of a given study

ProQuest. A searchable online database that contains not only research articles and conference papers but also thesis and dissertation studies

purpose of the study. Part of a research proposal; aims to clearly explain what the researcher proposes to study, as well as the goals for the research

purposeful sampling. Sampling strategies that involve the intentional selection of individuals and sites to learn about or understand the topic at hand

purposive sampling. Nonprobability sampling technique whereby people or other sampling units are selected for a particular purpose

p-value. Numerical index obtained from statistical analysis that indicates the probability of chance occurrences in our actual study

qualitative research. Research that involves the collection, analysis, and interpretation of data, largely narrative and visual in nature, to gain insights into a particular phenomenon of interest

quantitative research. Research that relies on the collection and analysis of numerical data to describe, explain, predict, or control variables and phenomena of interest

quartile deviation. Half the difference between the third quartile (i.e., the score that determines the top 25%) and the first quartile (i.e., the score that determines the bottom 25%) in a distribution of scores

quasi-experimental designs. Research designs that come the closest to true experiments; however, there is still no random assignment of the participants to groups

questionnaires. Surveys that are administered in written form

quota sampling. Often seen as a variation of convenience sampling; involves a process of selecting a sample based on precise numbers of individuals or groups with specific characteristics

random assignment. Assignment of participants such that every individual who has been randomly selected to participate in the experiment has an equal chance of being assigned to any of the groups (i.e., experimental or comparison groups) being compared in the study

random sampling techniques. See *probability sampling techniques*

random selection. The process of choosing, in random fashion, individuals for participation in a research study, such that every member of the population has an equal chance of being selected to be a member of the sample

range. The difference between the highest score and the lowest score in a distribution

ratio. Measurement scale that possesses the characteristics of nominal, ordinal, and interval measurements plus the additional characteristic of a true zero point

rationale for the study. See *justification for the study*

reconnaissance. Preliminary information gathering in action research studies

refereed research report. A written research report that has been subjected to a review by colleagues and experts in a particular field

references. List of articles or other sources of information cited as part of a research proposal or written report

reflection. The act of critically exploring what you are doing, why you decided to do it, and what its effects have been; critical component of action research

reflective teaching. Process of developing lessons or assessing student learning with thoughtful consideration of educational theory, existing research, and practical experience, along with analysis of the lesson's effect on student learning

reflexivity. Process of intermingling the researcher's own preliminary thoughts and interpretations with field notes

regression. See *linear regression*

reliability. Essential characteristic of quantitative data; measure of the consistency of those data

repeated measures *t*-test. See *repeated samples t-test*

repeated samples *t*-test. Statistical comparison test appropriate for a situation where one group is being measured twice; commonly used in pretest/posttest designs; also known as *repeated measures t-test* or *paired samples t-test*

research design. The plan that will be used by the researcher to carry out the study

research hypothesis. Hypothesis that is most often a statement of what the researcher actually expects to discover in the study; also known as an *alternative hypothesis*

research methods. Specification of exactly how a research study will be conducted

research problem. An initial concern for a research study that has been clarified and stated succinctly

research proposal. Written plan for conducting a research study

research questions. Carefully stated questions that guide the conduct of a research study

respondents. Sample of individuals selected to respond to a survey

restorying. In narrative research, the process of organizing a good deal of personal story data into a presentation that will make sense to the intended audience

return rate. Rate of response to a survey, usually expressed as a percentage

reversal design. See *A-B-A design*

rigor. The quality, validity, accuracy, and credibility of action research and its findings

sample. Subset of the population for an actual study, such that it is representative of the accessible population so the results can be generalized to the larger group

sampling bias. Systematic sampling error that is generally the fault of the researcher

sampling error. Discrepancies between a sample statistic and a population parameter

sampling interval. Distance in the population list between each individual selected for inclusion in the sample; used with systematic sampling

sampling validity. How well the items that appear on the test *represent* the total content area being tested

scatterplot. Visual representation of the relationship between two interval or ratio variables

school-level action plans. Action plans developed and implemented by the entire staff at a school

scientific method. The step-by-step process used to answer questions and resolve problems, and to conduct most educational research studies

search engines. Searchable Internet databases, used to locate websites as organized by keywords

secondary sources. Summaries, compilations, analyses, or interpretations of primary research conducted by other individuals

selection-maturation interaction. Threat to internal validity where the effects of differential selection of participants also interact with other threats, such as history, maturation, or testing

semistructured interviews. Interviews where the researcher asks several "base" questions but also has the option of following up a given response with additional questions, depending on the situation

semistructured observations. Observations that allow the researcher the flexibility to attend to other events or activities occurring simultaneously in the classroom or to engage in brief, but intense, periods of observation and note taking

sequential timing. Implementation of a mixed-methods study in two distinct phases; collection and analysis of one type of data occur only after collection and analysis of the other type of data

significance tests. Specific statistical criteria used to test null hypotheses

simple random sampling. Best way to obtain a representative sample; process is analogous to putting names on individual slips of paper, thoroughly mixing them, and blindly drawing out the number desired for the sample

single-subject experimental research designs. Experimental designs used to study and promote a change in behavior as exhibited by an individual

single-variable designs. Research designs that involve only one manipulated independent variable

snowball sampling. Sampling technique whereby the researcher observes or interviews participants and then asks them to recommend other individuals who they think would be a benefit to the study; used in qualitative and quantitative research

Solomon four-group design. Combination of the posttest-only control group design and the pretest–posttest control group design. First involves the random assignment of participants to one of four groups; two groups are pretested and two are not. One of the pretested groups and one of the non-pretested groups receive the experimental treatment, and the other two groups receive nothing or an alternative treatment. Finally, all four groups are posttested using the same measure.

Spearman rho correlation. Measure of the relationships between two ordinal variables; used with larger samples

split-half reliability. Type of internal consistency reliability used when testing a single group on two occasions is not feasible or when an alternate form of a test is not available

stability. See *test–retest reliability*

standard deviation. The average distance of the scores from the mean; calculated by finding the square root of the variance of a set of scores

standard error. The standard deviation of the sample means within the distribution of sample means

standard score. Calculation that expresses how far an individual score is from the mean, typically in standard deviation units

statement of the problem. Part of a research proposal; should provide ample background information and also a thorough description of the context in which the problem is occurring

static-group comparison design. Preexperimental research design where an experimental and comparison group are pretested and compared

statistical regression. Threat to internal validity consisting of the tendency for participants who score very high on one test (e.g., a pretest) to score lower on a second, similar test (e.g., a posttest), or for participants who score very low on a pretest to score much higher on a posttest

statistical significance. The decision made from the results of statistical procedures that enable researchers to conclude that the findings of a given study are large enough in the sample studied to represent a meaningful difference or relationship in the population from which the sample was drawn

statistics. Numerical indices and procedures that describe the sample and help the researcher make inferences about the population

stratified random sampling. Probability sampling technique in which certain subgroups are selected for inclusion in the sample

structural equation modeling. Substantially advanced analytical technique that can be thought of as a combination of path analysis and factor analysis

structured interview. Participant interviews consisting of a set of predetermined questions; those questions—and only those questions—are asked of each person being interviewed

structured observations. Data collection technique that requires the observer to do nothing but observe, looking usually for specific behaviors, reactions, or interactions

student journals. Type of data collection journals that perform a role similar to that of homework, in that they provide a sense of students' daily thoughts, perceptions, and experiences in the classroom

style guide. Written guides that provide assistance and recommendations for developing written research reports and other academic manuscripts

summative classroom assessments. Assessments that are administered after a substantial period of instruction (e.g., following completion of an instructional unit, at the end of a semester or course) to inform administrative decisions, such as assigning final grades, or simply to provide a broader overview of student achievement

survey. Group of quantitative data collection techniques that involve the administration of a set of questions or statements to a sample of people

survey research. Type of descriptive research focused on describing characteristics of a group or population

systematic sampling. Probability sampling strategy where every Kth individual in a population list is selected for inclusion in the sample

target population. The group of people to whom the researcher would like to generalize the results of the study

teacher journals. Type of data collection journal that can give teachers the opportunity to maintain narrative accounts of their professional reflections on practice

team action plans. Action plans developed by collaborative groups of teachers, who have worked together to address an area of common interest to all members of the team

telephone surveys. Method of administering surveys where the researcher must read each survey question to individual respondents

test–retest reliability. Method of determining reliability of quantitative data by administering a test to a group of participants and then, perhaps a week later, readministering the same test to the same people; also referred to as *stability*

testing. Threat to internal validity that may occur if pretests and posttests are used, because participants may learn enough from the pretest to improve performance on the posttest, even when the experimental treatment has no effect; also known as *pretest sensitization*

tetrachoric correlation. Measure of the relationships between two variables when both are artificial dichotomous variables

theoretical lens. A guiding perspective or ideology that provides structure that ultimately advocates for specific groups or individuals, during both the research and the writing of the final qualitative research report

theoretical validity. Extent to which a study, and its final report, relate the phenomenon being studied to a broader theory

theory sampling. Researcher samples individuals or sites because they can help generate or discover a new theory or concept; used in qualitative research; also known as *concept sampling*

time-series design. Quasi-experimental design where an extensive amount of data is collected on one group by first pretesting the participants repeatedly until the pretest scores become stable; the group is then exposed to a treatment condition and then posttested repeatedly

timing. The temporal relationship between quantitative and qualitative strands in a mixed-methods study

transferability. Technique for assessing trustworthiness in qualitative studies; involves the provision of descriptive and contextualized statements so that someone reading the study can easily identify with the setting

transformative design. Mixed-methods design whereby the researcher conducts the entire study within a transformative theoretical framework. All the researcher's key decisions are made within the context of a transformative framework

treatment group. See *experimental group*

trend study. A longitudinal survey study that examines changes within a specifically identified population over time

triangulation. The process of using multiple methods, data collection strategies, sources of data, and perhaps even researchers in qualitative research to establish their trustworthiness or verify the consistency of the facts while trying to account for their inherent biases

trustworthiness. Characteristic of qualitative data; established by examining the credibility, transferability, dependability, and confirmability of qualitative data, as well as the resultant findings

T-score. Standard score that has been transformed to a scale where the mean is equal to 50 and the standard deviation is equal to 10

two-stage random sampling. See *multistage random sampling*

two-way ANCOVA. Factorial ANCOVA with two independent variables

two-way ANOVA. Factorial ANOVA with two independent variables

Type I error. Statistical hypothesis testing error made if a researcher concludes that a null hypothesis is false when it is actually true

Type II error. Statistical hypothesis testing error made if a researcher concludes that a null hypothesis is true when it is actually false

typical sampling. Technique focused on the study of a person or site that is *typical* to outsiders who might be unfamiliar with a particular situation; used in qualitative research

unstructured observations. Observations that allow the researcher to shift focus from one event to another as new—and perhaps more interesting—events occur; more typical of qualitative data collection

validity (in quantitative research). Essential quality in quantitative research that has to do with whether the data are, in fact, what they are believed or purported to be

variables. Any factors that may affect the outcome of a study or characteristics that are central to the topic or problems being addressed

variance. The average distance of all the scores from the mean

web-based surveys. Surveys administered on a website after initial contact with respondents via e-mail

z-score. Most basic type of standard score, where 99% of the scores range between −3.00 and +3.00; the sign indicates whether the score is above or below the mean, and the numerical value indicates the distance—in standard deviation units—between the score and the mean

• References •

American Educational Research Association, American Psychological Association, & National Council on Measurement in Education. (1999). *Standards for educational and psychological testing.* Washington, DC: American Educational Research Association.

Bogdan, R. C., & Biklen, S. K. (2007). *Qualitative research for education: An introduction to theory and methods* (5th ed.). Boston, MA: Allyn & Bacon.

Brewer, J. K. (1978). *Everything you always wanted to know about statistics, but didn't know how to ask.* Dubuque, IA: Kendall/Hunt.

Clandinin, D. J., & Connelly, F. M. (2000). *Narrative inquiry: Experience and story in qualitative research.* San Francisco, CA: Jossey-Bass.

Cohen, J. (1988). *Statistical power analysis for the behavioral sciences* (2nd ed.). Hillsdale, NJ: Lawrence Erlbaum.

Creswell, J. W. (2005). *Educational research: Planning, conducting, and evaluating quantitative and qualitative research* (2nd ed.). Upper Saddle River, NJ: Merrill/ Prentice Hall.

Creswell, J. W. (2007). *Qualitative inquiry and research design: Choosing among five approaches* (2nd ed.). Thousand Oaks, CA: Sage.

Creswell, J. W., & Plano Clark, V. L. (2011). *Designing and conducting mixed methods research* (2nd ed.). Los Angeles, CA: Sage.

Czarniawska, B. (2004). *Narratives in social science research.* London: Sage.

Dillman, D. A. (2000). *Mail and Internet surveys: The tailored design method* (2nd ed.). New York: Wiley.

Fleischer, C. (1994). Researching teacher-research: A practitioner's retrospective. *English Education, 26,* 86–126.

Fraenkel, J. R., & Wallen, N. E. (2003). Action research. In *How to design and evaluate research in education* (5th ed., pp. 571–597). Boston, MA: McGraw-Hill.

Fraenkel, J. R., Wallen, N. E., & Hyun, H. (2012). *How to design and evaluate research in education* (8th ed.). Boston, MA: McGraw-Hill.

Gay, L. R., Mills, G. E., & Airasian, P. (2009). *Educational research: Competencies for analysis and applications* (9th ed.). Upper Saddle River, NJ: Merrill.

Glesne, C. (2006). *Becoming qualitative researchers: An introduction* (3rd ed.). New York: Longman.

Goodson, I. (1994). Studying the teacher's life and work. *Teaching and Teacher Education, 10,* 29–37.

Harris, M. B. (1998). *Basic statistics for behavioral science research* (2nd ed.). Boston, MA: Allyn & Bacon.

Institute of Education Sciences. (n.d.). *ERIC—Education Resources Information Center.* Retrieved September 19, 2013, from http://ies.ed.gov/ncee/projects/eric.asp

Johnson, A. P. (2008). *A short guide for action research* (3rd ed.). Boston, MA: Allyn & Bacon.

Leedy, P. D., & Ormrod, J. E. (2013). *Practical research: Planning and design* (10th ed.). Boston, MA: Pearson.

McMillan, J. H. (2012). *Educational research: Fundamentals for the consumer* (6th ed.). Boston, MA: Allyn & Bacon.

Melrose, M. J. (2001). Maximizing the rigor of action research: Why would you want to? How could you? *Field Methods, 13*(2), 160–180.

Mertens, D. M. (2005). *Research and evaluation in education and psychology: Integrating diversity with quantitative, qualitative, and mixed methods* (2nd ed.). Thousand Oaks, CA: Sage.

Mertler, C. A. (2002). *Web-based surveys: Guiding lessons for their use.* Paper presented at the annual meeting of the American Educational Research Association, New Orleans, LA. (ERIC Document Reproduction Service No. 464139)

Mertler, C. A. (2003). *Classroom assessment: A practical guide for educators.* Glendale, CA: Pyrczak.

Mertler, C. A. (2007). *Interpreting standardized test scores: Strategies for data-driven instructional decision making*. Los Angeles, CA: Sage.

Mertler, C. A. (2010). Teachers' perceptions of the influence of No Child Left Behind on classroom practices. *Current Issues in Education, 13*(3). Retrieved from http://cie.asu.edu/ojs/index.php/cieatasu/article/viewFile/392/31

Mertler, C. A. (2013). Classroom-based action research: Revisiting the process as customizable and meaningful professional development for educators. *Journal of Pedagogic Development, 3*(3), 39–43.

Mertler, C. A. (2014). *Action research: Improving schools and empowering educators* (4th ed.). Los Angeles, CA: Sage.

Mertler, C. A., & Charles, C. M. (2011). *Introduction to educational research* (7th ed.). Boston, MA: Pearson.

Mertler, C. A., & Vannatta, R. A. (2013). *Advanced and multivariate statistical methods: Practical application and interpretation* (5th ed.). Glendale, CA: Pyrczak.

Metz, M. H., & Page, R. N. (2002). The uses of practitioner research and status issues in educational research: Reply to Gary Anderson. *Educational Researcher, 31*(7), 26–27.

Mills, G. E. (2014). *Action research: A guide for the teacher researcher* (5th ed.). Boston, MA: Pearson.

Parsons, R. D., & Brown, K. S. (2002). *Teacher as reflective practitioner and action researcher*. Belmont, CA: Wadsworth/Thomson Learning.

Patton, M. Q. (2001). *Qualitative research and evaluation methods* (3rd ed.). Thousand Oaks, CA: Sage.

Plano Clark, V. L., & Creswell, J. W. (2010). *Understanding research: A consumer's guide*. Boston, MA: Merrill.

Pyrczak, F., & Bruce, R. R. (2003). *Writing empirical research reports: A basic guide for students of the social and behavioral sciences* (4th ed.). Los Angeles, CA: Pyrczak.

Radebaugh, B. (1994). Democratizing educational research or why is our nation still at risk after ten years of educational reform? *Thresholds in Education, 20*(2–3), 18–21.

Richardson, V. (1994). Conducting research on practice. *Educational Researcher, 23*(5), 5–10.

Schmuck, R. A. (1997). *Practical action research for change*. Arlington Heights, IL: SkyLight Professional Development.

Schwalbach, E. M. (2003). *Value and validity in action research: A guidebook for reflective practitioners*. Lanham, MD: Scarecrow Press.

Stake, R. (1995). *The art of case study research*. Thousand Oaks, CA: Sage.

Stringer, E. T. (2007). *Action research* (3rd ed.). Thousand Oaks, CA: Sage.

Wiersma, W., & Jurs, S. (2005). *Research methods in education: An introduction* (8th ed.). Boston, MA: Allyn & Bacon.

Wolcott, H. F. (1994). *Transforming qualitative data: Descriptions, analysis, and interpretation*. Thousand Oaks, CA: Sage.

Wolcott, H. F. (2001). *Writing up qualitative research* (2nd ed.). Thousand Oaks, CA: Sage.

Yin, R. K. (2009). *Case study research: Design and methods* (4th ed.). Thousand Oaks, CA: Sage.

• Index •